ECONOMIC AND SOCIAL COMMISSION FOR ASIA AND THE PACIFIC

# ECONOMIC AND SOCIAL SURVEY OF ASIA AND THE PACIFIC 2003

UNITED  NATIONS

New York
2003

UNITED NATIONS
ECONOMIC AND SOCIAL SURVEY OF ASIA AND THE PACIFIC
2003

ST/ESCAP/2233

UNITED NATIONS PUBLICATION

Sales No. E.03.II.F.11



ISBN: 92-1-120148-9 ISSN: 0252-5704

# FOREWORD

Most Asian and Pacific economies showed surprising strength in 2002, despite continued weaknesses in the world economy. Surging intraregional trade, combined with fiscal stimulus and monetary easing, lifted regional production by approximately 5 per cent, 2 points higher than the 2001 rate, and more than 3 points higher than the expansion of global output in 2002. This has raised hopes that the region would experience a modest uplift in economic growth in 2003. Still, the rate of economic expansion was several percentage points below that which prevailed before the crisis of 1997-1998, resulting in lower levels of job creation and new pressures on government budgets, including fiscal allocations for basic social services and poverty reduction.

This edition of the *Economic and Social Survey of Asia and the Pacific* includes an in-depth look at the efforts of the public sector in education and health, in particular to reach women, the poor, people living in rural and remote areas and others to whom greater attention must be paid. Given the large resources required for these key areas, the responsibility for funding cannot be that of the public sector alone; rather, the *Survey* indicates, multiple channels that involve civil society and the private sector have to be tapped.

The *Survey* also focuses on environmental degradation, which often accompanies rapid economic growth and adversely affects the lives of the poor in a disproportionate manner. In recognition of these tensions, the *Survey* examines the links between the environment and poverty as well as the policy options available for improving the environment while reducing poverty. It recommends actions that will help to ensure property rights for the poor, improve access to affordable, environmentally clean technologies and reduce vulnerability to natural disasters through better disaster-management planning.

The information and insights contained in this volume should prove useful to policy makers, scholars and anyone else concerned about the economic and social advancement of the ESCAP region. I hope that readers will also see, throughout the *Survey,* examples of the United Nations system at work helping the people of the ESCAP to region to reach the millennium development goals. In that spirit of partnership, I recommend this publication to the widest possible global audience.

Kofi A. Annan
Secretary-General

March 2003

# ACKNOWLEDGEMENTS

The *Economic and Social Survey of Asia and the Pacific 2003* was prepared under the direction of Raj Kumar and coordinated by N.V. Lam (chapters I and II) and Hiren Sarkar (chapters III and IV) of the Poverty and Development Division of ESCAP.

Experts from within and outside the ESCAP secretariat contributed to various stages in the preparation of the *Survey 2003*. The team of staff members of the Poverty and Development Division who prepared the *Survey 2003* comprised: Shahid Ahmed, Edgar Dante, Eugene Gherman, Fareeda Maroof Hla, Nobuko Kajiura, Muhammad Hussain Malik, Hiren Sarkar, Seok-Dong Wang and Marin Yari. Staff analysis was based on data and information available up to mid-February 2003. Research assistance was provided by Somchai Congtavinsutti, Kiatkanid Pongpanich and Amornrut Supornsinchai. All graphics work and the cover design were done by Somchai Congtavinsutti. The logistics of processing and production, and the organization of the meetings referred to below, were handled by Dusdeemala Kanittanon and Woranut Sompitayanurak.

Andrew Flatt, Chief of the Statistics Division, provided useful comments and suggestions on data presentation in all draft chapters of the *Survey 2003*. Inputs for the *Survey 2003* also came from Hirohito Toda, Least Developed Countries Coordination Unit, Office of the Executive Secretary; and Fuyo Jenny Yamamoto, Transport Infrastructure Section, Transport and Tourism Division.

Major inputs for the *Survey 2003* were received from the following external consultants: Mushtaq Ahmad, Tarun Das, Muhammad Allah Malik Kazemi, Mohammad Kordbache, Theodore Levantis, George Manzano, Ahmed Mohamed, Penjore, Djisman Simanjuntak, Vo Tri Thanh and Wang Tong.

Chapter I was the anchor paper for discussion at the Meeting of Eminent Persons on Current and Prospective Economic and Social Performance in the ESCAP Region held at ESCAP, Bangkok, on 24 and 25 October 2002. The eminent persons, who attended the Meeting in their personal capacity, were: Ronald Charles Duncan (Australia), Rehman Sobhan (Bangladesh), Jiahua Pan (China), M. Govinda Rao (India), Djisman Simanjuntak (Indonesia), Shinichi Ichimura (Japan), Ragayah Haji Mat Zin (Malaysia), Yuba Raj Khatiwada (Nepal), Ashfaque H. Khan (Pakistan), Wook Chae (Republic of Korea), Vladimir V. Popov (Russian Federation), Chia Siow Yue (Singapore), Pisit Leeahtam (Thailand) and Le Van Chau (Viet Nam). J.K. Robert England (UNDP, Bangkok) and Kazi Matin (World Bank, Bangkok) also participated in the Meeting.

Chapters III and IV were discussed at the Expert Group Meeting on Development Issues and Policies, held at Bangkok on 2 and 3 December 2002. The experts, who participated in the Meeting in their personal capacity, were: Aiguo Lu (China), Rajesh Chandra (Fiji), Swapna Mukhopadhyay (India), Daniel Kameo (Indonesia), S.M. Naseem (Pakistan), Bienvenido P. Nito (Philippines), Sang-Moon Hahm (Republic of Korea), Leonid M. Grigoriev (Russian Federation), Linda Low (Singapore), Dushni Weerakoon (Sri Lanka), Juree Vichit-Vadakan (Thailand), Sitanon Jesadapipat (Thailand) and Vo Tri Thanh (Viet Nam).

# CONTENTS

# CONTENTS *(continued)*

# BOXES

# TABLES

## TABLES *(continued)*

# TABLES *(continued)*

## TABLES *(continued)*

## FIGURES

## FIGURES *(continued)*

*Page*

## FIGURES *(continued)*

*Page*

# EXPLANATORY NOTES

The term "ESCAP region" is used in the present issue of the *Survey* to include Afghanistan; American Samoa; Armenia; Australia; Azerbaijan; Bangladesh; Bhutan; Brunei Darussalam; Cambodia; China; Cook Islands; Democratic People's Republic of Korea; Fiji; French Polynesia; Georgia; Guam; Hong Kong, China; India; Indonesia; Iran (Islamic Republic of); Japan; Kazakhstan; Kiribati; Kyrgyzstan; Lao People's Democratic Republic; Macao, China; Malaysia; Maldives; Marshall Islands; Micronesia (Federated States of); Mongolia; Myanmar; Nauru; Nepal; New Caledonia; New Zealand; Niue; Northern Mariana Islands; Pakistan; Palau; Papua New Guinea; Philippines; Republic of Korea; Russian Federation; Samoa; Singapore; Solomon Islands; Sri Lanka; Tajikistan; Thailand; Tonga; Turkey; Turkmenistan; Tuvalu; Uzbekistan; Vanuatu; and Viet Nam. The term "developing ESCAP region" excludes Australia, Japan and New Zealand.

The term "Central Asian republics" in this issue of the *Survey* refers to Armenia, Azerbaijan, Georgia, Kazakhstan, Kyrgyzstan, Tajikistan, Turkmenistan and Uzbekistan.

The designations employed and the presentation of the material in this publication do not imply the expression of any opinion whatsoever on the part of the Secretariat of the United Nations concerning the legal status of any country, territory, city or area, or of its authorities, or concerning the delimitation of its frontiers or boundaries.

Mention of firm names and commercial products does not imply the endorsement of the United Nations.

The abbreviated title *Survey* in footnotes refers to the *Economic and Social Survey of Asia and the Pacific* for the year indicated.

Many figures used in the *Survey* are on a fiscal year basis and are assigned to the calendar year which covers the major part or second half of the fiscal year.

Growth rates are on an annual basis, except where indicated otherwise.

Reference to "tons" indicates metric tons.

Values are in United States dollars unless specified otherwise.

The term "billion" signifies a thousand million. The term "trillion" signifies a million million.

In the tables, two dots (..) indicate that data are not available or are not separately reported, a dash (–) indicates that the amount is nil or negligible, and a blank indicates that the item is not applicable.

In dates, a hyphen (-) is used to signify the full period involved, including the beginning and end years, and a stroke (/) indicates a crop year, a fiscal year or plan year. The fiscal years, currencies and 2002 exchange rates of the economies in the ESCAP region are listed in the following table:

| *Country or area* | *Fiscal year* | *Currency and abbreviation* | *Rate of exchange for $1 as at November 2002* |
|---|---|---|---|
| Afghanistan | 21 March to 20 March | afghani (Af) | 3 000.00 |
| American Samoa | .. | United States dollar ($) | 1.00 |
| Armenia | 1 January to 31 December | dram | 585.81 |
| Australia | 1 July to 30 June | Australian dollar ($A) | 1.78 |
| Azerbaijan | 1 January to 31 December | Azeri manat (AZM) | 4 893.00 |
| Bangladesh | 1 July to 30 June | taka (Tk) | 57.90[a] |
| Bhutan | 1 July to 30 June | ngultrum (Nu) | 48.27 |
| Brunei Darussalam | 1 January to 31 December | Brunei dollar (B$) | 1.76 |
| Cambodia | 1 January to 31 December | riel (CR) | 3 930.00 |
| China | 1 January to 31 December | yuan renminbi (Y) | 8.28 |
| Cook Islands | 1 April to 31 March | New Zealand dollar ($NZ) | 2.02 |
| Democratic People's Republic of Korea | .. | won (W) | 2.20 |
| Fiji | 1 January to 31 December | Fiji dollar (F$) | 2.12 |
| French Polynesia | .. | French Pacific Community franc (FCFP) | 133.30[b] |

| Country or area | Fiscal year | Currency and abbreviation | Rate of exchange for $1 as at November 2002 |
|---|---|---|---|
| Georgia | 1 January to 31 December | lari (L) | 2.17 |
| Guam | 1 October to 30 September | United States dollar ($) | 1.00 |
| Hong Kong, China | 1 April to 31 March | Hong Kong dollar (HK$) | 7.80 |
| India | 1 April to 31 March | Indian rupee (Rs) | 48.27 |
| Indonesia | 1 April to 31 March | Indonesian rupiah (Rp) | 9 059.00 |
| Iran (Islamic Republic of) | 21 March to 20 March | Iranian rial (Rls) | 7 977.03 |
| Japan | 1 April to 31 March | yen (¥) | 122.30 |
| Kazakhstan | 1 January to 31 December | tenge (T) | 154.20 |
| Kiribati | 1 January to 31 December | Australian dollar ($A) | 1.78 |
| Kyrgyzstan | 1 January to 31 December | som (som) | 46.17 |
| Lao People's Democratic Republic | 1 October to 30 September | new kip (NK) | 10 750.00 |
| Macao, China | 1 July to 30 June | pataca (P) | 8.00 |
| Malaysia | 1 January to 31 December | ringgit (M$) | 3.80 |
| Maldives | 1 January to 31 December | rufiyaa (Rf) | 12.80 |
| Marshall Islands | 1 October to 30 September | United States dollar ($) | 1.00 |
| Micronesia (Federated States of) | 1 October to 30 September | United States dollar ($) | 1.00 |
| Mongolia | 1 January to 31 December | tugrik (Tug) | 1 122.22 |
| Myanmar | 1 April to 31 March | kyat (K) | 6.49 |
| Nauru | 1 July to 30 June | Australian dollar ($A) | 1.81 |
| Nepal | 16 July to 15 July | Nepalese rupee (NRs) | 78.30 |
| New Caledonia | .. | French Pacific Community franc (FCFP) | 133.30[b] |
| New Zealand | 1 April to 31 March | New Zealand dollar ($NZ) | 2.02 |
| Niue | 1 April to 31 March | New Zealand dollar ($NZ) | 2.02 |
| Northern Mariana Islands | 1 October to 30 September | United States dollar ($) | 1.00 |
| Pakistan | 1 July to 30 June | Pakistan rupee (PRs) | 58.53 |
| Palau | 1 October to 30 September | United States dollar ($) | 1.00 |
| Papua New Guinea | 1 January to 31 December | kina (K) | 3.39[b] |
| Philippines | 1 January to 31 December | Philippine peso (P) | 53.31 |
| Republic of Korea | 1 January to 31 December | won (W) | 1 208.80 |
| Russian Federation | 1 January to 31 December | rouble (R) | 31.84 |
| Samoa | 1 July to 30 June | tala (WS$) | 3.27 |
| Singapore | 1 April to 31 March | Singapore dollar (S$) | 1.76 |
| Solomon Islands | 1 January to 31 December | Solomon Islands dollar (SI$) | 5.30[b] |
| Sri Lanka | 1 January to 31 December | Sri Lanka rupee (SL Rs) | 96.59 |
| Tajikistan | 1 January to 31 December | somoni | 2.95[a] |
| Thailand | 1 October to 30 September | baht (B) | 43.35 |
| Tonga | 1 July to 30 June | pa'anga (T$) | 2.24 |
| Turkey | 1 January to 31 December | Turkish lira (LT) | 1 603 940.00 |
| Turkmenistan | 1 January to 31 December | Turkmen manat (M) | 5 200.00 |
| Tuvalu | 1 January to 31 December | Australian dollar ($A) | 1.81 |
| Uzbekistan | 1 January to 31 December | sum (sum) | 871.43 |
| Vanuatu | 1 January to 31 December | vatu (VT) | 134.99 |
| Viet Nam | 1 January to 31 December | dong (D) | 15 339.00[c] |

*Sources:* United Nations, *Monthly Bulletin of Statistics*, available at <http://esa.un.org/unsd/mbs/mbssearch.asp> (20 February 2003); IMF, *International Financial Statistics* (CD-ROM), February 2003; and Economist Intelligence Unit, *Country Reports*, available at <http://db.eiu.com/countries.asp> (24 February 2003).

[a] October 2002.

[b] Average 2002.

[c] September 2002.

# ABBREVIATIONS

| | |
|---|---|
| ADB | Asian Development Bank |
| AFTA | ASEAN Free Trade Area |
| ASEAN | Association of Southeast Asian Nations |
| c.i.f. | cost, insurance, freight |
| CD-ROM | compact disk read-only memory |
| CIS | Commonwealth of Independent States |
| EU | European Union |
| f.o.b. | free on board |
| FAO | Food and Agriculture Organization of the United Nations |
| FDI | foreign direct investment |
| FTAs | free trade agreements |
| GDP | gross domestic product |
| HIV/AIDS | human immunodeficiency virus/acquired immunodeficiency syndrome |
| ICT | information and communication technology |
| IMF | International Monetary Fund |
| IT | information technology |
| NPLs | non-performing loans |
| ODA | official development assistance |
| OECD | Organisation for Economic Cooperation and Development |
| OPEC | Organization of the Petroleum Exporting Countries |
| SAARC | South Asian Association for Regional Cooperation |
| SMEs | small and medium-sized enterprises |
| UNCTAD | United Nations Conference on Trade and Development |
| UNDP | United Nations Development Programme |
| UNESCO | United Nations Educational, Scientific and Cultural Organization |
| UNICEF | United Nations Children's Fund |
| VAT | value added tax |
| WHO | World Health Organization |
| WMO | World Meteorological Organization |
| WTO | World Trade Organization |

# GLOBAL AND REGIONAL ECONOMIC DEVELOPMENTS: IMPLICATIONS AND PROSPECTS FOR THE ESCAP REGION[1]

## OVERVIEW

*The optimism in early 2002 dissipated during the year*

Following the sharp slowdown of the global economy in 2001, signs of a return to more robust growth became evident in the first quarter of 2002. These encouraging signs, however, dissipated quickly and activity in the global economy lost momentum steadily against a backdrop of weakening consumer and business confidence as the year progressed. The risk of military conflict in Iraq and the nuclear situation in the Democratic People's Republic of Korea contributed to heightened uncertainty while the continuing fragility of corporate balance sheets led to more pronounced risk aversion on the part of investors and households in 2002. Stock markets virtually across the world experienced a third year of falling indices. Although countered by monetary easing in the main economies, both developed and developing, a strong recovery of the global economy consequently proved elusive in 2002. By and large, these factors are likely to persist and a significant improvement in the growth rate of the global economy is considered unlikely until well into 2003. Forecasts for the global economy and for trade, commodity prices, inflation and interest rates are summarized in table I.1.

*The ESCAP region was apparently immune to the worsening external environment*

In the ESCAP region the effects of these developments manifested themselves largely in swings in overall business sentiment and not in GDP growth in 2002 (see chapter II). Stock markets, which had risen strongly in the early part of the year in anticipation of a strong pick-up of the global economy later in the year, weakened considerably in the second half of 2002. Notwithstanding growing doubts about the strength of the global recovery and weaker business confidence, overall GDP growth in the region remained surprisingly strong. Indeed, the latest estimate by the United Nations *World Economic Situation and Prospects 2003* identifies Asia and the Pacific as the fastest-growing region in the world in 2002; the expansion in ESCAP developing economies' output was 3.4 percentage

[1] This is a revised and updated version of "Global and regional economic developments: implications and prospects for the ESCAP region", in *Bulletin on Asia-Pacific Perspectives 2002/03* (United Nations publication, Sales No. E.02.II.F.69).

**Table I.1. Selected indicators of global economic conditions, 1999-2003**

| | | 1999 | 2000 | 2001 | 2002[a] | 2003[b] |
|---|---|---|---|---|---|---|
| **Economic growth (percentage change of GDP)** | | | | | | |
| World | | 2.9 | 3.8 | 1.1 | 1.7 | 2.8 |
| Developed economies | | 2.7 | 3.2 | 0.7 | 1.3 | 2.3 |
| Japan | | 0.8 | 2.6 | −0.3 | −0.6 | 0.9 |
| United States of America | | 4.2 | 3.8 | 0.3 | 2.4 | 2.5 |
| European Union | | 2.4 | 3.3 | 1.5 | 1.1 | 2.3 |
| Developing economies | | 3.5 | 5.6 | 2.4 | 3.3 | 4.7 |
| Developing economies of the ESCAP region | | 6.4 | 7.1 | 3.2 | 5.1 | 5.4 |
| Economies in transition | | 6.3 | 7.0 | 3.1 | 5.0 | 5.7 |
| **Growth in volume of trade (percentage)[c]** | | | | | | |
| World | | 5.3 | 12.6 | −0.1 | 2.1 | 6.1 |
| Developed economies | Export | 5.2 | 12.0 | −1.1 | 1.2 | 5.4 |
| | Import | 7.8 | 11.8 | −1.3 | 1.7 | 6.2 |
| Developing economies | Export | 4.3 | 15.0 | 2.6 | 3.2 | 6.5 |
| | Import | 1.3 | 15.9 | 1.6 | 3.8 | 7.1 |
| **Commodity prices (annual percentage change; US dollar terms)** | | | | | | |
| Non-fuel primary commodities | | −7.0 | 1.8 | −5.4 | 4.2 | 5.7 |
| Oil | | 37.5 | 57.0 | −14.0 | 0.5 | −0.8 |
| **Inflation rate (percentage)[d]** | | | | | | |
| CPI in the developed economies | | 1.4 | 2.3 | 2.2 | 1.4 | 1.7 |
| CPI in the developing economies | | 6.9 | 6.1 | 5.7 | 5.6 | 6.0 |
| **Short-term interest rates** | | | | | | |
| United States | | 5.4 | 6.5 | 3.7 | 1.8 | 1.6 |
| Japan | | 0.2 | 0.2 | 0.1 | 0.1 | 0.0 |
| Euro area | | 3.0 | 4.4 | 4.2 | 3.3 | 3.0 |
| **Exchange rates (nominal units per US dollar)[e]** | | | | | | |
| Yen per US dollar | | 113.9 | 107.8 | 121.5 | 125.4 | 122.5 |
| Euros per US dollar | | 0.939 | 1.085 | 1.118 | 1.063 | 1.003 |

*Sources:* United Nations, "Project LINK World Economic Outlook: Aggregate Table" (October 2002); IMF, *World Economic Outlook* (Washington, September 2002) and *International Financial Statistics,* vol. LV, No. 11 (November 2002); OECD, *OECD Economic Outlook No. 72* (December 2002); *The Economist,* various issues; and national sources.

[a] Preliminary estimate.
[b] Forecast.
[c] Exports and imports (goods and services).
[d] Developed and developing economies ratios weighted at purchasing power parity.
[e] Period average.

points more than global output growth. This apparent immunity to the weakening external environment extended over much of the region. The observed variation in subregional growth patterns had more to do with the relative strength of domestic factors in the different subregions than the impact of global developments.

***Intraregional trade was an important factor in supporting growth***

A welcome development was the surge in intraregional trade, which, in turn, was the outcome of both external and internal causes. On the external front, regional and bilateral trading links fuelled trade dynamism in the region in both 2001 and 2002. FDI-induced componentization of production, especially in South-East Asia, served to enhance trade flows within the region. Moreover, the evidence also suggests that intraregional trade has moved beyond the trade in ICT components to embrace a wider range of non-ICT products and services as well. Above all else, the region is home to some of the most dynamic economies in the world and, in this context, there is ample evidence that trade accompanies growth just as much as growth accompanies trade. Notably, imports by Japan, the largest economy in the region, grew by 22 per cent in 2000 and then declined by 8 per cent in 2001. However, China (the second largest economy in the region) increased its imports by 35.8 per cent in 2000 and 8.2 per cent in 2001. The available evidence suggests that these trends were maintained in 2002 although the pace slackened somewhat. On the internal front, fiscal stimulus and monetary easing have supported the growth of domestic demand, though with some attendant risks.

***However, future prospects continue to be uncertain***

Prospects for 2003 for both the global economy and the ESCAP region embody a significant level of underlying uncertainty. The uncertainty is compounded by the threat of war in Iraq and the nuclear situation in the Democratic People's Republic of Korea, which could potentially exacerbate the prevailing weaknesses in the global economy.[2] The rise in oil prices, if it persists, will have a negative impact on the region's terms of trade, among other adverse ripple effects. There are some grounds for optimism that growth in the ESCAP region will remain largely unaffected by the weakening global economy, at least in the short term. Nevertheless, risks on the downside should not be ignored. In particular, global trade and the stimulus provided by expanding exports to the United States of America and Japan have been major factors in output growth for many economies in the region, especially following the 1997-1998 financial and economic crisis. Given this, the principal influences for the ESCAP region are essentially the following:

First, global conditions generally, and the outlook for the United States and Japanese economies in particular, remain a major determinant of the economic performance in the region. In this respect, confidence in

---

[2] For one view, see Jeffrey D. Sachs "Economic effects of a war with Iraq", *The Nation*, 3 October 2002.

a robust recovery in the United States and by inference in the global economy in 2003 has been significantly eroded in recent months, as noted earlier. Strong bearish forces have gripped stock markets in the United States and in much of the rest of the world, causing holders of wealth in the form of equities to suffer major losses. Rising house prices have been an offsetting factor helping to preserve household wealth, however.

Second, it is not possible to predict at this stage how these various forces will interact in 2003. The current consensus is that in the United States consumer confidence should remain largely intact in the months ahead, though with some risks on the downside. As such, a revival of corporate capital spending in 2003, the one missing element for a stronger recovery in that country, could provide a new impetus for output growth. Meanwhile, economic growth in the European Union (EU) is expected to pick up in 2003 after easing somewhat in the second half of the previous year. The consensus view as regards Japan is that its economy is likely to expand at a modest pace in 2003.

***ESCAP growth is likely to be on target in 2002 and to accelerate modestly in 2003***

Third, the balance of probabilities suggests that growth in the ESCAP region could experience a slight acceleration in 2003. Details of forecasts for output growth in the main economies of the region are discussed elsewhere in chapter II. At the same time, however, there are concerns that global and hence regional stock market weakness could persist well into 2003. Foreign investors are major participants in United States stock markets and any disorderly repatriation of liquidated investments from the United States would undermine global financial markets; this would, in turn, generate adverse repercussions on both corporate and consumer confidence virtually across the globe. In another context, persistent weaknesses in United States stock markets would hurt corporate capital spending, ultimately impacting on consumer confidence and spending in the region as well. Finally, in a weakening overall economic environment, risk aversion by investors could intensify, resulting in a sharply reduced availability of finance for non-investment grade borrowers, both corporations and countries.

What are the policy issues that arise for the region from the foregoing analysis? Some of the relevant issues were raised in the *Survey 2002,* but as is self-evident the implied policy trade-offs are constantly evolving and have to be examined afresh. They also vary between subregions and between countries. Their main features as viewed from the current perspective for the region as a whole are highlighted below:

- One, how can economies preserve the momentum of growth, and thus counter the consequent social distress arising from slower growth, in the face of a deteriorating global economic?

- Two, how effective is it to rely on fiscal and monetary stimulus, and what are the pitfalls of doing so, particularly in economies where the burden of public debt is already on the high side, as in South Asia; and what are the implications in economies where inflation is low and declining, as in East Asia?

- Three, what is the likely impact on the ESCAP region of external developments such as the realignment of the dollar exchange rate vis-à-vis other world currencies, and a rapid correction of the long-standing and now growing United States current account imbalance?

- Four, how can the stock markets of individual countries in the region and, indeed elsewhere, sustain the confidence of market participants in the face of intensified bearish trends in the United States and other developed country stock markets?

- Five, what are the areas and scope for national and regional policy initiatives, in both the short and long terms, with regard to the questions raised above? Interwoven with these issues are policy measures needed to mitigate the negative effects on employment and social distress of a slowdown in the ESCAP region.

These and other matters bearing upon global economic trends and their likely impact on the ESCAP region are considered at greater length in chapter II. The relevant policy options for consideration can be summarized here as follows:

- One, it is essential that there be a commitment to preserve growth through domestic demand stimulation but within a framework of sustained macroeconomic stability. In this context, there are major shortcomings in the physical infrastructure of many, if not most, developing ESCAP economies. Investment in infrastructure alongside expenditure on the multifaceted development of human resources will not fully offset the diminution in external demand but will contribute to short-term growth as well as to improving long-term competitiveness.

- Two, the maintenance of macroeconomic prudence depends greatly on having in place a credible approach to manage the risks of policy slippage. A low inflationary environment at present allows somewhat more policy leeway than in the past, but Governments should be alive to the likelihood of overshooting and/or undershooting macroeconomic objectives.

- Three, a volatile external environment and exchange rate instability should not interfere with the progress towards trade liberalization, whether or not this takes place on a multilateral or bilateral basis. In this context, the removal of the more mundane impediments to trade such as time-consuming customs clearance procedures and cumbersome trade-financing mechanisms would serve to stimulate domestic production and the restructuring process as well.
- Four, the highest standards in corporate governance should continue to be promoted and agreement sought within the region on the minimum standards of enforceability in corporate reporting.
- Five, regional cooperation in trade and financial matters should continue to be emphasized while national competitiveness is promoted at the same time.

## GLOBAL ECONOMIC DEVELOPMENTS

### Developed countries

***The global slowdown in 2001 was reflected in a sharp drop in world trade***

As reported in the *Survey 2002,* there was an unexpected and sharp slowdown in the developed countries, causing a sharp decline in the growth of world trade volume, and an absolute decline in world trade value, in 2001 compared with 2000. The slowdown was driven by an abrupt deceleration in corporate capital spending in ICT, which was itself caused by rising inventories, declining profits and growing indebtedness in corporations. A tentative turnaround in global output growth led by the United States occurred in the first quarter of 2002 but this was primarily the result of a cyclical inventory turnaround. There was little or no evidence of a revival in corporate capital spending, the main driver of growth in the United States in the second half of the 1990s. In fact, the balance sheets of corporations weakened in 2001-2002 and the worsening gearing ratios restricted access to finance for many, especially the less creditworthy, paradoxically in the face of very low interest rates.

***The slowdown was a result of the bursting of the asset price bubble in the United States***

The 2001-2002 slowdown has an important feature in that it was not the result, as has usually been the case in the past, of a deliberate policy tightening in the face of rapid growth leading to supply constraints and price pressures. Instead, it was a correction of an asset bubble in the shape of overinflated valuations of ICT-related stocks that had encouraged too many companies with only the rudiments of a business plan to raise capital in the stock markets. Encouraged by extravagant claims on behalf of ICT and the so-called new economy, investors themselves eschewed scepticism and were instrumental in inflating the bubble. Consequently, capital was misallocated on a massive scale and much of it will have to be, and is being, written off. These matters were alluded to in the

*Survey 2002,* where the risks facing the global economy from the bursting ICT bubble were also analysed. It was stressed then that the overhang of excess capacity and debt could take a long time to work itself out, generating in the process a prolonged period of volatility in the stock markets. This is proving to be the case.

The 2001 slowdown originating in the United States has certain peculiar characteristics that could shed light on the observable events in 2002. First, it was triggered by and concentrated in the ICT sector, for which the ESCAP region is a major supplier of inputs. Following the overinvestment in ICT and ensuing massive write-offs, corporate investment expenditure has, in effect, been suspended until corporate balance sheets are rebuilt. This will involve a painful period of restructuring with many probable corporate bankruptcies.

Second, in an environment of growing optimism, exaggerated profit expectations were also applied as benchmarks for other traditional sectors of the economy. In response, some companies in the United States began to inflate their earnings artificially, sometimes illegally, in contravention of accounting norms and standards. When these accounting malpractices were discovered, a severe crisis of confidence occurred that gravely undermined American stock markets, affecting both new- and old-economy shares alike. Stock markets have consequently been weakened virtually on a worldwide basis, including the ESCAP region, though with one or two notable exceptions.

***Low interest rates have kept consumption strong***

Third, the stock market bubble and its associated ripple effects occurred in an environment of negligible inflation and low interest rates. All evidence of an impending slowdown in the real economy in 2001 was met with successive reductions in interest rates in the United States, which now stand at 40-year historical lows. Interest rates also tumbled to very low levels in 2001 and 2002 in other developed countries. In Japan interest rates are, and have been, close to zero for some time. The European Central Bank, though constrained by its EU-zone inflation target, has reduced interest rates by more than a full percentage point. In consequence, private consumption has offset the investment and inventory-driven slowdown and prevented a more wide-ranging downturn. In addition, the wealth effect of rising housing equity has counterbalanced the declining value of share ownership in the United States. However, the external imbalance in the United States has worsened in the process, mainly through a surge in imports; this has thus introduced a new source of uncertainty into the global economy. In Japan and the EU, the interface between the real economy and the financial environment is somewhat different because of different institutional arrangements and individual characteristics, in terms of consumer behaviour and preferences. The following paragraphs attempt to shed light on the relevant trends in the main developed countries.

In the United States, as already noted, stock markets remain weak and volatile, despite low interest rates in 2002. In the real economy, for example, there were some tentative signs of a modest upturn in manufacturing activity in the middle of the year and private consumption remained strong generally. However, both lost some buoyancy in the second half of 2002. Low interest rates and a strong housing market have driven private consumption but these sources of consumer confidence cannot continue indefinitely. Investment expenditures by corporations, a better bellwether of medium-term prospects, contracted again in 2002 following the contraction in 2001.

***The inflow of capital to the United States is reversing itself***

Economic trends in the United States must be viewed against the fact that gross national saving fell again in 2002, the fiscal deficit re-emerged and the current account deficit widened from 4 to 5 per cent of GDP. Weak stock markets have led to a gradual but steady withdrawal from, and repatriation of, dollar-denominated assets held by foreigners. These have been partly reinvested in United States Treasury bonds but a significant portion has gone into European and United Kingdom government and corporate bonds. Bond prices consequently rose substantially, standing nearly 20 per cent higher at end-December 2002 compared with end-December 2001. During 2002 the dollar also depreciated against several currencies, primarily the euro, in an environment of increased volatility; the prices of precious metals also rose during the year.

***Economic growth in Japan continues to be hampered by long-standing domestic problems***

Interest rates have been reduced close to zero in Japan but demand remains subdued owing to, among other adverse long-term factors, chronically weak consumer confidence and structural impediments such as overcapacity and inadequate reform in the financial sector. The impact of certain short-term factors, such as the yen-dollar exchange rate, is a source of additional concern. To date, the decline in GDP has been caused by both external and domestic forces. In particular, export growth declined in 2001 and 2002 following the collapse in the ICT sector in the United States. Meanwhile, the massive and persistent loss of personal wealth over the last 10-12 years continued to depress consumption, a trend which is most visible in the endemic weakness in the property and stock markets. Business investment has followed an erratic course, rising briefly in response to improved export prospects but falling rapidly in 2001 and 2002. Despite interest rate reductions, savings remain high and the external current account surplus has begun to creep upwards again to 3 per cent of GDP. The latter phenomenon has major implications for the yen exchange rate and in terms of the sustainability of export-driven economic recovery in the near term.

***Growth performance in the European Union has been flaccid***

In the EU,[3] growth faltered palpably in 2002. Barely perceptible growth in Germany, Italy, Belgium and Austria was accompanied by below-trend growth in France and the United Kingdom of Great Britain and Northern Ireland. Reflecting high levels of unemployment and poor consumer confidence, retail sales showed a marginal decline up to September 2002 in the EU, with the exception of the United Kingdom and some of the smaller economies. Indeed, unemployment stood at 8.4 per cent in the euro zone in October 2002 compared with 8.0 per cent 12 months earlier. Overall, the EU-15 were unable to meet earlier economic expectations for 2002. On the plus side, however, the recent appreciation of the euro and the pound sterling in the face of monetary easing should counter any lingering threat of inflation overshooting official targets, thus giving some room for monetary easing. On the minus side, the overall climate of uncertainty generated by stock market turmoil, concerns about the strength of the United States economy and a rapid appreciation of the euro itself are likely to dampen both non-euro zone export growth and capital investment in 2002. Moreover, in the face of persistent high unemployment, consumer demand is unlikely to provide a major stimulus to economic activity in the short term. Only in Denmark, Sweden and the United Kingdom (the three economies outside the euro zone) is consumer spending showing a degree of buoyancy. The United Kingdom economy is very similar in this respect to that of the United States with rather low business confidence being offset in large measure by strong consumer spending on the back of a strong property market; both of the latter appeared to be losing strength towards the end of 2002, however.

***The major developed economies are unlikely to be engines of global growth in the near term***

Looking ahead over the next four quarters, the evidence available thus far seems to be evenly poised between higher or flat GDP growth in the developed countries. According to the United States Federal Reserve Board, recovery in the United States is likely to remain sluggish and probabilities, by and large, are weighted towards continuing weakness. Indeed, forecasts for 2003 have been scaled down for both the United States and the EU owing to the absence of a visible turnaround in business sentiment and, on the debit side, a greater likelihood of negative influences adversely affecting consumer spending, such as stock market turmoil or a weaker housing market. For Japan, however, there is consensus concerning positive economic growth in the country in 2003. Thus, the major developed countries are unlikely to have a noticeable positive influence on the global economy in the short term. Again, the

---

[3] An event worthy of note from a long-term perspective was the announcement by the European Commission on 8 October 2002 that negotiations for membership in the EU had been concluded with Cyprus, the Czech Republic, Estonia, Hungary, Latvia, Lithuania, Malta, Poland, the Slovak Republic and Slovenia. These countries should join the EU by June 2004 and will bring its membership to 25.

prospects for the developed countries must be viewed against an environment characterized by low and declining inflation and low interest rates, but also by some uncertainty as regards the fiscal situation. Specifically, the EU is constrained by its Growth and Stability Pact while Japan's public debt is already uncomfortably high.

## Developing countries

***Weak commodity prices worsened the impact of the global slowdown on developing countries in 2001***

The global economic slowdown in 2001 contributed to lower growth in output and further weakness in commodity prices, and implied terms of trade losses, of the developing countries. The all-items commodity index of *The Economist* had declined by nearly 15 per cent in the 12 months to December 2001. It has since risen somewhat but at 75.2 index points it stands almost 27 per cent below its 1995 level (see figure I.1). The loss of the external stimulus could only be partially compensated for by growth in domestic demand in 2001. In particular, there were severe output declines in economies with high export-to-GDP ratios generally or with a large preponderance of exports to the United States. Although this assessment was generally true for the region, there were important exceptions as well. Notably, China and India, and many subregional economies in North and Central Asia, were largely immune to the slowdown in 2001.

**Figure I.1. Indices of commodity prices, 1995-2002**

*(1995 = 100)*

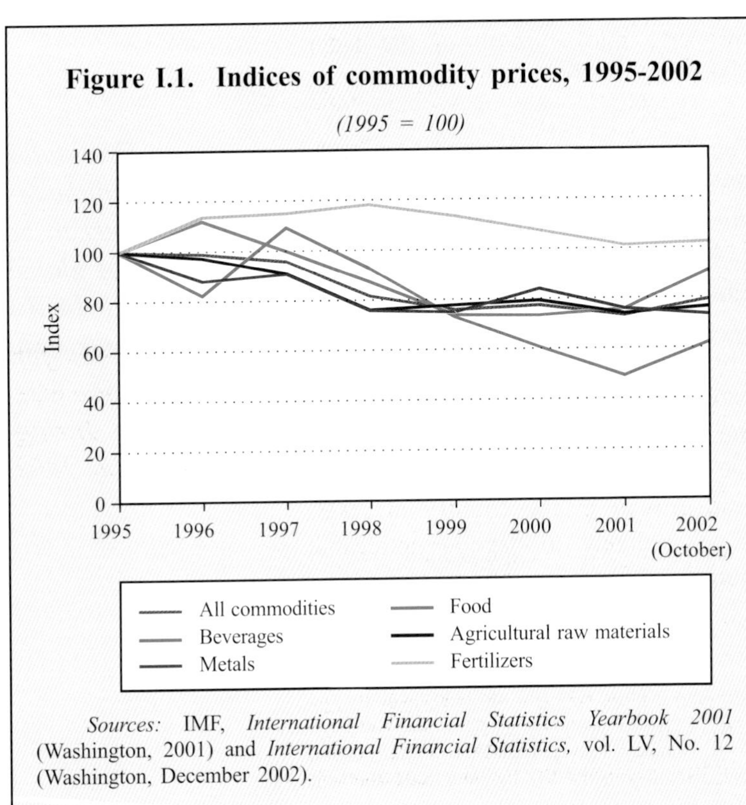


*Sources:* IMF, *International Financial Statistics Yearbook 2001* (Washington, 2001) and *International Financial Statistics,* vol. LV, No. 12 (Washington, December 2002).

In early 2002, however, indicators of activity in most developing countries strengthened in response partly to domestic stimulus measures (including the easing of fiscal and monetary policies), and partly to the apparent recovery of export demand, especially from the United States. Indeed, the economic turnaround in the United States in late 2001 led to significant upward revisions of growth forecasts for developing economies with large high-tech export sectors. Asia's slowdown in 2001 had been largely driven by the sharp decline in world demand for high-tech exports, which account for about 40 per cent of total manufactured exports from the region. A revival of demand in the developed economies generally and for high-tech exports in particular was expected to provide additional strength to the region's output growth but also to lead to a modest firming of commodity prices. The latest indications are that, for now, the external stimulus from the United States, Japan and the EU is likely to wane in the months ahead. All things considered, growth will need to be sustained primarily by domestic measures or through intraregional trade well into 2003.

***Domestic demand and an initial export recovery were behind strengthened performance in developing countries***

West Asia's economic fortunes in 2003 primarily rest on external energy demand and prices, the manifest intensity of the Israel-Palestine conflict and, for now, the danger of military action against Iraq. The most probable consequence of the latter two factors is for energy prices to rise. Higher energy prices might benefit the energy-producing economies in the region in the short term but will almost certainly have a negative impact on global recovery. The conflicts in the region have also sharply restricted investment activity and tourism in and around the countries immediately involved. Thus, any increase in their intensity would automatically depress economic activity in the entire region. On balance, therefore, it is unlikely that West Asia will be able to match its 2002 performance in 2003.

Meanwhile, the current economic situation in Latin America is dominated by events in Argentina and their fallout on the rest of the continent. Uruguay and Brazil have already fallen victim to the contagion from Argentina and both economies have needed to have recourse to external support in order to pre-empt a serious financial collapse. Brazil, for example, had to arrange a massive $30 billion standby facility with IMF in August 2002. The uncertain prospects for the United States economy, political tension in Venezuela and ongoing financial market turmoil suggest that economic performance is likely to deteriorate in the short run with low or even negative output growth in all the main economies in the region, with the possible exceptions of Mexico and Peru.

Economic performance in Africa held up relatively well in 2001 compared with other parts of the developing world, despite the global slowdown. Until early 2002, performance was expected to strengthen further, particularly among oil-producing countries, in the year in line with a stronger external environment. However, the short-term outlook became less positive in the second half of 2002 in the face of increasing uncertainty in the global economy. The interaction between weak commodity prices and output, the limited ability of most African Governments to take countervailing measures on the domestic front (against a deteriorating external environment) and the chronic nature of internal conflicts in many countries are key influences bearing on economic performance over much of the African continent. These considerations suggest little or no improvement or, more likely, even a slight deterioration in the economic outlook for 2003 over the 2002 performance.

***The outlook for African economies worsened during the course of 2002***

## Trade and financial market developments

An important element in the global slowdown in 2001 was the role played by international trade and financial flows in transmitting changes in economic activity within the world economy. The most notable feature in international trade is the coexistence of strong volume growth and weaknesses in prices almost across the board, with the exception of oil (see table I.2).

**Table I.2. World trade and prices,[a] 1991-2002**

| | *Annual percentage changes* | | | | |
|---|---|---|---|---|---|
| | *1991-2000* | *1999* | *2000* | *2001* | *2002[b]* |
| Trade volumes | 7.3 | 5.6 | 12.8 | −0.7 | 2.6 |
| Trade prices (United States dollars) | −0.8 | −2.0 | 0.3 | −3.5 | −1.5 |
| Manufactures | −0.9 | −1.9 | −5.1 | −2.4 | −0.5 |
| Oil | 2.1 | 37.5 | 57.0 | −14.0 | −5.3 |
| Other commodities | −0.9 | −7.0 | 1.8 | −5.5 | −0.1 |
| Terms of trade | | | | | |
| Developed economies[c] | 0.2 | 0.1 | −2.5 | 0.4 | 0.6 |
| Developing economies | 0.0 | 4.5 | 7.4 | −3.0 | −1.6 |

*Source:* IMF, *World Economic Outlook,* cited in Bank for International Settlements, *72nd Annual Report: 1 April 2001-March 2002* (Basel, July 2002).

a Goods only.

b IMF forecast.

c Advanced industrial economies plus newly industrializing Asian economies (Hong Kong, China; Republic of Korea; Singapore; and Taiwan Province of China).

Capital flows to the developing countries and to developing Asia are given in table I.3. They rose strongly up to 1996 but have been fluctuating at a considerably lower level since 1997. For example, in 2002 developing Asia was expected to receive only a quarter of the inward flows of private capital in 1996. No early revival of capital inflows is indicated from the available information.

***International trade in 2003 is likely to be little changed from the previous year***

As explained in the *Survey 2002,* trade flows have absorbed an increased proportion of output in today's economies. Moreover, vertical integration in production means that individual sectors are likely to be influenced by factors specific only to those sectors, and not necessarily by developments in the wider economies of the countries where the pertinent production facilities are located. However, international trade flows are not totally insulated from country-specific macroeconomic conditions. World trade growth declined sharply in 2001 in tandem with the global

**Table I.3. Net capital flows[a] to developing countries and to developing Asia, 1995-2003**

*(Billions of US dollars)*

| | 1995 | 1996 | 1997 | 1998 | 1999 | 2000 | 2001 | 2002 | 2003 |
|---|---|---|---|---|---|---|---|---|---|
| Total: all developing countries[b] | | | | | | | | | |
| Net private capital flows[c] | 211.5 | 228.8 | 102.2 | 62.1 | 84.8 | 29.4 | 24.9 | 62.4 | 64.9 |
| Net private direct investment | 98.2 | 114.4 | 141.7 | 153.6 | 164.0 | 158.0 | 172.1 | 151.3 | 160.9 |
| Net private portfolio investment | 42.7 | 90.2 | 46.7 | −0.1 | 34.3 | −4.3 | −42.6 | −3.0 | −4.0 |
| Other net private capital flows | 70.5 | 24.1 | −86.2 | −91.5 | −113.4 | −124.3 | −104.6 | −85.9 | −91.9 |
| Net official flows | 26.5 | −2.3 | 68.3 | 69.9 | 12.2 | 0.2 | 15.4 | 20.6 | 18.2 |
| Changes in reserves[d] | −118.2 | −108.1 | −68.8 | −48.2 | −87.9 | −113.2 | −119.9 | −146.6 | −129.7 |
| Developing Asia[e] | | | | | | | | | |
| Net private capital flows[c] | 96.9 | 122.1 | 7.1 | −45.9 | 6.8 | −12.9 | 16.7 | 31.6 | 7.9 |
| Net private direct investment | 52.6 | 53.4 | 56.8 | 59.7 | 61.2 | 54.2 | 47.1 | 58.7 | 59.0 |
| Net private portfolio investment | 22.7 | 32.8 | 7.3 | −17.9 | 14.4 | 4.3 | −13.5 | 0.7 | −9.7 |
| Other net private capital flows | 21.6 | 35.9 | −56.9 | −87.7 | −68.8 | −71.4 | −16.8 | −27.8 | −41.3 |
| Net official flows | 4.5 | −12.4 | 16.9 | 26.1 | 4.4 | 5.1 | −5.7 | −1.4 | 3.3 |
| Changes in reserves[d] | −43.3 | −46.9 | −15.4 | −67.4 | −78.9 | −48.7 | −84.7 | −97.4 | −67.8 |

*Source:* IMF, *World Economic Outlook* (Washington, September 2002).

[a] Net capital flows comprise net direct investment, net portfolio investment and other long- and short-term net investment flows, including official and private borrowing.

[b] Excluding Hong Kong, China.

[c] Because of data limitations, "Other net private capital flows" may include some official flows.

[d] A minus sign indicates an increase.

[e] Including Republic of Korea, Singapore and Taiwan Province of China.

slowdown and the best estimates for 2002 suggested an increase of only 2.1 per cent in volume terms; but this was likely to be offset by a decline of 1.5 per cent in prices. In value terms, world trade actually declined by 3.5 per cent in 2001 as a result of falling prices of internationally traded commodities and manufactures. Given the sluggish nature of the global economy and little upward pressure on prices, 2003 could well be a repeat of 2002, with an increase in volume offset by flat or declining prices.

***Low interest rates in developed countries have not stimulated capital outflows to developing countries***

A phenomenon observed in the 1990s was the rise in gross private capital flows from developed to developing countries as interest rates fell in the former. The evidence since 1999 suggests that this phenomenon has come to an end. For one thing, interest rates in many developing countries have also fallen to low levels owing to poor loan demand and monetary easing; thus they cannot fully compensate for increased risk aversion. For another, low interest rates have fuelled higher loan demand in some of the capital-exporting economies, particularly on the part of households.

Financial structures differ significantly across the world. Capital markets, as a source of investment finance, are typically stronger in the United States than in either Japan or the EU, where direct intermediation by banks is still common. Likewise, the housing market and housing mortgage finance are more important in household balance sheets in the United States than in Japan or the EU. This has implications for the wealth effect on consumer confidence. In fact, lower interest rates have diverted funds from the developing countries to consumers in the United States, partially financing the worsening current account deficit of the United States economy.

***Profit margins of manufacturing companies have been eroded in the United States***

Another feature of the global slowdown in 2001 and the fitful recovery in 2002 was the marked difference in performance between the domestic and externally oriented sectors in the developed countries. Manufacturing output growth has been weak in the United States while residential and public construction activity has remained strong. This reflects the differentiated responses of the trading and non-trading sectors to recent developments. Most notably in both 2001 and 2002, the profit margins of United States businesses in manufacturing came under increasing pressure. This phenomenon, visible in varying degrees in other developed economies as well, has been compounded by a build-up of excess capacity in several manufacturing activities. Firms have consequently lost their pricing power to a significant extent, a factor that has contributed to the low rates of inflation, and indeed a marginal degree of deflation, in the United States and in many other parts of the world.

***Lenders have become more discriminating in their choice of borrowers***

Low corporate profitability has, in turn, led to a marked shift in financing patterns both within and across different economies. Investment-grade borrowers have benefited from the easing of monetary conditions while those with non-investment status have experienced a widening of spreads, countering the effects of lower interest rates. In addition, lenders have not been averse to shifting finance from corporate and sovereign borrowers to the personal sector for housing mortgages and personal consumption. This trend has indirectly supported strong consumer spending in the United States and offset considerably the impact of lower corporate investment spending and rising unemployment. Such effects are less strong in Japan and the EU but they are not entirely absent either.

In the past, interest rate differentials had a major influence on the volume of capital flows, with developing countries typically receiving a higher volume of private capital flows when interest rates were low in the developed countries. In 2001 and 2002, however, declining interest rates coincided with a weakened global economy and higher investor risk aversion; the latter was further compounded by potentially disruptive financial crises in Turkey, Argentina and Brazil. Thus, low interest rates in developed countries did not lead to an increase in private capital flows to developing countries. In several Asian economies, however, cross-border lending turned positive in 2001-2002 for the first time since mid-1997. FDI flows to developing countries have remained steady in general but, as in previous years, they continue to be directed to a small number of countries, with China being the principal recipient of these flows.

***Credible macroeconomic policies can improve investor perceptions***

By and large, the overall capital flows to developing countries displayed a measure of resilience in 2001-2002. However, sentiment in international financial markets is highly sensitive to countries with high debt-to-GDP ratios, high debt-service requirements or a large element of short-term debt relative to reserves. The adoption of credible macroeconomic policies can mitigate the negative effects of, and external perceptions associated with, high indebtedness. This phenomenon is most visible in the EU candidate countries, which are perceived by investors as having policy frameworks or having to adopt a policy stance defined by the needs of EU entry. As such, they are judged less risky than other countries with similar external debt profiles.

The overall global economic and financial environment which prevailed in 2002 does not suggest that private capital flows to developing countries are likely to increase noticeably in the near future. Banks will remain cautious given that asset quality tends to deteriorate in an economic slowdown. Other investors are likely to be worried by the risks building up in Latin America. However, FDI flows are expected to remain broadly stable, and the relative immunity of Asian economies to a renewed slowdown in the United States could even lead to higher FDI flows to these countries in 2003 and beyond.

***Little real increase is likely in ODA***

ODA increased in 2001 but this was mainly on account of large disbursements by the IMF-led programmes for Argentina and Turkey. A similar phenomenon will occur in 2002 with IMF assistance recently announced for Brazil. In parallel, however, there is now increased awareness among donors of the importance of ODA for long-term development needs and the fight against poverty. This is a reflection of the Monterrey Consensus adopted at the International Conference on Financing for Development, held in March 2002. Nevertheless, given the overall economic and fiscal situation in the donor countries, this is unlikely to lead to significantly higher disbursements of ODA in 2002 or 2003, except for the special needs of Afghanistan and other exceptional cases.

## Implications for the ESCAP region

***Sustaining growth in the ESCAP region will depend on stimulating domestic demand***

The global economic slowdown in 2001 reduced the GDP growth of developing members of ESCAP from 7 per cent in 2000 to 3 per cent in 2001. The economic rebound in early 2002, combined with easier domestic policies, was expected to lead to a higher pace of growth than the 4.2 per cent rate that had been forecast for the ESCAP developing countries. In the event, however, the recovery lost steam in the United

States while growth failed to accelerate appreciably in either the EU or Japan. Indeed, it is now commonly agreed that the global economy is unlikely to show strong growth until well into 2003 or possibly later. In other words, the growth stimulus from a rebound in world trade and hence from net exports is likely to be moderate among the ESCAP developing countries over the next 12-18 months. Sustaining growth in 2003 at the rate achieved in 2002, around 5 per cent, will thus depend primarily on stimulating domestic demand. This could be sustained and, indeed, enhanced by higher intraregional trade flows.

***An outbreak of hostilities in the Middle East would undermine forecasts for 2003***

The evidence up to the third quarter of 2002 suggested that growth as forecast earlier in the year was broadly on track in much of the region. Such a performance, moreover, provides a base for the momentum to be sustained in the months ahead. However, this momentum is conditioned by the absence of: (a) major hostilities in Iraq, (b) a sustained increase in oil prices or significant disruptions in energy markets, (c) new or extended periods of turmoil in financial markets and (d) significant exchange rate realignments.

As mentioned elsewhere, the ESCAP developing region has managed to grow at a reasonable pace thus far through a combination of supportive domestic policies and greater intraregional trade. As far as the former are concerned, there are, of course, limits beyond which it may be difficult or less than prudent to stimulate activity further through public spending programmes or through monetary easing. One of the lessons emanating from Japan in the 1990s is that monetary easing in a low inflationary environment raises its own peculiar set of issues.

As regards trade, intraregional flows have expanded rapidly among countries of the ESCAP region. To what extent this impetus can be sustained remains a subject for debate, however. To some, intraregional trade is likely to slow soon because the demand for investment goods in the region, though expanding, remains essentially weak, a condition reflecting the overhang of excess manufacturing capacity in several economies. At the same time, domestic consumption demand, while currently buoyant, is expected to taper off in the absence of sustained increases in real income in the region. Indeed, much of such consumption is debt-financed and could thus pose systemic risks in some countries.

***The weakness of the United States dollar may not be entirely negative for the region***

A further influence on the region's export and growth performance over the next 12-18 months arises from the recent weakness of the dollar exchange rate and the strengthening of several regional currencies vis-à-vis the dollar. In theory, and on the face of it, this phenomenon could have a negative impact on these countries' competitiveness. In practice, the negative impact could be relatively small, however. The regional currencies may have strengthened against the dollar but they still remain cheaper on a trade-weighted basis than, say, before the 1997-1998 crisis.

In addition, the weaker dollar and lower interest rates serve to speed up the restructuring of dollar-denominated debt, thus freeing up resources in cash flow terms that would otherwise have been used in debt servicing. It is not clear, however, how competitive advantage has changed among economies whose exchange rates are fixed to the dollar and among those whose exchange rates are not fixed but have, nevertheless, experienced a degree of exchange rate appreciation.

## Policy issues and challenges

***Developing members of ESCAP have still to regain their pre-crisis momentum***

The developing countries of the region performed well in 2002 and could experience a modest improvement in 2003. Nevertheless, at these rates of growth, they would still be a good two percentage points or more below the rates achieved in 1996. The implied shortfall in output translates into lower levels of job creation and, through reduced tax yields, new pressures on government budgets. The immediate policy challenge, therefore, is to regain and sustain the pre-1997 momentum of growth in the region as a whole.

***Higher growth is needed to continue with poverty alleviation in the region***

A point to emphasize is that sustaining the momentum of growth is necessary not merely for its own sake but to provide Governments with the resources to address emerging social issues and problems and alleviate poverty and social distress progressively through the higher levels of employment made possible by durable growth. But economic growth is also needed to help in resolving issues pertaining to corporate and financial sector reform as enunciated in the *Survey 2002.* As discussed previously, significant progress has been made in dealing with these matters over the past five years. However, more decisive action would almost certainly be facilitated by an environment in which businesses, Governments and the public could all discern improvements taking place and reform efforts are not perceived or cease to be construed as an ongoing form of penance. It has to be recognized, too, that reforms are an essential, continuing process that needs to be securely anchored in a realistic framework of development and poverty reduction strategies in developing countries.

On the domestic front, given the higher or rising levels of public debt in many countries, a fundamental question is the degree to which fiscal stimulus can be maintained over the medium term without running the risk of getting caught in the debt trap, a situation where debt starts to grow faster than the means to service it. As discussed in the *Survey 2002,* the issue of fiscal sustainability arises in all economies, including those where the budget deficits have historically existed for some time and where public debt, as a ratio of GDP, has risen to a high level. The same consideration of fiscal sustainability applies to countries where rising public debt is a relatively new phenomenon.

***Lower interest rates have not always led to credit growth***

Monetary policy is also facing difficult choices in several economies.[4] Facilitated by lower interest rates in the developed countries and lower inflation locally, most economies in the region (except one or two) were able to keep interest rates low in 2002. However, lower interest rates have not led to higher credit growth, thus far at any rate. There is a view that despite low interest rates new capital expenditure is unlikely to be undertaken, given the excess capacity still in existence, and monetary easing could instead lead to a build-up of consumer debt in the months ahead.

Thus, monetary easing is as circumscribed in the real world as is fiscal policy, and its stimulating effects could be greatly nullified by a deflationary psychology. The monetary authorities have to ensure that the current phase of low and declining inflation is not transformed into a prolonged deflationary phase. It is also necessary to be aware of the forces causing downward pressure on prices and to fashion an appropriate response to the phenomenon.

On the external front, the size of the current account deficit of the United States along with financial market turmoil poses a major challenge not just for policy makers in the United States but in all open developing economies of the world. Present estimates suggest that the United States current account deficit is likely to increase from 4.7 per cent of GDP in 2002 to 5.0 per cent in 2003.

***Correcting the United States trade imbalance poses dangers for the global economy***

It has been argued for some time that the external imbalance in the United States is unsustainable. The imbalance rose from 1.5 per cent of GDP in 1995, a level at which it had stabilized in the previous two decades, to 4.7 per cent in 2002. Although alarmist talk regarding this deficit has tended to be consistently belied over the years, it is nevertheless true that such a sizeable shortfall cannot continue indefinitely. There would be a threshold above which foreigners would become unwilling to hold United States assets. Some observers argue that the subsequent rebalancing of investors' portfolios away from United States assets could involve a huge readjustment of the dollar exchange rate. Clearly, this might not happen suddenly but the rebalancing process would still pose a considerable challenge for participants in world financial markets and the regional economies as well.

***ESCAP region to maintain commitment to trade liberalization***

By and large, the first requirement is for countries in the region not to add to the uncertainty and possible dislocation in international transactions by taking restrictive measures in the areas of trade and

---

[4] Falling inflation automatically makes monetary conditions tighter even without an increase in interest rates. See Centre for European Policy Studies, *Fiscal and Monetary Policy for a Low-Speed Europe,* 4th Macroeconomic Policy Report of the CEPS Macroeconomic Policy Group, 2002.

financial flows. Regardless of actions being taken by other countries, countries in the ESCAP region should maintain their commitment to the agenda of liberalized trade and financial flows.

In this context, significant momentum has built up within the region independently of WTO through FTAs in the last two to three years. The ASEAN-China commitment to move to a free trade agreement in 10 years is one prominent example. FTAs between Singapore and Australia, Japan, New Zealand and the United States, and between Australia and the United States, for which negotiations have just commenced, are others. Singapore and the Republic of Korea are due to start negotiations later in 2003 for an FTA. From the perspective of the least developed countries, the Japanese Government announced in December 2002 that it would extend the generalized system of preferences to least developed countries, giving them duty-free and quota-free access to Japan starting in fiscal year 2003.

***Falling stock markets partly reflect a loss of investor confidence***

Financial market instability poses rather more complex issues. As at end-December 2002, the trade-weighted exchange rate of the dollar had depreciated by about 10 per cent and stock markets in the United States had fallen by about a fifth. The latter trend precipitated sell-offs virtually across the world, although markets in the ESCAP region have escaped some of the downside pressures. Forecasts are notoriously unreliable where stock markets are concerned and speculating about the next 6-12 months is hazardous in the extreme. However, if the decline in stock markets is prolonged, it could feed back negatively onto the global and regional economies.

With greater globalization, the world's stock markets have become much more correlated regardless of an individual country's fundamentals; and it would be futile to seek to shield individual markets from instability occurring in the bigger, more international markets. Nevertheless, countries in the region could redouble their efforts at enhancing standards of corporate governance and of transparency in corporate accounts. They should also take bold action concerning incidents of corporate malfeasance should they come to light in the future. Greater cooperation in maintaining exchange rate stability is worth exploring but the processes involved raise complex issues. Implementation would appear to be some years away.

***Countries in the region need to continue work on enhancing competitiveness***

As countries of the region gear up to tackle their short-term challenges, they must not lose sight of the need to maintain and, indeed, enhance their competitiveness in the medium term. Competitiveness has both macro and micro aspects and economic and non-economic determinants. Strong public and private contributions are needed to build and sustain the competitive edge.

***Cooperative action to tackle common problems of the world economy is the way forward***

Finally, all countries, whether developed or developing, should strive to tackle the common problems of the world economy in a new spirit of partnership and remain engaged to that end. This is a theme which, as has been suggested in various forums, including in particular the International Conference on Financing for Development, held at Monterrey, Mexico, in March 2002. At that meeting, Governments of developed and developing countries agreed that through ODA the benefits of globalization could reach people living in poverty in many low-income countries. To that end, partnerships between ODA donors and recipient countries must be enhanced and donor assistance structured around the recipient country's own strategy for development. Such partnerships could be extended to other areas, such as containing financial market volatility.

The World Summit on Sustainable Development, held at Johannesburg, South Africa, in August-September 2002, provides another good example of greater cooperation between the developed and developing countries. While falling short of the expectations of many, the World Summit nevertheless signified that developed and developing countries are dependent upon each other to achieve durable progress in solving the world's myriad economic, social and environmental problems. While the Summit has enhanced awareness of environmental issues, it remains true that without much greater cooperation between countries even the limited agreements reached at Johannesburg will be difficult to implement.

However, cooperation does not require that large events like the Johannesburg Summit be staged. Existing international and regional bodies provide forums and vehicles for cooperative endeavours to be identified and implemented. For their part, developed countries should be prepared to take more robust action in the areas of international financial flows, trade, debts and global governance. Developing countries, for their part, should make their domestic policies and institutional arrangements more development-friendly, a prerequisite to improving the utilization of ODA, reducing poverty and tackling deficiencies in the pursuit of these aims on the basis of durable "ownership". Effective ownership and participation require good governance at all levels of society based on realism and honesty, especially in matters concerning previous policy shortcomings in these areas.

As reported in the *Survey 2002,* through the Doha Development Agenda, WTO members agreed to launch a new round of trade negotiations. It is critically important for the global economy that the commitments made at Doha be honoured and that no slippage occur in the time frame for the completion of negotiations in different areas.

In this connection, it needs to be reiterated that the issues outlined by the Secretary-General in his report "Road a map towards the implementation of the United Nations Millennium Declaration" are both urgent and relevant to Doha. The issues are, inter alia, the need for developed nations to comply fully with commitments made under the Uruguay Round for access to their markets for the products of the developing countries in agriculture, textiles and clothing and to ensure that the next round of trade negotiations is truly a development round. It is vital, hence, that the Fifth WTO Ministerial Conference, which is to be held at Cancún, Mexico, in September 2003 and is to take stock of the post-Doha issues and concerns of the developing countries and the progress in negotiations, not get bogged down in discussions over procedural matters and deal constructively with substantive issues that lie at the heart of the Doha Development Agenda.

***The policy agenda for the ESCAP region is little changed from the previous year***

The overall conclusion for the ESCAP region thus consists of a reiteration of suggestions made in previous issues of the *Survey* to support sustainable growth by members over the next 12-18 months and beyond: (a) to speed up structural reforms to make their economies more competitive; (b) to prepare for and manage globalization better by a deeper understanding of the interactions between international and national policies and financial markets; (c) to continue to deepen financial markets and reduce dependence on any one source of finance for development; (d) to strengthen the formulation and implementation of policies, especially prudential macro policies; (e) to enhance the quality of governance in both the public and private sectors; and additionally (f) to minimize conflicts of interest in the field of governance.[5]

It is a truism that the course of events over the next 12 months or so will be conditioned not only by policies but also by unforeseen events. Experience, however, suggests that flexible public policies, based upon a credible and realistic framework of expectations, cannot only insulate economies considerably from adverse developments, but also cushion the impact on economic activities of unforeseen events when they happen. Not all adverse developments can be fully countered by policies and resource constraints remain a problem to be resolved by all economies, developed and developing, but, as has been seen, good policies can contribute to mitigating the adverse effects of disasters, natural or man-made, and to bringing about a quicker recovery in their aftermath. In hindsight, the ESCAP region has displayed considerable resilience in dealing with the 1997-1998 crisis and in meeting the challenges it posed in both the economic and social fields; this applies to the countries directly affected by the crisis as well as to others. The 2001-2002 slowdown provided another opportunity to fashion new policy responses to promote growth in 2003 and, for the region as a whole, to resume its pre-1997 pace of economic and social development.

---

[5] H. Kharas, "Staying on guard", *Bangkok Post*, 5 July 2002.

# MACROECONOMIC PERFORMANCE, ISSUES AND POLICIES

## REGIONAL OVERVIEW

***ESCAP region maintained a relatively strong momentum of growth in 2002 based on easier macroeconomic policies and buoyant intraregional trade***

In March 2002, the secretariat had noted discernible signs of recovery in the global and regional economies following the sharp slowdown in 2001. In the event, while the global economic recovery petered out in 2002 after an encouraging first quarter, the developing economies of the ESCAP region were able to maintain a relatively strong momentum of growth. GDP growth in 2001 by this group of economies was exceeded by nearly 2 percentage points in 2002. Indeed, at 5.1 per cent, it was the fastest-growing group of economies in the world in 2002. All the different subregions improved their growth performance in 2002 relative to 2001. The most impressive improvements in 2002 were recorded by East and North-East Asia and South-East Asia (see table II.1). The Pacific island economies recovered from a decline in GDP in 2001 to positive growth in 2002.

The improved growth performance was based partly on the stimulus provided by easier macroeconomic policies, principally lower interest rates, and partly on the growth of intraregional trade. Macroeconomic easing was facilitated by the low inflationary environment; the collective rate of inflation in developing economies of the ESCAP region declined from 3.5 per cent in 2001 to 2.2 per cent in 2002. International trade by developing countries of the region exceeded world trade growth in 2002 in value terms (plus 2.1 per cent up to August 2002 on a year-on-year basis versus minus 2.4 per cent on the same basis for the world as a whole). However, the increase was offset to some extent by price declines in manufactured goods so that, notwithstanding the improvement in some commodity prices, on an overall basis developing economies of the ESCAP region suffered terms-of-trade losses during the year.

In the later part of 2002, geopolitical uncertainties emanating from the possibility of military conflict in Iraq, the knock-on effects of the terrorist attack in Bali and the situation in the Democratic People's Republic of Korea served to further undermine already low corporate confidence across the globe. Although GDP growth in the region remained largely unaffected by these developments, the uncertainty they generated was discernible in most of the stock markets of the region. By and large, stock markets tended to weaken in 2002 with minor upward rallies.

**Table II.1. Selected economies of the ESCAP region: rates of economic growth and inflation, 2001-2005**

*(Percentage)*

| | Real GDP | | | | | Inflation[a] | | | | |
|---|---|---|---|---|---|---|---|---|---|---|
| | 2001 | 2002[b] | 2003[c] | 2004 | 2005[c] | 2001 | 2002[b] | 2003[c] | 2004[c] | 2005[c] |
| **Developing economies of the ESCAP region[d]** | 3.2 | 5.1 | 5.4 | 5.7 | 5.5 | 3.5 | 2.1 | 2.5 | 2.3 | 2.4 |
| **South and South-West Asia[e]** | 4.6 | 4.5 | 5.8 | 6.2 | 6.5 | 6.5 | 5.9 | 5.4 | 4.9 | 4.2 |
| Bangladesh | 5.3 | 4.8 | 5.2 | 5.7 | .. | 1.6 | 2.4 | 3.0 | 3.0 | .. |
| India | 5.6 | 4.4 | 6.0 | 6.5 | 6.8 | 4.3 | 3.5 | 3.5 | 3.0 | 3.0 |
| Iran (Islamic Republic of) | 4.8 | 6.5 | 6.7 | 6.8 | .. | 11.4 | 15.3 | 14.0 | 13.0 | .. |
| Nepal | 4.9 | 0.8 | 2.5 | 3.5 | .. | 2.4 | 2.9 | 4.5 | .. | .. |
| Pakistan | 2.5 | 3.6 | 4.5 | 5.0 | 5.5 | 4.4 | 3.5 | 4.0 | 4.0 | 4.0 |
| Sri Lanka | −1.4 | 3.0 | 5.3 | 5.9 | 6.3 | 14.2 | 9.5 | 6.7 | 6.6 | 6.4 |
| Turkey | −7.4 | 6.0 | 4.2 | 3.7 | 4.2 | 54.4 | 45.2 | 30.9 | 25.5 | 28.1 |
| **South-East Asia** | 2.2 | 4.0 | 4.7 | 4.7 | 4.5 | 5.9 | 3.7 | 3.9 | 3.8 | 3.9 |
| Cambodia | 5.5 | 4.5 | 6.4 | 6.0 | 6.5 | −0.5 | 3.0 | 3.5 | 3.3 | 3.0 |
| Indonesia | 3.3 | 3.2 | 4.1 | 4.4 | 4.3 | 11.5 | 10.5 | 9.0 | 8.6 | 8.8 |
| Lao People's Democratic Republic | 5.7 | 5.8 | 5.9 | 6.3 | .. | 7.8 | 10.6 | 5.5[f] | 5.0[f] | .. |
| Malaysia | 0.4 | 4.2 | 6.3 | 5.4 | 5.3 | 1.4 | 1.8 | 2.0 | 2.2 | 1.7 |
| Myanmar | 10.5 | 5.5 | 5.8 | 5.4 | .. | 21.1 | 51.3 | 38.2 | 24.9 | .. |
| Philippines | 3.2 | 4.6 | 4.6 | 4.9 | 5.5 | 6.1 | 3.1 | 4.0 | 3.5 | 3.1 |
| Singapore | −2.4 | 2.2 | 4.2 | 4.9 | 5.0 | 1.0 | −0.4 | 1.2 | 1.4 | 1.8 |
| Thailand | 1.8 | 4.9 | 4.5 | 4.4 | 3.4 | 1.7 | 0.7 | 1.5 | 1.3 | 1.9 |
| Viet Nam | 6.8 | 7.0 | 7.5 | 7.5 | 7.5 | −0.4 | 3.9 | 5.3 | 6.3 | 5.8 |
| **East and North-East Asia** | 3.3 | 5.7 | 5.6 | 6.0 | 5.7 | 1.4 | 0.3 | 1.0 | 1.0 | 1.3 |
| China | 7.3 | 7.9 | 7.7 | 7.8 | 7.7 | 0.7 | −0.8 | −0.5 | −0.3 | 0.0 |
| Hong Kong, China | 0.6 | 1.7 | 2.5 | 4.5 | 3.9 | −1.6 | −3.0 | −1.5 | −0.5 | 0.3 |
| Mongolia | 1.1 | 3.9 | 5.0 | .. | .. | 8.0 | 5.0 | 5.0 | .. | .. |
| Republic of Korea | 3.0 | 6.1 | 5.3 | 5.4 | 4.3 | 4.1 | 2.7 | 3.3 | 2.4 | 2.6 |
| Taiwan Province of China | −2.1 | 3.2 | 3.6 | 4.4 | 4.9 | 0.0 | 0.0 | 1.3 | 1.9 | 2.1 |
| **Pacific island economies** | −0.8 | 1.1 | 3.2 | 3.0 | 2.4 | 7.1 | 8.5 | 9.0 | 7.1 | 7.1 |
| Cook Islands | −3.3 | 1.4 | 2.4 | .. | .. | 8.7 | 4.0 | 2.5 | .. | .. |
| Fiji | 4.3 | 4.4 | 5.7 | 3.6 | 3.7 | 4.2 | 2.5 | 3.0 | 3.0 | 3.0 |
| Papua New Guinea | −3.4 | −0.5 | 1.8 | 2.7 | 1.6 | 9.3 | 12.0 | 13.2 | 10.0 | 10.0 |
| Samoa | 6.5 | 1.1 | 6.0 | 5.0 | 5.0 | 4.0 | 6.0 | 3.0 | 2.0 | 3.0 |
| Solomon Islands | −13.0 | 3.0 | 2.5 | 2.0 | 2.0 | 1.8 | 11.0 | 9.0 | 5.0 | 5.0 |
| Tonga | 3.0 | 3.0 | 4.5 | 3.0 | 3.0 | 6.3 | 4.0 | 3.0 | 3.0 | 3.0 |
| Vanuatu | −0.5 | −0.4 | 1.3 | 2.2 | 2.6 | 3.2 | 2.5 | 2.5 | 2.5 | 2.5 |
| **Developed economies of the ESCAP region** | −0.1 | −0.3 | 0.5 | 0.9 | 1.3 | −0.4 | −0.8 | −0.5 | −0.5 | −0.2 |
| Australia | 2.7 | 3.3 | 3.2 | 3.6 | 3.8 | 4.4 | 2.5 | 2.7 | 2.6 | 2.5 |
| Japan | −0.3 | −0.6 | 0.3 | 0.7 | 1.1 | −0.7 | −1.1 | −0.7 | −0.7 | −0.4 |
| New Zealand | 2.5 | 3.8 | 2.6 | 2.8 | 3.1 | 2.7 | 2.6 | 1.9 | 1.8 | 2.0 |

*(Continued on next page)*

**Table II.1** *(continued)*

*(Percentage)*

| | Real GDP | | | | | Inflation[a] | | | | |
|---|---|---|---|---|---|---|---|---|---|---|
| | 2001 | 2002[b] | 2003[c] | 2004[c] | 2005[c] | 2001 | 2002[b] | 2003[c] | 2004[c] | 2005[c] |
| **Memo** | | | | | | | | | | |
| Kazakhstan | 13.5 | 9.5 | 6.7 | 6.7 | 8.5 | 8.5 | 5.9 | 6.2 | 6.7 | 6.8 |
| Russian Federation | 5.0 | 3.9 | 4.0 | 4.1 | 4.5 | 21.6 | 15.1 | 13.6 | 11.9 | 10.0 |
| Uzbekistan | 4.5 | 3.0 | 3.5 | 4.0 | .. | 27.2 | 26.0 | 26.5 | 25.0 | .. |

*Sources:* ESCAP, based on IMF, *International Financial Statistics,* vol. LV, No. 12 (December 2002); ADB, *Key Indicators of Developing Asian and Pacific Countries 2002,* vol. XXXIII (ADB, 2002) and *Asian Development Outlook 2002 Update* (ADB, 2002); Economist Intelligence Unit, *Country Reports* and *Country Forecasts* (London, 2002 and 2003), various issues; web site of the Inter-State Statistical Committee of the Commonwealth of Independent States, <www.cisstat.com>; and national sources.

[a] Changes in the consumer price index.
[b] Estimate.
[c] Forecast/target.
[d] Based on data for 28 developing economies representing about 95 per cent of the population of the region (excluding the Central Asian republics); GDP figures at market prices in United States dollars in 1995 have been used as weights to calculate the regional and subregional growth rates.
[e] The estimates and forecasts for countries relate to fiscal years defined as follows: fiscal year 2002/03 = 2002 for India and the Islamic Republic of Iran; and fiscal year 2001/02 = 2002 for Bangladesh, Nepal and Pakistan.
[f] End-year figures.

There were few signs of a revival in corporate investment spending. Furthermore, as oil prices rose by some 50 per cent by the end of December 2002 on a year-on-year basis and with little evidence of durable growth in the United States, Japan and the EU, which together account for more than 50 per cent of the exports from the region, the outlook for regional growth in 2003 became less favourable.

***ESCAP region faces a daunting array of uncertainties***

As of now (early February 2003) the region is in the grip of a daunting array of uncertainties that render any assessment of the outlook for 2003 problematic in the extreme. Externally, until the situation relating to Iraq becomes clearer, demand for the region's exports in the developed economies could be much weaker than forecast even a few months ago as corporations delay new investment expenditure. Further, the world's financial markets, equities, bonds and foreign exchange, are likely to be buffeted by strong crosswinds of low and fragile investor confidence. This will manifest itself primarily in heightened risk aversion and exaggerated volatility in asset prices and trading volumes. A probable consequence of this could be greater instability in exchange rates, revolving around a weaker United States dollar, and investment funds flowing into safe haven-type outlets, such as precious metals, with deleterious effects even on trade-related cross-border financial transactions. Internally, a prolonged period of uncertainty would clearly have an adverse impact on business and consumer confidence, while the possibility of military conflict in Iraq could deflect Governments in the region from focusing on development issues and implementing their reform agendas owing to a narrower concern with security matters in the short term.

If other things remain the same, however, or if the uncertainties mentioned above resolve themselves quickly and trade and financial flows are not disrupted for a prolonged period, the underlying strength of the economies in the region suggests that the developing economies of the region should be able to maintain their current momentum of growth in 2003 or even enjoy a modest acceleration. But, in order to achieve this, the Governments of the region have to confront major policy issues and challenges. It should be stressed here that the balance of probabilities at the time of writing remains significantly weighted on the downside until the geopolitical situation and associated uncertainties are resolved. In the following paragraphs the recent performance and prospects for each subregion and the common policy issues and challenges facing the ESCAP region as a whole are discussed.

***Least developed and Pacific island countries did not match the rest of the ESCAP region in GDP growth in 2002***

In the least developed countries, GDP growth generally slowed in 2002. This was primarily caused by a slowdown in export growth and not, as in the past, by any adverse domestic developments. Least developed country exports are mainly destined for developed country markets and are still concentrated in a relatively narrow range of items, although newer exports such as garments have made a major contribution to exports and GDP growth in Bangladesh in recent years. Tourism was adversely affected as concerns about security kept tourists away from several of the least developed countries, and especially from countries such as Nepal, where the security situation worsened. On the plus side, inflationary pressures remained muted in the subregion with the exception of Myanmar. For the future, taking the least developed countries as a whole, much depends upon the recovery of global growth in 2003 and more particularly upon growth in the developed countries.

As in the case of the least developed countries, the Pacific island economies did not match the rest of the ESCAP region in showing a significant improvement in GDP growth in 2002. However, taking the economies as a whole, most of which have a narrow production and low population base, GDP stopped contracting and positive growth was attained in all the economies for which data are available, with the exception of Papua New Guinea and Vanuatu. The most visible turnaround occurred in Solomon Islands, where GDP grew in 2002 after experiencing a contraction of 13 per cent in 2001. The lacklustre GDP performance contributed to problems in macroeconomic management. As a result, the inflation rate went up in Papua New Guinea, Samoa and the Solomon Islands but came down in Fiji, Tonga and Vanuatu. Despite the fact that the Pacific island countries are away from the areas of tension, tourism displayed a mixed trend; it recovered in Fiji but not in other tourism-dependent economies. For 2003, overall prospects are for GDP growth to exceed the performance in 2002. The Pacific island economies are substantially influenced by developments in Australia and New Zealand, of which Australia is expected to achieve GDP growth in 2003 at, or close to that achieved in 2002.

***GDP growth in Central Asia remained broadly stable in 2002***

The economies of Central Asia were little affected by the global downturn in 2001 and the pace of GDP growth remained broadly stable in 2002. Growth in the subregion was achieved on the back of growing investor and consumer confidence that attracted enhanced external capital to resource-rich economies such as Kazakhstan and facilitated greater macroeconomic stability, particularly exchange rate stability, as production increased and inflation declined in virtually all the economies of the subregion. Against the overall trend, GDP growth tended to ease somewhat in 2002 relative to 2001 in the three largest economies, but was still maintained at a respectable pace. Central Asia remains heavily dependent upon the Russian Federation and strong growth in that country since the 1998 financial crisis has led to higher trade flows within the subregion on a more sustainable basis. The Russian Federation has been recognized as a market economy and its entry into WTO should boost not only its own development but that of the Central Asian economies, by locking them more firmly into the international economy. Prospects for 2003 are, however, subject to the uncertainty prevailing in the global economy at the present time. In particular, much will depend on the course of energy prices over the coming months.

***GDP growth picked up in South and South-West Asia in 2002 ...***

In South and South-West Asia, GDP growth picked up in 2002 compared with 2001. This was mainly on account of the recovery of Sri Lanka and Turkey from negative growth in 2001 and higher growth in Pakistan and the Islamic Republic of Iran. India, the largest economy in this subregion, saw a marginal decline in its GDP growth rate in 2002 relative to 2001; unfavourable weather affected agricultural production and was essentially responsible for the small overall decline in the GDP growth rate. Inflation in the subregion remained unchanged; it went up in the Islamic Republic of Iran but came down modestly from a very high level in Turkey and in Sri Lanka. On the external trade front, excepting India and Turkey, export growth remained subdued. However, with improved inflows of remittances and foreign capital, the foreign exchange reserve position improved significantly in nearly all countries of the subregion. In the case of India and Pakistan, higher inflows of foreign resources led to balance-of-payments current account surpluses. In 2003, the prospects are for a pickup in the overall GDP growth rate, especially in India, Pakistan and Sri Lanka. However, uncertainties remain: these are primarily external and could affect export growth adversely if growth in the global economy remains tentative or if prolonged military hostilities take place in Iraq. While the economies of the subregion are primarily domestic demand-driven, net exports make a significant contribution to GDP performance at the margin. In addition, other than the Islamic Republic of Iran, the subregion is a heavy importer of energy and higher energy prices would be a negative development for both growth and inflation in the subregion.

***... and in South-East Asia***

In South-East Asia, the rate of GDP growth improved from 2.3 per cent in 2001 to 4 per cent in 2002. Growth was strong in Malaysia and Thailand, driven, for the most part, by buoyant consumption aided by an upturn in electronics and electrical goods exports. Higher commodity prices were another positive feature in the subregion. These factors also applied to Viet Nam, where GDP growth remained buoyant in 2002. Growth was less strong in the Philippines and Indonesia, where the incidence of terrorist attacks tended to dampen business investment expenditures; the attacks, however, had a minimal impact on tourism in the subregion, which accounts for 4-5 per cent of GDP in South-East Asia generally.[1] Slower growth in the global economy in the second half of 2002 caused export growth to taper off in these economies and this phenomenon was responsible for the modest increase in output in Singapore in 2002 following a contraction in 2001. The outlook for 2003 is clouded by uncertainty on the external front. Even though exports to China increased rapidly in 2002 and should continue to grow in 2003, this may not be sufficient to offset the lack of robust growth in the United States, Japan and the EU. Domestically, strong consumption growth facilitated by easier macroeconomic policies is likely to be sustained but could come up against rising personal debt levels and the need to begin fiscal consolidation, given the rising public debt in several economies. Subject to these caveats and the uncertainties in the international situation, the subregion should enjoy stronger growth in 2003.

***Led by China East and North-East Asia was the best performing subregion in 2002***

East and North-East Asia was the best performing subregion in 2002, led by strong growth in China and the Republic of Korea. Mongolia, the smallest economy in the subregion, also improved its GDP growth rate in 2002. In China, growth was particularly robust in the first half of the year. Both domestic demand and exports supported growth in the subregion. Domestic demand is mainly investment-driven in China but rapidly rising middle-class incomes are boosting personal consumption expenditure as well, leading to the production of a wide array of consumer goods and a surge in FDI. In the Republic of Korea, domestic demand is both investment- and consumption-driven, the latter by the more liberal availability of personal credit from the financial system. Exports increased sharply in the first half of 2002 as a result of the upturn in the ICT sector. In the case of China, there was strong growth of imports from the region, with eight economies increasing the volume of exports to China by around 50 per cent in the first half of 2002. Growth was less strong in Taiwan Province of China and barely perceptible in Hong Kong, China. The former economy remains closely tied to the dynamics of

---

[1] World Bank, "Making progress in uncertain times: regional overview", *East Asia Update*, November 2002.

boom and slowdown in the global high-tech industry, while the latter, which is now primarily a services oriented economy, has been affected by the slowdown in cross-border financial transactions. Domestically, rising unemployment and falling property prices in Hong Kong, China, have shaken consumer confidence and, as in Japan, the economy has become mired in deflation, prices having fallen for four straight years. Deflation also affects China to some extent and Taiwan Province of China has seen no rise in prices for three years. Prospects for the subregion in 2003 are that GDP growth rates will be broadly maintained. This is likely to be the case in both China and the Republic of Korea, and some recovery in Hong Kong, China, and Taiwan Province of China.

***Japan experienced recession but Australia and New Zealand performed well in 2002***

Of the three developed countries of the region, in 2001 and 2002 Japan experienced its third and severest recession for several years. By contrast, Australia and New Zealand, with buoyant domestic demand, showed relatively strong growth at the upper end of growth within the OECD economies. This was despite drought in Australia, which reduced agricultural output substantially. There was deflation in Japan, while price pressures remained mild in Australia and New Zealand. The consensus view is that the Japanese economy appears to have bottomed out in 2002 and could see positive growth, albeit at a modest pace in 2003, as measures to speed up reforms in the banking sector begin to take effect. In Australia and New Zealand, strong domestic demand should preserve the current momentum of growth. However, with a deteriorating external environment and other uncertainties, there are risks on the downside. These are already reflected in lower consumer confidence in the two economies and a slower pace of output growth in the second half of 2002.

## POLICY ISSUES AND CHALLENGES

***Geopolitical uncertainties raise major policy issues and challenges***

The greatest threat to the region lies in the danger of a major military conflict in Iraq. In addition, the situation in the Democratic People's Republic of Korea or a major terrorist attack could markedly worsen prospects in the region. Indeed, to some degree the uncertainties thus generated are already manifesting themselves in higher oil prices and weak and volatile financial markets in the region, which, if prolonged, are likely to undermine both consumer and business confidence. In a worst-case scenario, a prolonged war in Iraq could set in train its own unpredictable security and sociopolitical dynamics and Governments would have to respond with policy adjustments as appropriate. The following paragraphs discuss the policy issues and challenges facing the region on the assumption that there will be no major and/or prolonged military action in Iraq.

Given the absence of any evidence of a strong pickup in the global economy, at least in the first half of 2003, sustaining growth in the region will depend primarily upon growth-stimulating domestic policies. Any impetus from higher intraregional trade flows would enhance the effects of such policies.

Sustaining a high momentum of growth is needed not merely for its own sake but to address the issues relating to poverty in the region and simultaneously assist economies in the region in continuing to make progress in tackling corporate and financial sector reform. In this regard, it should be stressed that higher public expenditure on domestic law and order and security, while clearly diverting resources from other uses in the short term, is actually essential for development because of its positive impact on levels of confidence in the relevant economies. It is particularly important in economies that have significant tourism sectors.

***Domestic demand stimulation needed to maintain the momentum of growth in most economies***

Domestic demand stimulus measures have relied on a mixture of fiscal and monetary policies. There is no doubt that with levels of public debt exceeding 50 per cent of GDP in most economies of the region the question of fiscal consolidation has to be tackled in earnest before too long. In the case of monetary policy also, interest rates have reached quite low levels as a result of falling inflation, so that the scope for further reduction is limited in most countries. Given the varying positions of individual economies of the region in this context, any general policy recommendation would clearly be inappropriate. However, there would appear to be a strong case for Governments to put both fiscal and monetary policies within a medium-term framework in which short-term flexibility can be combined with medium- or longer-term discipline. Countries could begin implementing a programme of refinancing older, higher-cost debt with lower-cost debt, given the lower interest rates currently available, and anchor it within a credible debt target, measured as a ratio to GDP, to be achieved, say, over the next five years taking into account currency and other risks.

With regard to monetary policy and the use of inflation targeting, there is some concern that the authorities may be erring on the side of keeping inflation low and thus sacrificing growth to some extent. Since very low rates of inflation, or even deflation, rather than high inflation are prevalent in a number of economies in the region and could potentially be as intractable as high inflation, the need for more flexible monetary policies is obvious. In particular, low inflation caused by a collapse in demand following the bursting of an asset bubble is likely to require rather more aggressive policy interventions than incremental adjustments in interest rates.

***Corporate and financial sector reform should be reinvigorated to sustain long-term growth***

The programmes of reform of the corporate and financial sectors that have been formulated in several countries over the last five years must continue to be implemented with renewed vigour. The problem of corporate restructuring involving major balance-sheet adjustments in terms of lower debt-equity ratios has made only slow progress thus far. This problem is intimately related to the NPL problem in banks, which, in turn, is an impediment to the revival of credit demand in many economies of the region. Ideally, both of these problems need to be substantially reduced over the next three to five years. It is worth noting that levels of investment in the private sector are still below pre-1997 levels in South-East Asia. Without a pickup in private investment, long-term growth is likely to be jeopardized.

***ESCAP economies must strive to enhance international competitiveness***

The reform effort applies equally to improved standards of governance and more efficient delivery of services in the public sector. Governments in the region need to instil much greater discipline, higher standards of accountability and more effective utilization of the limited resources available to them for the provision of public services. Waste and corruption not only lead to the poorer delivery of services but also lower the morale of providers and users alike and undermine productivity in the economy.

By the same token, as emphasized in the past, countries dependent upon ODA need to redouble their efforts to improve the utilization of external assistance by drawing up realistic projects for such funding and improving their aid management skills. The improved climate for ODA flows may suffer major harm if aid utilization skills do not match up to much higher expectations in the future.

One of the central challenges of globalization is that countries have to compete for markets. Globalization manifests itself in intensified competition among firms on a transnational basis, necessitating efficiency in the utilization of both capital and human resources. Governments must strive to provide a stable macroeconomic environment, realistic exchange rates and improvements in the physical infrastructure to enable firms to compete, and the firms themselves must promote innovation, improve product and service quality and become more receptive to change.

The momentum of trade liberalization, including action in trade facilitation, should be maintained. It is widely accepted that regional trading arrangements can be a useful complement to the multilateral trading system and enhance its effectiveness. Nevertheless, the recent increase in bilateral trade agreements in the region should not serve to reduce the commitment of Governments to promote the multilateral objectives of the Doha Development Agenda agreed at the fourth WTO Ministerial Conference, held at Doha, Qatar, in November 2001.

***Greater regional cooperation needed to counter terrorism, enhance security and maintain vigilance over financial markets***

The current weaknesses in the global economy and concerns with security issues such as terrorism and the use of the international financial system by terrorists require significantly enhanced cooperation at the regional level in the exchange of information, intelligence and policy-making in the area of security. In previous years the need for vigilance in pre-empting financial crises and containing their contagion has been stressed. Policy coordination to enhance growth is another area deserving attention and such coordination could be promoted initially through the various subregional organizations in the ESCAP region. An area in which this would be particularly appropriate is developing policy responses to the unravelling of the global balance-of-payments position involving major exchange rate adjustments in the months ahead.

# DEVELOPING ECONOMIES OF THE ESCAP REGION

## East and North-East Asia

### *Subregional overview and prospects*

***The economy of China remained robust and other economies of the subregion staged a strong economic performance***

The economic recovery in the subregion, which began late in 2001, continued to strengthen in the first half of 2002, but the momentum slowed mid-year as the global economic outlook became increasingly uncertain. China registered solid annual growth of 7.9 per cent, buttressed by strong domestic demand and improved external demand, while the Republic of Korea achieved a growth rate of 6.1 per cent in 2002, more than double the previous year's performance (figure II.1). Mongolia more than tripled the previous year's growth rate to reach 3.9 per cent in 2002, while the comparatively low growth rate of Hong Kong, China, at 1.7 per cent in 2002, was still significantly better than that in 2001.

**Figure II.1. Rates of GDP growth in selected East and North-East Asian economies, 1999-2002**

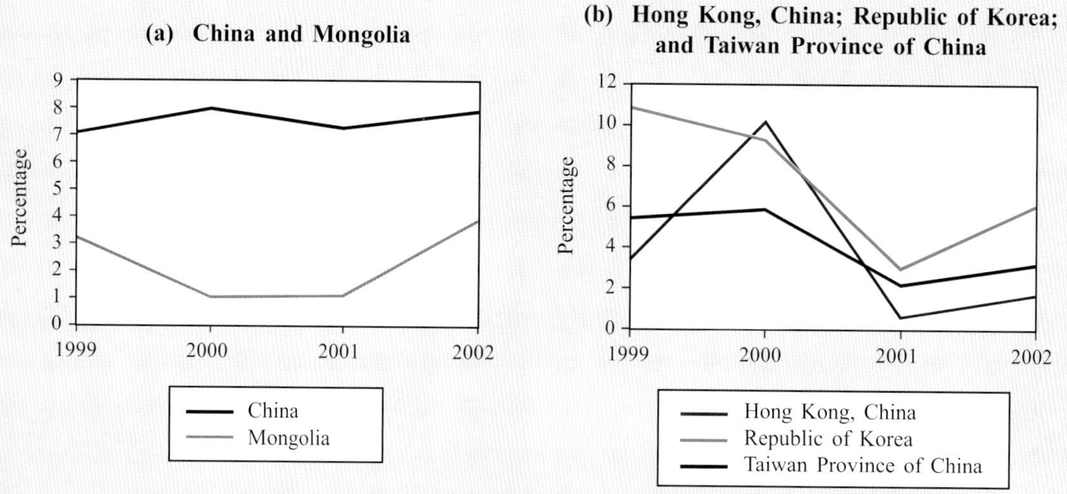

**(a) China and Mongolia**

**(b) Hong Kong, China; Republic of Korea; and Taiwan Province of China**

*Sources:* ESCAP, based on ADB, *Key Indicators of Developing Asian and Pacific Countries 2002,* vol. XXXIII (ADB, 2002) and *Asian Development Outlook 2002 Update* (ADB, 2002); Economist Intelligence Unit, *Country Forecasts* (London, 2002), various issues; and national sources.

*Note:* Data for 2002 are estimates.

Differences in the growth rates among the economies of the subregion reflected, in part, differences in the strength of domestic demand as stimulated by expansionary government policies. All countries pursued expansionary fiscal policies in 2002, which led to widening fiscal deficits. However, domestic demand was also boosted by increased incomes in urban households in China, while both fixed investment and consumption were strengthened by higher exports in the Republic of Korea. In Hong Kong, China, domestic demand remained sluggish owing to high unemployment, falling earnings, deflation and weak consumer confidence.

***China and Hong Kong, China, under deflationary pressure***

Consumer prices fell by 0.8 per cent in China in 2002, after low rates of inflation in the previous two years, owing to excess supply and general price cuts following the country's membership in WTO, which resulted in, among other things, tariff reductions and increased price competition (figure II.2). In Hong Kong, China, the marked deflation in 1999-2000, which had appeared to be slowing in 2001, continued in 2002 when prices fell by 3 per cent as the macroeconomic fundamentals and property prices remained weak. Inflation moderated noticeably in the Republic of Korea, but the continued upward trend in property

**Figure II.2. Inflation in selected East and North-East Asian economies, 1999-2002[a]**

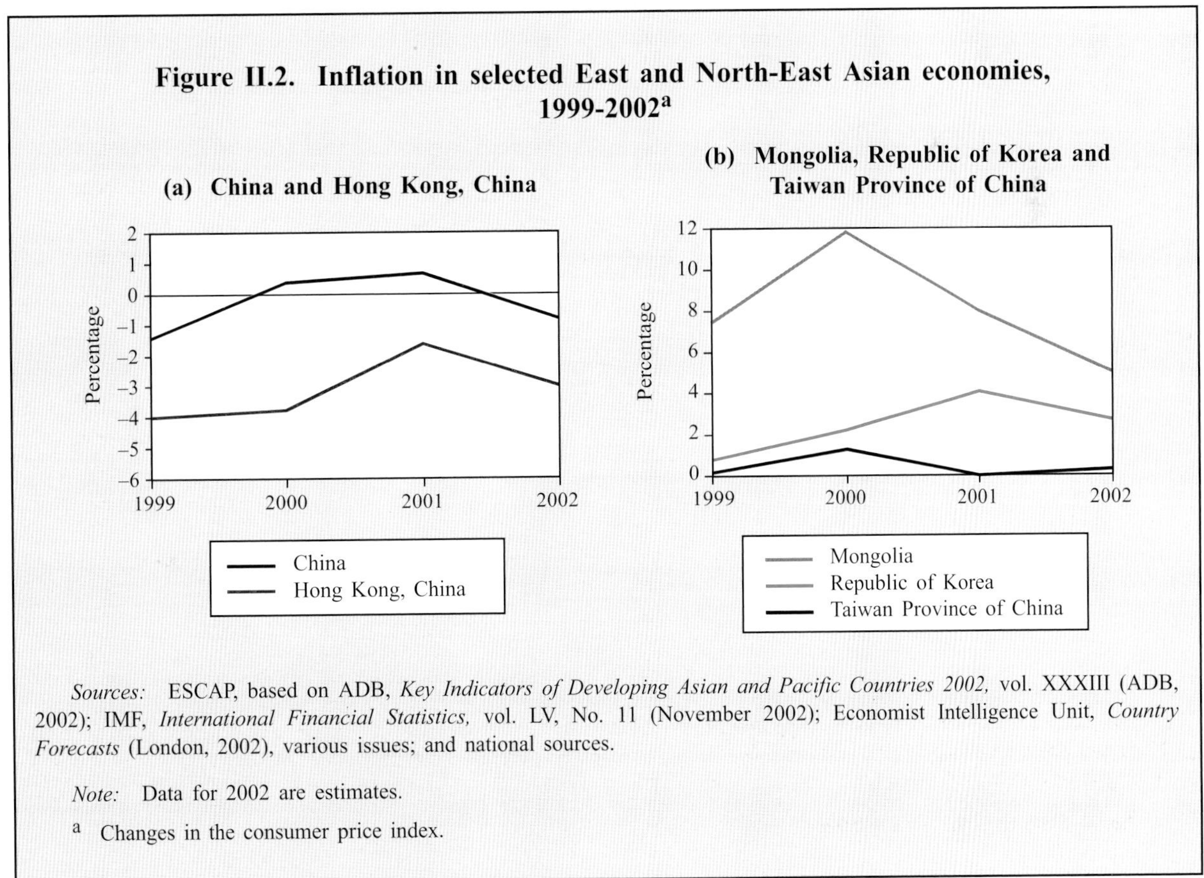


*Sources:* ESCAP, based on ADB, *Key Indicators of Developing Asian and Pacific Countries 2002,* vol. XXXIII (ADB, 2002); IMF, *International Financial Statistics,* vol. LV, No. 11 (November 2002); Economist Intelligence Unit, *Country Forecasts* (London, 2002), various issues; and national sources.

*Note:* Data for 2002 are estimates.

[a] Changes in the consumer price index.

rentals and a price hike for agricultural products largely influenced the annual price increase rate of 2.7 per cent in 2002. In Mongolia, inflation also slowed markedly to 5 per cent in 2002, thanks to stable food prices.

***China's exports soared and its robust economic performance pulled up intraregional trade***

Exports in most economies of the subregion picked up gradually with a recovery in global demand, including the high-tech sector, early in the year (figure II.3). Thanks to the strong performance of China, intraregional trading activities were also buoyant. China's merchandise exports soared by almost 30 per cent year on year during the first eight months of 2002, in part reflecting greater price competitiveness. This was accompanied by a widened trade surplus as imports grew at a much slower rate than exports (figure II.4). In particular, the expansion of export growth to the United States and developing countries in Asia as well as to Hong Kong, China, more than offset a slowdown in exports to Japan and the EU. Meanwhile, merchandise exports from Hong Kong, China, went up by 2.8 per cent year on year in the second quarter of 2002

**Figure II.3. Growth rates in merchandise export earnings of selected East and North-East Asian economies, 1999-2002**

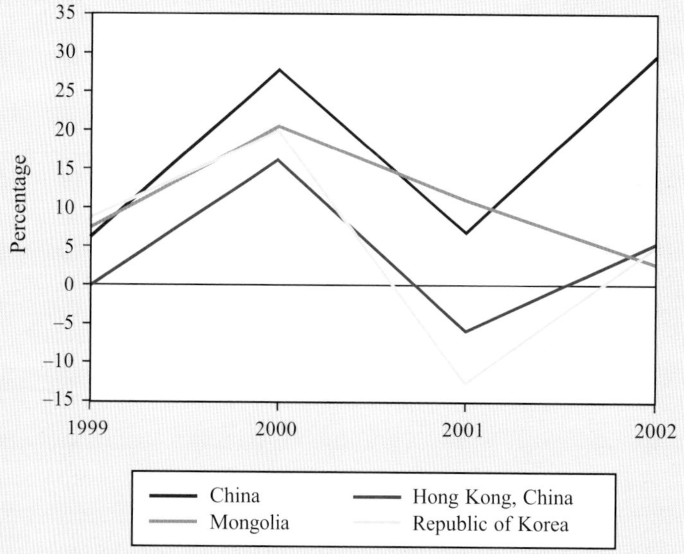

Percentage

35
30
25
20
15
10
5
0
-5
-10
-15

1999 2000 2001 2002

China
Mongolia
Hong Kong, China
Republic of Korea

*Sources:* IMF, *Direction of Trade Statistics* (CD-ROM), January 2003; web site of the Hong Kong, China, Census and Statistics Department, <http://www.info.gov.hk/censtatd/eng/public/index2_fp.html>, 28 January 2003; Ministry of Finance and Economy, *Republic of Korea Economic Bulletin* (Seoul), various issues; and national sources.

*Note:* Data for 2002 refer to January-August for China and Mongolia and to January-October for the Republic of Korea.

**Figure II.4. Growth rates in merchandise import spending of selected East and North-East Asian economies, 1999-2002**

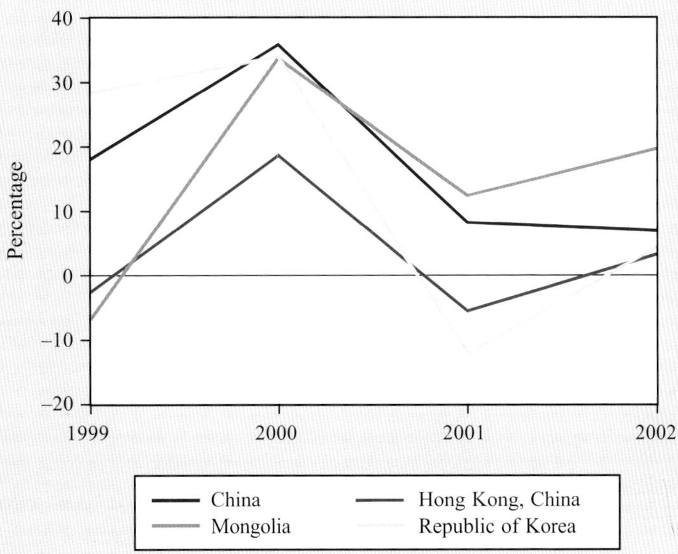


*Sources:* IMF, *Direction of Trade Statistics* (CD-ROM), January 2003; web site of the Hong Kong, China, Census and Statistics Department, <http://www.info.gov.hk/censtatd/eng/public/index2_fp.html>, 28 January 2003; Ministry of Finance and Economy, *Republic of Korea Economic Bulletin* (Seoul), various issues; and national sources.

*Note:* Data for 2002 refer to January-August for China and Mongolia and to January-October for the Republic of Korea.

after contracting for four consecutive quarters; the expansion was mainly driven by exports to Asia and North America. Merchandise imports increased marginally in the same quarter.

***High-tech exports rebounded in the Republic of Korea***

The Republic of Korea's exports returned to positive growth in 2002, with a rebound in demand for high-tech products such as semiconductors and wireless communications. Exports of electronic products and passenger cars also increased, by 13 and 10 per cent respectively, in the first eight months of 2002 compared with the same period a year earlier. Strong domestic spending also drew in more imports. Mongolia's exports crept up only marginally in the first eight months of 2002 as demand for copper, its major export commodity, remained weak owing to the incomplete recovery in the external high-tech sector. A significant expansion in imports caused the Mongolian trade deficit to reach $192 million in the first eight months of 2002.

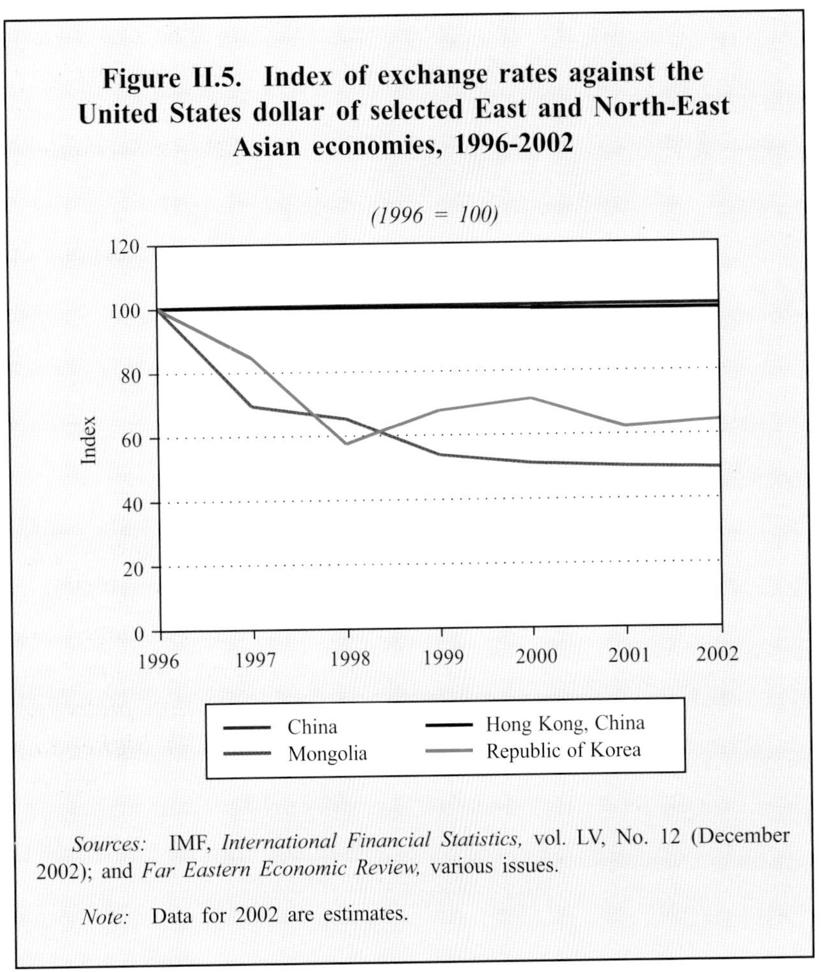


**Figure II.5. Index of exchange rates against the United States dollar of selected East and North-East Asian economies, 1996-2002**

*Sources:* IMF, *International Financial Statistics,* vol. LV, No. 12 (December 2002); and *Far Eastern Economic Review,* various issues.

*Note:* Data for 2002 are estimates.

With the exception of the Republic of Korea, exchange rates were generally stable in the subregion, with the authorities in China countering upward pressures on the exchange rate resulting from the strong balance-of-payments position and Hong Kong, China, maintaining its currency board arrangement with the United States dollar (figure II.5). Relative stability in the nominal exchange rate has also been maintained in Mongolia since 2000, whereas in the Republic of Korea there was a 10 per cent appreciation in the nominal exchange rate of the won against the United States dollar in 2002.

***Continued strong growth, accompanied by buoyant trade, is expected in China in 2003***

The economic outlook for the subregion is conditioned by several major risk factors, in particular, the possibility of a military conflict in the Middle East, leading to rising oil prices. Although the high price of oil appears to have had no significant impact on inflation in these economies so far, it is likely to have a negative impact on growth, especially in the countries that are almost entirely dependent on oil imports, including the Republic of Korea. China's growth prospects in 2003 are more or less the same as in 2002. Supported by a strong pace of investment expenditure, its economy is forecast to grow by 7-8 per cent in 2003, with stable or slightly lower prices. Expansionary policies are likely to be maintained by the Government, although the growing budget deficit could constrain the continued use of fiscal stimulus packages somewhat over the years. Private consumption is expected to continue to grow strongly, as is gross fixed investment, bolstered by both public sector investment and higher FDI inflows following China's entry into WTO. Inward FDI to China is projected to reach $58 billion in 2003, boosting export production capacity. Although the volume of imports is likely to rise, a large merchandise trade surplus is also expected in 2003.

*The export-led recovery in Hong Kong, China, is likely to be modest*

The economy of Hong Kong, China, is expected to experience an export-led recovery in 2003, with an annual growth rate of 2.5 per cent, on the back of strong growth in mainland China. The domestic recovery is expected to take time because of ongoing restructuring. Consumption growth will continue to be constrained by high unemployment and low property prices. Investment is also likely to be negatively affected by the weak property market and weak demand for fixed investment as some continuing deflation is likely to increase real interest rates.

Mongolia's economy is expected to grow by 5.0 per cent in 2003, with robust growth in the industrial and service sectors. Key risks to economic growth are weather-related losses in the agricultural sector, while investor and donor confidence needs to be sustained in the market-oriented structural reform process.

*Growth in the Republic of Korea will be somewhat slower in 2003 as inflation picks up with higher oil prices*

Growth in the Republic of Korea is expected to be strong but marginally slower, at 5.3 per cent, in 2003. Export performance is expected to remain robust, underpinned by a gradual pickup in the United States and Japanese economies and an acceleration in world trade growth. However, rising uncertainties over South-North relations on the Korean peninsula and the global economy could have a dampening effect, while domestic demand will be more muted than in 2002. Notwithstanding rising oil prices, the inflation rate is likely to be somewhat offset by the slowdown in consumer spending.

### GDP growth performance

*China continues to sustain high growth, with strong expansion in fixed investment and exports*

The Chinese economy is estimated to have grown at the rate of 7.9 per cent in 2002, faster than the 7.3 per cent growth rate recorded in 2001 (table II.2). A robust uplift in fixed investment, together with surging export earnings, were responsible for this striking economic performance in 2002. In the first eight months of 2002, for example, merchandise exports increased by almost 30 per cent as the global economy recovered moderately. Meanwhile, sustained by strong private sector investment and continued government spending on infrastructure, gross fixed investment went up by 24.5 per cent in January-August 2002, over 5 percentage points above the growth rate in the corresponding period of 2001. In particular, investment by State-owned enterprises and foreign-funded enterprises contributed substantially to boosting fixed asset investment; the investment ratio was up to 38.5 per cent of GDP in 2002 from just under 38 per cent in the previous year (table II.3). Property investment, accounting for almost a quarter of total fixed investment, increased by another one third in the first six months of 2002, in part as a result of the low interest rates. The total value of property sales was equivalent to 7.5 per cent of GDP, and housing mortgage loans constituted almost one tenth of the total outstanding loans of all financial institutions. There is

**Table II.2. Selected East and North-East Asian economies: growth rates, 1999-2002**

*(Percentage)*

| | | Rates of growth | | | |
|---|---|---|---|---|---|
| | | *Gross domestic product* | *Agriculture* | *Industry* | *Services* |
| China | 1999 | 7.1 | 2.8 | 8.1 | 7.5 |
| | 2000 | 8.0 | 2.4 | 9.6 | 7.8 |
| | 2001 | 7.3 | 2.8 | 9.9 | 7.4 |
| | 2002 | 7.9 | 3.0 | 12.6 | 6.8 |
| Hong Kong, China | 1999 | 3.4 | .. | .. | .. |
| | 2000 | 10.2 | .. | .. | .. |
| | 2001 | 0.6 | −2.6 | −2.5 | 1.3 |
| | 2002 | 1.7 | .. | .. | .. |
| Mongolia | 1999 | 3.2 | 4.2 | 1.1 | 3.5 |
| | 2000 | 1.1 | −14.4 | 1.3 | 18.3 |
| | 2001 | 1.1 | −16.0 | 13.0 | 8.2 |
| | 2002 | 3.9 | .. | .. | .. |
| Republic of Korea | 1999 | 10.9 | 5.4 | 12.8 | 9.9 |
| | 2000 | 9.3 | 2.0 | 11.9 | 7.9 |
| | 2001 | 3.0 | 1.4 | 2.6 | 3.6 |
| | 2002 | 6.1 | 0.5 | 7.0 | 5.2 |

*Sources:* ESCAP, based on ADB, *Key Indicators of Developing Asian and Pacific Countries 2002,* vol. XXXIII (ADB, 2002) and *Asian Development Outlook 2002 Update* (ADB, 2002); Economist Intelligence Unit, *Country Forecasts* (London, 2002), various issues; and national sources.

*Notes:* Data for 2002 are estimates. Industry comprises mining and quarrying; manufacturing; electricity, gas and power; and construction.

growing concern that the property market could become unstable and the Government has taken several precautionary measures, such as controlling new development projects by companies with poor financial standing.

***The rising incomes of urban households boosted consumption expenditure***

Consumption expenditure was also growing steadily, along with an increase in retail sales of over 10 per cent in real terms during the first nine months of 2002. As a result, the high savings rate decreased from an estimated 38.5 per cent of GDP in 2001 to 37.8 per cent in 2002. The robust consumer spending was largely due to higher urban household incomes, which rose 17.2 per cent in the first nine months of the year compared with an increase of 8.5 per cent during the same period in 2001. There was, however, a slower rate of expansion of income growth in rural areas, from 1.9 per cent in 2000 to 4.2 per cent in 2001 and further to 5.3 per cent during the first nine months of 2002. Such a pattern of earnings growth, if it persisted, could serve to widen the rural-urban income disparity.

**Table II.3. Selected East and North-East Asian economies: ratios of gross domestic savings and investment to GDP, 1999-2002**

*(Percentage)*

| | *1999* | *2000* | *2001* | *2002* |
|---|---|---|---|---|
| **Savings as a percentage of GDP** | | | | |
| China | 39.5 | 38.9 | 38.5 | 37.8 |
| Hong Kong, China | 30.9 | 32.9 | 31.6 | 33.6 |
| Mongolia | 20.0 | 18.0 | 18.0 | 19.0 |
| Republic of Korea | 36.9 | 35.6 | 33.3 | 33.7 |
| **Investment as a percentage of GDP** | | | | |
| China | 37.5 | 36.1 | 37.9 | 38.5 |
| Hong Kong, China | 25.3 | 28.1 | 26.5 | 24.4 |
| Mongolia | 27.0 | 29.0 | 28.0 | 29.0 |
| Republic of Korea | 29.4 | 30.8 | 29.5 | 32.0 |

*Sources:* ESCAP, based on ADB, *Key Indicators of Developing Asian and Pacific Countries 2002,* vol. XXXIII (ADB, 2002) and *Asian Development Outlook 2002* (Oxford University Press, 2002); and national sources.

*Note:* Data for 2002 are estimates.

***The high-tech sector made remarkable strides in China in 2002***

Agricultural production in China displayed the steady growth of recent years, expanding at an annual rate of 3 per cent in 2002, as it continued the transition to greater market-based orientation. Growth in industrial output showed a rising trend, reaching a rate of 12.6 per cent in 2002, compared with an average rate of just under 10 per cent a year in 2000-2001. Major sources of industrial value added were electrical products, transport equipment, especially automobiles, electronic communications equipment, such as personal computers and mobile phones, tobacco and steel products. The high-tech sector in China also recorded remarkable progress in 2002, particularly in the ICT industries, posting about 20 per cent in additional output in 2002. A third spaceship was successfully launched during the year. The growth rate in the service sector, however, slowed somewhat to 6.8 per cent in 2002, compared with an annual average of 7.6 per cent in 2000-2001. Part of the reason for this slower expansion could be the opening up of the domestic service markets after China's entry into WTO. In 2002, there were more foreign-funded companies in the fields of telecommunications, banking, insurance, retail trade and logistics than in 2001. The increased participation of well-known multinationals is expected to promote the development of China's service sector in the coming years owing to the transfer of expertise and increased competition.

***The strong growth in exports to mainland China offset the prolonged weakness in domestic demand in Hong Kong, China***

Hong Kong, China, has been recovering slowly from the global downturn that hit the subregion hard in 2001. The economy turned around to display a positive gain in total production in the second quarter of 2002; and a further gain in the third quarter. Helped by a stronger performance in exports of goods and services, the annual GDP growth rate reached 1.7 per cent in 2002, as against 0.6 per cent in 2001. Sustained strong demand from mainland China provided a substantial stimulus to merchandise exports, which also benefited from greater external price competitiveness owing to the weaker United States dollar. In contrast, domestic demand in Hong Kong, China, remained subdued; both private consumer spending and gross fixed capital formation declined from the last quarter of 2001 to the third quarter of 2002. A sharp decrease in investment spending on machinery, equipment and computer software outweighed the modest increase in building and construction, with negative effects on the productive potential of the economy. At the same time, weaknesses in the property market and corporate downsizing dampened consumer confidence with ripple effects on retail sales. The negative wealth effect resulting from the sluggish property and stock markets is expected to constrain domestic demand again in 2003.

***In Mongolia, stronger growth in 2002 was led by a robust performance in manufacturing***

Mongolia's economy performed better in 2002, expanding by 3.9 per cent, compared with just over 1 per cent in the previous year. The harsh winters of 2000 and 2001 caused large losses in animal herds as well as a significant decline in the output of the livestock sector, which accounted for about a quarter of GDP. Mongolia's agricultural sector has been an important source of economic growth, contributing more than half of the gains in total output during the 1990s. However, the sector is extremely vulnerable to climatic shocks, which can be only partially countered by adequate prior planning and other measures. In this context, a brighter note is that the industrial and service sectors have been contributing a greater share to overall GDP growth in recent years. Industrial output, for example, is estimated to have risen at an annual rate of 13 per cent in 2001 and an estimated 11.3 per cent year on year during the first eight months of 2002; a complementary pickup in the secondary or supportive industries is expected to push overall growth in the industrial sector higher. The best performing subsector continues to be manufacturing, registering an expansion of output by about two fifths year on year during the same period.

***The growth of the Republic of Korea rebounded with strong expansionary policies***

After experiencing a sharp decline in GDP growth in 2001 to 3 per cent from an average of 10.1 per cent a year in 1999-2000, the Korean economy rebounded strongly in the first quarter of 2002 and the gathering momentum resulted in an estimated expansion in aggregate output of 6.1 per cent growth for the year. The economic recovery was fuelled primarily by strong domestic demand; private consumption went up by

8 per cent year on year in the first six months of the year and fixed investment also rose very strongly in the second quarter of 2002. Monetary easing, which lowered interest rates, led to higher bank lending to households and hence stronger spending on consumer durables and housing investment. There was some concern about credit card delinquency, greater consumer debt and a potential housing price bubble in the cities, but the overall savings rate was maintained at 33.7 per cent of GDP in 2002, marginally higher than that of the previous year.

Merchandise exports also began to increase in the second quarter of 2002, led by high-tech products such as ICT manufactures, and growth in the first 10 months of 2002 is estimated at 4.9 per cent. The Republic of Korea was the largest producer of mobile telephones in the world, producing 112 million in 2002, of which 96 million were destined for export. Export earnings on ICT products maintained their robust growth, despite pervasive concerns over the delay in the economic recovery of the developed countries.

The low interest rate environment and robust economic recovery helped both the financial and corporate sectors to improve profitability, which was one of the goals of the ongoing economic restructuring. In turn, the improved business climate was reflected in a noticeable rise in the investment ratio to 32 per cent of GDP in 2002, from 29.5 per cent a year earlier. The industrial and service sectors expanded by 7 and 5.2 per cent respectively in 2002, reversing the declining trend in the growth rates of those sectors during the period 1999-2001. However, the agricultural sector, with a relative share of just 5 per cent of GDP in 2000, continued on a declining growth trend, expanding by only 0.5 per cent in 2002.

### *Inflation*

***Consumer prices in the subregion remained in check, or even declined***

In East and North-East Asia in 2002, inflation slowed in the Republic of Korea and Mongolia, while China, and Hong Kong, China, registered some measure of deflation (table II.4). Consumer prices in China declined by 0.8 per cent in 2002 after low or negative inflation in the period 1999-2001, the main reasons being oversupply and fierce price competition. Along with China's entry into WTO, large reductions in import tariffs were implemented at the beginning of 2002. This in effect forced local producers to cut prices in order to compete with imports and, together with the excess production capacity for most consumer products, contributed to downward pressure on consumer prices. According to the Domestic Trade Information Center, among more than 600 different industrial products, no item was in short supply. Of the various product categories that make up the consumption basket, only the costs of recreation, education and residential housing went up; the prices for other items,

**Table II.4. Selected East and North-East Asian economies: inflation and money supply growth (M2), 1999-2002**

*(Percentage)*

| | *1999* | *2000* | *2001* | *2002* |
|---|---|---|---|---|
| **Inflation**[a] | | | | |
| China | –1.4 | 0.4 | 0.7 | –0.8 |
| Hong Kong, China | -4.0 | –3.8 | –1.6 | –3.0 |
| Mongolia | 7.5 | 11.8 | 8.0 | 5.0 |
| Republic of Korea | 0.8 | 2.2 | 4.1 | 2.7 |
| **Money supply growth (M2)** | | | | |
| China | 14.7 | 12.3 | 15.0 | 19.1[b] |
| Hong Kong, China | 8.3 | 9.3 | -0.3 | –0.9[c] |
| Mongolia | 31.6 | 17.6 | 27.9 | 34.1[b] |
| Republic of Korea | 27.4 | 25.4 | 13.2 | 10.9 |

*Sources:* ESCAP, based on ADB, *Key Indicators of Developing Asian and Pacific Countries 2002,* vol. XXXIII, (ADB, 2002); IMF, *International Financial Statistics,* vol. LV, No. 11 (November 2002); Economist Intelligence Unit, *Country Forecasts* (London, 2002), various issues; and national sources.

*Note:* Data for 2002 are estimates.

[a] Changes in the consumer price index.
[b] January-August.
[c] January-July.

such as transport and communications services, household facilities and services and clothing, declined in 2002. Consecutive increases in grain production in the previous four years also helped to keep food prices stable. However, strong domestic demand, boosted by rapid economic growth in recent years, served to contain the fall in prices. As producer prices have started to stabilize recently and the Central Bank has begun to increase the money supply, the rate of deflation in China is expected to slow to approximately 0.5 per cent in 2003. In particular, interest rates were cut in February 2002, for the first time since 1999, in order to stimulate sustained economic growth.

***Falling property prices in Hong Kong, China, have been responsible for over half of the decline in consumer prices***

The rate of deflation accelerated to 3 per cent in Hong Kong, China, in 2002 after having shown some signs of stabilizing in 2001, when the fall in consumer prices was 1.6 per cent; deflation had averaged 3.9 per cent annually in 1999-2000. Among the main contributing factors to falling prices were weaknesses in the property market. According to an official source, falling property prices were responsible for 57 per cent of the deflation observed over the last four and a half years. The influence of subdued demand was evidenced mainly by a rapid fall in the prices of non-tradable services such as education and telecommunications. Import prices also contributed to the deflation, with the average cost of imports decreasing by 4.4 per cent year on year in the first nine months of 2002; such a decline, in turn, was influenced by deflationary pressure from mainland China.

Countermeasures taken by the Government, such as reductions in property rates and utility charges to ease the financial burden on households affected by the economic slowdown, also contributed to lower prices. As wage increases are expected to remain moderate, consumer prices are projected to keep falling in 2003 but at the slower rate of 1.5 per cent. The exchange rate of the Hong Kong dollar is pegged to the United States dollar. Such an arrangement, which has been held partly responsible for the continued deflation, does not allow much room for policy flexibility. The loosening of monetary policy in the United States has meant that interest rates have also remained low in Hong Kong, China, but domestic demand remains weak.

***Consumer prices were in check and food prices stabilized in Mongolia***

Mongolia experienced double-digit consumer price inflation of 12 per cent in 2000 owing to the effects of weather-related shortages in food supplies and higher public utility tariffs, as well as a 25 per cent general increase in civil service wages. However, the inflation rate has been brought down to single digits since 2001, as both the exchange rate and domestic food prices were relatively stable. Food prices, in particular, had fallen, thanks to the increased availability of meat and milk products during the summer, and this helped to reduce inflation to 5 per cent in 2002. Although recent drought conditions may result in higher food prices in the period ahead, Mongolia's inflation in 2003 is expected to remain at roughly the same rate as in 2002. Broad money supply (M2) expanded very sharply in 2001-2002, but without evidently worsening the inflation picture. However, the continuation of the high rates of monetary growth could worsen the outlook for consumer prices.

***The stronger won has mitigated the impact of higher oil prices in Republic of Korea***

The Republic of Korea succeeded in lowering the rate of inflation to 2.7 per cent in 2002, from 4.1 per cent in 2001, by stabilizing monetary growth and carrying out further market deregulation that encouraged the entry of, and hence competition from, more foreign companies, particularly in the service sector. Nevertheless, the within-year trend in consumer prices in 2002 indicated some increase in inflationary pressure as the economy continued to expand. More recently, higher food prices, following a weather-related drop in agricultural production, and rising housing costs, contributed to some pickup in inflation towards the end of the year. The strong won, however, has limited the impact of higher international oil prices on non-food prices so far. Inflation is expected to increase slightly to 3.3 per cent in 2003, along with higher prices for oil and raw materials, increased unit labour costs and a hike in public service fees.

## *Foreign trade and other external transactions*

### *External trade*

***Exports from China, particularly of high-tech products rebounded strongly in 2002***

After slowing for most of 2001, China's export earnings went up sharply in 2002. During the first eight months of the year, merchandise exports expanded by nearly 30 per cent year on year, compared with less than 7 per cent in 2001 (table II.5). During the same period, merchandise imports increased by almost 7 per cent, slower than the over 8 per cent growth in 2001 (table II.6), but import spending seemed to have picked up considerably in the latter half of the year. Exports of high-tech products went up particularly rapidly, at the annual rate of 44 per cent in the first six months of 2002, and have constituted a growing share of the country's total exports as more multinational companies move the production of technology-intensive goods to China to take advantage of low production costs.

***The contribution of foreign-funded enterprises to export growth was particularly important***

China has become the sixth largest country in the world in terms of foreign trade and is becoming more integrated into the world economy with an increasing share of overseas markets. The remarkable increase in China's trade dependence is attributable to trade liberalization in the run-up to WTO membership as more domestic firms become engaged in international trading activities. The non-State sector was mainly responsible for the rapid growth in trade achieved in 2002 and the contribution of foreign-funded enterprises was particularly important. Total exports by

**Table II.5. Selected East and North-East Asian economies: merchandise exports and their rates of growth, 1999-2002**

| | Exports (f.o.b.) | | | | |
|---|---|---|---|---|---|
| | Value (millions of US dollars) | Annual rate of growth (percentage) | | | |
| | 2001 | 1999 | 2000 | 2001 | 2002 |
| China[a] | 266 140 | 6.1 | 27.8 | 6.8 | 29.6 |
| Hong Kong, China | 190 069 | –0.1 | 16.1 | –6.0 | 5.4 |
| Mongolia[a] | 455 | 7.4 | 20.5 | 11.0 | 2.7 |
| Republic of Korea[b] | 150 439 | 8.6 | 19.9 | –12.7 | 4.9 |

*Sources:* IMF, *Direction of Trade Statistics* (CD-ROM), January 2003; web site of the Hong Kong Special Administrative Region, Census and Statistics Department, <http://www.info.gov.hk/censtatd/eng/public/index2_fp.html>, 28 January 2003; Ministry of Finance and Economy, *Republic of Korea Economic Bulletin* (Seoul), various issues; and national sources.

[a] Data for 2002 refer to January-August.

[b] Data for 2002 refer to January-October.

**Table II.6. Selected East and North-East Asian economies: merchandise imports and their rates of growth, 1999-2002**

| | Value (millions of US dollars) | Imports (c.i.f.) Annual rate of growth (percentage) | | | |
|---|---|---|---|---|---|
| | 2001 | 1999 | 2000 | 2001 | 2002 |
| China[a] | 243 613 | 18.1 | 35.8 | 8.2 | 6.9 |
| Hong Kong, China | 201 444 | –2.7 | 18.6 | –5.5 | 3.3 |
| Mongolia[a] | 661 | –6.9 | 33.8 | 12.4 | 19.7 |
| Republic of Korea[b] | 141 098 | 28.4 | 34.0 | –12.1 | 4.5 |

*Sources:* IMF, *Direction of Trade Statistics* (CD-ROM), January 2003; web site of the Hong Kong Special Administrative Region, Census and Statistics Department, <http://www.info.gov.hk/censtatd/eng/public/index2_fp.html>, 28 January 2003; Ministry of Finance and Economy, *Republic of Korea Economic Bulletin* (Seoul), various issues; and national sources.

[a] Data for 2002 refer to January-August.
[b] Data for 2002 refer to January-October.

those enterprises were up by about 24 per cent year on year in the first nine months of the year, accounting for more than half of the total earnings on exports. By contrast, State-owned firms were able to increase their exports by just over 7 per cent, while their spending on imports increased by almost 8 per cent year on year in the first nine months of 2002.

***Nevertheless, exports of traditional labour-intensive products dominate China's merchandise trade surplus***

The three major categories of China's merchandise exports in 2002, accounting for 73 per cent of the total export value during the first nine months of 2002, were machinery and electrical appliances, with a relative share of almost 35 per cent of the total, electrical machinery and equipment, nearly 20 per cent, and textiles, about 18 per cent. Although exports of technology-intensive goods were growing fast, exports of traditional labour-intensive products tended to dominate the merchandise trade surplus. However, China has a structural trade deficit in some key products such as oil, minerals, chemicals and plastics, as well as in the import-inducing and export-related sectors, such as electronics. As the economy grows in the future, these structural trade deficits are likely to widen and an eroding trade surplus is likely to be a result. However, with exports expanding faster than imports, the trade surplus soared to about $25 billion in the first 10 months of 2002; this was two fifths higher than the level in 2001. The current account surplus as a percentage of GDP expanded from 1.5 per cent in 2001 to an estimated 2.2 per cent in 2002 (table II.7).

**Table II.7. Selected East and North-East Asian economies: budget and current account balance as a percentage of GDP, 1999-2002**

*(Percentage)*

| | *1999* | *2000* | *2001* | *2002* |
|---|---|---|---|---|
| **Budget balance[a] as a percentage of GDP** | | | | |
| China | –2.9 | –2.8 | –2.6 | –3.0 |
| Hong Kong, China | 0.8 | –0.6 | –5.2 | –6.3 |
| Mongolia | –11.4 | –7.0 | –4.7 | –4.2 |
| Republic of Korea | –3.0 | 1.4 | 1.3 | 0.3 |
| **Current account balance as a percentage of GDP** | | | | |
| China | 2.1 | 1.9 | 1.5 | 2.2 |
| Hong Kong, China | 7.3 | 5.5 | 7.2 | 7.1 |
| Mongolia[b] | –14.1 | –15.8 | –15.9 | –14.0 |
| Republic of Korea | 6.0 | 2.7 | 2.0 | 1.5 |

*Sources:* ESCAP, based on ADB, *Key Indicators of Developing Asian and Pacific Countries 2002,* vol. XXXIII (ADB, 2002) and *Asian Development Outlook 2002* (Oxford University Press, 2002); IMF, *International Financial Statistics,* vol. LV, No. 11 (November 2002); Economist Intelligence Unit, *Country Forecasts* (London, 2002), various issues; and national sources.

*Note:* Data for 2002 are estimates.

[a] Excluding grants.
[b] Excluding official transfers.

***Sales to other economies in the region accounted for the revival in exports from Hong Kong, China***

After declining for four consecutive quarters, the export performance of Hong Kong, China, which had begun to deteriorate sharply in the first half of 2001, strengthened in the second quarter of 2002, and merchandise exports were up by 5.4 per cent in 2002 after a decline of 6 per cent in 2001. The turnaround was largely due to stronger exports to economies in Asia and the Pacific. In particular, total merchandise exports to such East Asian countries as mainland China, the Republic of Korea, Malaysia, Thailand, the Philippines and Singapore, picked up remarkably to reach double-digit growth year on year in the third quarter of 2002. Exports to Japan, which had been declining steadily for some time, reverted to positive growth in the third quarter of 2002, while those to North America and the EU were helped by improved relative price competitiveness. Service exports were also buoyant, with a surge in inbound tourism and in offshore trade and transport services in 2002.

***The current account surplus as a percentage of GDP remained steady in Hong Kong, China***

Imports of goods, which had declined by over 5 per cent in 2001, began to pick up in 2002, stimulated by stronger domestic demand and an increase in re-exports; import spending recorded positive growth over 3 per cent in 2002. Imports of services also rose moderately. Hong Kong, China's current account surplus is estimated to have been

7.1 per cent of GDP in 2002, substantially similar to the surplus of 7.2 per cent in 2001. However, as external demand in key export markets appears to have picked up faster than domestic demand, the trade deficit is projected to narrow and the current account surplus to widen in the immediate future.

***Mongolia's merchandise exports benefited from the rise in the price of gold***

Mongolia's export receipts depend heavily on global demand conditions and the terms of trade commanded by its principal export commodities, copper, gold, cashmere products, hides and skins, meat and other animal products. The outlook for copper exports worsened markedly as the slowdown in high-tech industries depressed world prices for copper. Meanwhile, the demand for finished cashmere in major industrial countries, such as the United States and Japan, has also slowed. However, the impact of those adverse developments on total export earnings has been moderated by a rise in the price of gold. Although merchandise exports increased by only 2.7 per cent year on year in the first eight months of 2002, Mongolia's export earnings are projected to have increased by about 20 per cent in 2002 as a whole on the back of higher gold prices. The United States and China are the principal export destinations and are likely to have accounted for approximately 40 and 34 per cent of Mongolia's export earnings in 2002.

Merchandise imports grew remarkably, by almost 34 per cent in 2000, before moderating to a 12.4 per cent annual growth rate in 2001. However, in the first eight months of 2002, spending on imports expanded by nearly 20 per cent year on year owing to higher imports of food, textiles, machinery and equipment, and spare parts. The Russian Federation is the principal source of imports for Mongolia, with an estimated 30 per cent share in 2002, followed by China, at around 18 per cent. Mongolia's trade deficit is projected to have widened in 2002, registering $192 million during the first eight months of the year or some 64 per cent higher than the trade shortfall in the same period of 2001. The ratio of the current account deficit to GDP is, however, expected to have improved somewhat in 2002, to 14 per cent from almost 16 per cent in 2001, reflecting the improved performance of GDP.

***China has become an important market for exports from the Republic of Korea***

Merchandise exports from the Republic of Korea decreased sharply in 2001, by over 12 per cent, after robust growth of almost 20 per cent in 2000. However, there were signs that a revival was under way in 2002, and exports were up by almost 5 per cent year on year in the first 10 months of the year. Strong sales to China contributed to the export recovery, and the Chinese market accounted for almost 14 per cent of total exports in 2002, up from 12 per cent in 2001. Exports to Japan, however, fell by another 7 per cent in the first eight months of 2002 from their level a year earlier, following a 20 per cent drop in 2001 as a whole. Exports to the United States were up by 4 per cent in the same period of 2002 compared with a year earlier, following an 18 per cent decline in

2001 as a whole. Notably, growth in merchandise exports accelerated from 5 per cent in the second quarter of 2002 to an estimated 17 per cent in the third quarter compared with a year earlier. The export growth reflected a rebound in exports of such high-tech goods as semiconductors and wireless communications, particularly to China; after a 24 per cent decline in 2001, exports of electronic products were more than 13 per cent higher in the first eight months of 2002 from a year earlier. Exports of passenger cars increased at an annual rate of 10 per cent over the same period following 3 per cent growth in 2001, boosted by the relatively strong demand for motor vehicles in the United States, although sales to Europe were sluggish.

***Strong consumer goods imports narrowed the trade and current account surpluses in the Republic of Korea***

Merchandise imports, which had fallen by around 12 per cent in 2001 after remarkable growth of 34 per cent in 2000, increased by 4.5 per cent year on year in the first 10 months of 2002. Strong domestic spending raised the value of imports in the third quarter, by 15 per cent from the level a year earlier, following 8 per cent annual growth in the second quarter and an annual decline of more than 11 per cent in the first quarter (all on a year-on-year basis). Import spending on consumer goods went up by 22 per cent in the first eight months of 2002 compared with the same period in 2001, after 3 per cent growth in 2001 as a whole. The growth in imports reduced the trade surplus slightly to $9.6 billion in the first eight months of 2002 from $9.7 billion a year earlier. In addition, higher net service payments and transfer outflows raised the service trade deficit to $6 billion in the first eight months of 2002 from $2.9 billion a year earlier. The lower trade surplus and the higher net payments for services reduced the current account surplus to $3.5 billion in the first eight months of 2002 from $6.8 billion a year earlier. The external current account surplus is estimated to have reached about $7 billion, or 1.5 per cent of GDP, in 2002, down from $8.6 billion, or 2 per cent of GDP, in 2001. The surplus is expected to go down further in 2003 because of a decline in the merchandise trade surplus, as steady growth in domestic demand is likely to increase imports faster than exports.

*Capital flows and exchange rates*

***Increased FDI in China boosted productive capacity and supported the strong export performance***

China's entry into WTO has spurred further inward foreign investment, which, in turn, has contributed greatly to expanding the country's productive capacity and strong export performance. As noted earlier, foreign-funded companies now account for over 50 per cent of total exports, up from 40 per cent five years earlier. Gross inflows of FDI reached $48 billion in the first 11 months of 2002, compared with $42 billion in the same period a year earlier, while new investment commitments amounted to $77 billion, an increase of more than 27 per cent over the previous year. In contrast, the downturn in global equity markets limited new offshore listings of Chinese companies in the first 11 months of 2002, while foreign bank exposure in China has been on a declining trend. No new international bonds were issued in the first 10 months of 2002, although higher investor confidence is reflected in the narrowing of the spread on the dollar-denominated sovereign bond issue of May 2001, to 90 basis points in November 2002 from 140 basis points at issue. The total external debt, which fell to $170 billion at the end of 2001 from $174 billion at the end of 2000, had fallen further to $160 billion by August 2002. Debt service amounted to less than 5 per cent of the value of exports of goods and services and China's net debt repayments have also been quite moderate. Meanwhile, rising per capita incomes have meant that both new commitments and net disbursements from the World Bank have shown a downward trend over the past few years. China's official foreign reserves increased to $257.2 billion in August 2002 from $215.6 billion at the end of 2001. The country has maintained a "managed float" exchange rate regime since 1994, with the yuan renminbi fluctuating in a narrow band of around 8.27 to the United States dollar. The strong balance-of-payments position has generated some upward pressure on the exchange rate; the pressure has been countered by the authorities and little change is expected in the near term.

***In contrast to mainland China, Hong Kong, China, experienced net outflows of FDI***

Hong Kong, China's net FDI outflows reached $1.3 billion in the first quarter of 2002, compared with a net inflow of $7.6 billion a year earlier. The large net inflows in 2001 preceded China's entry into WTO and coincided with a sharp rise in foreign investment commitments in that country, suggesting that funds were moved to Hong Kong, China, to position investors for the opening of China's markets under WTO, resulting in the net outflow in 2002. Share issues by red-chip companies in Hong Kong, China, in 2001 and 2002 contributed to the large foreign equity inflows, which were reversed when the funds were remitted to China. A higher level of direct equity investment in China, a weak stock market and continued reduction in foreign bank lending activity suggested that capital outflows had partially offset the current account surplus. Official foreign exchange reserves were up slightly to $112.3 billion in August 2002 from $111.2 billion in December 2001. Hong Kong, China, maintains a currency board system with the United States dollar, to which the Hong Kong dollar is pegged; this long-standing arrangement is likely to continue in the foreseeable future, given the ample amount of official reserves.

***External borrowing from private creditors increased in the Republic of Korea***

The Republic of Korea's economic rebound and relatively low interest rates available in international capital markets led to higher external borrowings, reversing the large debt repayments that had been a drain on the capital account over the past few years. Private creditors were the main sources of new lending, while official creditors continued to receive net repayments. In particular, foreign banks registered a sharp rise in their exposure in 2002 after being the recipients of net repayments in each of the previous five years. The bulk of new lending was in short-term trade and inter-bank credits. New international bond issues went up to $5.3 billion in the first nine months of 2002, from $1.1 billion a year earlier, as the decline in spreads over the past year lowered borrowing costs for Korean entities, thus encouraging them to tap the international bond market. For example, the spread on the 10-year sovereign issue maturing in April 2008 fell to 110 basis points in September 2002 from 190 basis points a year earlier. By contrast, in 2001 IMF received the outstanding balance of $5.7 billion of the funds provided under the 1997 standby programme. The World Bank, which has made no new commitments since the Structural Adjustment Loan at the onset of the financial crisis in 1997, continued to receive small net repayments. Official export credit agencies, however, appeared to have been a source of small net lending again in 2002, with increased trade credits following net inflows of less than $0.5 billion in 2001.

***The large equity inflows of the past few years have reverted to outflows in the Republic of Korea***

By contrast, foreign investors retreated from the Korean stock market, with net outflows of portfolio equity of $3 billion in the first eight months of 2002, compared with net inflows of almost $10 billion in 2001. Gross inflows of FDI also dropped to $1 billion in the first eight months of 2002 from $2.7 billion a year earlier, reflecting in part the weakening in investor sentiment globally. New investment commitments, however, rose to $6.7 billion in the first eight months of 2002 from $5.7 billion a year earlier. Total external debt amounted to $130.4 billion at the end of November 2002, up from $117.7 billion at the end of 2001, while debt-service payments due in 2002 were equivalent to about 8 per cent of exports of goods and services. Official foreign exchange reserves increased to $116.5 billion in August 2002, or about 13 per cent higher than the level in 2001. The exchange rate of the won has been under some upward pressure given the weakening of the United States dollar and the continuing current account surplus. In fact, the won had appreciated by about 10 per cent relative to the United States dollar by the end of 2002, compared with its value a year earlier. Strong export performance and a healthy foreign exchange reserve position are expected to support the stability of the won exchange rate in 2003.

***Mongolia's reliance on official foreign capital inflows continues to be heavy***

Mongolia relies on private capital markets to a limited extent and is thus less exposed to the risks stemming from a possible drying-up of commercial loans. The country is heavily dependent on foreign aid and official loans to cover a large proportion of the current account deficit of around 14-16 per cent of GDP in recent years. Such a shortfall is expected to remain stable with the help of the existing pipeline of concessional external loans in 2002. The total amount of external debt since 1991, which consists mainly of government debt secured on concessional terms, declined to 83 per cent of GDP in 2001; the debt-service ratio has so far remained manageable. However, the ongoing heavy reliance on foreign capital inflows to finance a large current account deficit makes the economy highly vulnerable to changes in donor and investor sentiment. Mongolia's FDI is expected to decline in the near future, reflecting the worsening prospects for the copper and cashmere industries. However, the investment inflows associated with the recent privatization of the Trade and Development Bank are projected to have been of the order of at least $12 million, or 1 per cent of GDP, in 2002. The decline in new FDI inflows may be exacerbated by a reduction in official loan disbursements if the Government does not take timely action to bring its reform programme back on track. In order to maintain donor confidence and attract inward FDI, the pursuit of sound macroeconomic policies would need to be complemented by prudent external debt management and market-friendly reforms.

Mongolia maintained a virtually stable exchange rate between its currency and the United States dollar between late 2000 and mid-2002. Upon IMF advice and in the light of weakening export growth and a worsening global environment, greater exchange rate flexibility has been introduced to encourage export-led investment and growth; in particular, beginning in July 2002, the buy-sell margin around the intervention rate was widened and consideration was being given to setting the intervention rate on a daily, rather than a weekly, basis.

### *Key policy issues*

***The pursuit of expansionary fiscal policies created pressures on the fiscal balance in some parts of the subregion in 2002***

There were higher fiscal deficits in some economies, owing in part to the various fiscal stimulus measures taken in 2002 (table II.7). Notwithstanding a significant increase in public spending in connection with the World Cup and the Asian Games, the Republic of Korea was the only economy in the subregion to run a budget surplus in 2002; at 0.3 per cent of GDP, however, it was much smaller than the average surplus of around 1.4 per cent of GDP a year in 2000-2001. Lower public expenditure, along with increased revenue from strong economic growth, can be expected to improve the budget position in the Republic of Korea in 2003-2004, thus facilitating a further reduction in the country's relatively low stock of public debt, which stood at 19 per cent of GDP at the end of 2000.

Public expenditure in China was up by almost 18 per cent in the first half of 2002 compared with the same period a year earlier, while fiscal receipts increased by just over 9 per cent in the same period year on year. China's budget deficit expanded to 3 per cent of GDP in 2002 from 2.6 per cent in the previous year. In Hong Kong, China, weak economic performance and the introduction of some tax relief measures are projected to make the budget deficit swell to 6.3 per cent of GDP in 2002. This high and widening level of fiscal shortfall has been a matter of concern; the deficit was equivalent to 5.2 per cent of GDP in 2001 and there was an approximate fiscal balance on average for 1999 and 2000. Mongolia managed to reduce the budget deficit to 4.2 per cent of GDP in 2002 from 4.7 per cent in 2001. However, lower revenues from the copper mining and cashmere sectors may necessitate further cuts in public expenditure in 2003-2004 to achieve fiscal sustainability.

***Contingent liabilities could raise the public debt ratio considerably in China***

China's public debt has increased significantly in recent years as a result of continued fiscal pump-priming. As a percentage of GDP, public debt is estimated to have remained below 20 per cent, which is low in comparison with the corresponding ratios in other countries in the region. However, the ratio could be much higher especially with the inclusion of contingent liabilities of the public sector; for example, a high level of NPLs among State-owned banks, and the need for increased contributions to the country's pension system in the coming years to support a large number of urban retirees, and for higher funding for social safety net arrangements in view of the expected large increase in the number of unemployed workers. Such contingent liabilities could narrow the scope and room for fiscal manoeuvre, although the overall level of public debt in China is believed by most experts to be sustainable over the medium and long terms given the country's substantial stock of convertible assets. The Government is moving to reform China's taxation system to broaden, deepen and strengthen its revenue base; divestiture of State-owned assets could also generate substantial funds to meet expected future obligations.

***China has made the largest single contribution of any country to global poverty reduction in the past two decades***

China's achievement in lifting hundreds of millions of people out of absolute poverty in the past 20 years has been extremely impressive, with sustained high rates of economic growth being a major underpinning force. The country has thus made the largest single contribution to global poverty reduction of any country in the last two decades. Beyond income growth, market-oriented reforms have dramatically improved the dynamism of both the rural and the urban economies and contributed to a substantial improvement in the indicators of human development.

Nevertheless, formidable challenges remain. It is estimated by the World Bank that some 200 million people, many in remote and resource-poor areas in the western and interior regions, still live on less than $1 per day. They often lack adequate access to clean water, arable land or health and education services. Regional and rural-urban income inequalities and the emergence of vulnerable urban groups have been a matter of policy concern. In parallel with its agenda for economic reform and growth, the Government has been pursuing the Western Region Development Strategy for some years to assist the 12 western and inland provinces, where per capita income is less than half that of the more developed coastal provinces and illiteracy is higher and where the largest proportion of China's very poor resides.

Since agriculture will continue to be the mainstay of the rural economy for some time to come, agricultural research and technology development geared to the specific needs of the typically poor western areas are viewed as an imperative. Environmental protection and sustainable development should also be important goals for both economic development and poverty reduction in China. There are interrelationships between poverty and environmental degradation, specifically as regards severe soil erosion, deforestation and desertification in rural areas. Promoting clean coal energy sources and technologies in urban areas could make a considerable contribution to reducing water and air pollution.

As China continues its economic restructuring and enterprise reform processes, the number of persons in unemployment and disguised unemployment is likely to rise, particularly in urban areas, at least in the short term and possibly the medium term. Official statistics showed that the registered number of unemployed workers in urban areas was 7 million at the end of June 2002, or about equal to the number at the beginning of the year, and the official unemployment rate, at 4 per cent, was below the Government's target of 4.5 per cent in 2002. However, many analysts believe that the actual unemployment rate is likely to be higher. Meanwhile, a variety of responsive measures have been introduced to help laid-off workers to obtain new jobs. The Government has also indicated that it would help to promote the development of labour-intensive enterprises with the market potential to absorb the unemployed.

***Employment generation is at the top of the policy agenda in Hong Kong, China***

Since the current level of unemployment is relatively high in Hong Kong, China, the issue of employment creation is among the top priorities on the Government's agenda. Measures imposed in response include encouraging private organizations to provide more employment opportunities, improving the business environment and facilitating market activities. At the same time, improvements in job training and retraining schemes and career advisory services are being carried out to ensure the greater employability and adaptability of workers seeking job opportunities. Other areas of policy focus are the maintenance of institutional strength that is conducive to market development; some reduction in the size and involvement of the Government; the promotion of closer economic ties with mainland China; the upgrading of human resources; the establishment of high-quality infrastructure, the development of high value added sectors and activities; and the stabilization of the property market.

***Mongolia is also dealing with widening income disparities in its market-based transition process***

Although a vibrant private sector is emerging in Mongolia, market forces have increased somewhat the disparities in the living standards between the rural and urban populations and the income gap between the haves and the have-nots. According to the World Bank, 23 per cent of the population lives in extreme poverty. The urban poor are in an especially vulnerable position, given the high costs of housing and of staple food.

Access to schooling and health services has apparently declined, particularly among the poor. While key social indicators are good in comparison with other countries at a similar stage of development and generally have not deteriorated, large differences have nevertheless emerged between the rural and urban sectors and between low- and high-income households. According to the 2000 census, 95.4 per cent of urban children aged 10-14 attended schools, while the rate was only 84.8 per cent for children living in rural areas. There are also signs that the quality of health and education may have deteriorated. With the support of multilateral institutions, the Government of Mongolia has drawn up rural development and poverty reduction strategies for which funding will be sought in 2003.

***Strengthening the financial sector is another important policy issue for China***

It was reported in June 2002 that the NPLs of the four State banks in China amounted to 23 per cent of total loans and 17 per cent of GDP. Progress in addressing the problem was first made in 1999 and 2000, when NPLs worth 1.4 trillion yuan renminbi ($169 billion) were transferred to asset management companies. After the transfer, there was a reduction by banks of 90.7 billion yuan renminbi ($11 billion) in the NPLs left on their books in 2001 and a further 36.9 billion yuan renminbi ($4.5 billion) between December 2001 and June 2002. The Government expects banks to reduce their NPL ratio to 15 per cent of total loans by 2006, when the banking sector is fully opened to foreign competition. The reduction is to be achieved through both the recovery of existing NPLs and the improved quality of new lending. The loan recovery process, however, has been slow and is becoming increasingly difficult as it is hampered by the lack of property markets and an underdeveloped legal system, among other things. The large amount of NPLs and the fragility of the banking sector in China are major factors in the official decision to pursue capital account liberalization gradually and cautiously.

***Although NPLs are comparatively high in China, there is little likelihood of a systemic crisis and liquidity remains ample***

There are no plans at present to transfer more NPLs to the asset management companies. This, however, has its risks because the amount of NPLs could rise rapidly with slower economic growth. Banks' credit analysis remains weak and a further acceleration in lending could result in higher NPLs. In addition, NPLs remain a heavy burden even if the ratio is reduced to 15 per cent, limiting the banks' ability to compete when banking business in the local currency is opened to foreign banks. The Government will also need to strengthen its supervisory functions significantly as an essential step towards maintaining financial stability and preventing future financial crises. While domestic banks' NPLs are large by international standards, the prospect of an immediate systemic crisis is unlikely, given the ample liquidity within the banking system. Confidence in the Government as well as limited investment alternatives have prompted residents to continue to deposit large amounts of savings in State banks. Meanwhile, domestic banks are also making concerted efforts to improve operational efficiency and asset quality, including through the closure of most of their loss-making branches in rural and less developed areas, and streamlining of the workforce.

***The Republic of Korea needs to go further in financial and corporate restructuring***

Although restructuring efforts in the corporate and banking sectors in the Republic of Korea have resulted in greater economic flexibility and adaptability of firms, further improvements can still be made in the areas of corporate governance, transparency and accountability. The restructuring of the financial sector is one of the key issues that the country is facing. In order to improve the Korean banking sector, the Government is pressing ahead with the sale of its shares in nationalized banks, for example, a merger agreement between Hana Bank and Seoul Bank was signed in August 2002; Seoul Bank had been nationalized in 1998 after the Government injected 5.6 trillion won in public funds into it. The process is expected to imply further bank consolidation, which will serve to bolster the competitiveness of domestic banks. The Government has also resolved to step up the pace and complete bank privatization over the next three years as faster economic growth has led to improved profitability in the banking sector. In the insurance industry, comprising 42 companies, 9 companies with solvency margins of less than 100 per cent have been restructured. To date, 20.8 trillion won of public funds have been injected into the insurance industry. NPLs of commercial and specialized banks fell to 2.4 per cent of total loans at the end of June 2002, from 8 per cent a year earlier. However, those in the non-bank sector remained relatively high, at 10 per cent of total loans as at June 2002, although there was some progress in reducing the ratio over the past year. The NPL ratio for the financial system as a whole stood at 4.2 per cent in mid-2002. With regard to the issues of rising consumer debt and credit card delinquency, measures have been introduced to make financial institutions more cautious about lending and managing consumer loans.

Another important policy priority in the Republic of Korea is to ensure a healthy and profitable corporate sector by expediting the exit of the remaining non-viable companies and by subjecting those corporations that are distressed, but viable, to workouts involving debt write-downs and operational restructuring. As China's entry into WTO will increase competitive pressures and open up new opportunities, Korean corporations will need to adjust and continue to move up the export ladder in terms of quality, technological sophistication, innovation and cost competitiveness.

***Market-based reforms are also needed in the banking sector in Mongolia***

Banking sector reform is an important policy agenda in Mongolia. Among the major areas for policy focus are strengthened bank supervisory capabilities, the restructuring of State-owned banks, the reform of non-financial public enterprises, the ongoing introduction of an open trade and investment system, reinforcement of a market-oriented regulatory framework and progressive reduction of public sector arrears along with the steady removal of indirect subsidies.

## North and Central Asia

### Subregional overview

*GDP growth was sustained for the fourth successive year in 2002*

The nine countries of North and Central Asia pulled through the global economic downturn in 2001 with remarkably little damage. In 2002, they headed for the fourth successive year of GDP growth, the longest sustained expansion since the beginning of their gradual transformation to a market-based economic system in 1992; Kyrgyzstan was an exception. The ongoing reform of policies and structures implemented by these economies in transition bolstered consumer and investor confidence, thus sustaining inward external resource transfers (both private and public) and steady growth in domestic demand. In particular, the flows of FDI into the subregion were unaffected by the global slowdown and expanded by 30 per cent to a record $5.87 billion in 2001. Kazakhstan became the first country in the subregion to reach investment-grade status in 2002, a rating achievement that owed much to an ongoing surge in FDI and generally strong export performance. The necessary preparations, including reserve accumulation, were made by many countries to reduce their vulnerability to short-term fluctuations in resource prices and meet the relatively high foreign debt payments due in 2003. Central Asia also received a greater flow of international aid in return for its support in the war against terrorism in Afghanistan.

*Two large economies of the subregion were recognized as fully-fledged market economies ...*

The strong economic expansion in most parts of the subregion was underpinned by the continuing growth in the Russian Federation, where GDP had risen by more than 20 per cent since the 1998 financial crisis. This solid economic performance created demand for imports, including those from the subregional producers. It also encouraged domestic companies to seek market and investment opportunities in the other economies of North and Central Asia. Indeed, the Russian Federation was recognized in 2002 as a fully-fledged market economy, thus providing a favourable climate for inward investments and WTO negotiations, among other things. Market-economy status was also accorded to Kazakhstan, another large economy of the subregion. In October 2002, the Russian Federation was removed from the blacklist of the Financial Action Task Force on Money-Laundering, an international body that monitors money-laundering. This embodied concrete recognition of the successful efforts made by the Government to combat money-laundering in 2000-2002.

*... and two other economies exceeded their 1989 GDP level*

The economic policy stance of countries in North and Central Asia in 2002 continued to focus on ensuring durable and stable growth through, among other avenues, the maintenance of a more balanced budget, low inflation rates and relatively steady currencies. A matter of some concern, however, was the output of most subregional economies, which remained 25-30 per cent below the 1989 level. Only Turkmenistan and Uzbekistan managed to exceed their 1989 GDP level, by 8 and 2 per cent respectively in 2001. The challenges faced by the subregion in the short to medium terms remained multifaceted. These ranged from energy sector reform, banking modernization and employment creation to poverty alleviation. In addition, concurrent efforts would have to be made to further enhance the subregion's competitiveness in international trade and investment markets, diversify its economic production and promote greater private sector participation in economic activities, including through the removal of bureaucratic barriers and a reduction of State involvement in the economy.

***However, labour market conditions deteriorated in some countries***

Along with the sustained economic recovery of the countries in North and Central Asia in the aftermath of the 1998 financial crisis in the Russian Federation there was a reduction in unemployment and, by extension, some progress in poverty alleviation. During the period 1999-2001, for example, the registered unemployment rate fell from 11.5 to just under 10 per cent in Armenia, from 3.9 to 2.8 per cent in Kazakhstan, from 12.2 to 8.7 per cent in the Russian Federation and from just over 3 to 2.6 per cent in Tajikistan. The rates of unemployment remained largely unchanged at a relatively low level in Azerbaijan and Kyrgyzstan. Notably, Uzbekistan reported the lowest unemployment rate (less than 1 per cent) among the subregional economies.

As a whole, however, the volume of employment in the North and Central Asian economies in 2001 was still 15-25 per cent below its 1989 level. Other factors contributing to the economic and social hardship of the unemployed included low levels of unemployment benefits and longer periods without jobs. Of particular concern was the large rise in unemployment of women and youth. The labour market conditions in 2002 tended to deteriorate somewhat, with unemployment going up in agriculture in some countries owing to poor weather conditions, and in the industrial sector as a result of the slow pace of restructuring and privatization. The number of registered unemployed in Kyrgyzstan and Tajikistan, for example, increased by 5.2 and 4.2 per cent respectively in the first half of 2002. There was some improvement in the labour market of the Russian Federation owing to the new labour legislation introduced by that country in 2002. The unemployment rate, at 7.7 per cent in the first six months of 2002, was about 1 per cent lower than in 2001.

### *GDP performance*

***A solid economic performance was recorded by most economies of the subregion***

Positive growth was recorded virtually across the subregion, with Armenia, Azerbaijan, Kazakhstan, Tajikistan and Turkmenistan registering GDP expansion of 9-16 per cent in 2002 (figure II.6). The largest subregional economy, the Russian Federation, also showed a solid economic performance. GDP growth in 1999-2001 was mainly fuelled by exports, especially the high international prices of oil and gas, by new investment, including FDI, and by domestic consumption. Total output went up by 3.9 per cent in 2002 largely on the strength of industrial production, which grew by 3.7 per cent in the same period (table II.8). The agricultural sector as a whole performed moderately well, grain

**Figure II.6. Rates of GDP growth in North and Central Asian economies, 1999-2002**

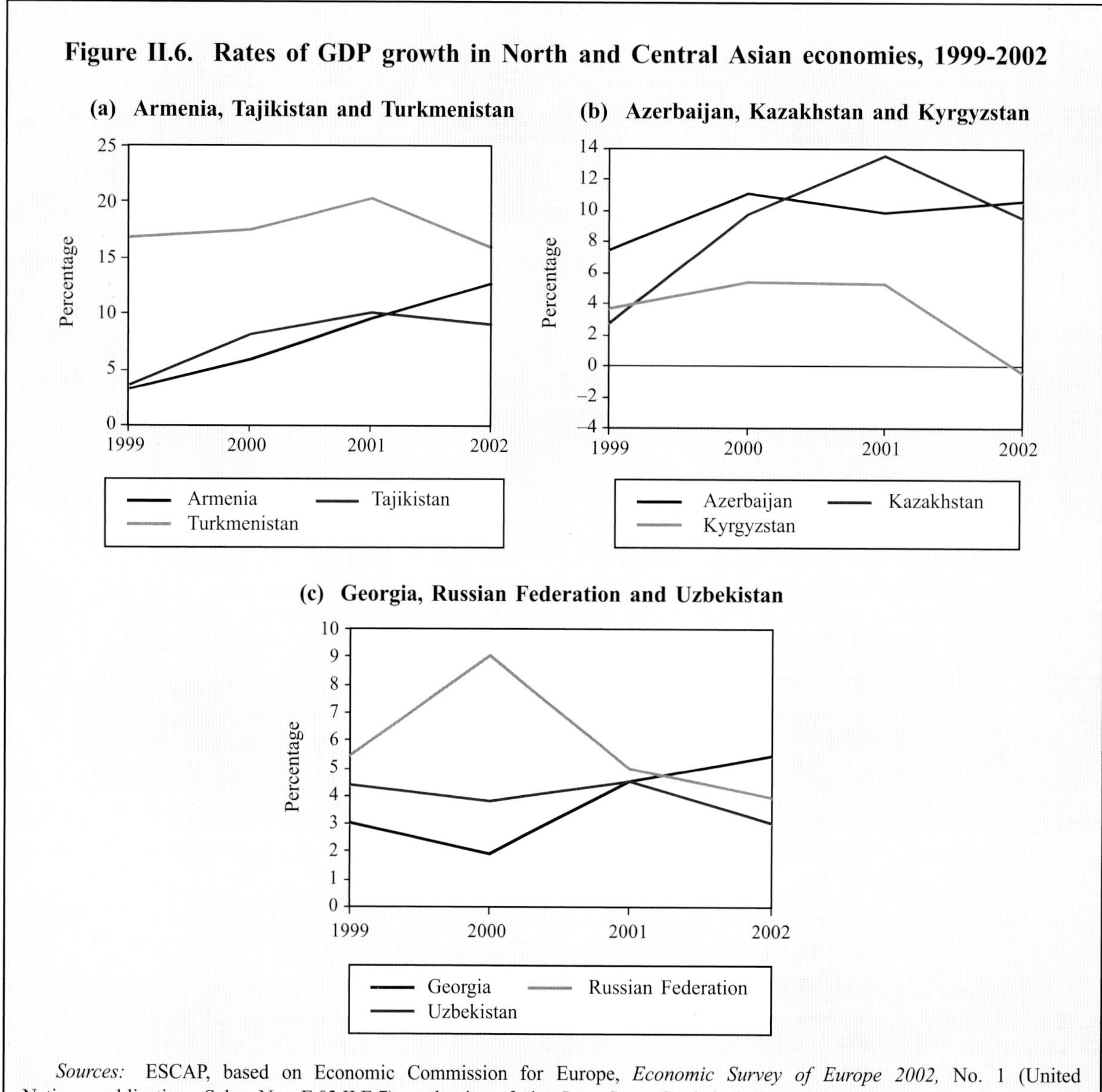


*Sources:* ESCAP, based on Economic Commission for Europe, *Economic Survey of Europe 2002,* No. 1 (United Nations publication, Sales No. E.02.II.E.7); web site of the Inter-State Statistical Committee of the Commonwealth of Independent States, <www.cisstat.com>, 12 February 2003; and Economist Intelligence Unit, *Country Reports* (London, 2002), various issues.

*Note:* Data for 2002 are estimates.

production was maintained at a high level with a harvest of more than 85 million tons, and the modest amount of grain exports continued. Oil production reached 207 million tons, an increase of 8.2 per cent in the first seven months of 2002. It was expected to continue to grow over the next few years to enable the development of a strategic oil reserve to meet the country's domestic needs and help to stabilize prices in the international energy markets.

**Table II.8. North and Central Asian economies: growth rates, 1999-2002**

*(Percentage)*

| | | Rates of growth | | |
|---|---|---|---|---|
| | | Gross domestic product | Gross agricultural output | Gross industrial output |
| Armenia | 1999 | 3.3 | 1.0 | 5.3 |
| | 2000 | 5.9 | –2.0 | 5.9 |
| | 2001 | 9.6 | 12.0 | 3.8 |
| | 2002 | 12.9 | 4.0 | 14.2 |
| Azerbaijan | 1999 | 7.4 | 7.0 | 3.6 |
| | 2000 | 11.1 | 12.0 | 6.9 |
| | 2001 | 9.9 | 11.0 | 5.1 |
| | 2002 | 10.6 | 6.0 | 3.6 |
| Georgia | 1999 | 3.0 | 8.0 | 7.4 |
| | 2000 | 2.0 | –15.0 | 11.0 |
| | 2001 | 4.5 | 6.2 | –5.0 |
| | 2002 | 5.4 | 7.0 | 4.9 |
| Kazakhstan | 1999 | 2.7 | 28.0 | 2.7 |
| | 2000 | 9.8 | –4.0 | 15.5 |
| | 2001 | 13.5 | 16.9 | 13.5 |
| | 2002 | 9.5 | 3.0 | 9.8 |
| Kyrgyzstan | 1999 | 3.7 | 8.0 | –4.3 |
| | 2000 | 5.4 | 3.0 | 6.0 |
| | 2001 | 5.3 | 6.8 | 5.4 |
| | 2002 | –0.5 | 3.0 | –13.1 |
| Russian Federation | 1999 | 5.4 | 4.0 | 11.0 |
| | 2000 | 9.0 | 8.0 | 12.0 |
| | 2001 | 5.0 | 7.0 | 4.9 |
| | 2002 | 3.9 | 2.0 | 3.7 |
| Tajikistan | 1999 | 3.7 | 3.0 | 5.6 |
| | 2000 | 8.3 | 13.0 | 10.3 |
| | 2001 | 10.2 | 11.0 | 14.8 |
| | 2002 | 9.1 | 10.6[a] | 8.2 |
| Turkmenistan | 1999 | 16.9 | 26.0 | 15.0 |
| | 2000 | 17.6 | .. | 30.0 |
| | 2001 | 20.5 | .. | 11.0 |
| | 2002 | 16.0 | 17.0[b] | 19.0[b] |
| Uzbekistan | 1999 | 4.4 | 6.0 | 6.1 |
| | 2000 | 3.8 | 3.0 | 6.4 |
| | 2001 | 4.5 | 5.0 | 8.0 |
| | 2002 | 3.0[c] | 2.0[c] | 7.8[c] |

*Sources:* ESCAP, based on Economic Commission for Europe, *Economic Survey of Europe 2002,* No. 1 (United Nations publication, Sales No. E.02.II.E.7); web site of the Inter-State Statistical Committee of the Commonwealth of Independent States, <www.cisstat.com>, 12 February 2003; and Economist Intelligence Unit, *Country Reports* (London, 2002), various issues.

*Note:* Data for 2002 are estimates.

[a] January-August.
[b] January-June.
[c] January-September.

***Armenia and Azerbaijan had fast rates of GDP growth***

GDP in Armenia grew by 12.9 per cent in 2002, one of the fastest rates in the subregion. Strong expansion in industrial output, by more than 14 per cent during the same period, was attributable mainly to increased domestic and foreign investment, which, in turn, enabled restructuring in the sector and the resumption of production in formerly idle enterprises in the metallurgy and chemical sectors. New investment also contributed to greater efficiency in the energy sector and to improvements in agricultural infrastructure. In the process, it was estimated that some 20,000-25,000 new jobs were created in the country in 2002, mostly in industry and construction.

Azerbaijan faced the problems of weak bankruptcy procedures and accumulated inter-enterprise arrears in the State-owned enterprises. Falling output in that sector and inadequate structural reforms resulted in modest growth of 3.6 per cent in industrial production in 2002. The hydrocarbon sector, which was the main driver of industrial growth, was the principal beneficiary of inward FDI. Agricultural growth, although relatively healthy at 6 per cent in 2002, was considerably lower than the expansion of 11 per cent recorded in 2001. Poor weather and severe flooding adversely affected part of the 2002 harvest. GDP in Azerbaijan, however, continued to show a strong performance, gaining over 10 per cent in 2002.

***Modest GDP increase in Georgia***

There was a comparatively modest increase, just over 5 per cent, in Georgia's GDP in 2002, compared with 2001. Agriculture contributed almost one fifth of GDP; the gain was attributed primarily to higher agricultural production, although flooding in certain areas of the country damaged part of the agricultural harvest in 2002. Generally, however, the agricultural sector faced a variety of constraints and bottlenecks, including a chronic shortage of credit, modern agricultural machinery and high-quality inputs. Overall growth was expected to accelerate to 6.5 per cent in 2003, owing mainly to a rapid rise in investment related to the construction of a gas pipeline from Azerbaijan to Turkey via Georgia.

***Continued strong economic performance in Kazakhstan***

In Kazakhstan, GDP had grown by over 11 per cent a year on average in 2000-2001 owing to the positive impact of continued institutional and banking reforms and strong inflows of FDI. Despite the global slowdown, the strong economic performance was expected to continue; in particular, GDP increased by 9.5 per cent in 2002, compared with 2001. Both industrial and agricultural production displayed solid gains. Agricultural production grew by 3.0 per cent in 2002. A good harvest in 2002, in particular, brought the economy over 9 million tons of high quality wheat for export. Industrial output rose by almost 10 per cent in Kazakhstan in 2002 as a result of rising oil and gas output and heavy FDI in new oilfield and pipeline construction projects. In particular, oil production was expected to expand, from 40 million tons in 2001 to 45 million tons in 2002 and further to 60 million tons by 2005. Oil revenues alone directly made up more than a quarter of the country's GDP and a more diversified economy remained a policy priority for the Government. Engineering plants were also restructured to better serve the booming oil and gas industry and other construction projects. However, the large burden of inter-enterprise debts and arrears remained a central problem for the corporate sector. The Government was expected to strengthen bankruptcy procedures as a remedial measure.

***A marginal decline in GDP in Kyrgyzstan***

Kyrgyzstan was expected to show a contraction in GDP in 2002. In fact, GDP declined marginally by 0.5 per cent in 2002, a setback due largely to a decline of more than 13 per cent in industrial production. Agricultural output could not offset the slackening activities as it went up by 3 per cent in 2002, owing in part to insufficient liquidity for agricultural producers. Economic growth was constrained by a slowdown in market-oriented reforms and industrial restructuring, post-privatization reforms in the agricultural sector and the after-effects of a monetary squeeze. At the same time there was growing social tension, a problem induced partly by rising unemployment. As a result, GDP growth for 2002 as a whole, originally targeted at 4.5 per cent, contracted marginally. GDP was projected to expand by 5.8 per cent in 2003 and industrial production to increase by almost 10 per cent.

***The industrial sector was an engine of GDP growth in Tajikistan ...***

The GDP of Tajikistan went up by 9.1 per cent in 2002 compared with 2001. Industrial production, up by 8.2 per cent over the same period, benefited from the continued growth in the aluminium sector. This sector had accounted for up to 60 per cent of industrial output in previous years and for more than half of the country's total export earnings. Agricultural output increased by 10.6 per cent in the first eight months of 2002, making it the fastest-growing economic sector. However, the growth prospects in Tajikistan were somewhat constrained by low levels of capital investment and relatively large deficits in the external current accounts.

***... and the oil and gas sector in Turkmenistan***

Driven by the continued expansion of the oil and gas sector and a boom in construction, the GDP of Turkmenistan was forecast to go up by 16 per cent in 2002. In the first six months of 2002, value added by the various sectors of GDP went up by 17-19 per cent (table II.8). Within the industrial sector, priority was accorded to developing the oil and gas sector, construction activities and textile manufacturing. Hydrocarbons remained the principal engine of economic growth in Turkmenistan and energy-based activities have received the bulk of both State and foreign investment over the last few years. The agricultural sector met the production target of 2.3 million tons of wheat, a record grain harvest, in 2002. However, the cotton crop was poor owing to adverse weather conditions. Only about 0.5 million tons of cotton, or a quarter of the planned target, had been harvested by November 2002.

***Steady economic progress maintained in Uzbekistan***

Uzbekistan recorded steady economic progress, with GDP growing by 3 per cent during the first nine months of 2002. The expansion was driven by higher industrial production, by almost 8 per cent compared with the same period in 2001, and agricultural output, by 2 per cent in the first nine months of 2002. In particular, the grain harvest increased from 4 million tons in 2001 to 5.3 million tons in 2002. However, heavy rain jeopardized the 2002 cotton harvest. Services comprised the fastest-expanding sector, growing by 12.7 per cent in the first half of 2002. To foster greater private activities and services, measures have been introduced to crack down on interference by local officials in the operations of small and medium-sized businesses and to lighten their tax burden.

### *Inflation*

***Inflation was on a downward trend in most economies of the subregion ...***

A tight monetary policy and domestic currency stability contributed to relatively low rates of inflation in Armenia, Azerbaijan and Kyrgyzstan (figure II.7). In 2002, for example, consumer prices rose by only 1 to less than 3 per cent in the three countries (table II.9). This represented one of their remarkable achievements, given their high rates of inflation in the late 1990s and/or up to 2000. In particular, Azerbaijan has sustained great price stability in the subregion for the last four years. However, the elimination of preferential tariffs for energy and transport services in January 2002 and the increase in real wages by about 15 per cent in the first half of 2002 pushed up consumer price inflation marginally from 1.6 per cent in 2001 to 2.8 per cent in 2002. Kyrgyzstan recorded a year-on-year price deflation of 0.3 per cent in May 2002. However, the monthly consumer prices were pushed up in June 2002 as a result of higher prices for food products, which constituted a major part of the consumption basket in the country. Similarly, higher prices for food products and imported raw materials were expected to exert some inflationary pressure in Armenia, thus pushing consumer prices up more than 1 per cent by the end of 2002. Inflation could be higher in 2003, owing to large increases in the prices of Armenia's main import commodities.

***... despite higher rates for basic utilities in several countries***

There were sharp increases in utilities tariffs, such as communal services, rail transport, telephone calls and medicines, in the Russian Federation in January 2002. However, inflation had been on a downward trend since the late 1990s; the rate of increase in consumer prices fell further from almost 22 per cent in 2001 to 15.1 per cent in 2002 owing to easier supply conditions for food and other consumer goods, and more stable exchange rates. A rise in the utilities tariffs was one of the main reasons behind an increase in inflation in Georgia. In 2002, for example, consumer prices increased by 5.6 per cent, compared with less than 5 per cent in 2001.

**Figure II.7. Inflation in North and Central Asian economies, 1999-2002[a]**

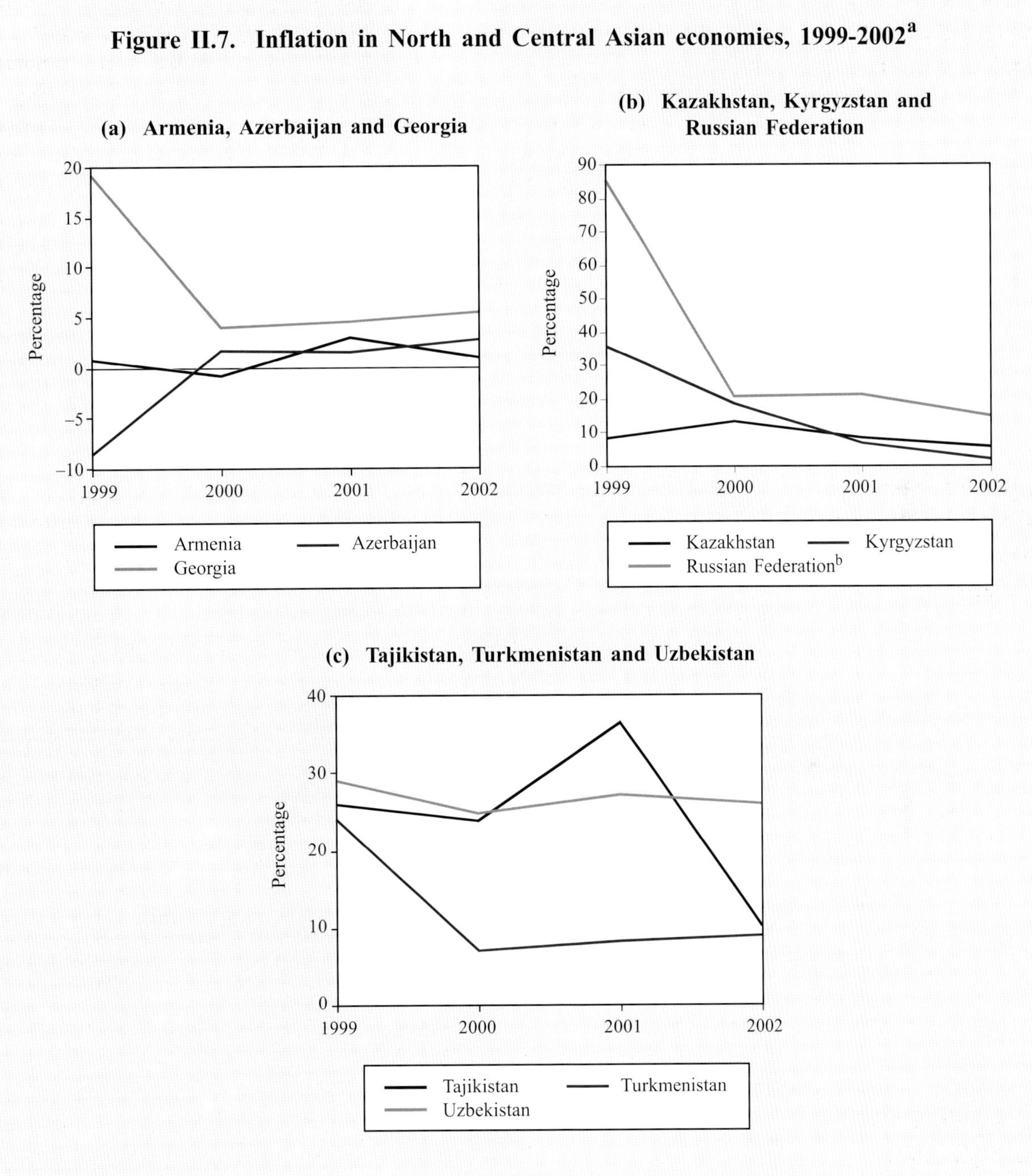


*Sources:* ESCAP, based on Economic Commission for Europe, *Economic Survey of Europe 2002,* No. 1 (United Nations publication, Sales No. E.02.II.E.7); web site of the Inter-State Statistical Committee of the Commonwealth of Independent States, <www.cisstat.com>, 12 February 2003; and Economist Intelligence Unit, *Country Reports* (London, 2002), various issues.

*Notes:* Data for 2002 are estimates.

[a] Percentage changes in the consumer price index.

[b] December 2001 compared with December 2002 for the year 2002.

Higher pensions and public sector wages in Uzbekistan could push inflation up to 26 per cent in 2002. The country had been experiencing high rates of inflation for several years. However, monthly inflation was on a downward trend in the middle of 2002 owing to a seasonal fall in food prices and an increase in the production of consumer goods. In fact, Uzbekistan experienced deflation of almost 4 per cent in June 2002. Relatively stable domestic food prices and government price controls in Turkmenistan have helped to keep inflation at the relatively stable level of 7-9 per cent in the last few years. Consumer prices were expected to rise by 9 per cent in 2002, a sharp decline from inflation of 24 per cent in 1999.

Inflation was also on a downward trend in Kazakhstan, falling from 13.5 per cent in 2000 to 8.5 per cent a year later and to around 6 per cent in 2002. The Government aims to bring inflation down to between 4 and 6 per cent in 2003-2004. In 2002, however, consumer prices went up by 5.9 per cent, reflecting rising wages, large-scale hard-currency inflows and an amnesty for capital repatriation; the last two factors contributed to an expansion in the money supply, which served to fuel inflation in 2002. A tight monetary policy and a stable level of food stocks resulted in a substantial reduction of inflation in Tajikistan, from 36.5 per cent in 2001 to 10.2 per cent in 2002. However, higher domestic fuel prices and a rise in public sector salaries were expected to produce a moderate increase in consumer prices in 2003.

**Table II.9. North and Central Asian economies: inflation, 1999-2002[a]**

*(Percentage)*

| | *1999* | *2000* | *2001* | *2002* |
|---|---|---|---|---|
| Armenia | 0.8 | −0.8 | 3.1 | 1.1 |
| Azerbaijan | −8.6 | 1.8 | 1.6 | 2.8 |
| Georgia | 19.2 | 4.1 | 4.6 | 5.6 |
| Kazakhstan | 8.4 | 13.5 | 8.5 | 5.9 |
| Kyrgyzstan | 35.9 | 18.7 | 6.9 | 2.1 |
| Russian Federation | 85.7 | 20.8 | 21.6 | 15.1[b] |
| Tajikistan | 26.0 | 24.0 | 36.5 | 10.2 |
| Turkmenistan | 24.1 | 7.2 | 8.2 | 9.0 |
| Uzbekistan | 29.0 | 24.9 | 27.2 | 26.0 |

*Sources:* ESCAP, based on Economic Commission for Europe, *Economic Survey of Europe 2002,* No. 1 (United Nations publication, Sales No. E.02.II.E.7); web site of the Inter-State Statistical Committee of the Commonwealth of Independent States, <www.cisstat.com>, 12 February 2003; and Economist Intelligence Unit, *Country Reports* (London, 2002), various issues.

*Note:* Data for 2002 are estimates.

[a] Percentage changes in the consumer price index.

[b] December 2001 compared with December 2002 for the year 2002.

## *Foreign trade and other external transactions*

### *External trade*

The value of external trade (both exports and imports) was on a substantial upswing virtually across North and Central Asia (figures II.8 and II.9). For the first 11 months of 2002, the expansion in trade was, by and large, at a double-digit rate. This provided a sharp contrast to the previous more subdued trade conditions in the subregion in 2001.

**Figure II.8. Growth rates in merchandise export earnings of North and Central Asian economies, 1999-2002**

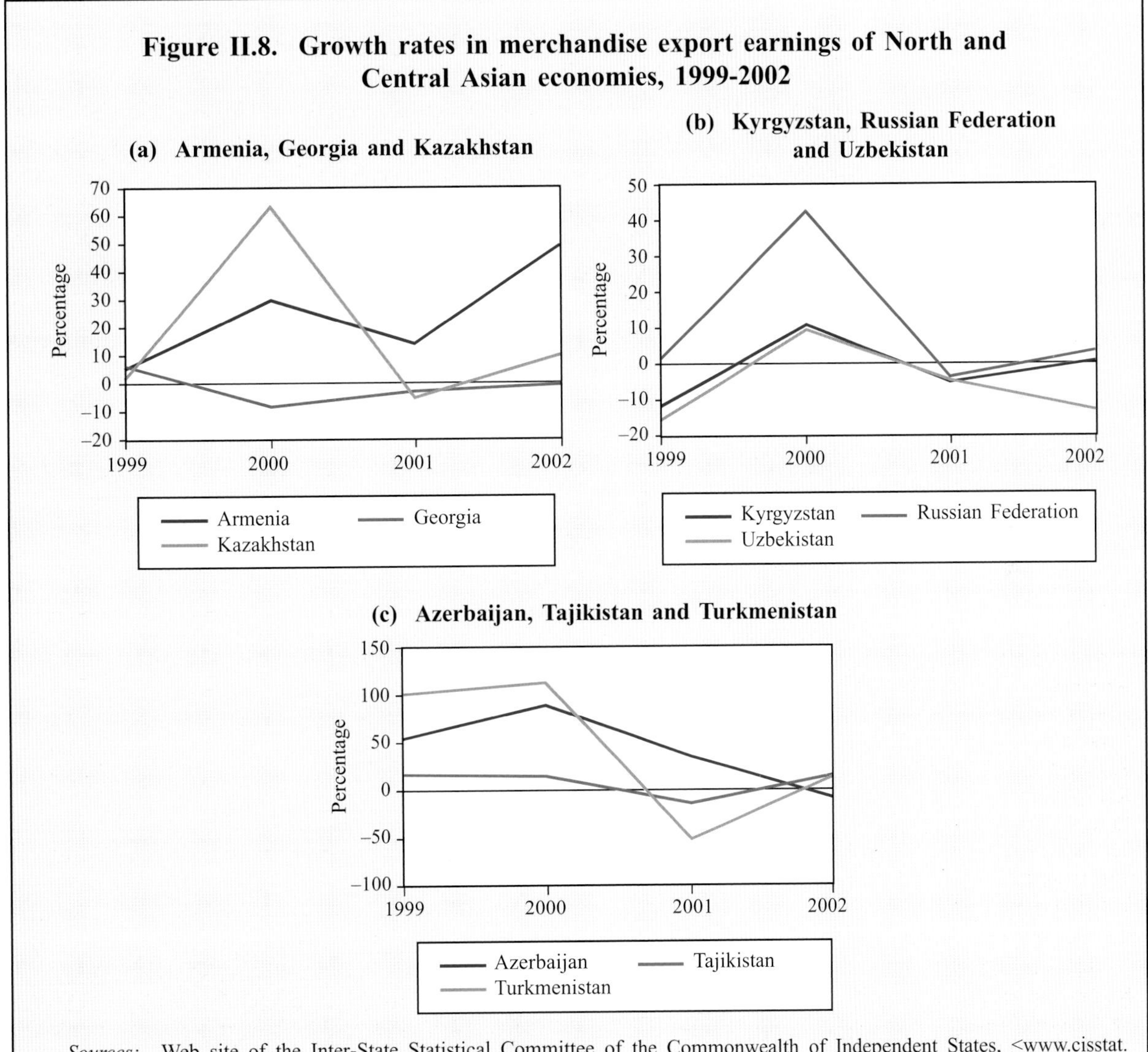


*Sources:* Web site of the Inter-State Statistical Committee of the Commonwealth of Independent States, <www.cisstat.com>, 13 February 2002, 30 December 2002 and 14 February 2003; and Economist Intelligence Unit, *Country Reports* (London, September 2002).

*Note:* Data for 2002 refer to the January-June for Turkmenistan and Uzbekistan and January-November for the other countries.

***Armenia is a new WTO member***

A recovery in the domestic processing of diamonds and other precious and semi-precious stones, plus an increase in world prices for these important export products, boosted the value of exports by about 50 per cent (to $457 million) in Armenia during the first 11 months of 2002 (table II.10). The trade deficit was also lowered, from $483 million in the first 11 months of 2001 to $420 million in the same period of 2002, because of a moderate rise of around 12 per cent in import spending (to $877 million) (table II.11). The country remained dependent on external fuel supplies and other mineral products, which together accounted for

**Figure II.9. Growth rates in merchandise import spending of North and Central Asian economies, 1999-2002**

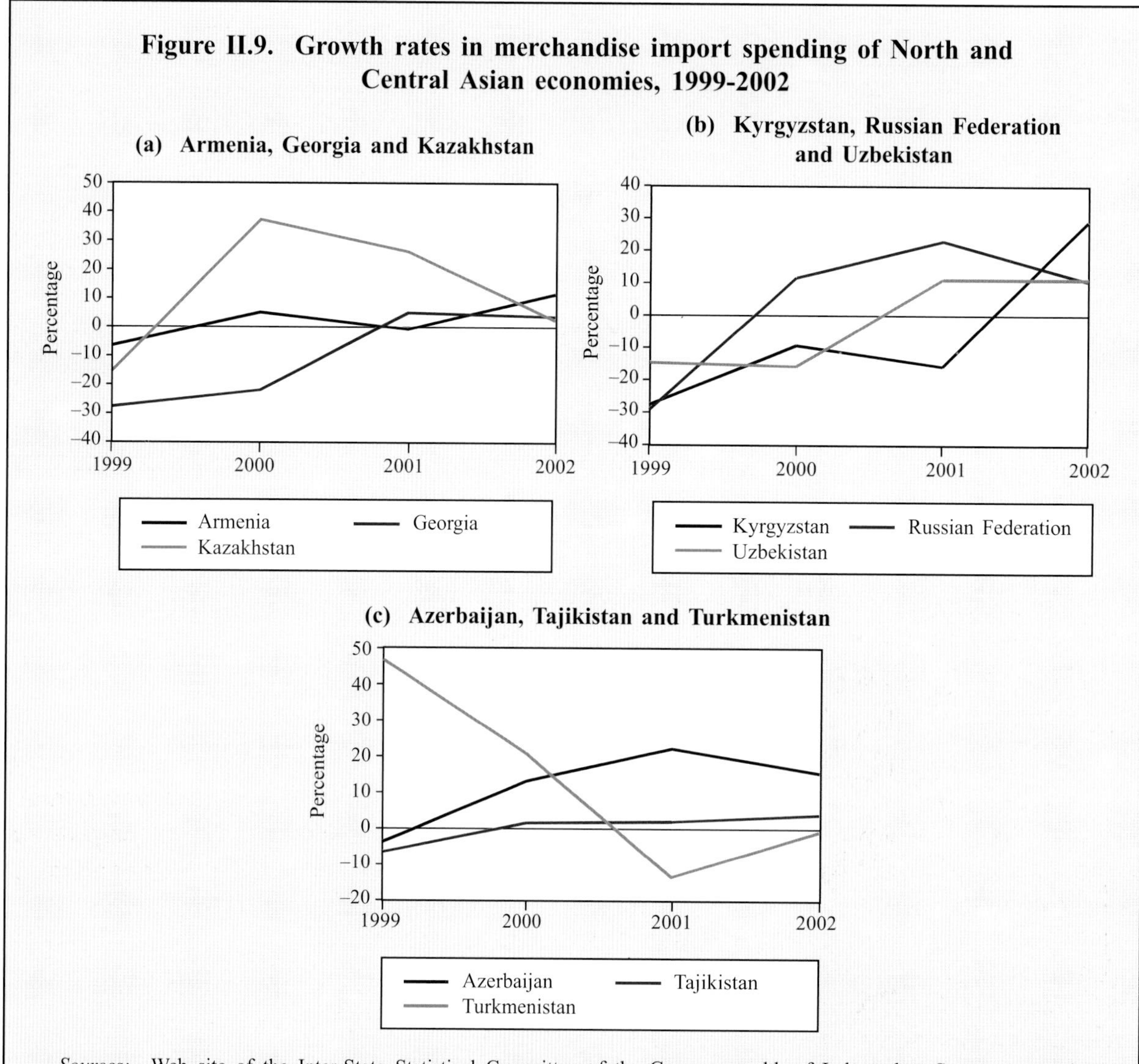


*Sources:* Web site of the Inter-State Statistical Committee of the Commonwealth of Independent States, <www.cisstat.com>, 13 February 2002, 30 December 2002 and 14 February 2003; and Economist Intelligence Unit, *Country Reports* (London, September 2002).

*Note:* Data for 2002 refer to the January-June for Turkmenistan and Uzbekistan and January-November for the other countries.

**Table II.10. North and Central Asian economies: merchandise exports and their rates of growth, 1999-2002**

| | Exports (f.o.b.) | | | | |
|---|---|---|---|---|---|
| | Value (millions of US dollars) | Annual rate of growth (percentage) | | | |
| | 2001 | 1999 | 2000 | 2001 | 2002 Jan.-Nov. |
| Armenia | 342 | 5.1 | 29.7 | 14.0 | 49.1 |
| Azerbaijan | 2 314 | 53.1 | 87.8 | 32.6 | –11.0 |
| Georgia | 320 | 6.4 | –8.4 | –3.0 | –0.5 |
| Kazakhstan | 8 647 | 1.6 | 63.2 | –5.2 | 9.8 |
| Kyrgyzstan | 476 | –11.6 | 10.6 | –5.6 | 0.2 |
| Russian Federation | 99 198 | 1.5 | 42.2 | –3.8 | 3.3 |
| Tajikistan | 652 | 15.4 | 13.9 | –16.8 | 14.1 |
| Turkmenistan | 1 184 | 100.0 | 111.0 | –52.7 | 11.0[a] |
| Uzbekistan | 2 025 | –15.5 | 9.0 | –5.0 | –13.3[a] |

*Sources:* Web site of the Inter-State Statistical Committee of the Commonwealth of Independent States, <www.cisstat.com/>, 13 February 2002, 30 December 2002 and 14 February 2003; and Economist Intelligence Unit, *Country Reports* (London, September 2002).

[a] January-June 2002.

the bulk of import spending in 2002. In preparation for accession to WTO, Armenia amended its Customs Code and laws on VAT and excise taxation to comply with WTO requirements. In addition, new agreements on the outstanding issues of agricultural subsidies, customs procedures and the protection of intellectual property were reached between WTO and Armenia in 2002. The country became a member of WTO in December 2002.

***A lower trade surplus in Azerbaijan ...***

Azerbaijan ran a trade surplus of $281 million in the first 11 months of 2002, which was significantly lower than that recorded for the corresponding period of 2001 ($705 million). In part, this decline was due to the strong expansion in imports (by over 15 per cent) in the first 11 months of 2002 on account of higher spending on machinery and equipment used for the construction of two new oil pipelines. There was also a hike in food imports in response to rising domestic demand, a development which partly reflected rising real wages in the oil and related sectors. However, there was a considerable fall of some 11 per cent in export revenue, from $2,012.5 million in the first 11 months of 2001 to $1,777.5 million in the same period in 2002. This setback was due mainly to lower oil prices and the restrictive measures introduced in 2002 to prevent oil export leakages.

**Table II.11. North and Central Asian economies: merchandise imports and their rates of growth, 1999-2002**

| | *Value (millions of US dollars)* | *Imports (c.i.f.) Annual rate of growth (percentage)* | | | |
|---|---|---|---|---|---|
| | *2001* | *1999* | *2000* | *2001* | *2002 Jan.-Nov.* |
| Armenia | 877 | -6.6 | 5.0 | -0.9 | 11.6 |
| Azerbaijan | 1 431 | -3.8 | 13.2 | 22.1 | 15.6 |
| Georgia | 684 | -28.0 | -21.8 | 5.1 | 3.9 |
| Kazakhstan | 6 363 | -15.7 | 37.0 | 26.0 | 2.5 |
| Kyrgyzstan | 467 | -27.4 | -9.2 | -15.7 | 28.7 |
| Russian Federation | 41 528 | -29.5 | 11.8 | 22.6 | 10.7 |
| Tajikistan | 688 | -6.7 | 1.8 | 1.9 | 3.9 |
| Turkmenistan | 1 554 | 46.8 | 20.9 | -13.1 | -1.0[a] |
| Uzbekistan | 2 341 | -14.7 | -15.8 | 11.0 | 11.0[a] |

*Sources:* Web site of the Inter-State Statistical Committee of the Commonwealth of Independent States, <www.cisstat.com>, 13 February 2002, 30 December 2002 and 14 February 2003; and Economist Intelligence Unit, *Country Reports* (London, September 2002).

[a] January-June 2002.

***... and a higher trade deficit in Georgia***

Georgia experienced a higher trade deficit, from $328.3 million in the first 11 months of 2001 to $354.5 million in the same period of 2002, which was attributable to lower export earnings (by 0.5 per cent). Owing to a temporary ban from July 2002 on one of its main export items, namely, non-ferrous scrap metal, export revenue reached $293.1 million during the first 11 months of 2002, compared with $294.6 million for the corresponding period of 2001. Import spending in the first 11 months of 2002 (at $648 million) rose by about 4 per cent compared with the same period in 2001; energy was the main import item.

***There were also higher trade turnovers in other subregional economies***

Despite a narrow export base and lower oil prices, export earnings in Kazakhstan rose from $7.95 billion in the first 11 months of 2001 to $8.73 billion in the corresponding period of 2002. Imports continued to be dominated by technological goods and the value of import spending increased by 2.5 per cent in the first 11 months of 2002 to $5.9 billion. The direction of trade was largely unchanged, with the Russian Federation being the largest trading partner of Kazakhstan, supplying more than half of the imports and taking over one fifth of the exports.

The value of Kyrgyzstan's foreign trade grew by 11.4 per cent during the first 11 months of 2002, to $971.1 million. There was a marginal increse in export earnings (by 0.2 per cent), so that the large increse in import spending of about 29 per cent contributed to a negative trade balance of $94.5 million. However, higher world prices for gold and several agricultural exports from Kyrgyzstan and a recovery in electricity sales to neighbouring countries were expected to bring a modest pick-up in export earnings for 2002 as a whole.

Intensive negotiations for accession between the Russian Federation and WTO in 2002 were focused on the so-called systemic issues, including especially the harmonization of the country's trade standards with global norms. In addition, the Government made a number of policy and structural adjustments in several sectors of the economy, such as agriculture, energy, transport and tourism. Agricultural issues remained the most difficult obstacle to WTO membership. The reform of natural monopolies undertaken in 2002 was aimed at harmonizing domestic and export energy prices. A range of new legislation covering customs and tax codes as well as technical and sanitary standards was also adopted as part of the preparatory process for accession to WTO.

With regard to the foreign trade of the Russian Federation, there was a reduction in the trade surplus, from $54.5 billion in the first 11 months of 2001 to $53.3 billion in the corresponding period of 2002. However, the trade balance was expected to remain strong, thus contributing to higher international reserves and the recapitalization of the banking sector. Notably, the country limited its oil exports in order to prevent a sharp decline in world oil prices. Export revenue increased by 3.3 per cent, to $94.5 billion, in the first 11 months of 2002. At the same time, imports increased by more than 10 per cent to $41 billion.

Tajikistan's trade deficit was lowered from $50.2 million recorded in the first 11 months of 2001 to $7.5 million in the first 11 months of 2002. There was an increase of 14.1 per cent and about 4 per cent in export revenue and import spending, respectively. The trade surplus with CIS countries amounted to $20 million in the first 11 months of 2002, compared with a trade deficit of $12 million with other countries in the world. Tajikistan relied heavily on imported energy and raw materials from CIS countries for its aluminium production. Aluminium and cotton remained the principal sources of export earnings, accounting for up to seven tenths of total export earnings. In 2002, trading activities benefited considerably from the resumption of rail links with, and the lowering of transit tariffs in neighbouring countries.

Turkmenistan and Uzbekistan implemented their import-substituting industrialization policies in 2002 through the introduction of trade restrictions such as import licences, government certificates and limits on hard currency sales. During the first half of 2002, import spending from

***Import-substituting industrialization policies in Turkmenistan and Uzbekistan***

Uzbekistan nevertheless rose by 11 per cent owing mainly to an increase in imported machinery and equipment, which accounted for 44 per cent of all imports of goods and services. Export earnings declined from \$1.58 billion in the first half of 2001 to \$1.37 billion for the corresponding period of 2002, mainly owing to a decline in the value of cotton, food and energy exports.

The implementation of the import-substituting industrialization policy in Turkmenistan contributed to a reduction in the share of imports of machinery and equipment for construction and agriculture in total imports, from almost four fifths in the first six months of 2001 to just under two-thirds in the same period of 2002. The country was also developing its textile industry to raise domestic employment and add value to cotton-processing capacity and manufacturing activities. The share of textiles in total export revenue went from 2 per cent in 2001 to 6 per cent in the first half of 2002. However, the gas and oil sectors remained the main contributors to export earnings, with a relative share of more than four fifths. Turkmenistan's receipts from exports rose by 11 per cent to reach \$1.4 billion in the first half of 2002.

*Exchange rate developments*

***National currencies remained stable in most economies***

Tight monetary and sound fiscal policies, moderate and moderating inflation, and an improved or stable balance in the external current accounts enabled most countries of North and Central Asia to ensure considerable stability of their national currencies in 2002 (table II.12 and

**Table II.12. North and Central Asian economies: current account balance as a percentage of GDP, 1999-2002**

*(Percentage)*

| | *1999* | *2000* | *2001* | *2002* |
|---|---|---|---|---|
| Armenia | -17.1 | -14.6 | -9.6 | -7.8 |
| Azerbaijan | -13.0 | -3.2 | -0.9 | -8.0 |
| Georgia | -4.5 | -5.6 | -4.2 | -5.5 |
| Kazakhstan | -1.0 | 2.3 | -7.8 | -6.0 |
| Kyrgyzstan | -15.0 | -5.5 | -1.3 | -6.0 |
| Russian Federation | 12.8 | 17.9 | 11.2 | 8.7 |
| Tajikistan | -3.3 | -6.3 | -7.2 | -9.2 |
| Turkmenistan | -22.2 | 13.9 | -2.5 | -2.8 |
| Uzbekistan | -1.0 | 0.5 | -0.5 | -1.0 |

*Source:* ESCAP, based on Economist Intelligence Unit, *Country Reports* (London, 2002), various issues.

*Note:* Data for 2002 are estimates.

figure II.10). The exchange rates in Azerbaijan, Kazakhstan, the Russian Federation and Turkmenistan also benefited from the robust growth in oil and gas exports and the considerable inflows of foreign investment resources. Both Armenia and Tajikistan pursued a liberal foreign exchange regime with full convertibility of their currencies. In general, most currencies in North and Central Asia experienced some marginal depreciation relative to the dollar in 2002.

**Figure II.10. Index of exchange rates against the United States dollar of selected North and Central Asian economies, 1996-2002**

*(1996 = 100)*

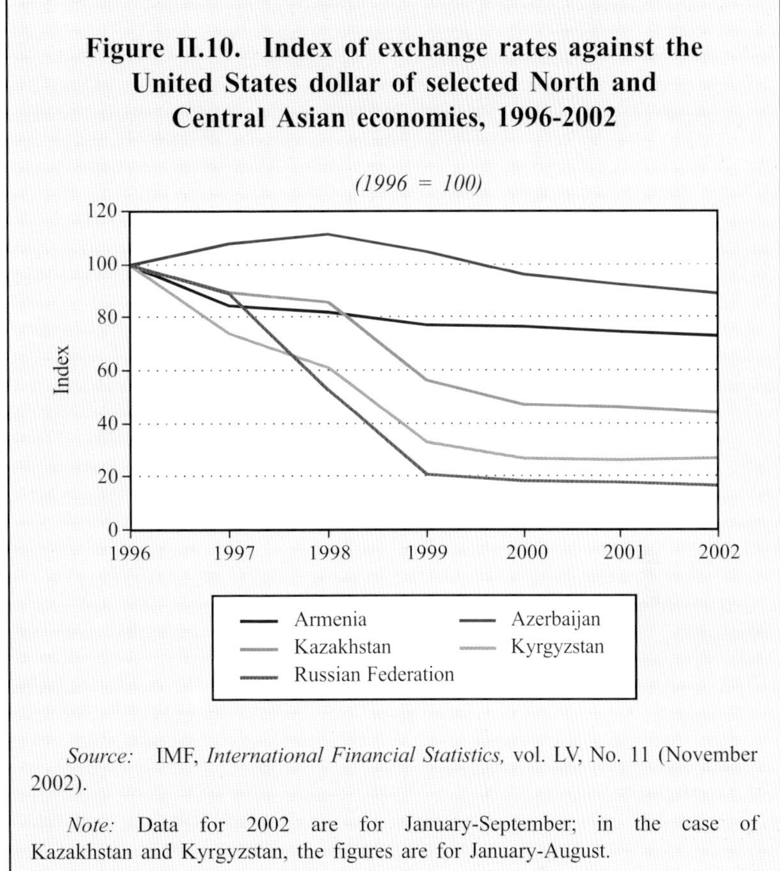


*Source:* IMF, *International Financial Statistics*, vol. LV, No. 11 (November 2002).

*Note:* Data for 2002 are for January-September; in the case of Kazakhstan and Kyrgyzstan, the figures are for January-August.

There were, however, some sharp adjustments in exchange rates. The exchange rate in Kyrgyzstan went up from just over 48 to 46 som to the dollar in the first nine months of 2002. In contrast, the Uzbekistan sum plunged from 920 to 1,400 per dollar in April 2002, a depreciation made to bring the official rate closer to the so-called parallel market rate. In the first quarter of 2002, for example, the spread between the official exchange rate and the black market rate was over 100 per cent. Unification of currency exchange rates was a key requirement of IMF in the implementation of structural reform and to remove the existing restrictions on the free convertibility of the national currency in the country. The use of foreign currency to pay for goods or services was also banned in July 2002 in order to strengthen the sum.

### *Capital inflows*

***Higher capital inflows in Kazakhstan and the Russian Federation ...***

The growing confidence of foreign investors was underpinned by the liberalization of FDI policy regimes, a generally stable macroeconomic environment, a generally improved or stable balance on the external current accounts and better business conditions. Such confidence was manifested in higher inflows of external resources in several countries of North and Central Asia. In particular, FDI amounted to about $6 billion in 2001, or more than twice the level of the mid-1990s.

The hydrocarbon sector remained of great interest to foreign investors. For example, over four fifths of the FDI received by Kazakhstan in the first half of 2002 went to the energy sector, especially for the development of the offshore oil fields in the Caspian Sea, which was the biggest new project in the subregion. In absolute terms, net FDI into Kazakhstan rose from $1.2 billion in 2000 to $2.8 billion in 2001 and by a further 90 per cent to over $2.1 billion in the first six months of 2002 compared with the same period in 2001. Such massive resources enabled the country to cover its large current account deficits in 2001-2002. However, Kazakhstan has also made a concerted effort to broaden its economic base by encouraging investment in other sectors, such as ferrous and non-ferrous metallurgy, transport, telecommunications and other infrastructure. Another large recipient of FDI, the Russian Federation, was able to attract $2.5 billion in 2001. FDI increased by a further 25 per cent in the first half of 2002 over the same period in 2001.

***... and modest inflows in some other subregional economies***

FDI flows to other countries of the subregion were much more modest in magnitude. There was a higher level of FDI in Turkmenistan, from $100 million in 2000 to $130 million in 2001. The bulk of such resources were directed towards textile manufacturing and the construction sector. FDI had been on a relatively stable trend, averaging about $100 million a year over the last decade. In the next 10 years, however, Turkmenistan was planning to attract some $350 million in FDI annually to develop the oil and gas industry. In contrast, FDI flows into Armenia, Kyrgyzstan, Tajikistan and Uzbekistan in 2000-2001 were the lowest among the economies of North and Central Asia owing mainly to their geographical isolation and weak infrastructure.

***FDI flows remained low in Armenia, Kyrgyzstan and Georgia***

A considerable fall in FDI into Armenia, from $104 million in 2000 to $70 million in 2001, contributed to a lower surplus of its capital and financial accounts in 2001. The increase in FDI, by 14 per cent to $19 million in the first quarter of 2002, was channelled mainly to the tobacco industry, the financial sector and exploration for copper and molybdenum ores. Kyrgyzstan was aiming to bring in $150 million in FDI in 2002, compared with only $25 million in 2001. Such resources were needed to sustain the public investment programme and enhance the efficiency of the services trade, in such areas as banking, insurance, information technology and tourism. However, FDI inflows rose by about 15 per cent only in the first six months of 2002, which was much below the government target. To encourage foreign investment, Tajikistan improved its legislation and adopted a three-year strategy of privatization of State assets, including the sale of airlines and railways. Uzbekistan was the destination of only $70 million of FDI in 2001. New external resources to be secured for 2002 were expected to be in the form of debt to implement the import-substituting industrialization programme.

In other countries of the subregion, FDI in Georgia fell from $131 in 2000 million to $110 million in 2001 owing to the lack of adequate legal protection for external investment, the arbitrary application of regulations and the poor state of the energy sector in the country. However, higher FDI inflows were expected in 2002 in the light of more favourable incentives such as unlimited tax-free repatriation of capital and profits and of foreign-currency account holdings. Foreign investment laws in Azerbaijan were also improved in 2002 so as to strengthen the rule of law and reduce the vast number of regulations, totalling more than 600, applicable to FDI. The fundamental problem for the country was structural distortions and overconcentration of investment in the energy sector.

***Considerable assistance of IMF and the World Bank to the subregional economies***

In addition to FDI, the countries in North and Central Asia also received credits and grants from multilateral organizations. In 2002, IMF and the World Bank allocated over $600 million to Kyrgyzstan to cover government spending requirements and meet the debt-service burden. Kazakhstan was expected to receive $700 million from the World Bank in 2002 to support the development of small and medium businesses, the private sector, public education, the health service and agricultural production. The World Bank was also assisting Tajikistan financially in completing the construction of two large hydroelectric power stations. A new system of dams and reservoirs would ensure better water supply for the whole region of Central Asia, reduce the deterioration of the drying Aral Basin and provide a better mechanism to deal with droughts, which had devastated the agricultural sector of Tajikistan in the last three years. Since joining the World Bank in 1992, Uzbekistan had received $494 million to implement macroeconomic policy adjustments and structural reforms. In 2002-2004, the country was to be allocated loans worth $350 million to fund projects in the health, agriculture, banking and water resources sectors.

## *Key policy issues*

The economic priorities for countries in North and Central Asia in 2002 were to maintain macroeconomic stability, carry out ongoing implementation of structural and institutional reforms, improve budgetary performance and reduce unemployment and poverty. A variety of policy measures were implemented, and the following brief review focuses on a number of key policy issues and policy outcomes.

### *Fiscal performance*

The budgets of Azerbaijan, Kazakhstan and Turkmenistan remained vulnerable to shifts in world prices for their key exports (table II.13). Oil, gas and minerals contributed, for example, more than one quarter of fiscal

***Vulnerable budgets in some economies***

revenue in Kazakhstan in 2001. The budget deficit of the country, at 0.2 per cent of GDP in 2001, was expected to reach 2.5 per cent in 2002. For the period 2003-2005, the budget shortfall was targeted at 2 per cent of GDP. VAT remained the most important source of fiscal revenue in Azerbaijan, with a relative share of almost one third in the first four months of 2002. Despite higher public sector wages, the budget deficit target of 1.2 per cent of GDP was met on account of more buoyant oil prices. Likewise, oil and gas revenue enabled Turkmenistan to continue to supply gas, water, electricity and salt to the population free of charge, in addition to the subsidies allocated to the agricultural and industrial sectors in 2002. The budget deficit for 2002 was expected to be at the relatively low level of 0.7 per cent of GDP.

Revenue shortfalls had constrained Georgia's budget for several years. The actual tax collection was estimated to be about one half of the potential revenue owing mainly to a variety of exemptions of important goods from VAT. In 2002, the Government was expected to limit the budget deficit to 2.0 per cent of GDP through the pursuit of stricter financial discipline, the abolition of tax privileges, broadening of the tax base and better revenue collection. In particular, the tax code was amended and the Finance and Tax Ministries were merged to improve coordination and transparency and reduce tax evasion. Concerted efforts were also made in Armenia to crack down on tax evasion, including

**Table II.13. North and Central Asian economies: budget balance as a percentage of GDP, 1999-2002**

*(Percentage)*

| | *1999* | *2000* | *2001* | *2002* |
|---|---|---|---|---|
| Armenia | –5.5 | –4.6 | –4.0 | –3.2 |
| Azerbaijan | –2.8 | –1.9 | –2.0 | –1.2 |
| Georgia | .. | .. | –4.0 | –2.0 |
| Kazakhstan | –4.8 | –1.8 | –0.2 | –2.5 |
| Kyrgyzstan | –2.5 | –2.6 | 0.4 | 0.6 |
| Russian Federation | –1.2 | 2.4 | 2.9 | 0.7 |
| Tajikistan | –3.1 | –0.6 | –0.6 | –1.0 |
| Turkmenistan | 0.9 | 0.4 | 0.9 | –0.7 |
| Uzbekistan | –3.2 | –3.9 | –3.6 | –3.4 |

*Sources:* ESCAP, based on Economic Commission for Europe, *Economic Survey of Europe 2002,* No. 1 (United Nations publication, Sales No. E.02.II.E.7); and Economist Intelligence Unit, *Country Reports* (London, 2002), various issues.

*Note:* Data for 2002 are estimates.

through the introduction of a bill that set clear limits on cash transactions in payment for goods and services; three fourths of all domestic business transactions were estimated to have been conducted in cash. Higher fiscal receipts were expected and the budget shortfall was limited to 3.2 per cent of GDP in 2002. In the draft budget for 2003, tax revenues were forecast to rise by more than 13 per cent, thus contributing to a lower deficit of 2.6 per cent of GDP.

Kyrgyzstan experienced a better fiscal out-turn in 2001, when a surplus of 0.4 per cent of GDP was recorded. A consolidated budget surplus of 0.6 per cent of GDP was generally feasible in 2002. However, the low economic growth could undermine the fiscal performance of the country. Moreover, social spending to alleviate widespread poverty raised government expenditure by 23 per cent during the first four months of 2002. A draft budget set the same level of surplus at 0.4 per cent of GDP for 2003.

***A new approach in fiscal policy in the Russian Federation***

There has been a substantial increase in tax collections in the Russian Federation over the last three years. The improved fiscal performance resulted in a further budget surplus of 2.9 and 0.7 per cent of GDP in 2001 and 2002 respectively (table II.13). As a follow-up to the introduction of a flat 13 per cent income tax rate in 2000, taxes on small and medium-sized businesses were also simplified significantly in March 2002. In particular, these enterprises were provided with the option of paying a 20 per cent tax on profit or an 8 per cent tax on turnover values. The new approach was expected to satisfy both the needs of fiscal revenue generation and the interests of entrepreneurs, who had to pay VAT, sales tax, property tax and income tax under the previous tax regime. The draft 2003 budget envisaged a surplus of 0.8 per cent of GDP, thus conserving resources for the servicing of foreign debt.

***Varying budget deficits in Tajikistan and Uzbekistan***

Tajikistan had had low budget shortfalls of less than 1 per cent for several years. However, there was a surplus of 2.5 per cent of GDP in the first half of 2002, an outcome attributable largely to improved revenue collection following reform measures in tax administration, the establishment of a new Ministry of State Revenues and Duties and the introduction of progressive income taxation. Nevertheless, higher spending on social welfare and infrastructure in the second half of 2002 to meet the damage caused by several natural disasters could result in an overall deficit of 1 per cent for 2002.

Uzbekistan had sustained a budget deficit of around 4 per cent of GDP for some years. Corporate profit tax had been lowered from 35 per cent in 1998 to 24 per cent in January 2002 so as to induce greater tax compliance and more corporate investment. Consequently, there was a fall in the relative share of corporate profit taxation in the total budget revenue, from 12 per cent in the first half of 2001 to 10 per cent in the corresponding period of 2002. The consolidated budget deficit could be marginally lower at 3.4 per cent of GDP for 2002 as a whole.

*Financial and banking reforms*

***The banking sector was consolidated in most parts of the subregion***

The Central Bank of Armenia approved the first merger of two large commercial banks in February 2002 as part of banking sector consolidation, a process necessitated by the failure of many commercial banks to meet the normal industry standards for size and capital adequacy. A similar development was observable in Azerbaijan, where the number of the banks was reduced from 51 to 46 in 2002 after an increase in the minimum capital requirement from $2 million to $2.5 million. Further consolidation could be expected; on average, the capitalization of each of the remaining banks, at $2.3 million, was still below the requirement. The total number of banks in Georgia also declined, from 228 in 1994 to 28 in 2002; of these, 10 accounted for the bulk of the assets, loans and total capital of the banking sector.

Further progress recorded by the Russian Federation in 2002 included the gradual deregulation of currency controls, the ongoing recapitalization of the banking system, the adoption of accepted international accounting and auditing standards and the introduction of a government-guaranteed deposit-insurance system. The new Federal Law on the Central Bank of the Russian Federation, adopted in 2002, preserved the independence of the Bank and increased the transparency of its operations. New and tighter measures on financial monitoring and supervision could lead to the closure of many of the existing 1,300 banks, as those institutions would have to meet tough capital adequacy requirements, internal control procedures and tests of management quality. As a further liberalization measure, the amount of corporate earnings of foreign currency to be sold to the Central Bank was lowered from one half to 30 per cent.

*Foreign debt*

***High ratios of foreign debt to GDP in some economies ...***

Armenia, Georgia, Kyrgyzstan and Tajikistan had relatively high debt-to-GDP ratio levels of around 60-70 per cent in 2002. Most of the debt was owed to multilateral lenders, such as IMF and the World Bank, plus the Paris Club of international creditors. Two subregional economies, the Russian Federation and Turkmenistan, were also among the bilateral lenders, mainly through their energy exports to other countries in North and Central Asia. Armenia managed to reduce almost one tenth of its foreign debt of $900 million in a debt-equity swap. The Russian Federation agreed to write off debt worth some $100 million in exchange for a controlling stake in four large enterprises. However, without new external borrowing, debt service could pose a problem in 2003 owing to the limited mobilization of domestic resources through taxation and export earnings. The restructuring of Kyrgyzstan's foreign debt by the Paris Club in March 2002 not only alleviated a potential debt payment crisis in 2003 but also improved the prospects for economic growth in the country. Georgia also secured some assistance to reschedule its debt with the Paris Club in 2002: to keep debt levels in check, new debt would be contracted only on concessional terms. Owing to low levels of FDI and limited domestic resources, Tajikistan financed its budget and current account deficits through external borrowings. As a result, the stock of external debt exceeded $1 billion in 2002. Debt restructuring was apparently necessary to resolve foreign debt payment problems in the near term.

***... and stabilized debt stock in others***

Kazakhstan and Uzbekistan had a relatively strong position in servicing their external debt owing to the strong export performance by the former country, and large resource inflows in both countries. Uzbekistan stabilized its foreign debt stock, which accounted for about 50 per cent of GDP in 2002. Kazakhstan's external debt was down from $3.7 billion to $3.15 billion in 2002. External resource inflows, including new bond issues, were expected to help to diversify the economy away from its heavy reliance on hydrocarbon resources. The foreign debt of the Russian Federation, at $134 billion in 2001, was reduced by around 10 per cent in the following year; the necessary resources were being incorporated in the federal budget to meet the scheduled payments in 2002-2003. The external market for the Russian Federation's sovereign debt was noticeably improved with the spread on 10-year bonds dropping from 1,500 to 350 basis points over US treasuries in 2002. In this context, new international bonds of $2 billion with maturities in 2010 and 2030 were issued by the Government in exchange for the residual foreign trade debt that had not yet been restructured. However, two large domestic companies started to tap resources in the international bond markets in April 2002. The State Debt Management Agency was created to administer and control the foreign debt incurred at the regional levels and in the corporate sector.

*Structural reforms*

***Continued reforms of natural monopolies***

The more difficult steps in the implementation of structural reform undertaken by the countries of North and Central Asia in 2002 included reforming the so-called natural monopolies and fostering the development of SMEs and private business activities. Among the reform measures in the energy sector of Azerbaijan were the elimination of preferential consumer tariffs for electricity, gas and heating. Efforts were also made to improve tariff collection and privatize the energy distribution companies. Further liberalization of the energy sector was carried out by the Russian Federation, although overall control of the sector remained with the Government. The domestic tariff rates for natural gas were raised by 35 per cent and those for electricity by 32 per cent in January 2002. Higher revenue would help to improve the infrastructure and communal services and, at the same time, reduce excess consumption.

***Further progress in promoting SMEs in some subregional countries ...***

Private business activities and services were given further impetus in Kazakhstan, the Russian Federation and Uzbekistan through the efforts made to promote SMEs in 2002. Kazakhstan removed a number of business restrictions and also simplified the tax procedures for SMEs, including those for the registration of new businesses. Uzbekistan took several steps to establish a solid legislative framework for the development of SMEs. In particular, the share of SME production in GDP, which was estimated at 1.5 per cent at the beginning of 1990s, was to reach 31 per cent in 2000. In 2002, the Law on Guarantees of Freedom of Entrepreneurial Activity in Uzbekistan was adopted to protect business persons, establish new sources of credit for entrepreneurs and eliminate unnecessary government involvement in the SME sector. Taxes and red tape concerning SMEs were also reduced and streamlined in the Russian Federation. Small business accounted for around one tenth of GDP and employed some 12 million people (about 12 percentage of the total employment) in 2002.

***... and limited progress in some others***

Progress with structural reforms was slow in Kyrgyzstan and Georgia in 2002. In Kyrgyzstan, there were limited possibilities for export diversification except into gold production, while there was also a slow pace of restructuring and privatization. Georgia almost completed its privatization of small-scale businesses, but the privatization of large enterprises remained stalled owing to a lack of investor interest, which, in turn, reflected the tough conditions set for bidding. As mentioned earlier, Tajikistan's newly adopted three-year privatization programme envisaged the divestiture in 2002-2003 of small-scale industrial enterprises, including cultural and health-care facilities, construction companies, poultry and fish production units and pharmaceutical firms. The privatization of large-scale industrial enterprises such as Tajik Airlines, Tajik Aluminum and Tajik Railways was expected to be completed in 2004.

***Improved business environment in the Russian Federation***

The privatization programme of the Russian Federation for 2002 included the sale of 450 out of 9,810 State-owned companies and government stakes in 600 out of 4,354 other enterprises. The divestiture programme was expected to generate $1.7 billion for the budget in 2003.

The focus of the programme was on the privatization of oil, gas, telecommunications and transport companies in which potential investors had a strong interest. At the same time, the Russian Federation took significant steps to improve the domestic business environment, such as adopting a new law on bankruptcy and amending the law on money-laundering in 2002. In particular, the former legislation established a clear basis for declaring a debtor bankrupt and spelled out the rights and obligations of debtors and creditors throughout the bankruptcy and financial recovery processes. The country was removed from the watch list of the Financial Action Task Force on Money-Laundering with the amended laws on money-laundering, as already noted.

### *Poverty reduction efforts*

***Extensive agenda in poverty alleviation***

Poverty is another issue of significant policy concern in North and Central Asia. The process of market-based transition undertaken by these countries over the past decade has necessitated a series of ongoing economic and structural reforms and adjustments, some of which were discussed earlier. The changes in policy orientation, economic production and marketing have created considerable economic and, by extension, social disruptions and dislocations in the short and medium terms. Some of these transitional problems and difficulties have included, at one time or another, higher unemployment, lower purchasing power and disparities in the distribution of wealth and access among various socio-economic strata. The ongoing and, in several countries, strong economic recovery of the last few years has had a positive impact on social and human welfare. However, the agenda for poverty alleviation in consonance with the United Nations millennium development goals remains extensive in the subregion and, for that matter, in most developing countries in the world.

***Challenging tasks in poverty reduction in some subregional economies***

In 2002, around 82 per cent of the family units in Kyrgyzstan lived below the poverty line. In 2002, a loan of $16 million was made by IMF under a three-year Poverty Reduction and Growth Facility to finance the country's poverty reduction strategy. The main objective in poverty alleviation was to reduce the poverty rate by 15-17 percentage points annually so that by 2005 no more than 30 per cent of the population would fall into the above category. As part of the process, social allowances were raised by an average of 20 per cent in April 2002 to help to counter an increase of 25 per cent in electricity tariffs. Average wages grew by around 15 per cent in the first half of 2002 in nominal terms owing to the deceleration in inflation. Despite continued growth in real wages, earnings in absolute terms remained very low compared with those in Kazakhstan and the Russian Federation.

The number of registered unemployed persons in Kyrgyzstan remained at just over 3 per cent over 2001-2002. Half of those unemployed were women and unemployment benefits amounted to around $9.50 per month, or a little over one third of the monthly minimum subsistence level of $32.

Over the last decade, the population of Tajikistan increased by 14 per cent to 6.2 million in 2002, while GDP fell by 64 per cent, resulting in higher unemployment and poverty. Policy efforts have been made to slow the rate of population growth, improve the general socio-economic situation and reduce disparities in the distribution of wealth. Official unemployment was at a relatively low level of 4.2 per cent of the workforce in 2002. Over half of the unemployed were women and the rate of unemployment was two thirds among young people in the age group 15-29. About 500,000 people were estimated to have left Tajikistan in search of seasonal employment in neighbouring countries. However, unemployment appeared to be on an upward trend in the short term owing to the low speed of restructuring and privatization in the industrial sector, which employed about 35 per cent of the workforce. In addition, poor weather conditions contributed to unemployment in the agricultural sector. In response, the Government was expected to create 41,000 new jobs in 2003. The minimum wage in Tajikistan was one of the lowest in CIS. The average monthly salary in Georgia was $41 in 2001, although that level of earnings was still about a quarter lower than the minimum subsistence level. Unemployment in the country was 4 per cent in the first quarter of 2002; the standard unemployment benefit paid during the six-month period was about $6 per month.

***Improved standards of living in the Russian Federation and Kazakhstan***

In 2002, the standard of living in the Russian Federation returned to the levels attained prior to the economic crisis in August 1998. Since that year, real incomes had increased by 24 per cent, real wages by 55 per cent and pensions by 28 per cent. However, one third of the population still lived below the minimum subsistence level, defined as less than $55 per month. Around 28 per cent of the poor were men in the age group 31-59, while another 44 per cent were children aged 16 or younger. The death rate in the Russian Federation exceeded the birth rate by 70 per cent, resulting in a reduction in life expectancy from 70 years in the 1980s to 65 years in 2001. If these trends were to continue, the population would decline from 145 million in 2002 to 128-138 million by 2016. Among countries of the subregion, Kazakhstan came third behind the Russian Federation and Turkmenistan in per capita income, which was expected to rise to $1,600-1,700, while the percentage of the population living below the poverty line was expected to be reduced to under 20 per cent over the period 2002-2004.

## Pacific island economies

### *Subregional overview and prospects*

***Economic performance remained lacklustre in 2002***

The economic performance of the Pacific island economies remained generally lacklustre in 2002, with GDP growth in the range of –0.5 to 4.4 percentage points (figure II.11). In particular, the Solomon Islands economy grew by 3 per cent compared with an absolute contraction, caused by internal strife, averaging 14.5 per cent a year in 2000-2001. Meanwhile, the sharp expansion in Samoa's economy, averaging 6.7 per cent a year in 2000-2001, lost steam in 2002; GDP went up marginally by just over 1 per cent owing to irregular weather conditions and the completion of major construction activities. By contrast, Papua New Guinea and Vanuatu recorded a contraction in total output for the year. In Papua New Guinea, this was mainly due to the falling production of mineral commodities, and in Vanuatu, declines in agricultural and service sector outputs.

The subdued economic performance contributed to problems in macroeconomic management, including persistent budget deficits, in a number of countries. Papua New Guinea, Solomon Islands and Vanuatu all had some difficulty in funding such services as primary education,

**Figure II.11. Rates of GDP growth in selected Pacific island economies, 1999-2002**

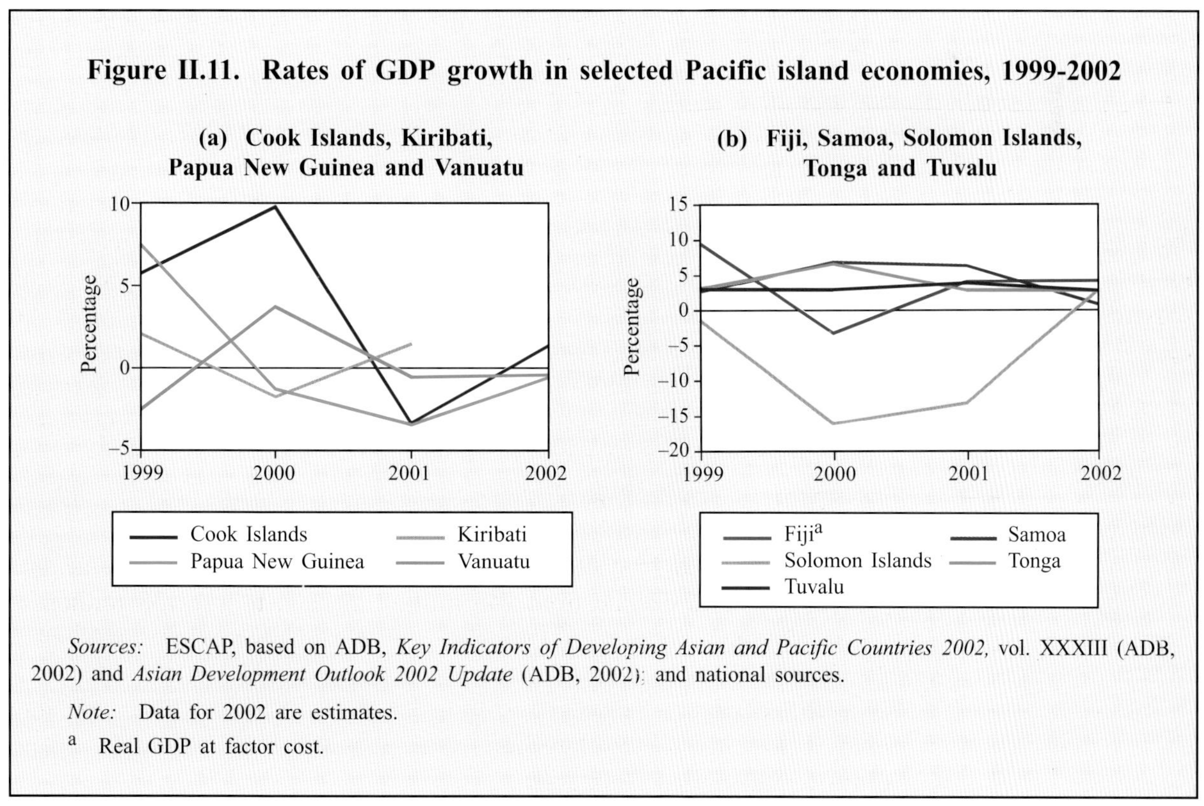


*Sources:* ESCAP, based on ADB, *Key Indicators of Developing Asian and Pacific Countries 2002,* vol. XXXIII (ADB, 2002) and *Asian Development Outlook 2002 Update* (ADB, 2002); and national sources.

*Note:* Data for 2002 are estimates.

[a] Real GDP at factor cost.

basic health care and the maintenance of security for persons and property. Solomon Islands is recovering slowly from the coup in 2000 with the Peace Agreement signed at Townsville, Australia, later in that year. There are reports of a rise in poverty levels in some Pacific island countries, including Fiji, Papua New Guinea and Solomon Islands. Population growth, at the rate of approximately 3 per cent a year in Papua New Guinea, Solomon Islands and Vanuatu, is high by developing country standards and this demographic trend is putting increasing demands on the delivery of basic services as well as pressure on the available services.

***Consumer prices varied in several countries***

Consumer prices varied in Pacific island countries in 2002 (figure II.12); this outcome was mainly due to declining world commodity prices and stable exchange rates. The double-digit inflation in Papua New Guinea and Solomon Islands was caused by currency depreciation, while the continued weakness in local food supplies lifted prices in Samoa. Inflation in Pacific island countries is highly dependent on movements in exchange rates and, to a lesser extent, the price of fuel. The latter has inched upwards as a result of tension in the Middle East, and any persistent price hike would not augur well for price stability in the subregion in 2003.

**Figure II.12. Inflation in selected Pacific island economies, 1999-2002[a]**

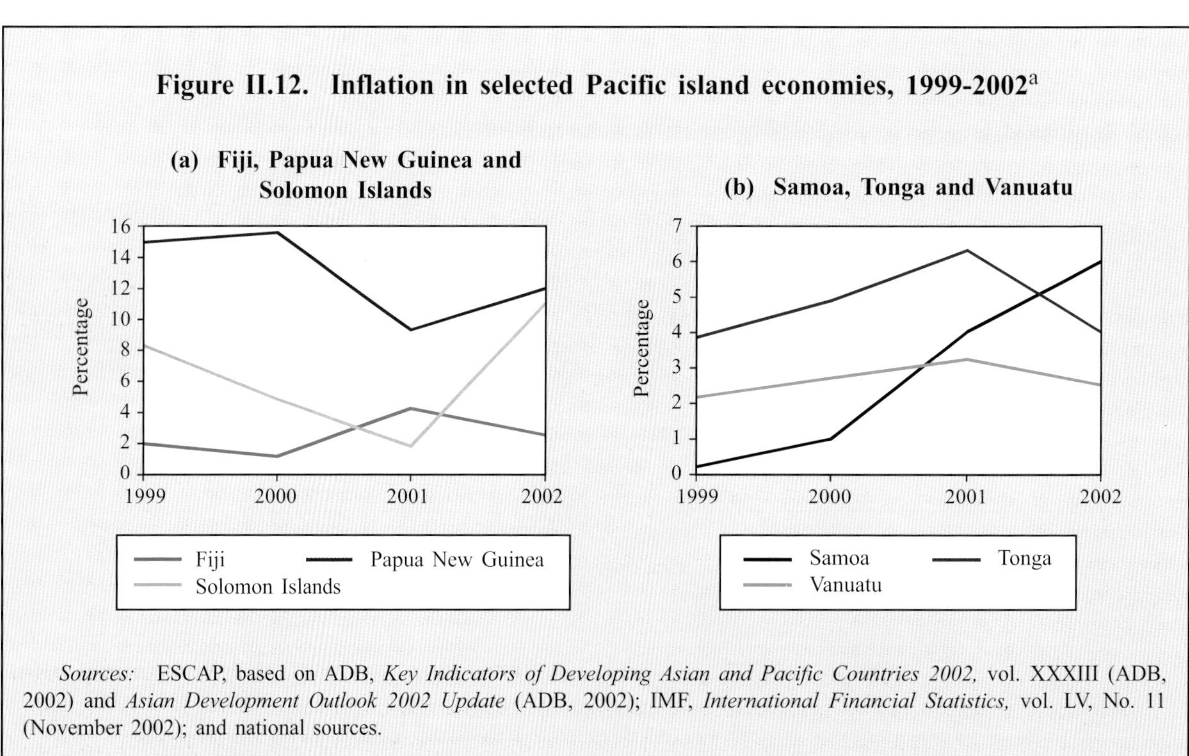


*Sources:* ESCAP, based on ADB, *Key Indicators of Developing Asian and Pacific Countries 2002,* vol. XXXIII (ADB, 2002) and *Asian Development Outlook 2002 Update* (ADB, 2002); IMF, *International Financial Statistics,* vol. LV, No. 11 (November 2002); and national sources.

*Note:* Data for 2002 are estimates.

[a] Changes in the consumer price index.

***Most countries recorded increases in exports and imports in 2002***

There were positive developments on the trade front, and Fiji, Solomon Islands, Tonga and Vanuatu were expected to record some increases in their merchandise export earnings in 2002. However, Papua New Guinea and Samoa registered an unfavourable trade performance, with the former experiencing an export contraction for the second year in a row. Import spending went up in most parts of the subregion, except notably in Solomon Islands and Vanuatu. This upward trend reflected, among other things, the pickup in oil prices and a recovery of demand after some import compression in the previous two years.

***Mixed performance in the tourism sector***

The coup in Fiji in 2000 served to push intending visitors to Vanuatu, but this was a temporary diversion; the tourist flows returned as political problems ebbed in Fiji, and Vanuatu began to have its own problems. The impact of the October 2002 terrorist attack in Bali remains uncertain, but there is some possibility of a positive ripple effect on tourism in the Pacific island subregion. Again, such a diversion may be only a short-term gain until Bali, as an important tourist destination, makes a comeback. Terrorist activities and the fear of air travel may pose some risks to long-term investment and growth in the tourism industry for the subregion as a whole. An option is for the tourism-dependent economies to revamp and strengthen their security precautions as a competitive factor in inward tourism services.

### *GDP performance*

***Several economies managed modest economic expansion in 2002***

The pattern of low and uneven GDP growth characteristic of the Pacific island subregion in recent years continued into 2002 with a GDP contraction of about 0.5 per cent in Papua New Guinea and, at the other end of the spectrum, an expansion of 4.4 per cent in Fiji (table II.14). In particular, both Papua New Guinea and Vanuatu experienced output contraction for two years in a row but Cook Islands and Solomon Islands recovered positively in 2002 after experiencing a decline in total production a year earlier. However, Solomon Islands had suffered from a significant fall in GDP, averaging some 14.5 per cent annually in 2000-2001; thus, the economic expansion of 3 per cent in 2002 was a useful achievement although the restoration of the pre-1999 standard of living remains a long-haul process.

***Fiji's economy grew by over 4 per cent in 2001 and 2002***

After output contraction of 3.2 per cent in 2000 following the political coup of that year, Fiji's economy rebounded, showing a GDP growth of over 4 per cent a year in 2001 and 2002. Growth prospects in excess of 5 per cent for 2003 are perceived as good by the Reserve Bank of Fiji. However, the emigration of skilled and professional workers continues and this may impose some constraints on the upward growth

**Table II.14. Selected Pacific island economies: growth rates, 1999-2002**

*(Percentage)*

| | | Rates of growth | | | |
|---|---|---|---|---|---|
| | | *Gross domestic product* | *Agriculture* | *Industry* | *Services* |
| Cook Islands | 1999 | 5.8 | −27.5 | 7.0 | 13.5 |
| | 2000 | 9.8 | 32.4 | 6.8 | 6.5 |
| | 2001 | −3.3 | .. | .. | .. |
| | 2002 | 1.4 | .. | .. | .. |
| Fiji[a] | 1999 | 9.5 | 16.0 | 9.8 | 7.7 |
| | 2000 | −3.2 | −0.9 | −7.4 | −1.8 |
| | 2001 | 4.3 | 1.7 | 7.4 | 3.6 |
| | 2002 | 4.4 | 1.1 | .. | .. |
| Kiribati | 1999 | 2.1 | 8.8 | 38.0 | 3.4 |
| | 2000 | −1.7 | 7.9 | −32.4 | 2.1 |
| | 2001 | 1.5 | .. | .. | .. |
| Papua New Guinea | 1999 | 7.6 | 4.3 | 5.7 | 12.4 |
| | 2000 | −1.2 | 9.1 | −4.8 | −7.0 |
| | 2001 | −3.4 | −5.4 | −3.3 | 1.9 |
| | 2002 | −0.5 | 3.6 | −5.5 | 1.3 |
| Samoa | 1999 | 2.6 | −3.5 | 1.4 | 5.5 |
| | 2000 | 6.9 | 0.3 | 11.3 | 7.5 |
| | 2001 | 6.5 | −4.6 | 11.1 | 8.4 |
| | 2002 | 1.1 | 0.5 | −3.0 | 3.0 |
| Solomon Islands | 1999 | −1.4 | −7.2 | 41.8 | −3.6 |
| | 2000 | −16.0 | −20.0 | −18.0 | −8.0 |
| | 2001 | −13.0 | −15.0 | −20.0 | −8.0 |
| | 2002 | 3.0 | 6.0 | 3.0 | 0.5 |
| Tonga | 1999 | 3.1 | −3.1 | 12.4 | 4.2 |
| | 2000 | 6.7 | 10.8 | 3.0 | 5.6 |
| | 2001 | 3.0 | 1.3 | 5.4 | 3.2 |
| | 2002 | 3.0 | 2.0 | 4.0 | 2.5 |
| Tuvalu | 1999 | 3.0 | .. | .. | .. |
| | 2000 | 3.0 | .. | .. | .. |
| | 2001 | 4.0 | .. | .. | .. |
| | 2002 | 3.0 | .. | .. | .. |
| Vanuatu | 1999 | −2.5 | −9.3 | 5.2 | −1.7 |
| | 2000 | 3.7 | 2.5 | 8.4 | 3.3 |
| | 2001 | −0.5 | −14.9 | −1.1 | 3.3 |
| | 2002 | −0.4 | −0.5 | 0.4 | −0.5 |

*Sources:* ESCAP, based on ADB, *Key Indicators of Developing Asian and Pacific Countries 2002,* vol. XXXIII (ADB, 2002), *Asian Development Outlook 2002* (Oxford University Press, 2002) and *Asian Development Outlook 2002 Update* (ADB, 2002); and national sources.

*Notes:* Data for 2002 are estimates. Industry comprises mining and quarrying; manufacturing; electricity, gas and power; and construction.

[a] Real GDP at factor cost.

path. The savings rate recovered from 18 per cent of GDP in 1998 to around 20 per cent in 2000 in the wake of the rebound in agricultural sector income after the prolonged drought of 1997 and 1998. The prognosis for investment and growth for 2002 onwards was dependent on a return of investor confidence in the economy and stability on the political front.

***The struggling sugar industry has severe implications for future growth***

The sugar industry has historically accounted for approximately four fifths of the value added of Fiji's marketable agricultural commodities. However, its relative importance declined considerably from around 11 per cent of GDP in the mid-1990s to just over 6 per cent in 2002. Expiring leases for land on which sugar cane is grown, combined with poor performance in sugar-milling, will cause production to fall in 2002. Meanwhile, Fiji Sugar Corporation Ltd., has been operating at a substantial loss since 1999, although its financial collapse, which would have had severe, economy-wide ramifications, was headed off by budgetary support in the form of soft loans and government guarantees. All in all, agricultural sector growth of around 1 per cent is expected in 2002, compared with 1.7 per cent in 2001.

Tourism is by far the largest industry in Fiji, with relative shares of 10 per cent of GDP, 30 per cent of formal sector employment and 30 per cent of gross foreign exchange earnings. Its outlook is generally favourable provided that security is maintained and access to land for tourist developments is securely available. In this context, large investments in new hotels and the related infrastructure are needed; only a few projects have materialized, although a number of others are in the pipeline. Tourist arrivals in 2002, at 409,000 persons, are nearly the same as those recorded prior to the coup of 2000. Much of the observed recovery in tourism is due to successful marketing campaigns and heavy price discounting by service providers to reduce excess capacity. Tourism growth accounted for the sectoral expansion in services, which went up by 3.6 per cent in 2001 and by an estimated 3 per cent in 2002.

Fiji's large and rapidly growing garment industry, which had been severely affected by international union boycotts in 2000, has been on the rebound following the lifting of restrictions and revival of orders. However, a deteriorating law and order situation is constraining growth in the industry, given its large female workforce. Reductions in tariff preferences as a result of trade liberalization in such export markets as Australia and New Zealand are eroding the profitability of Fijian suppliers and have made it necessary for them to search for alternative and additional markets, among other things. Meanwhile, several large publicly funded projects, plus the building of a large hotel complex, will provide a much-needed injection into construction activity, which had been subdued since 2000. However, the prospects for the continued growth of this industry and of manufacturing activities in general are closely linked with the resolution of political uncertainties and access to land. By and large, the industrial sector is expected to grow by 4 per cent in 2002, a considerable deceleration from the level of 7.4 per cent reached in 2001.

***Papua New Guinea's economy is on a declining path***

Economic activities have been generally subdued in Papua New Guinea since the mid-1990s. After a brief recovery, with GDP growth reaching 7.6 per cent in 1999, the economy contracted three years in a row by a total of around 5 percentage points. This represented a large setback in living standards, given the relatively high population growth rate of 2.7 per cent. After many years of delay, a $3.5 billion gas pipeline is to be built from the Southern Highlands of Papua New Guinea to Northern Australia in 2003. The associated economic stimulus is expected to lift GDP growth to over 2 per cent in 2003 and 2-3 per cent in the following years. Elsewhere in the economy, however, the business and investment environment is relatively poor because a number of important issues, such as the deteriorating law and order situation, still have to be addressed and a number of mineral operations are due to be closed in the second half of the decade.

***Agricultural output picked-up in 2002***

After a big upsurge in 2000, growth in agricultural production in Papua New Guinea became marginal the following year owing to a combination of adverse factors. Deteriorating infrastructure and continuing law and order problems have reduced farmers' access to markets. Poor prices for several export commodities, coffee in particular, reduced earnings and the incentive to produce. Agricultural output is expected to grow by 3.6 per cent in 2002 owing to a stronger growth in palm oil, cocoa and log production with modest improvements in copra, copra oil, coffee and rubber.

The industrial sector in Papua New Guinea contracted by a total of over 13 per cent during the period 2000-2002. Among the main contributing factors were shrinking oil reserves and hence production, and a rapid fall of over 9 per cent annually in the construction industry in 2000-2001. These declining trends in turn reflected the poor business and investment climate as well as the lack of new mineral developments. At the same time, mining output also fell in 2002 owing to the drought-induced difficulties experienced in the two largest mines: low river-water levels prevented the transport of ore. The value added in Papua New Guinea's service sector increased by almost 2 per cent in 2001 and is expected to further increase by 1.3 per cent in 2002, principally because of a rapid expansion in government expenditure in the first half of the year.

***Stalled economic activities in Samoa in 2002***

After sustained strong growth averaging over 6 per cent a year in 2000-2001, the Samoan economy stalled in 2002, with total output edging up by just over 1 per cent. However, the outlook is for a sharp economic rebound of around 6 per cent in 2003 and a growth path of around 5 per cent in future years. The main contributors and stimuli are expected to be manufacturing, construction and tourism. However, Samoa's subsistence agriculture has continued to decline, with virtually no growth forecast for the primary sector over the coming years. Indeed, negative outcomes in agriculture are possible in view of Samoa's vulnerability to natural disasters. Wet weather conditions early in 2002 hindered agriculture, with adverse effects on most fruit and vegetable crops. An offsetting stimulus came from the expanded fishery output; the export-oriented fishing industry constituted almost half of the value added in primary production. Overall, the marginally positive production in the primary sector expected for 2002 was a turnaround from a sharp drop of 4.6 per cent in 2001 owing mainly to crop disease and a slump in the exports of coconut products and kava, the latter being due in part to problems in the receiving countries.

Samoa's industrial sector experienced particularly strong growth of over 11 per cent a year in 2000 and 2001 as a result of the construction boom, which, in turn, was supported by a strong public investment programme. In 2002, however, a decline of about 3 per cent was expected in industrial output because a number of investment projects were wound up or delayed in order to cool what the Government regarded as an overheating economy. This contributed to a slump in the construction industry and served to weaken the manufacturing sector, owing to its close linkages to construction activities, and domestic demand. A strong rebound in the construction and manufacturing sectors could follow the renewed impetus in public investment in 2003. The service sector, accounting for nearly three fifths of GDP, had experienced strong growth of almost 8 per cent annually in 2000-2001. The momentum could not be sustained, however, because of a tapering off in private sector demand and a tightening of the Government's fiscal position. Growth fell to about 3 per cent in 2002, although a renewed expansion in inward tourism and a more expansive fiscal policy stance could drive service sector growth to 7 per cent in 2003.

***The Solomon Islands economy was on the rebound in 2002***

In Solomon Islands, the civil unrest that had erupted in 1999 became extensive through 2000, causing severe economic devastation and social dislocation. GDP, for example, fell by an average of 14.5 per cent a year in 2000-2001; per capita income was reduced to around $490 in 2001, compared with a peak of $1,120 in 1997. Among other things, palm oil production ceased in June 1999 and some 2,000 workers lost their jobs at the processing mill. Much of the idle equipment has sustained extensive damage from the weather and militia activities and would thus require heavy new investment before operations could resume.

The Gold Ridge Mine Tailings Storage Facitity, the only mining company, ceased production in June 2000 because of law and order problems, resulting in a loss of 300 jobs and the discontinuation of ancillary services, including those from a health clinic and a primary school. This mine is not expected to reopen in the near future.

Copra and coconut oil production was also in a decline owing to poor commodity prices and the financial problems suffered by the Commodities Export Marketing Authority. Logging has moved out of Guadalcanal to regions less affected by violence, thus further lowering income and reducing access to the ancillary social services that were once provided by the companies. Fish production is also quite subdued, the catch in 2001 being some 15 per cent lower than that of the previous year. Driven by a resurgence in fishery production, GDP growth is expected to reach 3 per cent in 2002. This may mark the start of an economic rebound for Solomon Islands, although heavy reinvestment and new investment are needed to sustain the momentum and reduce the sharp decline in living standards, an outcome compounded by the country's relatively rapid rate of population growth.

***Tonga's economy showed relatively strong sustained growth***

Aggregate production went up by about 3 per cent in Tonga in 2001-2002, a positive outcome in terms of per capita income as the population is estimated to be increasing by 0.5 per cent per annum. In fact, a devastating cyclone at the beginning of 2002 prevented even faster growth, while inward tourism is expected to lift GDP growth by another percentage point in 2003, with relatively healthy economic expansion in the vicinity of 3 per cent annually in the medium term. Tonga is another island economy greatly vulnerable to natural disasters, the damage from which is borne largely by the agricultural sector. This sector, however, has performed reasonably well in recent years, reflecting concerted government efforts to open up new niche markets overseas. There is considerable potential for expanding the export of off-season agricultural products to Japan and other countries, particularly from organic cultivation. Against a declining rural population and tempered by a damaging cyclone early in 2002, the agricultural sector, which includes fishing, nevertheless managed to expand by about 2 per cent during the year. Growth in the agricultural sector in future years is forecast to be in the range of 2-2.5 per cent, assuming no major natural disasters.

A surge in construction, supported mostly by aid funding, had pushed up Tonga's industrial sector output by 5.4 per cent in 2001, but with weaker growth in construction activities the industrial sector is expected to have expanded at a slower pace of about 4.0 per cent in 2002. Current initiatives taken to broaden the scope of food processing will increase manufacturing activities in future years, and the industrial sector as a whole could grow at an annual rate of 2-3 per cent beyond 2002. The service sector, which comprises 45 per cent of the economy, has long benefited from a substantial, and generally higher, flow of remittances from Tongans working abroad as well as significant earnings from inward tourism. The events in Bali in October 2002 are expected to help to strengthen tourism in Tonga in 2003. Tourism receipts amounted to $6.5 million in 2001.

***Domestic output contracted again in Vanuatu in 2002***

Economic production in Vanuatu was marginally lower (by 0.5 per cent) in 2001 and is expected to show another marginal fall (about 0.4 per cent) in 2002. The average medium-term expansion in GDP was therefore just over 1 per cent a year in the five years to 2002, compared with 2.6 per cent annually for population growth. In addition to the implied decline in per capita income, pressures on government resources (from subdued economic activities) were compounded by natural disasters; in particular, the capital, Port Vila, was struck by an earthquake measuring 7.6 points on the Richter scale early in 2002.

Agriculture accounts for just over one fifth of GDP but supports around four fifths of the population. Commercial farming is dominated by copra, beef and kava production. Copra (and coconut oil) output is set to rise in the wake of a price increase from VT 10,000 to VT 25,000 per ton made possible by a government subsidy. This could be a short-term respite, because of budgetary implications, but it has provided some impetus to the agricultural sector. That sector had performed poorly, with output declining by a total of about 22 per cent during the period 1999-2002. The sharp fall of almost 15 per cent in 2001 was largely due to two devastating cyclones which hit Vanuatu early in 2001. Kava production recovered strongly from the damage but its further growth may be affected by the global slump in demand. Several European countries have banned the sale of kava-based medicinal products, while the United States and the United Kingdom have asked for a voluntary withdrawal of kava products by their suppliers. Even though Fiji and New Caledonia are the destination of about two thirds of Vanuatu's kava exports, a fall in demand for kava in the industrial countries will have an adverse impact on prices and therefore on the growth of the domestic industry. Cocoa production declined with the suspension of the activities of a large plantation estate that traditionally accounted for some two fifths of total output. Organic beef-raising has good prospects for niche marketing; success on this front has been mixed, in part for lack of the organic certification that is necessary to earn the price premium and in part for lack of economies of scale in packaging and transport.

Vanuatu's industrial output varied marginally in 2001-2002. Recent investment in the industrial sector is dominated by the development by the private sector of a mini oil refinery with inputs of crude oil to be imported at international prices from Papua New Guinea and Australia. The objective is to provide domestic fuels at a discount on the prices currently prevailing in the market. The service sector is underpinned by tourism and financial services. Vanuatu is host to around 50,000 tourists each year in addition to 50,000 people who visit for one or two days ashore as cruise ship passengers. Around three quarters of the visitors come from Australia and there was a surge in tourists from New Zealand recently after the opening of a flight to Auckland. The tourism sector was buoyant in 2001, with relatively high hotel occupancy rates; it is also the dominant recipient of private sector lending in Vanuatu. Other things being equal, inward tourism was expected to improve the current account balance in 2002.

### Inflation

***Inflation remained relatively high in Papua New Guinea and Solomon Islands***

The picture as regards consumer prices was mixed in the Pacific island subregion in 2002 (table II.15). There was, in particular, lower inflation in Fiji, Tonga and Vanuatu and, except for Papua New Guinea and Solomon Islands, which showed double-digit increases in consumer prices, inflation remained largely muted at less than 6 per cent in that year. In Fiji, the drought is expected to generate some pressure on prices

**Table II.15. Selected Pacific island economies: inflation and money supply growth (M2), 1999-2002**

*(Percentage)*

| | *1999* | *2000* | *2001* | *2002* |
|---|---|---|---|---|
| **Inflation**[a] | | | | |
| Fiji | 2.0 | 1.1 | 4.2 | 2.5 |
| Papua New Guinea | 14.9 | 15.6 | 9.3 | 12.0 |
| Samoa | 0.2 | 1.0 | 4.0 | 6.0 |
| Solomon Islands | 8.3 | 4.8 | 1.8 | 11.0 |
| Tonga | 3.9 | 4.9 | 6.3 | 4.0 |
| Vanuatu | 2.2 | 2.7 | 3.2 | 2.5 |
| **Money supply growth (M2)** | | | | |
| Fiji | 14.2 | –2.1 | –3.1 | 4.9[b] |
| Papua New Guinea | 9.2 | 5.0 | 1.6 | 6.7[b] |
| Samoa | 15.7 | 16.3 | 6.1 | 3.6[c] |
| Solomon Islands | 7.0 | –0.7[d] | .. | .. |
| Tonga | 11.9 | 18.8 | 14.9 | 0.7[e] |
| Vanuatu | –9.2 | 5.5 | 5.7 | –3.4[e] |

*Sources:* ESCAP, based on ADB, *Key Indicators of Developing Asian and Pacific Countries 2002,* vol. XXXIII (ADB, 2002); IMF, *International Financial Statistics,* vol. LV, No. 11 (November 2002); and national sources.

*Note:* Data for 2002 are estimates.

[a] Changes in the consumer price index.
[b] January-July.
[c] January-June.
[d] January-September.
[e] January-August.

in 2003 but stability in the exchange rate will exert a stabilizing influence, with the result that inflation was expected to be at the rate of 3 per cent in 2003, compared with 2.5 per cent in 2002.

**Figure II.13. Index of exchange rates against the United States dollar of selected Pacific island economies and Australia and New Zealand, 1996-2002**

*(1996 = 100)*

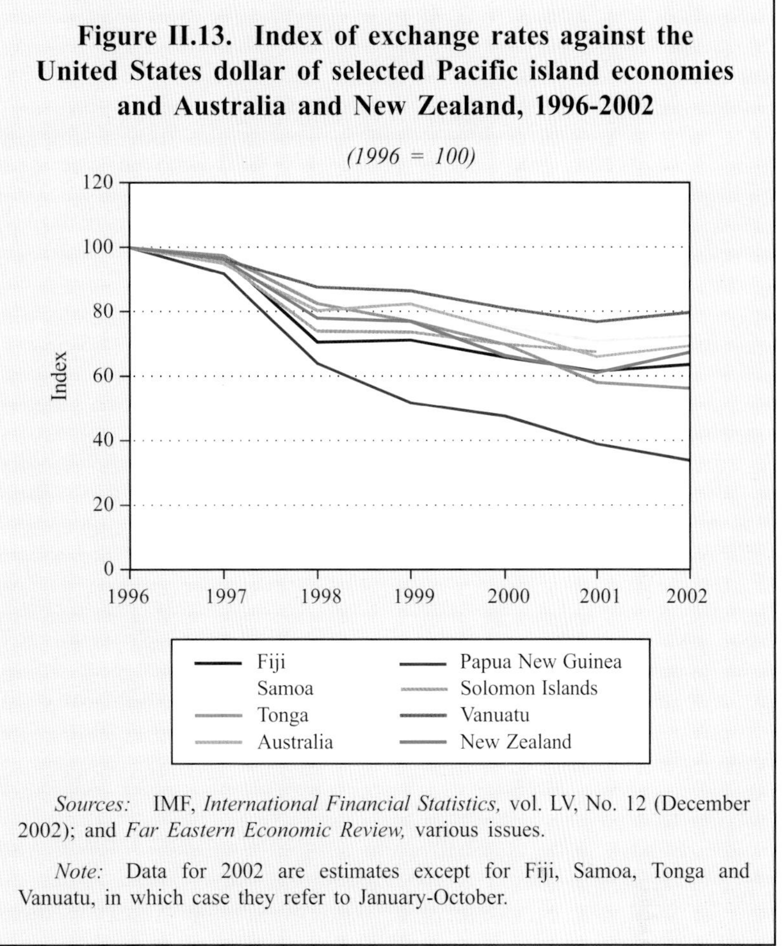


*Sources:* IMF, *International Financial Statistics,* vol. LV, No. 12 (December 2002); and *Far Eastern Economic Review,* various issues.

*Note:* Data for 2002 are estimates except for Fiji, Samoa, Tonga and Vanuatu, in which case they refer to January-October.

Despite a prolonged recession, inflation in Papua New Guinea is both relatively high and volatile; it also stands out as having been among the highest in the subregion for several years. The exchange rate was floated in 1995 and the currency has depreciated significantly against those of the main import suppliers (figure II.13). Inflation dropped to 9.3 per cent in 2001, from almost 16 per cent a year earlier, largely owing to greater stability in the exchange rate in the second half of 2000 and the first half of 2001. Consumer prices are expected to have risen by around 12 per cent in 2002 and, following a sharp depreciation of the kina in the second half of 2002, inflation is likely to be much higher in 2003.

The Central Bank of Samoa targets an inflation rate consistent with that of its main trading partners; the import content has a relative weight of about half of the typical consumption basket. However, prices in Samoa are also vulnerable to the state of domestic agriculture and the cost of overseas fuels; many sectors of the domestic economy depend heavily on imported energy products. In particular, a surge in the prices of domestic agricultural products in the second half of 2001 contributed to a hike in the inflation rate to 4 per cent from just 1 per cent in the previous year. The continued weakness in fruit and vegetable supplies caused a further sharp rise in food prices and inflation is expected to have risen to 6 per cent in 2002. Consumer prices could rise more modestly in the following year, perhaps by 3 per cent, as a result of the improved supply of local food produce, although this was offset in part by the flow-on impact of higher oil prices in the second half of 2002.

The inflation situation in Solomon Islands was improving as a result of fiscal tightening, given severe budgetary problems, the reluctance of the Central Bank to fund further deficits and a relatively more stable exchange rate. Consumer prices, for example, were on a downward trend, rising by less than 5 per cent in 2000 (compared with over 8 per cent during the previous year) and by less then 2 per cent in 2001, the lowest level for two decades. However, the inflation outlook worsened in 2002, with consumer prices forecast to rise by 11 per cent, largely because of the sharp mid-year depreciation of the local currency against all major trading currencies. For example, the local currency depreciated against the Australian and New Zealand dollars by 17.6 and about 22 per cent respectively.

Inflation in Tonga in 2001 bucked the moderate trend of earlier years, and reached 6.3 per cent, the highest level in the decade. The main cause of this uplift in consumer prices was a sharp depreciation of the exchange rate from late 2000 into parts of 2001. However, a more stable exchange rate in 2002 served to temper inflation, which was expected to return to the normal trend of around 4 per cent during the year.

Vanuatu has characteristically maintained a remarkable record of price stability throughout the 1990s and into the new millennium as well; annual increases in consumer prices were, by and large, limited to within a low band of 2 to 3 per cent. Inflation moderated from 3.2 per cent, which was approaching the threshold for the Reserve Bank of Vanuatu to tighten monetary policy, to 2.5 per cent in 2001-2002. A comfortable level of foreign exchange reserves should ensure continued stability in the exchange rate and hence in consumer prices, barring unexpected natural disasters. The Reserve Bank has limited discretion in shifting the composition of and weights within the basket which serves as the peg for the vatu exchange rate; changes in the weights were made only twice, once in 1998 and again in 2001, to induce a de facto depreciation of the currency against the United States dollar.

### *Foreign trade and other external transactions*

#### *External trade*

***Several Pacific island countries recorded increases in export earnings in 2002***

The available data up to the first half of 2002 indicate an improved trade performance in most parts of the subregion during the year; the exceptions to this pattern were Papua New Guinea and Samoa (tables II.16 and II.17). This represented a reversal in the trend for Fiji, Solomon Islands and Vanuatu, which experienced some decline in export earnings in 2001. However, Papua New Guinea's export earnings fell sharply by almost one quarter in 2002 (figure II.14). The 24 per cent decline in Papua New Guinea was mainly owing to the depletion of mineral oil reserves.

**Table II.16. Selected Pacific island economies: merchandise exports and their rates of growth, 1999-2002**

| | Exports (f.o.b.) | | | | |
|---|---|---|---|---|---|
| | Value (millions of US dollars) | Annual rate of growth (percentage) | | | |
| | 2001 | 1999 | 2000 | 2001 | 2002 (two quarters) |
| Fiji | 530 | 19.4 | −6.8 | −6.8 | 2.0 |
| Papua New Guinea[a] | 1 817 | 9.1 | 7.3 | −13.7 | −23.7 |
| Samoa[a] | 14 | −2.3 | −25.6 | 3.3 | −10.3 |
| Solomon Islands | 47 | 3.8 | −53.2 | −31.9 | 6.5 |
| Tonga[b] | 12 | 1.6 | −9.5 | 9.5 | 76.9 |
| Vanuatu | 20 | −24.3 | 6.0 | −27.0 | 5.6 |

*Sources:* Central Bank of Samoa, *Bulletin* (Apia, 2002), various issues; National Reserve Bank of Tonga, *Quarterly Bulletin* (Nuku'alofa, 2001-2002), various issues; Central Bank of Solomon Islands, *Quarterly Review* (Honiara, 2002), various issues; Reserve Bank of Vanuatu, *Quarterly Economic Review* (Port Vila, 2002), various issues; Reserve Bank of Fiji, *Quarterly Review* (Suva, 2002), various issues; and Bank of Papua New Guinea, *Quarterly Economic Bulletin* (Port Moresby), various issues.

[a] Data for 2002 are estimates for the whole year.
[b] Fiscal year.

**Table II.17. Selected Pacific island economies: merchandise imports and their rates of growth, 1999-2002**

| | Imports (c.i.f.) | | | | |
|---|---|---|---|---|---|
| | Value (millions of US dollars) | Annual rate of growth (percentage) | | | |
| | 2001 | 1999 | 2000 | 2001 | 2002 (two quarters) |
| Fiji | 783 | 25.3 | −11.2 | −2.6 | 7.1 |
| Papua New Guinea[a] | 942 | −0.1 | −7.0 | −6.4 | 2.1 |
| Samoa[a] | 119 | 20.8 | −8.5 | 12.7 | 9.2 |
| Solomon Islands | 81 | −15.5 | −14.8 | −11.5 | −15.3 |
| Tonga[b,c] | 62 | −28.9 | 12.8 | −1.6 | 18.6 |
| Vanuatu[c] | 78 | 9.3 | −7.3 | 0.5 | −0.7 |

*Sources:* Central Bank of Samoa, *Bulletin* (Apia, 2002), various issues; National Reserve Bank of Tonga, *Quarterly Bulletin* (Nuku'alofa, 2001-2002), various issues; Central Bank of Solomon Islands, *Quarterly Review* (Honiara, 2002), various issues; Reserve Bank of Vanuatu, *Quarterly Economic Review* (Port Vila, 2002), various issues; Reserve Bank of Fiji, *Quarterly Review* (Suva, 2002), various issues; and Bank of Papua New Guinea, *Quarterly Economic Bulletin* (Port Moresby), various issues.

[a] Data for 2002 are estimates for the whole year.
[b] Fiscal year.
[c] Import value f.o.b.

Except for Solomon Islands and Vanuatu, spending on imports in other Pacific island countries are expected to increase in 2002 (figure II.15). The continued contraction of imports in Solomon Islands reflects the poor state of the country's economy during the year.

***Fiji's trade deficit widened in 2002 owing to strong demand for intermediate goods***

Fiji's merchandise export earnings fell by almost 7 per cent in 2001, to $530 million, largely as a result of a 14 per cent drop in sugar exports and a reduction of 16 per cent in garment export value; the healthy growth of gold and fish exports prevented a sharper fall in total exports. Sugar exports had gone down by 16 per cent in 2000 and the performance of this once-dominant industry is expected to be weak in future years owing to continued uncertainty over the land tenure of sugar farmers. Merchandise imports fell by 2.6 per cent in 2001 to $783 million but there was a 3 per cent contraction in the merchandise trade deficit compared with the previous year's level. The merchandise trade deficit is expected to widen in 2002 as a result of strong demand for intermediate and consumer goods that more than offset the small decline in payments for imported machinery and equipment, mineral fuels and raw materials, and a marginal increase in exports. The prognosis for merchandise trade

**Figure II.14. Growth rates in merchandise export earnings of selected Pacific island economies, 1999-2002**

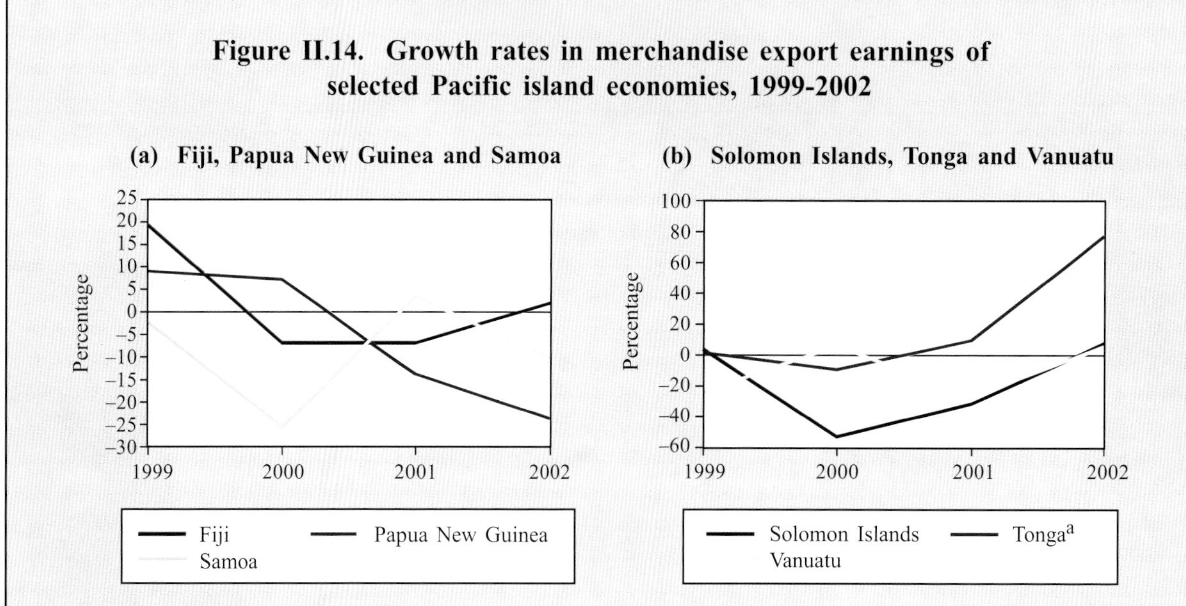


*Sources:* Central Bank of Samoa, *Bulletin* (Apia, 2002), various issues; National Reserve Bank of Tonga, *Quarterly Bulletin* (Nuku'alofa, 2001-2002), various issues; Central Bank of Solomon Islands, *Quarterly Review* (Honiara, 2002), various issues; Reserve Bank of Vanuatu, *Quarterly Economic Review* (Port Vila, 2002), various issues; Reserve Bank of Fiji, *Quarterly Review* (Suva, 2002), various issues; and Bank of Papua New Guinea, *Quarterly Economic Bulletin* (Port Moresby), various issues.

*Note:* Data for 2002 are for two quarters only, except for Papua New Guinea and Samoa, in which case they are estimates for the whole year.

[a] Fiscal year.

**Figure II.15. Growth rates in merchandise import spending of selected Pacific island economies, 1999-2002**

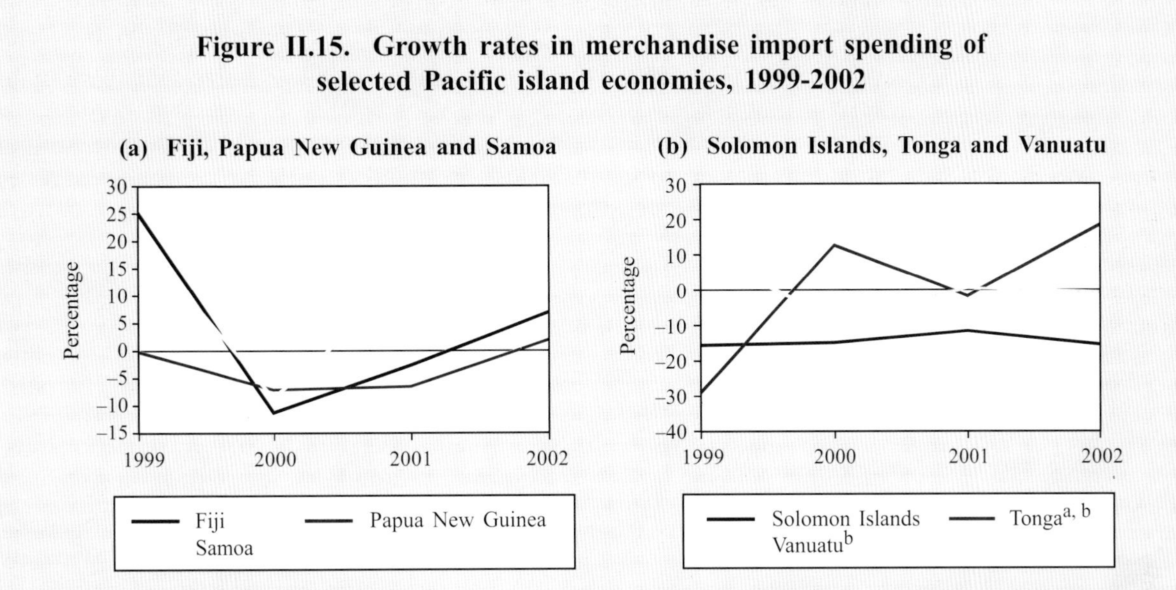


*Sources:* Central Bank of Samoa, *Bulletin* (Apia, 2002), various issues; National Reserve Bank of Tonga, *Quarterly Bulletin* (Nuku'alofa, 2001-2002), various issues; Central Bank of Solomon Islands, *Quarterly Review* (Honiara, 2002), various issues; Reserve Bank of Vanuatu, *Quarterly Economic Review* (Port Vila, 2002), various issues; Reserve Bank of Fiji, *Quarterly Review* (Suva, 2002), various issues; and Bank of Papua New Guinea, *Quarterly Economic Bulletin* (Port Moresby), various issues.

*Note:* Data for 2002 are for two quarters only, except for Papua New Guinea and Samoa, in which case they are estimates for the whole year.

[a] Fiscal year.
[b] Value f.o.b.

is improving given a recovery in garment exports to Australia and New Zealand following the lifting of trade bans imposed by trade unions in those countries.

The coup-induced slump in tourism drove down service exports by over 7 per cent in 2001, after an earlier fall of 9.5 per cent in 2000. Tourism is by far Fiji's most important source of foreign exchange earnings and, all in all, service exports amounted to 29 per cent of GDP in 1999. The strong recovery in tourism accounted for the expansion of over 11 per cent in service exports in 2002. The overall current account deficit rose marginally in 2001 to 3.6 per cent of GDP. In 2002, the improvement in the service balance more than compensated for a higher trade deficit, thus contributing to a slightly lower current account deficit of 3.1 per cent of GDP.

***A sharp decline in Papua New Guinea's merchandise exports in 2002***

Papua New Guinea's merchandise exports went down by almost 14 per cent in 2001, to $1.82 billion, and declined further, by almost 24 per cent, during the first half of 2002. All major export sectors performed poorly. Agricultural export earnings fell by 25 per cent in 2000 and by another 30 per cent in 2001; they were expected to decrease by a further 28 per cent in 2002. The main source of this persistent slump is coffee, which registered sharp falls in both export volumes and export prices. As a result, earnings on this commodity in 2001 were just one third of the level received in 1999; more seriously, it was expected that such earnings would be halved again in 2002. Palm oil exports have been steady and have now become the country's most important agricultural export.

Mineral oil exports are also on a declining trend owing to the depletion of reserves. Despite favourable external prices, gold and copper exports were expected to be lower in 2002 as a result of supply disruptions at the two largest mines caused by drought conditions. Forestry exports went down in 2001 and 2002 owing to a restrictive export tax regime. Merchandise imports, which had fallen by 6.4 per cent in 2001, to $942 million, recovered to grow by around 2 per cent during the first half of 2002. The share of merchandise imports as a percentage of GDP remained relatively steady at 31.4 per cent, compared with that of merchandise exports, which reached 60 per cent of GDP in 2001.

The merchandise trade surplus, at almost 29 per cent of GDP in 2001, was relatively steady when compared with the previous year but, because of the contraction in GDP, it was $164 million lower in absolute terms. Because of the poor export performance, the trade surplus was estimated to have shrunk further, by some $329 million, to less than one fifth of an already falling GDP. The deficit on external services and incomes fell steadily, from $713 million in 2000 to $608 million in 2001, and was expected to fall to around $527 million in 2002. This trend was due to lower outflows on services and other incomes earned because of the recessional conditions of the domestic economy, including the export sector. The overall current account surplus was over 9 per cent of GDP in both 2000 and 2001, but with the sharp shrinkage of the trade surplus the out-turn for 2002 was expected to be just about 1 per cent of GDP.

Samoa's merchandise exports recovered strongly to grow by 3.3 per cent, or $14 million in 2001, after the steep decline by over a quarter suffered in 2000. The turnaround was, by and large, due to increased fish exports, which accounted for some two thirds of the merchandise export value. Also in 2001, garment exports took over from coconut products to become the country's second most important earner of foreign exchange. This fledgling industry first commenced exports in 2000 and there is considerable scope for greater earnings in this sector. Receipts from the traditional mainstay of the export sector, coconut products, in 2001 were half their 1999 level because of a temporary closure of the coconut oil mill. Operations were scheduled to resume late in 2002, and this would provide a welcome boost to exports in the years to follow. In addition, kava exports nearly disappeared owing to the cessation of orders from the German and American pharmaceutical markets. Taro exports were on the rise after the recovery of the crop from a devastating blight in 1993.

All in all, merchandise exports were expected to be down by 10 per cent in 2002, with the value of fish, garments and coconuts changing little from their 2001 export levels.

***Samoa's merchandise trade deficit expected to have worsened in 2002***

Merchandise imports in Samoa rose strongly in 2001 to $119 million, or 53 per cent of GDP, owing to higher oil prices and buoyant local demand. The merchandise trade deficit of $105 million, or over 46 per cent of GDP, is expected to have worsened further to 49 per cent of GDP, or about $130 million, in 2002. These massive trade deficits were offset by equally substantial surpluses in the service account balance and inflows of private remittances. The value of exported services dropped slightly in 2001 to $63.6 million, but was expected to expand by over 11 per cent in 2002. The uplift was largely due to tourism, which accounted for three fifths of service exports; indeed, it was likely that revenues from inward tourism would be nearly three times greater than the total earnings on merchandise exports in 2002.

In 2001, the overall surplus on the service account was almost $41 million, or just under 17 per cent of GDP. Net private remittances were relatively stable, adding another $44.3 million in 2001, although this figure was marginally lower, by 2 per cent, than the previous year's level. The strengthening of the currencies of New Zealand and Australia, which are the main sources of private remittances for Samoa, was expected to boost inward remittances by almost one fifth in 2002. The overall current account deficit is also generally stable. It deteriorated in 2001 to an amount equal to 11.2 per cent of GDP, from 5 per cent in the previous year. A further marginal shortfall equivalent to 12.3 per cent of GDP was forecast for 2002.

***Solomon Islands' export sector expected to have rebounded in 2002***

The export sector was the most severely hit by the civil unrest in Solomon Islands. Merchandise exports fell by 53 per cent in 2000 and by another 32 per cent in the following year, to $47 million, but rebounded with positive growth of over 6 per cent during the first half of 2002. Copra, palm oil and gold exports had disappeared completely and fish exports were at a fraction of their previous level. Log exports were the only commodity to have held up and constituted four fifths of earnings on merchandise exports. The stability of log exports will provide a foundation for trade earnings, which, other things being equal, would recover in the renewal and rehabilitation process.

Balance on the merchandise trade account revealed the severe deterioration in the external trade sector in Solomon Islands. The country had enjoyed a merchandise trade surplus of 14 per cent of GDP in 1999. This became a deficit equivalent to 9.4 per cent of GDP in 2000 and worsened to equal 16.7 per cent during the following year. An improved outcome was expected in 2002 as merchandise exports picked up and imports continued to fall. The external current account also swung sharply from surplus to deficit and amounted to just over 18 per cent of

GDP in 2000. However, a sharp turnaround in inward transfers from abroad more than compensated for the deterioration in the merchandise and service accounts in 2001 and, as a result, shortfalls in the external current account were lowered to 13.3 per cent of GDP; it was expected that the deficit for 2002 would be less than 7 per cent of GDP.

***Tonga's efforts in finding new niche markets have yielded dividends in recent years***

In Tonga, concerted efforts made by the Government to widen the export base, including the provision of better conditions for the fishing industry and the exploration of new niche markets in agriculture, have yielded dividends in recent years. Merchandise exports went up by 9.5 per cent in 2001, following a decline of almost the same magnitude in the previous year; an even larger upswing of almost 77 per cent was achieved for the first half of 2002. Fish and squash continued to be the principal foreign exchange earners, accounting for 65 per cent of the total export earnings in 2000.

Tonga continues to carry a sizeable merchandise trade deficit, which was equal to almost 43 per cent of GDP in 2001, compared with a relative share of 14.6 per cent in the case of merchandise exports. However, the value of imported merchandise was just over 57 per cent of GDP, compared with 54 per cent in 2000; the marginal decline of 1.6 per cent in import spending in United States dollar terms was offset by the depreciation of the local currency in 2001. Surpluses in the external service account, which amounted to 7.5 per cent of GDP in 2001, compensated in part for the large trade deficit. However, as in the case of Samoa, by far the most important item in the external current account was private unrequited transfers, which, in 2001, brought in $52 million, or almost 39 per cent of GDP. The level of such transfers was twice as high as that of the mid-1990s, although their expansion was expected to taper off in 2002 mainly owing to the adverse impact of the economic slowdown on Tongan workers in the United States. Tonga has recorded a current account deficit since the early 1990s, and the shortfall amounted to 10.7 per cent of GDP in 2001.

***Export earnings expected to improve in Vanuatu in 2002 with the recovery in cocoa and copra output***

Vanuatu's merchandise exports slumped by 27 per cent, to $20 million or just one tenth of GDP, in 2001, owing principally to the effects of the two devastating cyclones early in the year on cocoa and copra production. Export earnings increased by 5.6 per cent in the first half of 2002, along with the recovery in cocoa and copra output. As in the case of several other Pacific island economies, spending on imports far exceeded receipts from exports, so that the merchandise trade deficit was equivalent to just over a quarter of GDP in Vanuatu in 2001. However, by far the most important exchange earner is inward tourism, which also brought in an amount equal to a quarter of GDP for the same year. Such earnings were thus the main factor accounting for the surplus of just under 1 per cent of GDP in the external current account for 2001; it was likely that the continuing growth in inward tourism would result in a surplus in the external current account for 2002.

*Capital flows*

Fiji's capital account surplus shrank in the aftermath of the May 2000 coup but, with restored confidence, external capital was again flowing in. The capital account showed a sizeable surplus of $40 million, or 2.4 per cent of GDP, in 2001. This translated into a lower deficit, equal to 1.8 per cent of GDP, in the overall balance of payments in 2001, compared with a shortfall of 3.1 per cent of GDP in the previous year. The stock of foreign reserves stood at F$770 million as at September 2002; this amount was sufficient to cover 3.7 months of imports. In the aftermath of the coup, the Reserve Bank of Fiji introduced capital transaction control measures to stem capital flight and minimize the likelihood of a foreign exchange crisis. Among the notable measures were a reduction in transaction ceilings on foreign exchange, an increase in interest rates on the use of the Reserve Bank's lending facilities, an increase in the documentary requirements involving foreign exchange and the withdrawal of some delegations given to commercial banks on approving foreign exchange transactions.

***Fiji has one of the lightest external debt service burdens in the subregion***

Along with the improving domestic environment, control measures were being withdrawn in January 2003 with the aim of bringing the foreign exchange control regime to pre-coup conditions. Meanwhile, Fiji's external debt has been in steady decline for a number of years and was around 8 per cent of GDP in 2000. Much of this debt was concessional in nature and external debt-servicing took up only 1.5 per cent of GDP, making it one of the lightest debt-service burdens in the subregion.

In Papua New Guinea, the external capital account deficit shrank from 5.3 to 2.6 per cent of GDP in 2000-2001 on account of a large official drawdown of funds made available under the Structural Adjustment Programme. Partly as a result, the balance-of-payments surplus expanded to $196 million, or 6.5 per cent of GDP, and led to a build-up of foreign exchange reserves, which, at $458 million, were enough for nearly six months of import cover. The small capital account surplus of $49 million, or 1.8 per cent of GDP, in 2002 was principally due to the reorganization of equity ownership in the mineral sector. Despite the lower trade surplus in 2002, the balance of payments was also expected to remain in surplus, although its magnitude would be lower, equivalent to around 3 per cent of GDP.

***External debt on the rise in Papua New Guinea***

External debt attributable to mining and oil companies has been on the decline because of little new investment and reductions in outstanding loan positions. However, the external debt of the government sector has been on the rise and this accounted for the considerable increase in the level of Papua New Guinea's foreign public debt in 2001 to almost 49 per cent of GDP, compared with 40 per cent in 2000. The debt-service burden jumped to 10 per cent of GDP in 2001, compared with just over 8 per cent in 2000 and 5.4 per cent in 1999.

***External debt service remained manageable in Samoa in 2002***

Samoa's capital account surplus rose sharply in 2001 to almost $26 million, or almost 11 per cent of GDP, from $12.5 million in the previous year. The capital account is dominated by official flows and the higher surplus reflected the rise in external concessional loans for public investment programmes. The capital account surplus for 2002 was expected to be marginally lower, at around 10 per cent of GDP. The overall balance of payments continued to be in good shape, with a small surplus of 0.4 per cent of GDP in 2000 and a small deficit of 0.6 per cent of GDP in the following year. However, the overall shortfall for 2002 was likely to have been greater, at around 2.7 per cent of GDP. The level of foreign reserves was, by and large, reasonably reassuring at more than four months of import cover. Samoa's external debt levels stabilized at around $145 million in the period 1997-2000, but continued to fall as a percentage of GDP; the level was 55 per cent in 2002, compared with 59 per cent in 2001. The burden on external debt service remained manageable at 2.5 per cent of GDP in 2002.

***External debt-servicing is a major problem in Solomon Islands***

Solomon Islands recorded capital account surpluses in 2000 and 2001, owing in large measure to the building-up of payment arrears. The overall balance of payments showed a deficit of $19 million in 2000 but a small surplus of $2 million in the following year. The foreign reserve level, at $24 million as at the end of 2001, was less than one half the 1999 level but was enough for three months of cover for lower import demand. External debt increased sharply, from 57 per cent to an estimated 77 per cent of GDP between 1999 and 2001. The slump in GDP was the reason for the surge in the relative importance of external debt, which remained relatively stable in United States dollar terms. Debt-servicing was contained to 4.8 per cent of GDP in 2001, although the decline in export earnings meant that debt-service payments absorbed 21.3 per cent of merchandise export receipts in 2001, compared with 7.4 per cent in 1999.

The overall balance of payments was kept under control in Tonga, with small surpluses recorded for 2000 and 2001. The higher capital inflows expected in 2002 in support of the Public Sector Reform Programme would lead to a larger surplus of around 4 per cent of GDP. Foreign reserve levels were stable and sufficient for four months of import cover. As a share of GDP, external debt went up to just over 43 per cent of GDP in 2001, compared with 39 per cent in 2000, because of the depreciation of the local currency relative to the United States dollar. Debt-servicing was manageable at 2.4 per cent of GDP.

The balance of payments of Vanuatu has been characterized by extended periods of merchandise trade deficits financed by large surpluses on the external service account and sustained inflows of foreign aid and FDI. Since 1998, funds disbursed from multilateral agencies and bilateral donors under the Comprehensive Reform Programme have been a significant source of capital inflows. Overall, the capital account showed only a small deficit in both 2000 and 2001, and the overall position in external payments came very close to balance, recording a deficit of only 0.2 per cent of GDP in both years. Official reserve levels were healthy at 5.3 months of import cover. In principle, the level of external debt in Vanuatu is protected by a safeguard requirement that the Government maintain a prudent level in its external debt position. External debt was low compared with that of other Pacific countries, at under 30 per cent of GDP, and debt-servicing has been less than 1 per cent of GDP in recent years.

## *Key policy issues*

### *Governance*

***Governance issues are compounding socio-economic difficulties in several subregional economies***

Several Pacific island economies have faced severe social difficulties in recent years, including civil unrest, law and order problems and political disturbances. In large part such difficulties are the symptoms of an unsatisfactory economic performance, the inadequacy of basic services to meet the growing needs of an expanding population, unrelenting pressure on government resources and persistent and sizeable budget shortfalls (table II.18). The importance of good governance in both the

**Table II.18. Selected Pacific island economies: budget and current account balance as a percentage of GDP, 1999-2002**

*(Percentage)*

| | *1999* | *2000* | *2001* | *2002* |
|---|---|---|---|---|
| **Budget balance as a percentage of GDP** | | | | |
| Fiji | −5.4 | −6.6 | −6.9 | −6.9 |
| Papua New Guinea | −2.7 | −2.0 | −3.6 | −3.5 |
| Samoa | 0.3 | −0.7 | −2.3 | −2.0 |
| Solomon Islands[a] | −3.7 | 2.9 | −8.0 | −3.0 |
| Tonga[a] | −0.3 | −0.4 | −2.6 | −4.0 |
| Vanuatu | −3.1 | −7.4 | −4.0 | −3.0 |
| **Current account balance as a percentage of GDP** | | | | |
| Fiji | −4.5 | −6.3 | −3.6 | −3.1 |
| Papua New Guinea | 2.7 | 9.9 | 9.4 | 1.1 |
| Samoa | −8.1 | −5.0 | −11.2 | −12.3 |
| Solomon Islands | .. | −18.1 | −13.3 | −6.8 |
| Tonga | −12.8 | −10.8 | −10.7 | −9.7 |
| Vanuatu | −5.4 | 2.1 | 0.8 | 1.7 |

*Sources:* ESCAP, based on ADB, *Key Indicators of Developing Asian and Pacific Countries 2002,* vol. XXXIII (ADB, 2002) and *Asian Development Outlook 2002* (Oxford University Press, 2002); IMF, *International Financial Statistics,* vol. LV, No. 11 (November 2002); and national sources.

*Note:* Data for 2002 are estimates.

[a] Excluding grants.

public and the private sectors, as well as a synergistic development partnership between these two sectors, cannot be overemphasized. There is, moreover, a clear need to enhance the role of the private sector in socio-economic activities and services to improve efficiency in resource utilization and, in the process, take some of the load off the public sector. In fact, while extensive structural reforms have been initiated by several Pacific island countries in recent years, the outcome has not always been satisfactory, in part because of inadequate response from the private sector. Consequently, a number of countries have actually abandoned or postponed some scheduled reform measures, such as the privatization of selected public enterprises.

*Budget deficits*

An external debt burden is not a major problem for most Pacific island countries because the debt stock, relative to, say, GDP, is comparatively modest and a large proportion of external obligations are on highly concessional terms. On the whole, budget deficits as a percentage of GDP have been increasing for some of these countries, including the small, atoll economies (see box II.1), in recent years. However, (non-inflationary) deficit-financing mainly from domestic sources implies the crowding-out of private sector activities.

***Fiji's fiscal position deteriorated in 2002***

In Fiji, for example, the fiscal position has deteriorated, and the budget deficit was forecast to reach 7 per cent of GDP in 2002 and 4 per cent in 2003. Consequently, debt levels that were on a downward trend prior to the coup in 2000 are on the rise once again, reaching 45 per cent of GDP in 2001. The bulk of this debt is held domestically, and foreign obligations amount to approximately 15 per cent of the total. The medium-term forecasts for the budget and debt levels remain largely sanguine. The actual outcomes, however, will be largely dependent on the success of expenditure reforms and the effectiveness of several newly introduced measures to raise tax compliance while also broadening the tax base. Total expenditure as a proportion of GDP in 2002, for example, stood at 31 per cent, compared with the target of 28 per cent. The priorities for allocations have been changed, with public investment slated to rise from 20 to 30 per cent of the budget. Total government revenue is currently low, standing at just 22.8 per cent of GDP in 2001 and 24.1 per cent in 2002.

Since the tax reforms of 1999 in Papua New Guinea and despite the new revenue measures introduced in 2000, tax revenue has been on a declining trend as a share of GDP. This is due in part to the limited success of VAT, which was introduced as part of the 1999 reforms. Among the causal factors for this lack of success are the inadequate resources committed to enforcing VAT compliance. Further difficulties for

## Box II.1. Difficult issues for economic management in small, atoll economies in the Pacific

The available data indicate GDP growth in the range of 0.2-4 per cent in Cook Islands, Kiribati, the Marshall Islands, the Federated States of Micronesia and Tuvalu in 2002. Cook Islands' economy rebounded in that year, after registering a contraction in overall production in 2001, while Kiribati, the Marshall Islands and Tuvalu sustained an average economic expansion of 2.9 per cent a year in 2001-2002. The public sector continues to be a major growth-inducing force in most of these atoll economies. For example, the Marshall Islands economy benefited from the temporary boost in funding and other forms of assistance provided through United States Government programmes under the Compact of Free Association with the United States. Grant funding amounted to about 71 per cent of total government revenue in 2002. The first 15-year phase of the Compact for the Marshall Islands expired in September 2001. Provisions for the next phase, currently under negotiation, are expected to be finalized in 2003; meanwhile, the Compact provides for two years of interim financing.

The Federated States of Micronesia and Palau also benefit from funds received under the Compact of Free Association with the United States. In fact, economic growth in the former economy has been driven largely by the expansionary fiscal policy made possible by the successful adjustment to the reduction in Compact funds that occurred in the mid-1990s. The Federated States of Micronesia and the United States have also been negotiating the nature and extent of continued financial support under the Compact since 1999. The commitments for the first 15 years ended in 2001; on 1 October 2001, additional transitional funds became available for a further two years while negotiations continued. Palau signed its Compact of Free Association with the United States in 1995; it is not due for renegotiation until 2009.

As in the larger Pacific island countries, the small and atoll economies in the subregion face even bigger problems with increasing budget deficits. In the case of the Federated States of Micronesia, the budget surplus in 2002 was a welcome change from the deterioration in consolidated government finances which had been reflected in sizeable budget deficits since 1988; the shortfalls ranged between 4 and 6 per cent of GDP in each year from 1997 to 2001. Local revenue generation is weak in smaller Pacific island economies, a reflection not only of problems with tax collection but also of the low levels of private sector development in those economies. It is therefore welcome news for Cook Islands, the Marshall Islands, the Federated States of Micronesia, Nauru, Niue and Palau that they are to receive a total of 20.9 million euros from the EU during the next five years; the Federated States of Micronesia will be allocated about one third of those funds. All six island economies are new members of the African, Caribbean and Pacific group aid, trade and development partnership with the EU, joining it under the new Cotonou Agreement signed in June 2000. Eight other Pacific island countries have already been included in the Lomé conventions. These funds are to be used by the six countries for developing renewable energy sources, improving health and education services and dealing with drought and cyclone emergencies.

Most Pacific island countries continue to be affected by various natural disasters, including cyclones, drought and earthquakes, which have caused significant damage to property and, in several cases, loss of lives. Several economies, including Fiji, Guam, Solomon Islands, Tonga and Vanuatu, were victims of natural disasters in 2002 alone. In the case of Guam, the overall cost of the damage from Typhoon Pongsona is estimated at $70 million, a substantial sum for a small island economy. This disaster came at a time when the Government of Guam was facing some financial difficulties. It plans to lay off hundreds of workers, increase some taxes and possibly borrow $120 million to balance the budget in 2003.

tax administration were then added by a court ruling late in 2002 that the VAT rate as currently applied was unconstitutional. Meanwhile, VAT revenues in 2001 had reached only one third of the original projections and amounted to less than 9 per cent of the tax revenue for the year, instead of becoming the Government's most important source of revenue, as had been hoped initially.

***A mini-budget in Papua New Guinea in 2002 was aimed at reducing the revenue shortfall***

Total government revenue fell to 28.4 per cent of GDP in 2001, from over 31 per cent during the previous year. This drop was due to the slump in VAT revenue collections and a fall in realized taxes on log exports and corporate incomes. Total government expenditure amounted to just under one third of GDP in 2001, but one seventh of such spending was absorbed by debt-service payments. The budget deficit exceeded projections and, at 3.6 per cent of GDP in 2001, was the highest shortfall in a decade. It expanded rapidly in 2002, in part because of increased spending relating to the general elections and in part because of the ongoing recession. A mini-budget introduced by the incoming Government for the second half of 2002 aimed at reducing the fiscal deficit to under 3.5 per cent of GDP for 2002, compared with earlier expectations of more than 6 per cent.

***Samoa plans to increase the VAT rate by 2.5 per cent to address a persistent fiscal deficit***

Samoa continues its prudential fiscal management with the budget deficit for the financial year to June 2002 set at 2 per cent of GDP, down slightly from the previous year's outcome, which was equivalent to 2.3 per cent of GDP. For future years, however, the Government is targeting a balanced budget. Tax revenue in financial year 2001/02 was rising in line with GDP growth and stood at around 21 per cent of GDP. A matter of concern for the Government is the declining trend in non-tax revenue, which fell a further 29 per cent in 2002 to its lowest level since the early 1990s. This persistent fall is due partly to the implementation of the Public Sector Reform Programme and partly to weakened enforcement. Thus, in an effort to maintain a strong revenue base, plans are being made to increase the VAT rate in Samoa from 10 to 12.5 per cent.

External grants to Samoa rose sharply in 2002 to $27.6 million, or almost one third of government revenue, and were the main contributor to the observed rise in total revenue to almost one third of GDP in 2002, from just under 31 per cent in 2001. However, there was a modest rise in public spending, from 33.1 to 34.8 per cent of GDP in 2001-2002, mainly because of advanced allocations on an aid-funded programme plus higher public sector wages and salaries. There was, in fact, an implied tightening of expenditure, especially in the second half of 2002. Loan-funded infrastructure projects were held back to contain expenditure and cool off the economy. Government debt had reached almost 62 per cent of GDP in 2000, but dropped to under 59 per cent in the following year owing to a strong economic performance. The debt-service burden was highly manageable in 2001 at just 2.4 per cent of GDP.

***The budgetary position of Solomon Islands remains fragile***

By contrast, the budgetary position of Solomon Islands remains precarious. This is the net result of large and persistent past deficits combined with sizeable losses of government revenue caused by declining economic activities and the rise in civil unrest, which had begun in 1999. Expenditure went up considerably to accommodate higher public sector wages and salaries; the estimated deficit for 2001 was 8 per cent of GDP. In addition, large arrears in payments had been building up and some public sector salaries were not being paid. The security situation was improving but the increased efforts to curb law and order problems could be hampered by overdue payments. Domestic debt was approaching one third of GDP in 2001, but the true debt position may be higher when account is taken of accumulated overdue payments.

***Tonga's overall budget deficit is on an upward trend***

In Tonga, tax revenue fell short and expenditure exceeded the budget in 2001, the latter being attributable to a rise in public sector salaries and support for loss-making public trading enterprises. Total government revenue as a share of GDP rose slightly to 28 per cent in 2001, while expenditure expanded sharply from just under 29 per cent to almost 32 per cent of GDP in 2000-2001. Consequently, the overall budget deficit was on an upward trend; it was equivalent to 0.4 per cent of GDP in 2000 but went up to 2.6 per cent in the following year and was expected to reach 4 per cent of GDP in 2002. This has been a matter of significant concern to the Government and responsive measures are being taken to address the problem through the Public Sector Reform Programme introduced in mid-2002. For some time, ways and means have been considered to find alternatives to tariffs as a principal source of revenue. Tax revenue has declined marginally as a share of GDP but this has been offset by the relatively healthy growth of non-tax revenues.

***The budget deficit, although relatively high, moderated in Vanuatu in 2002***

Vanuatu recorded relatively large fiscal deficits, averaging 5.7 per cent of GDP in 2000-2001. The budget shortfall, although becoming lower at 3 per cent of GDP, in 2002, persisted despite a variety of measures implemented by the Government to rein in expenditure. Optimistic revenue projections for gambling taxes and VAT are primarily responsible for these deficits. But the revenue base is narrow and broadening efforts are called for so that total revenue can reach 27 per cent of GDP, as intended, from the current level of around 24 per cent. However, the recommendations of a committee to review revenue are yet to be accepted or implemented. Total government debt built up to nearly 40 per cent of GDP in 2001, and debt-servicing payments reached 3.5 per cent of GDP and absorbed more than 16 per cent of government revenue.

### *Money and finance*

***Demand for credit in Fiji remained subdued, with the Government absorbing the bulk of the available funds***

The Reserve Bank of Fiji has maintained an accommodative stance on monetary policy, with the indicator rate on its 91-day bonds at 1.25 per cent as at September 2002. A relatively healthy foreign exchange position has enabled the Reserve Bank to relax controls on cross-border capital flows. Commercial bank interest rates were also on a downward trend as a result of the build-up of excess liquidity in the year. In particular, the weighted average lending rate on outstanding loans and advances had fallen in 2002 to 8 per cent, compared with 8.3 per cent in 2001 and 8.4 per cent in 2000. However, demand for credit remained subdued, with the Government absorbing the bulk of the available funds. One issue is that, despite the excess liquidity in the system, interest rate margins remained large and lending rates high relative to those in the neighbouring industrialized countries, Australia and New Zealand. There were signs of recovery in the demand for credit by the private sector, which could result in interest rates either stabilizing or edging upwards in 2003.

***The downward trend in private sector credit in Papua New Guinea was a reflection of the poor business and investment environment***

Credit extended to the private sector in Papua New Guinea fell by 1.3 per cent in 2001 in local currency terms. As a share of GDP, it declined from 16.2 per cent in 2000 to 15.3 per cent in 2001 and further to 13 per cent in 2002. This downward trend reflected the poor business and investment environment and persisted despite an easing of interest rates. Lower borrowings from agriculture and commerce were the main factor responsible for the credit slump. However, money supply registered a strong expansion in 2002 owing to rises in government credit. Lending rates eased in 2001 to 14.6 per cent, the lowest levels since 1998, from 15.5 per cent in 2000. However, the interest rate margin expanded, with average deposit rates falling from 6.7 in 2000 to 4.1 per cent in 2001.

***Financial sector liberalization in Samoa has contributed to improving private sector access to credit***

The programme of financial sector liberalization in Samoa began in 1998 and has proved particularly successful in improving private sector access to credit and, by extension, facilitating greater participation of the private sector in development. Private sector credit has grown rapidly since liberalization. At the same time, government credit demand has been lowered; in fact, the Government continues to be a big net lender in the monetary system. Private sector credit, which had grown by 14.5 per cent to reach 31.3 per cent of GDP in 2001, slowed somewhat and expanded by 5 per cent in the following year. This was a reflection of successful government efforts to cool off the economy, as noted earlier. The building and construction industry continued to be a major borrower, with the agricultural sector absorbing just 4 per cent of private sector credit in 2002. Nominal interest rates have been stable in recent years, with the weighted average lending rate going down marginally from 11 per cent in 2000 to 9.9 per cent in 2001 and to an expected 9.8 per cent in 2002. The deposit rate declined in a similar manner over those years and the interest rate spread remained steady at around 4.4 per cent.

***The high lending rates in Solomon Islands reflected higher commercial risks***

There are difficult issues to resolve in Solomon Islands' financial system. Its net foreign asset position fell by 60 per cent as at the end of 2001, compared with 1999. Private sector demand for credit fell by 22 per cent in 2001, and this contributed to sharp increases in liquidity. Domestic financial institutions and the Central Bank have declined to purchase any Treasury Bills, thereby imposing severe discipline on the budget. There were signs of revival in credit demand by the private sector towards the end of 2002 along with the improved security situation. Reflecting higher commercial risks, among other things, the (average) lending rate went up to 15.5 per cent in 2000 from 14.5 per cent in 1999; the interest rate margin also increased to more than 13 percentage points in 2000 compared with levels of around 11.6 percentage points in 1999.

There is a comparatively low interest rate spread in Tonga, in part because of the regulation on interest rates. Deposit and lending rates have remained largely unchanged for a number of years so that the interest rate spread remained between 4.8 and 5.2 per cent during the period 1998-2002. In 2001, the private sector accounted for 86 per cent of domestic credit, which expanded by just under 10 per cent compared with almost 18 per cent in 2000. The rapid growth in money supply (M2) in 2000-2001, averaging almost 17 per cent annually, was of some concern. Lower public sector borrowing is expected to contribute to a sharp decline in money supply growth in 2002.

In response to the slowdown in economic activities in the second half of 2001, the Reserve Bank of Vanuatu eased monetary conditions. Private sector credit went down by almost 5 per cent in 2000 but rebounded in 2001 to grow 6.4 per cent. Vanuatu continues to have high lending rates, which increased to 10.2 per cent up to September 2002 from 9.1 per cent in 2001; the interest rate spread has been increasing in recent years and reached over 9 per cent in 2002.

### *Combating money-laundering issues*

***Addressing concerns that countries in the subregion may be easy targets for people and organizations involved in money-laundering activities is a major challenge for subregional economies***

FDI and other forms of external capital inflows are crucial for economic and social development in the Pacific island economies, especially given the low levels of domestic savings in the subregion. However, concerns that these economies may be an easy target for money-laundering activities have brought a new perspective to the whole issue of capital flows. Money-laundering, defined as the process of disguising proceeds from criminal acts as legitimate income, is posing a new threat to Pacific island countries.[2] Central bankers from Pacific island countries have agreed to be specially vigilant in dealing with capital transfers and related transactions so as to weed out criminal proceeds and funds used to support terrorist activities. Fiji and Vanuatu are in the process of establishing a Financial Intelligence Unit responsible for gathering, storing and disseminating information to relevant authorities on financial transactions associated with criminal activities.

[2] See *Survey 2001*, box II.2.

*Development of statistics*

The chronic lack of reliable and up-to-date data on Pacific island economies has been a major problem for policy makers and government planners. At the initiative of the Secretariat of the Pacific Community (SPC), a broad range of statistical indicators, including those for the millennium development goals, will soon be available for the first time in a regional Internet-based information system which the national statistical offices in the Pacific subregion will be able to update. The Pacific Regional Information System (PRISM) is currently been developed by SPC and is expected to go online in May 2003. Although PRISM may not generate fresh data, it is expected to provide a cheaper, wider and easier way to disseminate essential data from the subregion.

***The Secretariat of the Pacific Community's new initiative with the Pacific Regional Information System is likely to address data problems in Pacific island countries***

PRISM offers new scope for enhancing capacity in the Pacific by providing regional solutions to common problems and disseminating key information on the extent, causes and dynamics of such issues as poverty, healthy lifestyles and the environment to a wide range of users within the Pacific island subregion and beyond. One of the features of this new project is that it contains not only statistical data but also the sources of these data and information on how they were compiled. Another distinguishing feature of PRISM is that the national statistical offices will be the main beneficiaries; the national Internet web sites will be built and maintained by national statistical office staff, with major emphasis on ensuring national ownership of the information to be stored in PRISM. SPC will be developing PRISM in consultation with other subregional organizations, thereby improving the quality, coverage and dissemination of information throughout the subregion.

The primary aim of PRISM is to give national statistical offices the tools and skills needed to develop, publish and maintain their own Internet web sites, containing key statistical indicators, statistical summaries, reports, concepts, definitions and other documentation relating to the statistical indicators. The PRISM web site will act as a portal to the national statistical web sites to be developed and maintained by the national statistical offices in cooperation with SPC. Where countries lack the capacity to host their own web sites locally, these web sites will be hosted at SPC. All the information on the national web sites will be compiled on the SPC PRISM web site, which will also contain a number of additional resources for users. In this way, PRISM will provide the national statistical offices with more cost-effective data dissemination and storage facilities and eliminate much of the costly duplication of effort now faced by Pacific island countries in responding to numerous queries and requests for information and statistics.

## South and South-West Asia

### A. Developing economies of the subregion

#### *Subregional overview and prospects*

***Improved growth performance across the subregion***

GDP growth was stronger in most countries of the subregion in 2002, despite continuing weather disturbances and unfavourable external factors (figure II.16). The recovery in the agricultural sector, the revival of trading activities in Sri Lanka, and strong foreign investments, coupled with an improved business climate in Turkey, contributed to the economic expansion in these countries. India and Pakistan showed some resilience against the severe drought that occurred in 2002. Robust growth in the industrial and service sectors in India, and a higher flow of overseas remittances and foreign aid into Pakistan, as well as the improved performance of the service sector, partly offset the poor out-turn in the agricultural sector in those two countries. Meanwhile, a higher level of activities in the oil sector, rising domestic demand, increased business confidence and recovery in agricultural output helped to maintain a robust rate of economic growth in the Islamic Republic of Iran.

**Figure II.16. Rates of GDP growth in selected South and South-West Asian economies, 1999-2002**

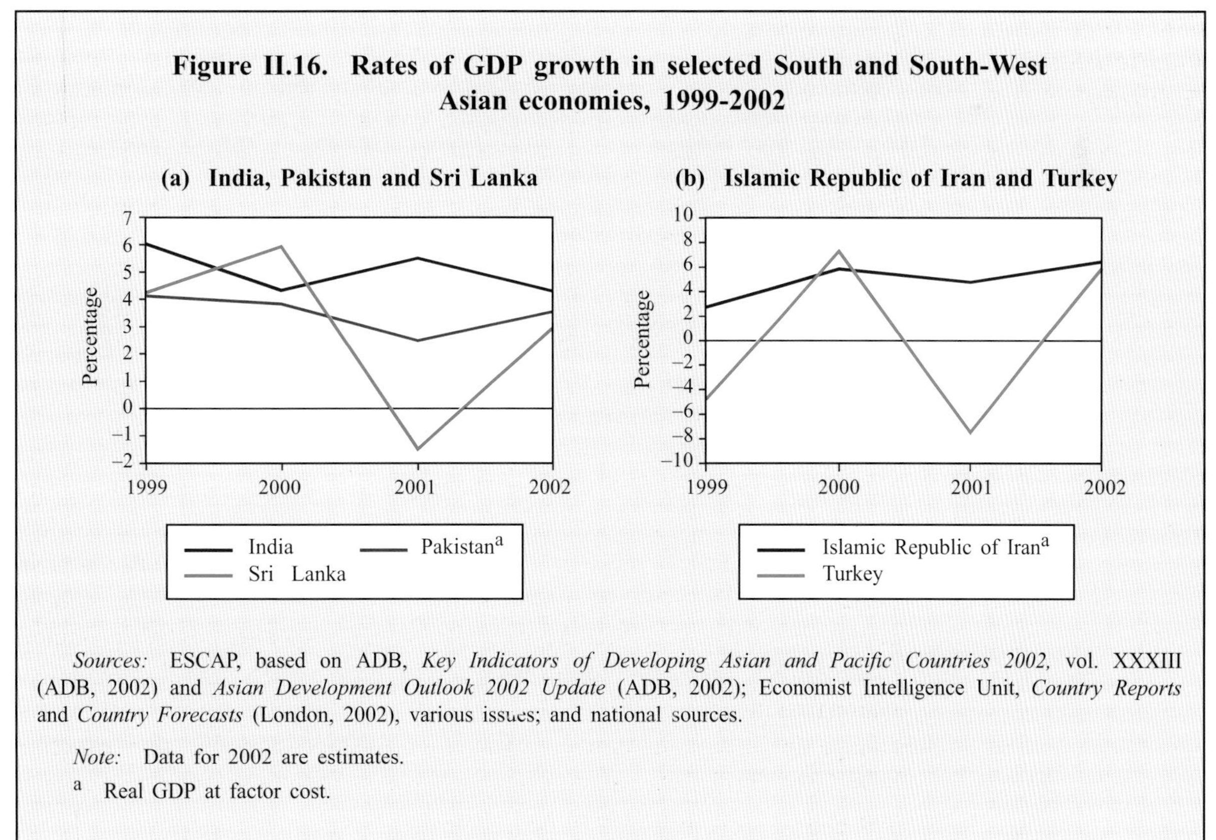


*Sources:* ESCAP, based on ADB, *Key Indicators of Developing Asian and Pacific Countries 2002,* vol. XXXIII (ADB, 2002) and *Asian Development Outlook 2002 Update* (ADB, 2002); Economist Intelligence Unit, *Country Reports* and *Country Forecasts* (London, 2002), various issues; and national sources.

*Note:* Data for 2002 are estimates.

[a] Real GDP at factor cost.

The agricultural sector plays an important role in income and employment generation, and hence in poverty reduction in the subregion. However, it is still primarily dependent on weather conditions owing to insufficient irrigation and drainage facilities. In 2002, a severe drought, one of the worst and most widespread, struck a large part of the subregion, causing significant losses in agricultural output. Aggregate foodgrain output in India, for example, was estimated to have dropped by about 7.5 per cent and the agricultural sector as a whole contracted by 3.1 per cent in 2002. In Pakistan, the output from major crops also fell, but the impressive performance by the livestock subsector helped the agricultural sector to show marginal growth. The economic performance and prospects of the least developed countries in the subregion, Bangladesh, Bhutan, Maldives and Nepal, are discussed separately below.

***Inflation rates came down but remained a source of concern in some countries***

The inflation situation improved in 2002, but continued to be a matter of concern in some countries (figure II.17). In 2001, consumer prices had risen by over 54 and 14 per cent respectively in Turkey and Sri Lanka. Although some moderation occurred in 2002, inflation remained worrisome in Turkey (at some 45 per cent). Meanwhile, India continued to record relative price stability with inflation at around 3.5 per cent;

**Figure II.17. Inflation in selected South and South-West Asian economies, 1999-2002[a]**

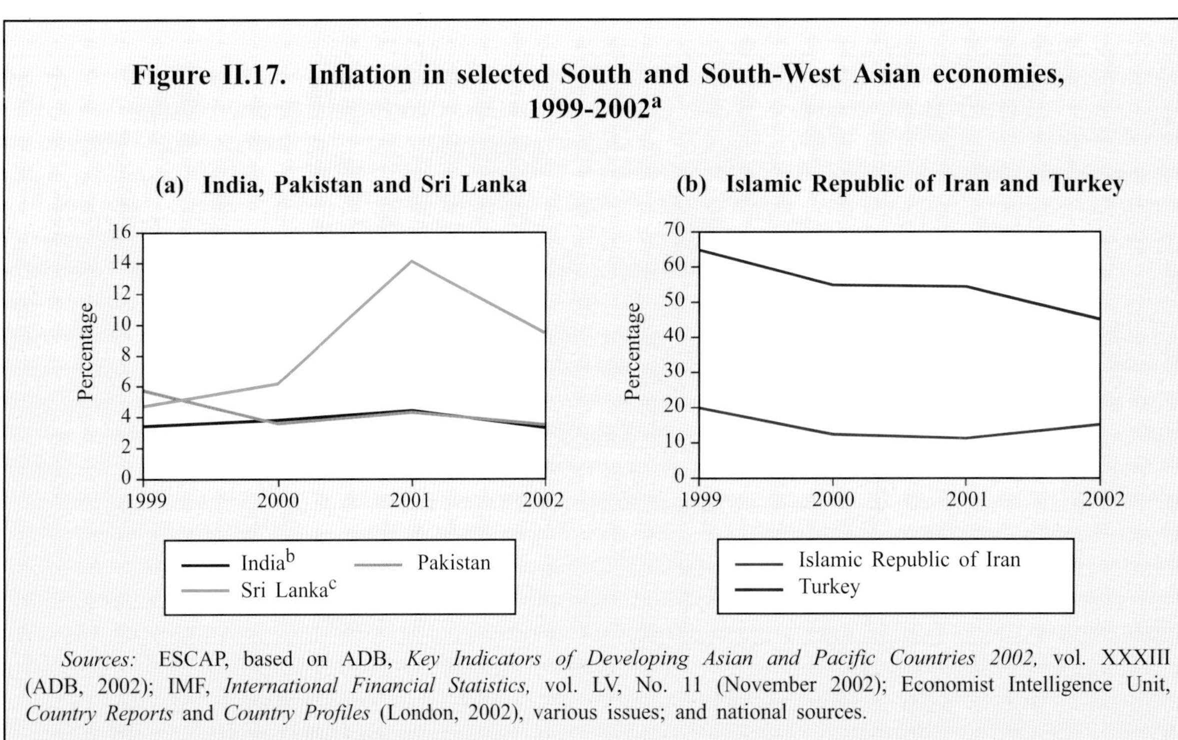


*Sources:* ESCAP, based on ADB, *Key Indicators of Developing Asian and Pacific Countries 2002,* vol. XXXIII (ADB, 2002); IMF, *International Financial Statistics,* vol. LV, No. 11 (November 2002); Economist Intelligence Unit, *Country Reports* and *Country Profiles* (London, 2002), various issues; and national sources.

*Note:* Data for 2002 are estimates.

[a] Changes in the consumer price index.
[b] Consumer price index for industrial workers.
[c] Colombo only.

the huge food stocks from the previous year's bumper crop, a recovery of industrial output and greater competition from liberalized imports were contributing factors. Consumer prices went up by 3.5 per cent in Pakistan in 2002, compared with 4.4 per cent in 2001, owing to comfortable food supplies, weak international prices for petroleum in the first half of the year, lower prices of cotton and the appreciation of the Pakistani rupee. There was some pickup in consumer prices in the Islamic Republic of Iran.

***The depreciation of domestic currencies slowed***

The rate of depreciation of the Turkish lira and Sri Lankan rupee tapered off in 2002, although the lira exchange rate became quite volatile during part of the year owing to political uncertainties. In Sri Lanka, reduced inflation rates, an improved fiscal performance, a manageable current account deficit and the relatively stable political environment slowed depreciation of the domestic currency. The Indian rupee displayed a fluctuating trend in 2002 and appreciated for some time relative to the United States dollar. However, it was expected to depreciate slightly by 0.5 per cent in 2002 compared with 4.4 per cent in the previous year. The Pakistani rupee appreciated by 6.8 per cent in 2002 compared with a 19 per cent depreciation in 2001. The appreciation was supported by a large current account surplus, a substantial increase in overseas workers' remittances, and debt relief. Continuing its exchange rate reforms, the Islamic Republic of Iran unified its two-tier exchange rate in March 2002. The unified exchange rate remained relatively stable during the remaining part of the year.

***The export performance remained subdued, except in India and Turkey***

External trade was adversely affected by the ripple effects following the events of 11 September 2001 and by the slower economic growth in major export markets (figures II.18 and II.19). Pakistan's exports fell marginally in 2002, while in Sri Lanka exports continued to decline, albeit at a slower rate. The export earnings of the Islamic Republic of Iran decreased by 7.5 per cent during the first six months of 2002. However, higher oil prices and strong non-oil exports were expected to result in some positive growth in exports for the full year. India's exports remained stagnant in 2001 but staged a strong recovery and grew by 15 per cent in 2002. Similarly, exports from Turkey expanded by about 15 per cent in 2002.

***The prospects for improved growth were good***

A return to more normal weather conditions and a recovery in the global economy, albeit at a slower pace, should further improve economic performance in the subregion in 2003. The consequent resurgence of world trade could also translate into stronger external demand for exports from the subregion. On the assumption that there were no major internal or external shocks or military conflicts, India could achieve higher GDP growth of about 6 per cent in 2003. Agricultural output contracted in 2002; a recovery in that sector, supported by the sustained robust performance of both the industrial and service sectors, was expected to

**Figure II.18. Growth rates in merchandise export earnings of selected South and South-West Asian economies, 1999-2002**

**(a) India, Islamic Republic of Iran and Pakistan**

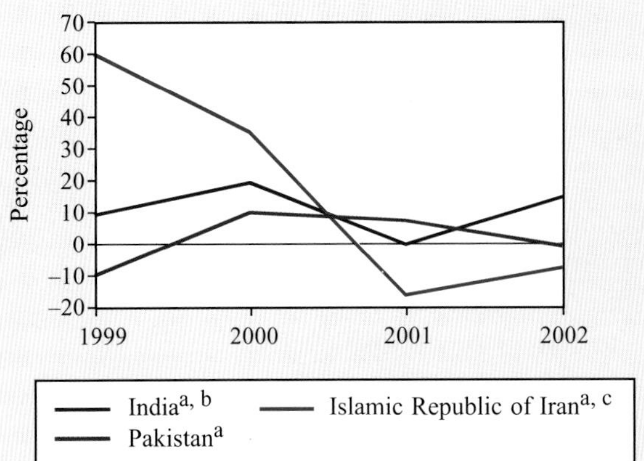


India[a, b]
Pakistan[a]
Islamic Republic of Iran[a, c]

**(b) Sri Lanka and Turkey**

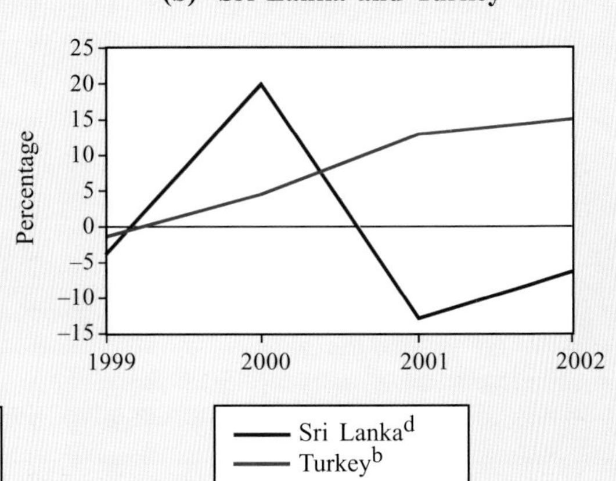


Sri Lanka[d]
Turkey[b]

*Sources:* Web site of the State Bank of Pakistan, <http://www.sbp.org.pk/eimports.htm>, 7 January 2003; web site of the Central Bank of Sri Lanka, <www.lanka.net/centralbank>, 8 January 2003; web site of the Central Bank of the Islamic Republic of Iran, <http://www.cbi.ir/>, 9 January 2003; Economist Intelligence Unit, *Country Reports* (London, 2002), various issues; and national sources.

[a] Fiscal year.
[b] Data for 2002 are estimates.
[c] Data for 2002 refer to the first six months of the fiscal year.
[d] Data for 2002 refer to January-October.

accelerate growth in 2003. In Pakistan, a significant improvement in economic performance became visible in the final months of 2002, including higher export earnings and inward remittances from overseas workers. Improvement in the availability of water would contribute to a substantial recovery in agriculture, with positive knock-on effects on the industrial and service sectors. GDP is targeted to grow by 4.5 per cent in 2003 against 3.6 per cent actual growth in 2002. Sri Lanka could also rely on a sharp rebound in the export sector to fuel economic growth to reach 5.3 per cent in 2003, compared with 3 per cent in 2002. Political stability, improved security conditions, an acceleration in tourism and progress in the implementation of economic reforms would also play a major role in the uplifted growth process.

The economic outlook for the Islamic Republic of Iran and Turkey is somewhat uncertain, amid tensions and the possible adverse impact of a military conflict with Iraq. In Turkey, the massive stock-building, which acted as a large stimulus to GDP growth in 2002, was expected to decrease sharply, serving as a drag on economic growth in the

**Figure II.19. Growth rates in merchandise import spending of selected South and South-West Asian economies, 1999-2002**

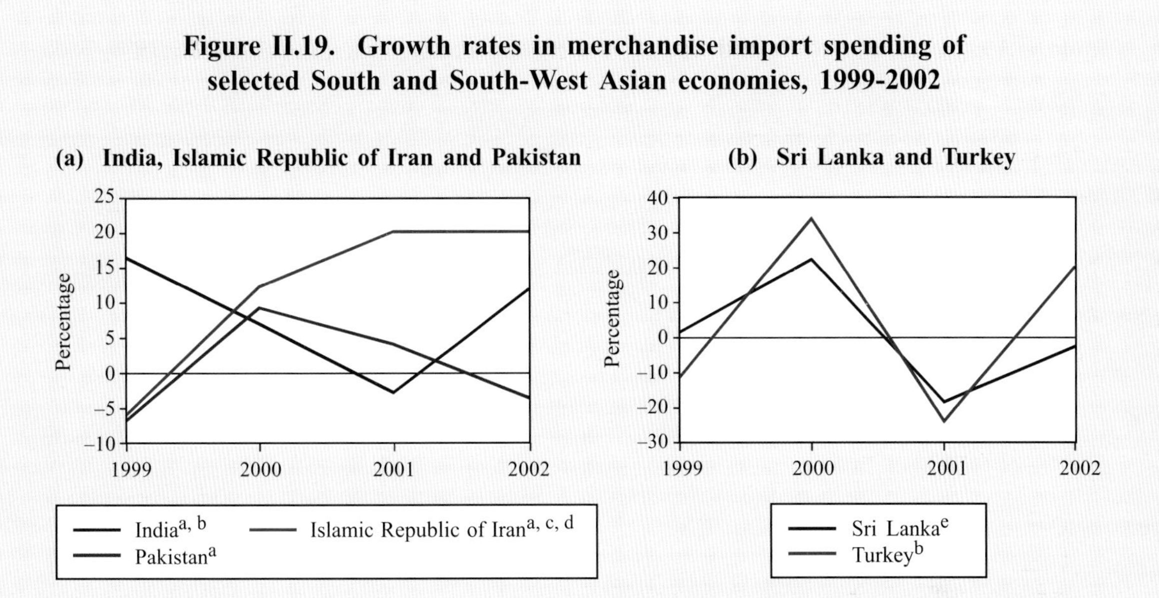


*Sources:* Web site of the State Bank of Pakistan, <http://www.sbp.org.pk/eimports.htm>, 7 January 2003; web site of the Central Bank of Sri Lanka, <www.lanka.net/centralbank>, 8 January 2003; web site of the Central Bank of the Islamic Republic of Iran, <http://www.cbi.ir/>, 9 January 2003; Economist Intelligence Unit, *Country Reports* (London, 2002), various issues; and national sources.

[a] Fiscal year.
[b] Data for 2002 are estimates.
[c] Data for 2002 refer to the first six months of the fiscal year.
[d] Import value f.o.b.
[e] Data for 2002 refer to January-October.

coming year. Other constraints on the growth process included the persistently high unemployment rates, outstanding problems related to banking and corporate debt and the need to contain budget shortfalls. In the Islamic Republic of Iran, GDP growth was expected to accelerate along with firm oil prices and the ongoing implementation of economic reform programmes to encourage more investment in the oil and non-oil sectors.

## *GDP performance*

***The growth momentum in India remained strong***

Despite many unfavourable factors, the economies of the subregion displayed impressive resilience. The growth momentum in India remained relatively strong; GDP expanded by 4.4 per cent in 2002, compared with 5.6 per cent in the previous year (table II.19). Higher levels of economic activity came largely from the industrial and service sectors, which, in turn, were underpinned by government spending, and by measures to boost industrial production and infrastructure development as well as to liberalize capital and money markets and encourage private and

**Table II.19. Selected South and South-West Asian economies: growth rates, 1999-2002**

*(Percentage)*

| | | *Rates of growth* | | | |
|---|---|---|---|---|---|
| | | *Gross domestic product* | *Agriculture* | *Industry* | *Services* |
| India[a] | 1999 | 6.1 | 0.3 | 4.8 | 10.1 |
| | 2000 | 4.4 | −0.4 | 6.6 | 5.6 |
| | 2001 | 5.6 | 5.7 | 3.3 | 6.8 |
| | 2002 | 4.4 | −3.1 | 6.1 | 7.1 |
| Iran, Islamic Republic of[a, b] | 1999 | 2.8 | −5.6 | 2.3 | 4.5 |
| | 2000 | 5.9 | 3.8 | 9.1 | 5.0 |
| | 2001 | 4.8 | 4.7 | 5.0 | 4.8 |
| | 2002 | 6.5 | 5.5 | 7.1 | 7.4 |
| Pakistan[a] | 1999 | 4.2 | 1.9 | 5.0 | 5.0 |
| | 2000 | 3.9 | 6.1 | −0.1 | 4.8 |
| | 2001 | 2.5 | −2.5 | 4.2 | 4.4 |
| | 2002 | 3.6 | 1.4 | 2.8 | 5.1 |
| Sri Lanka | 1999 | 4.3 | 4.5 | 4.8 | 4.0 |
| | 2000 | 6.0 | 1.8 | 7.5 | 7.0 |
| | 2001 | −1.4 | −3.0 | −2.0 | −0.5 |
| | 2002 | 3.0 | 2.8 | 1.3 | 3.9 |
| Turkey | 1999 | −4.7 | −5.0 | −6.2 | −3.6 |
| | 2000 | 7.4 | 3.9 | 5.8 | 9.3 |
| | 2001 | −7.4 | −6.1 | −7.3 | −7.8 |
| | 2002 | 6.0 | 3.0 | 2.0 | 9.4 |

*Sources:* ESCAP, based on ADB, *Key Indicators of Developing Asian and Pacific Countries 2002,* vol. XXXIII (ADB, 2002) and *Asian Development Outlook 2002 Update* (ADB, 2002); Economist Intelligence Unit, *Country Reports* and *Country Forecasts* (London, 2002), various issues; and national sources.

*Notes:* Data for 2002 are estimates. Industry comprises mining and quarrying; manufacturing; electricity, gas and power; and construction.

[a] Real GDP at factor cost.
[b] Industry comprises oil; mining and manufacturing; water, power and gas; and construction.

foreign investment. Six core infrastructure industries, electricity, coal, steel, cement, crude oil and petroleum products, achieved average growth of 6.4 per cent from April to November 2002; it was expected to reach 6.5 per cent in the full fiscal year 2002. Reconstruction activities related to drought, greater movement of foodgrains to food-deficit regions and higher government expenditure on rural development also raised output in the industrial sector. Meanwhile, a rapid increase in expenditure on public administration, social services, rural extension services and defence had a stimulating impact on the service sector, which expanded by 7.1 per cent in 2002 compared with 6.8 per cent in the previous year. However, agricultural output contracted by 3.1 per cent in 2002 owing to the widespread and severe drought, contributing to a decline in the share of agriculture in GDP, from 23.8 to 22.2 per cent between 2000 and 2002. Barring major internal and external shocks and adverse climatic conditions, India is likely to sustain GDP growth rates in the range of 6 to 7 per cent from 2003 to 2005.

***Improved economic performance in Pakistan***

In Pakistan, agriculture was also constrained by a severe drought, despite relatively good irrigation facilities and improved water management practices. A marginal decline of 0.5 per cent was recorded in the output of the major crops in 2002, compared with a contraction of almost 10 per cent in the previous year. However, the strong performance of the livestock subsector enabled the agricultural sector as a whole to expand by 1.4 per cent. By contrast, the manufacturing sector, which contributed 18 per cent to GDP, suffered from weak global demand relating to the ripple effects of the events of 11 September 2001 and higher oil prices. Value added grew by 7.6 per cent in 2001 but by only 4.4 per cent in 2002. The service sector remained robust, in part owing to large increases in public administration and defence spending. It expanded by just over 5 per cent in 2002, lifting GDP growth to 3.6 per cent, from 2.6 per cent in 2001.

***Recovery in Sri Lanka and Turkey***

Sri Lanka and Turkey had suffered a sharp downturn in 2001. In 2002, however, GDP growth in Sri Lanka was estimated at 3 per cent, a recovery fuelled largely by a higher level of value added in services and agriculture; both sectors had contracted in 2001 owing to severe drought and a power crisis. However, recovery in the industrial sector was relatively weak owing to depressed earnings of key industrial exports. Demand for garments, for example, remained subdued, although a slight recovery was expected during the second half of 2002. Meanwhile, Turkey managed to reverse a GDP contraction of over 7 per cent in 2001 and achieve an economic expansion of 6 per cent in the following year. Growth was fuelled by an improvement in the business environment, which, in turn, benefited from declining interest rates and the relative strengthening of the Turkish lira as a result of large inflow of foreign funds, including from IMF, in the first half of the year. Despite uncertainties related to the election in November 2002 and concerns about a possible war in Iraq, economic growth was stronger than expected during the second half of 2002.

***Faster GDP growth in the Islamic Republic of Iran***

The Islamic Republic of Iran had experienced marginally slower GDP growth of 4.8 per cent in 2001, largely owing to declining oil production and exports, which, in turn, were attributable to a downward revision in the OPEC quota. Non-oil activities, however, expanded by 6 per cent in real terms but registered unemployment remained high at 16 per cent at the end of 2001, as the creation of 450,000 jobs lagged behind the volume of new entrants into the labour force. GDP expansion was on an upward trend, reaching an expected rate of 6.5 per cent in 2002. The upturn was underpinned by relatively favourable oil market conditions, rising domestic demand and a recovery in agricultural output. Non-oil activities also increased and were more robust because of strong public sector demand, increased business confidence and higher investment (table II.20). Construction and manufacturing, in particular, were expected to be much strengthened in line with sharply higher investment and consumer demand.

**Table II.20. Selected South and South-West Asian economies: ratios of gross domestic savings and investment to GDP, 1999-2002**

*(Percentage)*

| | *1999* | *2000* | *2001* | *2002* |
|---|---|---|---|---|
| **Savings as a percentage of GDP** | | | | |
| India | 23.1 | 23.4 | 24.0 | 25.0 |
| Iran (Islamic Republic of) | 25.4 | 26.8 | 27.4 | 28.0 |
| Pakistan | 12.3 | 15.6 | 15.9 | 15.2 |
| Sri Lanka | 19.5 | 17.4 | 15.3 | 15.5 |
| Turkey | 21.4 | 18.3 | 16.0 | .. |
| **Investment as a percentage of GDP** | | | | |
| India | 24.2 | 24.0 | 23.7 | 23.9 |
| Iran (Islamic Republic of) | 26.0 | 27.1 | 28.3 | 29.5 |
| Pakistan | 15.6 | 16.0 | 15.9 | 13.9 |
| Sri Lanka | 27.3 | 28.0 | 22.0 | 24.1 |
| Turkey | 24.0 | 24.9 | 16.7 | .. |

*Sources:* ESCAP, based on ADB, *Key Indicators of Developing Asian and Pacific Countries 2002,* vol. XXXIII (ADB, 2002) and *Asian Development Outlook 2002* (Oxford University Press, 2002); and national sources.

*Note:* Data for 2002 are estimates.

## *Inflation*

***Inflation decelerated in Turkey and Sri Lanka***

Inflation eased in both Turkey and Sri Lanka in line with improved supply and demand conditions. It remained high in absolute terms, at over 45 per cent, in Turkey in 2002 but this was some 9 percentage points lower than the previous year's level (table II.21). The decline was attributed to the limited monetary expansion through the Central Bank's strict adherence to the monetary programme, wage and salary increases in the public sector having been kept in line with the programmed targets, and the relative stability of the Turkish lira. To further contain inflationary pressures, the Central Bank planned to adopt a fully fledged policy of inflation-targeting in 2003. In Sri Lanka, consumer prices rose

**Table II.21. Selected South and South-West Asian economies: inflation and money supply growth (M2), 1999-2002**

*(Percentage)*

| | 1999 | 2000 | 2001 | 2002 |
|---|---|---|---|---|
| **Inflation**[a] | | | | |
| India[b] | 3.4 | 3.8 | 4.3 | 3.5 |
| Iran (Islamic Republic of) | 20.1 | 12.6 | 11.4 | 15.3 |
| Pakistan | 5.7 | 3.6 | 4.4 | 3.5 |
| Sri Lanka[c] | 4.7 | 6.2 | 14.2 | 9.5 |
| Turkey | 64.9 | 54.9 | 54.4 | 45.2 |
| **Money supply growth (M2)** | | | | |
| India | 17.1 | 15.2 | 14.3 | 17.2[d] |
| Iran (Islamic Republic of) | 21.5 | 22.4 | 27.6 | 26.5[e] |
| Pakistan | 4.3 | 12.1 | 11.7 | 14.8[d] |
| Sri Lanka | 13.3 | 12.8 | 14.4 | 19.5[d] |
| Turkey | 98.3 | 40.0 | 87.2 | .. |

*Sources:* ESCAP, based on ADB, *Key Indicators of Developing Asian and Pacific Country 2002,* vol. XXXIII (ADB, 2002); IMF, *International Financial Statistics,* vol. LV, No. 11 (November 2002); Economist Intelligence Unit, *Country Reports* and *Country Forecasts* (London, 2002), various issues; and national sources.

*Note:* Data for 2002 are estimates.

[a] Changes in the consumer price index.
[b] Consumer price index for industrial workers.
[c] Colombo only.
[d] January-June.
[e] January-July.

at a slower rate, from over 14 per cent in 2001 to 9.5 per cent in 2002, owing to increased imports and domestic supplies of agricultural products, a relatively slower depreciation of the domestic currency and government intervention to control the prices of key commodities, including cooking gas, dairy foods, flour and petroleum. There was also some easing in the budget deficit, although it remained high (table II.22). Further progress in liberalizing the domestic market, together with improved agricultural growth in 2002, could cause inflation to fall further in 2003.

***Price stability continued to prevail in India and Pakistan***

Inflation remained at relatively low levels in both India and Pakistan compared with other countries of the subregion. Consumer prices in those countries eased to 3.5 per cent in 2002. In India, the inflation rate for food products, with a relative weight of 57 per cent in the consumption basket, remained modest at 3 per cent, down from 3.4 per cent in 2001, owing to the large surplus stock of foodgrains in the country. The price of manufactured products also rose moderately in line with the global decline in the prices of manufactured items, the removal of quantitative

**Table II.22. Selected South and South-West Asian economies: budget and current account balance as a percentage of GDP, 1999-2002**

*(Percentage)*

| | *1999* | *2000* | *2001* | *2002* |
|---|---|---|---|---|
| **Budget balance as a percentage of GDP** | | | | |
| India | −5.4 | −5.6 | −5.9 | −6.5 |
| Iran (Islamic Republic of)[a] | −0.2 | −0.2 | −0.1 | −0.2 |
| Pakistan[a] | −6.1 | −6.4 | −5.3 | −7.0 |
| Sri Lanka | −6.9 | −9.5 | −10.5 | −8.5 |
| Turkey | −11.7 | −10.3 | −15.7 | −14.1 |
| **Current account balance as a percentage of GDP** | | | | |
| India | −1.1 | −0.6 | 0.3 | 1.1 |
| Iran (Islamic Republic of) | 12.2 | 18.0 | 6.5 | 3.5 |
| Pakistan | −4.1 | −1.9 | −0.9 | 2.2 |
| Sri Lanka | −3.6 | −6.4 | −1.7 | −3.6 |
| Turkey | −0.7 | −4.9 | 2.3 | 0.6 |

*Sources:* ESCAP, based on ADB, *Key Indicators of Developing Asian and Pacific Countries 2002,* vol. XXXIII (ADB, 2002) and *Asian Development Outlook 2002 Update* (ADB, 2002); IMF, *International Financial Statistics,* vol. LV, No. 11 (November 2002); Economist Intelligence Unit, *Country Reports* and *Country Forecasts* (London, 2002), various issues; and national sources.

*Note:* Data for 2002 are estimates.

[a] Excluding grants.

restrictions and the continual reduction in import duties in India. Inflation in Pakistan fell to 3.5 per cent in 2002 from 4.4 per cent in 2001, owing to the better availability of essential commodities as a result of improved production of food and non-food products and the ample stocks carried over from previous years. Other stabilizing factors included appreciation of the domestic currency, which lowered the costs of imported products, and concerted government efforts to monitor consumer prices and take remedial action when needed; price stability is directly linked with the country's poverty reduction strategy.

***There was a pickup in consumer prices in the Islamic Republic of Iran***

Inflation had been on a downward trend during the past few years in the Islamic Republic of Iran but went up from just over 11 per cent in 2001 to more than 15 per cent in 2002. This upturn was due in large part to the unification of the exchange rate on the prices of a wide range of imported goods that had been purchased previously at the lower official exchange rate. In addition, domestic demand was expected to remain strong, adding to inflationary pressures, although the rate of increases in consumer prices could be eased in 2003 as monetary policy reforms continued and the impact of currency unification stabilized.

## *Foreign trade and other external transactions*

### *External trade*

***The export earnings of Sri Lanka and the Islamic Republic of Iran continued to contract***

Exports in Sri Lanka continued their second year of decline, with earnings in the first 10 months of 2002 falling by 6.3 per cent compared with the same period in 2001. The textile and garment sector, which accounted for a little over half of the total receipts on merchandise exports, remained depressed. It experienced a large contraction in 2001 and production further declined by 8 per cent in 2002. Tea exports, which accounted for about 15 per cent of the total export earnings, also fell, although at a slower pace, in 2002. The export earnings of the Islamic Republic of Iran showed a decline, by 7.5 per cent, during the first half of fiscal year 2002, but aggregate export receipts could register a slight increase by the end of the fiscal year (March 2003) owing to higher non-oil exports. Earnings on carpets, in particular, were particularly strong, expanding by 8 per cent during the first four months of the fiscal year.

Pakistan's export earnings, which fell marginally by 0.7 per cent to $9.1 billion in 2002 (table II.23), were on track to reach the target of $10 billion until the weakening of the international market in the aftermath of the events of 11 September 2001. There were cancellations of export orders, particularly those destined for United States and European markets, and higher freight charges on all cargo entering and leaving Pakistan.

**Table II.23. Selected South and South-West Asian economies: merchandise exports and their rates of growth, 1999-2002**

| | Value (millions of US dollars) | Exports (f.o.b.) Annual rate of growth (percentage) | | | |
|---|---|---|---|---|---|
| | *2001* | *1999* | *2000* | *2001* | *2002* |
| India[a,b] | 44 915 | 9.5 | 19.6 | 0.0 | 15.0 |
| Iran (Islamic Republic of)[a,c] | 23 904 | 60.3 | 35.3 | −16.0 | −7.5 |
| Pakistan[a] | 9 202 | −9.8 | 10.1 | 7.4 | −0.7 |
| Sri Lanka[d] | 4 817 | −3.9 | 19.8 | −12.8 | −6.3 |
| Turkey[b] | 31 334 | −1.4 | 4.5 | 12.8 | 14.9 |

*Sources:* Web site of the State Bank of Pakistan, <http://www.sbp.org.pk/eimports.htm>, 7 January 2003; Web site of the Central Bank of Sri Lanka, <www.lanka.net/centralbank>, 8 January 2003; Web site of the Central Bank of the Islamic Republic of Iran, <http://www.cbi.ir/>, 9 January 2003; Economist Intelligence Unit, *Country Reports* (London, 2002), various issues; and national sources.

[a] Fiscal year.
[b] Data for 2002 are estimates.
[c] Data for 2002 refer to the first six months (April-September) of the fiscal year.
[d] Data for 2002 refer to January-October.

Earnings on primary commodity exports (e.g., rice, raw cotton, fish and fruits) registered the largest contraction at almost 15 per cent. Meanwhile, the earnings from textile products and other manufactured goods showed a marginal increase of 0.4 and 1.3 per cent, respectively.

***Exports surged strongly in India and Turkey***

India and Turkey recorded relatively high rates of export growth in 2002. India experienced stagnant exports, at $44.9 billion, in 2001 but earnings on exports were expected to rise by around 15 per cent by the end of fiscal year 2002 (March 2003), thus outperforming the government target of 12 per cent. This upsurge was due to various export-facilitating measures, the stability of the Indian rupee and strong performance in such key sectors as ready-made garments, engineering goods, chemicals, leather and leather products, ore and minerals, basic metals and petroleum products. Computer software and the service industry have emerged as the major export earners, contributing an estimated $10 billion in 2002. However, the share of agricultural exports declined to 12 per cent in 2002 from 20 per cent in 1996. In Turkey, export earnings, after growing at the rate of 12.8 per cent in 2001, were expected to expand by some 15 per cent in the following year.

***Import spending varied among countries of the subregion***

The value of merchandise imports contracted in Pakistan by 3.6 per cent and in Sri Lanka by 2.5 per cent in 2002 (table II.24). The contributing factors included the imposition of additional shipment insurance and lower imports of fuel and food in Pakistan, and subdued

**Table II.24. Selected South and South-West Asian economies: merchandise imports and their rates of growth, 1999-2002**

| | *Imports (c.i.f.)* | | | | |
|---|---|---|---|---|---|
| | *Value (millions of US dollars)* | *Annual rate of growth (percentage)* | | | |
| | *2001* | *1999* | *2000* | *2001* | *2002* |
| India[a,b] | 57 618 | 16.5 | 7.0 | −2.8 | 12.0 |
| Iran (Islamic Republic of)[a, c, d] | 18 129 | −6.0 | 12.3 | 20.2 | 20.1 |
| Pakistan[a] | 10 729 | −6.8 | 9.3 | 4.1 | −3.6 |
| Sri Lanka[e] | 5 974 | 1.5 | 22.4 | −18.4 | −2.5 |
| Turkey[b] | 41 399 | −11.4 | 34.0 | −24.0 | 20.3 |

*Sources:* Web site of the State Bank of Pakistan, <http://www.sbp.org.pk/eimports.htm>, 7 January 2003; Web site of the Central Bank of Sri Lanka, <www.lanka.net/centralbank>, 8 January 2003; Web site of the Central Bank of the Islamic Republic of Iran, <http://www.cbi.ir/>, 9 January 2003; Economist Intelligence Unit, *Country Reports* (London, 2002), various issues; and national sources.

[a] Fiscal year.
[b] Data for 2002 are estimates.
[c] Data for 2002 refer to the first six months (April-September) of the fiscal year.
[d] Import value f.o.b.
[e] Data for 2002 refer to January-October.

economic activities as a result of the power crisis and drought in Sri Lanka. Pakistan registered lower import expenditure on food items, with the value of imported sugar and soybean oil falling by over 90 and 70 per cent, respectively. This decline was due largely to higher domestic production of sugar and large shipments of soybean oil from the United States under the Public Law (P.L.) 480 food assistance programme. However, imports started to pick up towards the latter part of 2002 and were expected to reach a new record level of $11 billion in 2003. In Sri Lanka, import expenditure fell by 2.5 per cent during the first 10 months of 2002.

Import spending was more buoyant in other countries of the subregion. After a slight contraction in 2001, India experienced an estimated expansion of 12 per cent in imports in 2002. There were higher imports of edible oil, crude petroleum, export-related products and capital goods. In the Islamic Republic of Iran, imports have been growing at high rates during the last three years following the gradual relaxation of import restrictions, the liberalization of the foreign exchange regime and other measures for economic recovery. Import spending went up by another one fifth during the first six months of fiscal year 2002. In Turkey, a rebound in import spending occurred in 2002 owing to stronger growth in private consumption and gross fixed investment and to higher prices of non-oil commodities. Imports grew by 20.3 per cent in 2002 compared with a contraction of 24.0 per cent in 2001.

### *Capital flows and exchange rates*

***The foreign exchange reserve position strengthened in India and Pakistan***

Despite the continuing weakness in the global economy, FDI flows into India grew by 2.4 per cent, to $4 billion, in 2002, reflecting the ongoing improvement in infrastructure, further liberalization of foreign investment policies and the removal of economic sanctions on India by the United States. The bulk of FDI went into ICT activities, engineering industries, services, electronics and electrical equipment, chemicals and allied products, food and dairy products. In Pakistan, FDI surged by 50 per cent, from $322 million in 2001 to $485 million in 2002. About two thirds of such investment went to the oil and gas and power sectors. There was, however, a downturn in portfolio investment in India owing to the downgrading of Indian stocks by the international credit-rating agencies and bearish domestic share markets. The modest outflow of portfolio capital from Pakistan was, in fact, a significant improvement over the massive level in the previous year.

The foreign exchange positions of India and Pakistan strengthened as a result of higher foreign investment, the improved current account balance and, specifically in the case of Pakistan, the debt-relief package from the Paris Club. In Pakistan, foreign exchange reserves were on an upward trend, totalling over $9 billion in January 2003. Meanwhile, the local currency appreciated by 6.8 per cent against the United States dollar in 2002, in contrast to a depreciation of almost one fifth in 2001.

India's foreign exchange reserves had reached an estimated $74.7 billion by the end of fiscal year 2002, compared with the previous year's level of $54.1 billion, and were equivalent to nearly 14 months of imports. Apart from booming ICT exports (see box II. 2), the increase in reserves reflected higher remittances, the quicker repatriation of export proceeds and non-debt inflows of capital. In particular, the higher interest rates had

## Box II.2. Indian information technology: a success story

IT is of increasing importance in the Indian economy, in terms of both export revenue and employment generation. The highly dynamic IT industry grew at an average annual rate exceeding 50 per cent from 1991 until 2001. In that year, computer software and services, which are the main drivers of the industry and account for the bulk of IT products, generated over $10 billion in sales revenue, up from a mere $150 million 10 years earlier. In addition, the industry created 92,000 new jobs and provided 250,000 people with indirect employment during that period.[a] The industry is highly export-oriented; its export revenue was $7.6 billion in 2001. With a projected growth of 30 per cent in 2002, export revenue could reach $10 billion. Overall, IT software and service exports accounted for over 16 per cent of India's total exports in 2001. It is expected that by 2008 the industry will account for 7.7 per cent of India's GDP and 35 per cent of its total exports. India's IT software and service industry represents a mere 2 per cent of the global software market. The Government and the software industry, however, have set an ambitious goal for software exports of $50 billion by 2008, a share equivalent to 6 per cent of the relevant global market.[b]

The United States, Canada and Latin America continue to be India's foremost computer software and service export destinations, accounting for 63 per cent of its export revenue, followed by the EU at 26 per cent, Japan at 4 per cent and the rest of the world at 7 per cent. The performance of the Indian IT industry therefore depends largely on global economic conditions, particularly the United States market. This became evident in 2001, when a slowdown in the American economy had an adverse impact on the Indian IT software and service industry. Diversification of the market for Indian IT exports could reduce the industry's external vulnerabilities. Plans have been made to expand exports to Germany, France and Italy in Europe, Singapore, the Republic of Korea and Malaysia in Asia, and Chile, Mexico, Uruguay and Brazil in Latin America. The variety of IT services would also be expanded. In particular, increasing attention is being given to business process outsourcing as client firms are ceasing to buy software and are instead engaging software firms to manage their IT-intensive functions, such as operations, accounts and manpower management.

The Government of India has played an important role in providing critical inputs and removing major bottlenecks in the path of software development in order to achieve the export target of $50 billion by 2008. It is also a major client of IT products and services in line with its effort to computerize government processes and implement e-government applications. Indian spending on IT is currently around 1.7 per cent of GDP and is expected to reach 3 per cent by 2008.[c]

---

[a] OffshoreDev.com, "2003: year of revival for Indian firms: Nasscom", <http://offshoredev.com/jsp/features_details?fid=124>, 27 January 2003.

[b] Government of India, Department of Information Technology, *Annual Report 2001-2002,* <http://www.mit.gov.in>, 27 January 2003.

[c] The US Commercial Service, *India Country Commercial Guide, Fiscal Year 2002,* <http://www.usatrade.gov/website/CCG.nsf/CCGurl/CCG-INDIA2002-CH-5:-006C4DCB>, 27 January 2003.

attracted large amounts of foreign exchange from non-resident Indians. The appreciation of the United States dollar vis-à-vis major international currencies led to a depreciation of the Indian rupee by 4.4 per cent in 2001; the Indian rupee exchange rate had gone down by a mere 0.5 per cent by the end of 2002 (figure II.20).

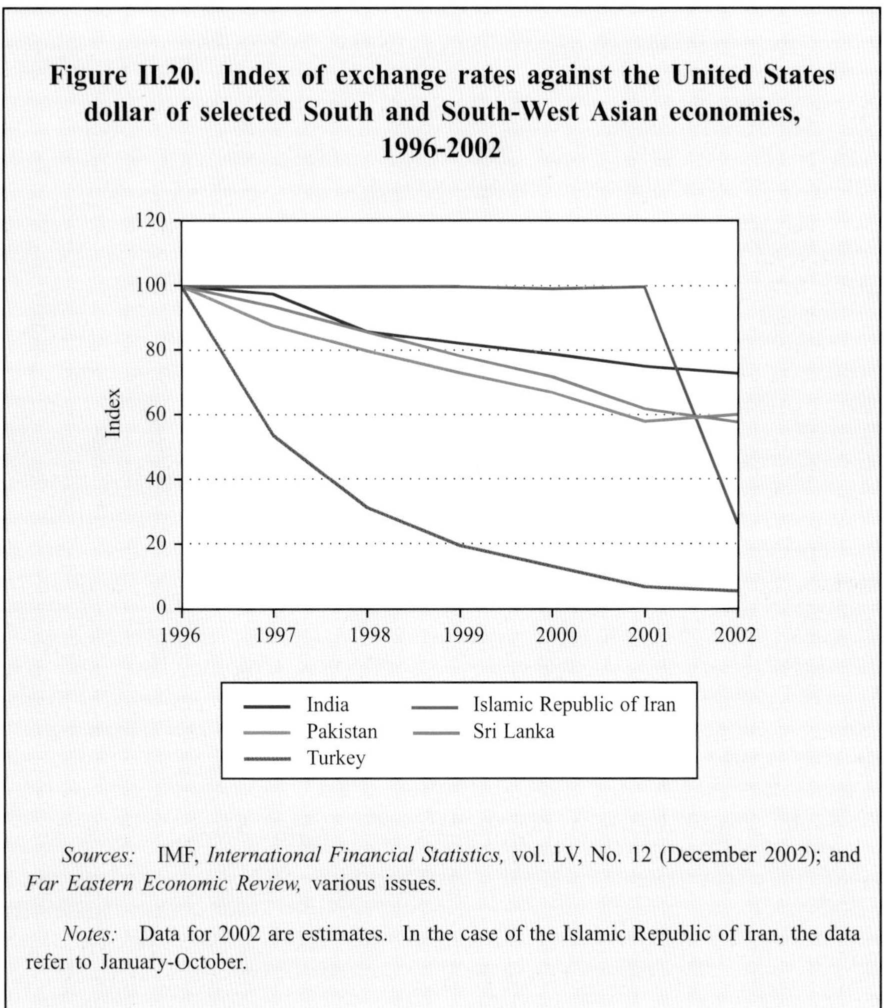


**Figure II.20. Index of exchange rates against the United States dollar of selected South and South-West Asian economies, 1996-2002**

*Sources:* IMF, *International Financial Statistics,* vol. LV, No. 12 (December 2002); and *Far Eastern Economic Review,* various issues.

*Notes:* Data for 2002 are estimates. In the case of the Islamic Republic of Iran, the data refer to January-October.

***The improved political climate was bringing more FDI and stability to exchange rates in Sri Lanka and Turkey***

FDI into Sri Lanka was expected to recover in 2002 along with a better political climate and an active government promotion programme. Meanwhile, volatility in the exchange rate of the Turkish lira, which had been high in parts of 2002, eased somewhat following the decision of the then Government to hold an early election. The new Government, installed in November 2002, affirmed its support for the IMF-backed programme and its commitment to joining the EU. This brought much stability to the exchange rate, a crucial part of the IMF programme and the economic recovery process.

***Major reforms of the exchange rate system in the Islamic Republic of Iran***

In 2001 and 2002, the Islamic Republic of Iran managed to raise foreign exchange reserves, which were expected to reach $20.2 billion by the end of March 2003. The process of exchange rate unification continued along with the elimination of all the restrictions on current account transactions which had existed prior to March 2002. A single rate replaced the multi-tier exchange rate regime from the beginning of fiscal 2002. All foreign exchange transactions that had formerly taken place in the Tehran Stock Exchange market were shifted to a newly established inter-bank market; the exchange rate was unified at the rate prevailing in the Tehran Stock Exchange market before the unification. The unified exchange rate should remove uncertainties and help to ensure greater stability in the exchange rate market.

### *Foreign debt*

***Various indicators showed an improved external debt situation in India, the Islamic Republic of Iran and Pakistan***

Pakistan achieved a distinct improvement in its external debt profile, reflecting the country's adherence to the debt reduction and management strategy. The successful completion of the IMF standby arrangement had paved the way for a medium-term IMF assistance programme and higher aid inflows from other international financial institutions. Moreover, Pakistan also obtained a stock re-profiling of bilateral debt from the Paris Club of creditors on generous terms. While the absolute decline in external debt and liabilities of $607 million was marginal, the debt re-profiling and the replacement of expensive commercial loans by cheaper credits led to a significant drop in the net current value of the outstanding external debt and liabilities, between 28 and 44 per cent depending on the interest rate negotiations with individual creditors.

There was also a marked improvement in the external debt position of India, which, according to a World Bank classification, had been transformed from a "moderately indebted country" to a "low indebted country" as of 1999. The debt-to-GDP ratio declined continuously from 38 per cent in 1991 to just over 20 per cent in 2002 and the debt-service ratio from 35 per cent in 1990 to 13.3 per cent in 2002. It is estimated that India's external debt, both short-term and long-term will amount to around $102.3 billion at the end of March 2003.

In the Islamic Republic of Iran, external debt fell by 11 per cent to $7.1 billion in 2001. The ratio of outstanding external debt to GDP dropped from 8.4 to 6.3 per cent in 2000-2001. Correspondingly, the debt-service ratio fell from 12.5 per cent in 2000 to 7.8 per cent in the following year; it was expected to decline further to 3.7 per cent in 2002.

***Some increase was seen in the foreign debt of Sri Lanka and Turkey***

The foreign debt positions of Sri Lanka and Turkey worsened in 2002. In Sri Lanka, external debt in 2002 was estimated at $9.6 billion, up from $8.8 billion in 2001. Public debt, including external debt, has become a matter of great concern but the strengthened peace process could help to reduce military spending. Turkey's estimated external debt reached $119 billion, or almost two thirds of GDP, in 2002, compared with $112 billion in 2001.

### *Key policy issues*

***The poverty reduction strategies of countries in the subregion have been based on ensuring sustained and rapid economic growth complemented by targeted programmes and the provision of social protection***

In support of the millennium development goals, Governments of the subregion have reiterated their commitment to poverty reduction as an overarching development goal. Measures have been taken, for example, in India, Pakistan and Sri Lanka, to assess the poverty situation and identify pertinent policies and strategies. The broad range of policies and interventions which have been pursued in the economic and social areas can be categorized under two major themes. The first is based on the assumption that sustained economic growth is a prerequisite to achieving real progress in poverty reduction, and the second is that direct interventions targeted to benefit the poor in particular and to provide social protection in general are vital to ensure that gains from economic growth trickle down quickly to the poor and the disadvantaged groups.

The first assumption is based on past experience showing that poverty levels fall more rapidly during periods of rapid economic growth. Consequently, countries of the subregion have focused, to a large extent, on spurring economic growth and sustaining macroeconomic stability. Following the economic slowdown in 2001, the most urgent challenge to poverty reduction in 2002 was rejuvenating the economy and preparing the conditions for higher economic growth in the coming years. There are two general agenda for boosting economic growth; the first is to reduce the budget deficit and the second to enhance investment and trade through market liberalization programmes. The first was reviewed at length in the *Survey 2002;* the following discussion focuses on the progress of market liberalization, including privatization, in the subregion.

***Enhancement of investment and trade through market liberalization programmes***

Countries of the subregion have promoted the path to market liberalization and private sector-led growth in varying degrees. Pakistan has opened up a significant part of its economy to the private sector and offered various incentives to foreign investors, including external participation in industrial projects on a 100 per cent equity basis without any need to secure permission from the Government. A recent landmark in the privatization programme was the divestiture of the Government's minority working interests in seven oil and gas concessions, and the sale of Pak Saudi Fertilizers. That was the largest industrial transaction in the history of Pakistan's privatization programme.

However, the privatization process has generally been slow, despite the existence of numerous enabling policy frameworks. Among the causal factors are the lack of investor confidence and of a clear and fair regulatory framework, opposition from those with vested interests, and public misconceptions of and distrust for the objectives and process of privatization.[3] The Government has identified the following key measures to speed up the pace of privatization: restoring investor confidence by improving the macroeconomic situation; further deregulation and liberalization; establishing and/or strengthening regulatory frameworks; and improving transparency and public understanding of the privatization process.

Trade liberalization, simplification of the trade investment regime and further reductions in export and import restrictions are prominent in India's economic reform programmes to boost growth momentum and domestic and foreign investment. Privatization is at the forefront of these reforms and is seen a benchmark of the Government's commitment to economic reforms. Consequently, more sectors, including power, steel, oil refining and exploration, road construction, air transport, telecommunications, ports, mining, pharmaceuticals and financial services are being thrown open to private investors. Sectors such as garments and textiles, previously reserved for small-scale industries, were also delicensed to encourage competition. The Government's decision in December 2002 to resume the divestment of its stakes in two large State-owned oil companies, Hindustan Petroleum and Bharat Petroleum, is an encouraging sign of concerted government efforts towards privatization, despite heavy opposition from domestic industrial and nationalist groups. The current wave of privatization has benefited India's large-scale private sector. However, the overall success of the privatization programmes depends to a large extent on removing major infrastructure bottlenecks, including poor transport networks and insufficient and erratic power supplies, in which there is limited private investment.

The trade and investment liberalization process in Sri Lanka gained momentum in 2002 in line with government efforts to attract foreign investment. The port, electricity and petroleum sectors have been deregulated and, with effect from April 2002, 100 per cent foreign ownership has been permitted in previously regulated sectors, such as in the construction of buildings, roads, water supply, mass transport, telecommunications, banking, financial services, including stockbroking, and insurance, and the production and distribution of energy. Further

---

[3] Government of Pakistan, Privatisation Commission, *Annual Report 2001* <http://www.privatisation.gov.pk>, 27 January 2003.

liberalization was planned for 2003 and 2004, including the removal of limits on inward foreign investment and expansion in the scope of privatization to more sectors, such as manufacturing (cement), services (hotels, lotteries), mining (graphite companies) and trade. The Government has also stepped up its efforts to remove impediments to trade and pursued a free trade accord with other countries, such as India and Pakistan. However, concrete progress in the resolution of the civil war will go a long way to boost trade, investment and economic growth in the country (box II.3).

The Government of Turkey enhanced the pace of liberalization in 2001 following a slowdown in its traditionally public sector-led economy. The reform focuses on market liberalization in the energy and telecommunication sectors, the privatization of State-owned enterprises, including Turk Telekom, the national airline, petroleum refineries, and iron and steel companies, and liberalization of the agricultural sector, including shifting from price subsidies to direct income payments to farmers. The reform is expected to bring down inflation and interest rates, paving the way for increased business activities and investments.

Market liberalization is also in progress in the Islamic Republic of Iran, albeit at slower pace; a privatization programme is being pursued within the framework of the current five-year plan, 2000-2004. The Government has sought to open its power and telecommunication sectors to the private sector, but issues relating to legal restrictions against privatization have yet to be fully resolved. In July 2002, the Government ended State monopoly on the import of sugar, thus opening up trade to the private sector. The move followed the lifting of the State monopoly on the import of tobacco, tea and vegetable oil.

***Unemployment remained a serious problem***

In the area of social protection, there has been growing concern about the rising unemployment rates in the subregion in recent years, which could seriously undermine efforts to reduce poverty. The economic slowdown in several of the economies in 2001 was obviously a factor contributing to this trend. However, an examination of long-term data revealed that, in some countries, unemployment rates continued to expand even during years of rapid economic growth. For example, unemployment rates in India widened from 6 per cent in 1993/94 to 7.3 per cent in 1999/2000 in spite of higher GDP growth, averaging 6.1 per cent a year between 1993/94 and 1999/2000. Similarly, unemployment rates in Pakistan increased from 5.9 per cent in 1998 to 7.8 per cent in 2000, while GDP growth averaged 3.4 per cent a year during that period.

## Box II.3. The economic implications of the Sri Lankan peace process

After two decades of conflict, the Government of Sri Lanka successfully entered into a ceasefire agreement with the Liberation Tigers of Tamil Eelam (LTTE) in February 2002, with the assistance of the Government of Norway as a facilitator.[a] As a result, a fair degree of normalcy has been restored in the northern and eastern parts of this island country. The economic embargo on these areas has been lifted, allowing for the resumption of economic activity. Following the agreement, direct peace talks between the Sri Lankan Government and LTTE have so far yielded satisfactory outcomes. The first round of talks, in September 2002, centred around the establishment of regional autonomy. The second round, in October 2002, brought the peace process further forward with the setting up of three joint committees of the Government and LTTE to deal with economic, political and military affairs. In the third round, in December 2002, the peace talks yielded another major breakthrough: an agreement to study a federal structure of government which could be the basis for a final political solution to the conflict. The fourth round, in January 2003, tackled the details of resettlement and reconstruction in war-hit areas. Although a major breakthrough in the key area of disarmament was not expected, the fact that the talks have reached this stage can be considered a significant step towards achieving peace, and thus provide a fillip to the enhancement of economic activities.

The success of the peace process will have an immense positive impact on the economy. The large expenditure on defence contributed to government budget deficits in the 1990s. The peace process provides hope that budget deficits can be reduced and sustained at lower levels. Moreover, the cessation of hostilities would also lead to a rising influx of tourists, which is a major source of foreign exchange for the country. Sri Lanka already has tourist facilities of an international standard and therefore the potential for tourism growth would be significant. In particular, the peace process helped to raise tourist arrivals by 17 per cent in 2002;[b] a further increase of 20 per cent in 2003 would be possible through aggressive marketing.

Furthermore, real progress in the peace process has triggered a massive inflow of aid for reconstruction, particularly in war-torn areas, with significant spin-offs expected for the national economy at large. In November 2002, for example, the World Bank released $31 million to Sri Lanka for that purpose.[c] This financial assistance was to restore primary health care, repair urban water schemes, provide returning families with opportunities for income generation and employment, and build the capacity to undertake a multi-donor-funded reconstruction programme in the future. More lending was expected from the World Bank as well as from bilateral donors and other international organizations as the peace talks yielded significant progress. In January 2003, at the fourth round of talks, the World Bank became the custodian of the funds raised through international forums to be administered by the Subcommittee on Immediate Humanitarian and Rehabilitation Needs.[c] The improved prospects for peace therefore have far-reaching benefits for the economic development of the country.

Finally, as the peace process is showing significant progress, expectations are now running high among Sri Lankans and the international community that a political solution to the conflict, which has caused the death of around 64,000 people in some 20 years of fighting, will evolve. The international community has an important role to play in sustaining the momentum of the peace process and providing resources for resettlement and reconstruction.

---

[a] "Peace process of Sri Lanka", official web site of the Sri Lankan Government's Secretariat for Coordinating the Peace Process, <http://www.peaceinsrilanka.org>, 17 January 2003.

[b] Reuters Foundation, Newsdesk, "Sri Lanka, on back of peace bid, eyes tourism record", <http://www.alertnet.org/thenews/newsdesk/COL174334>, 17 January 2003.

[c] World Bank, "Sri Lanka: World Bank to support reconstruction and peace building", press release No. 2003/149/SAR, 21 November 2002, <http://www.worldbank.org/lk>, 17 January 2003.

[d] World Bank, "World Bank invited to administer Sri Lanka reconstruction fund", <http://www.worldbank.org/lk>, 17 January 2003.

***The targeted programme for the poor was strengthened, new modalities for providing social security were introduced, and attention was paid to generating resources for poverty reduction***

In order to mitigate the impact of insufficient employment generation in the formal sector, social protection programmes in India and Pakistan have been strengthened in recent years with the expansion of existing programmes and the launching of new ones. Pakistan launched two new major initiatives, a comprehensive poverty intervention aimed at generating economic activity through public works, and a microcredit bank, as nationwide efforts to address poverty and vulnerability problems. In January 2003, to help the poor, the Prime Minister's "Falahi package" was approved by the Cabinet. Under that programme, 2.5 million families would be provided with financial assistance of 2,500 rupees each year; 5 billion rupees were allocated for this purpose. At the same time, the new civilian Government was working on additional relief packages for the benefit of the poor and low-income groups.

Similarly, India launched a number of social protection programmes during the period 2000-2002, for example, Integrated Village Employment Programme, providing wage employment and food security in rural areas, the Prime Minister's village development scheme for village-level development, the Food for Work Programme, and schemes providing foodgrains at highly subsidized prices, social security benefits to agricultural labourers and educational allowances to the children of parents living below the poverty line. At the budget presentation on 28 February 2003, the Government of India explicitly placed poverty reduction, covering health, housing, education and employment, among the five priority areas for fiscal 2003-2004. Concerns about the well-being of the poor are also being pursued in other closely interrelated priority areas, namely agriculture, where a large majority of the poor depends for their livelihood, and infrastructure development, particularly improvements in rural roads.

In Turkey, with the exception of the Bag Kur social insurance plan for the self-employed, a major part of the social security system is linked to benefits associated with holding a formal job. The Government has recently embarked upon an economic reform programme that includes action to improve the social protection system significantly. For example, Parliament approved a major policy reform introducing an unemployment insurance scheme in April 2002.

The Islamic Republic of Iran has given special emphasis to human development and social protection and has made significant progress so far. As a result of major public sector investments in the social sector over the last 20 years, with virtually universal education and extensive health coverage and an active government distributive strategy through direct transfers and indirect subsidies, the proportion of the population living below the poverty line has fallen significantly, from 47 per cent in 1978 to about 16 per cent in recent years. Virtually all social indicators have shown improvement. Of particular note is the closing of the gender gap in education, where enrolment rates for boys and girls show only small differences, in literacy and in political representation.

## B. Least developed countries in the subregion

### *Overview and prospects*

***The slowdown in economic growth in the least developed countries of South Asia was largely led by a decline in the external sector***

Economic growth in the least developed countries of South Asia generally moderated in 2002 from the levels reached the previous year; however, Nepal experienced a sharp fall in GDP expansion (figure II.21). Unlike previous periods of economic slowdown, which were largely the result of poor agricultural performance, the current decline is a reflection of the overall slowdown in the external sector. Setbacks were registered by garment exports from Bangladesh and Nepal and tourism receipts by Bhutan, Maldives and Nepal, leading to a fall in manufacturing and services linked to external trade. Agriculture remained the most important sector for Bangladesh, Bhutan and Nepal in terms of the associated volume of domestic employment and contribution to GDP. However, the composition of sectoral output in the least developed countries of the subregion confirmed the long-term, slow shift towards industry and services. In all of these countries, the persistent reliance on a small range of economic

**Figure II.21. Rates of GDP growth in selected least developed countries in South and South-West Asia, 1999-2002**

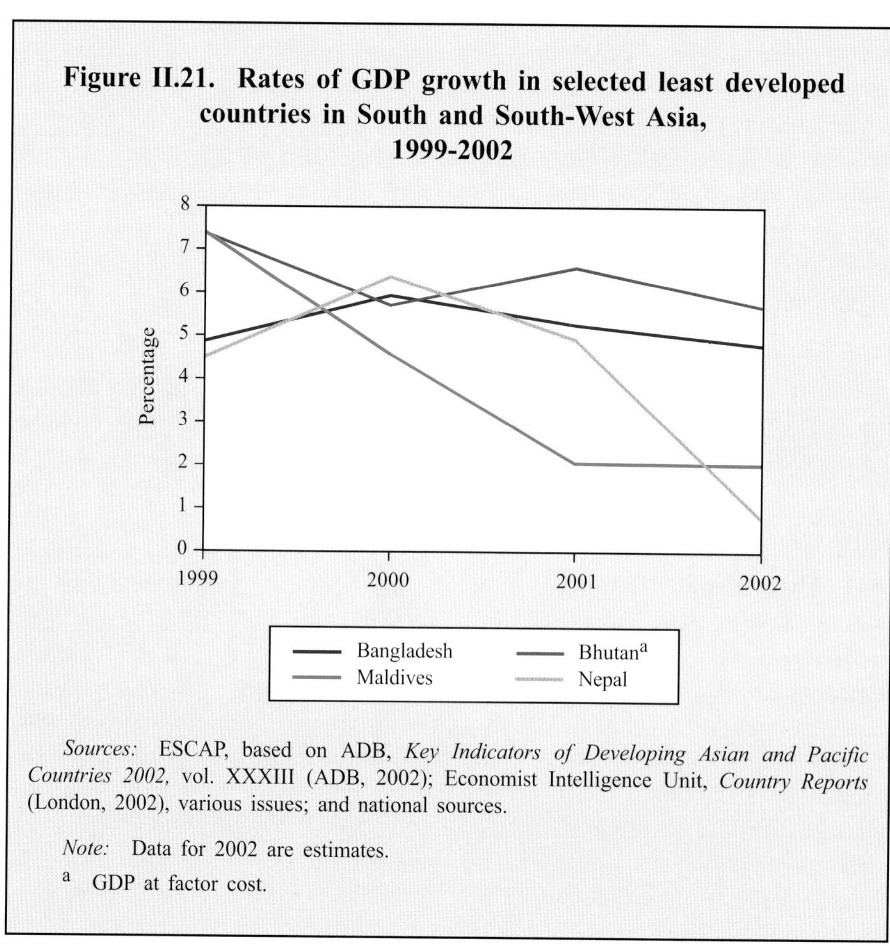


*Sources:* ESCAP, based on ADB, *Key Indicators of Developing Asian and Pacific Countries 2002,* vol. XXXIII (ADB, 2002); Economist Intelligence Unit, *Country Reports* (London, 2002), various issues; and national sources.

*Note:* Data for 2002 are estimates.

[a] GDP at factor cost.

activities and a few key trading partners highlights their vulnerability to adverse external developments and underscores the need for them to achieve greater diversification in economic production and trade.

***However, the outlook is for faster growth***

In Bangladesh, based on steady growth in agriculture and stronger demand from foreign markets, GDP growth was projected to be on an upward trend of 5.2, 5.8 and 6.5 per cent, respectively in 2003, 2004 and 2005. Progress on structural and economic reforms would be another stimulus to private sector activity. The Ninth Five-Year Plan of Bhutan forecasts a faster rate of annual economic growth of 8.2 per cent in the period 2003-2007, considerably higher than the 6.7 per cent projected in the Eighth Plan period, owing to the ongoing construction of major hydroelectric projects which are scheduled for completion during the Plan period, the establishment of new industrial estates and greater inflows of FDI. The economic outlook for Maldives depends heavily on inward tourism, the mainstay of economic activities and related services in this island country. GDP growth was expected to be somewhat higher, at 4.2 per cent, in 2003, as tourism recovers in line with the expected stronger economic growth and revival of export demand in the EU and the United States. An additional stimulus to construction and transport comes from work on some public sector projects. Nepal expects GDP to recover and expand by 1.5 per cent in 2003 and by another 3.5 per cent in 2004, given the restoration of law and order, favourable weather conditions and external trade, continuing strong economic performance in India and progress in domestic reforms to provide a more conducive environment to private sector development.

**Figure II.22. Inflation in selected least developed countries in South and South-West Asia, 1999-2002[a]**

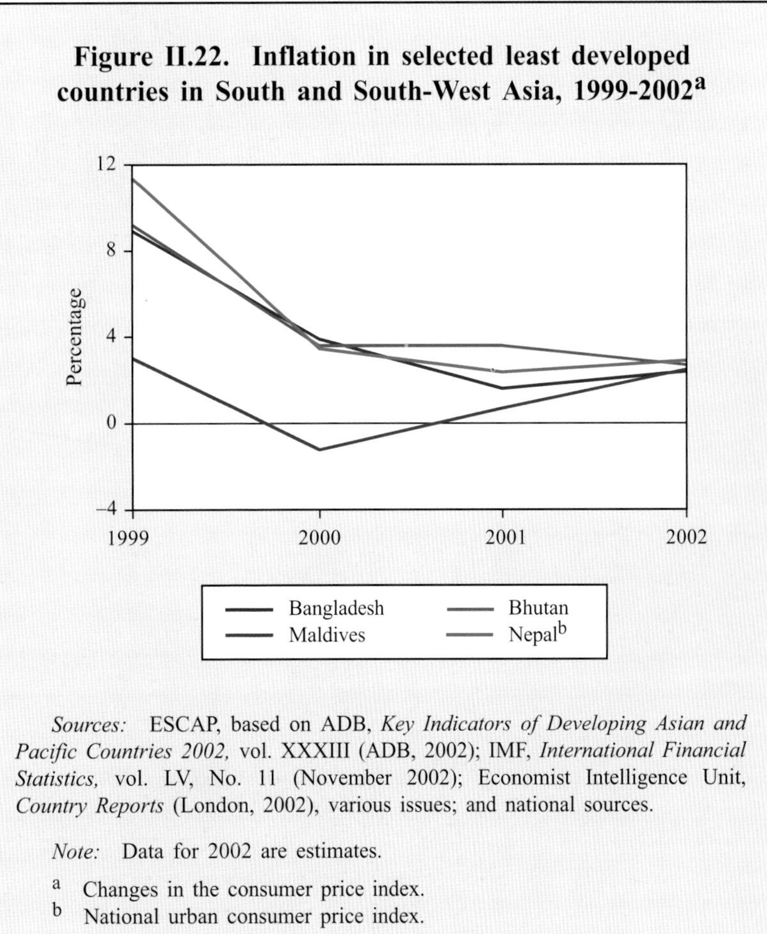


*Sources:* ESCAP, based on ADB, *Key Indicators of Developing Asian and Pacific Countries 2002,* vol. XXXIII (ADB, 2002); IMF, *International Financial Statistics,* vol. LV, No. 11 (November 2002); Economist Intelligence Unit, *Country Reports* (London, 2002), various issues; and national sources.

*Note:* Data for 2002 are estimates.

[a] Changes in the consumer price index.
[b] National urban consumer price index.

Inflation was contained at less than 3 per cent in 2002 in the least developed countries in South Asia (figure II.22). Among the contributing factors to this

***Inflation was contained below 3 per cent***

relative price stability were improved food supplies owing to favourable weather conditions and stable exchange rates leading to little change in import prices; some upward pressure, however, was felt with rising world oil prices.

Merchandise exports, mainly of garments, from Bangladesh declined noticeably in fiscal 2002 (figure II.23). Imports associated with those exports as well as for domestic consumption were also on a downward trend (figure II.24), leading to lower trade and current accounts deficits. Nepal's experience was similar. Inward migrant remittances, which exceeded merchandise export earnings in the case of Nepal, increased noticeably in the two countries and contributed to a more favourable overall balance of payments. Meanwhile, Bhutan's external trade, which is strongly conditioned by developments in the hydropower sector, continued to be heavily dependent on energy demand from India in 2002. In Maldives, the weakness of merchandise exports and inward tourism reflected less than fortuitous global economic conditions, taking their toll on the current account deficit. Foreign exchange reserves in the four least developed countries of the subregion ranged from less than 3 months of

**Figure II.23. Growth rates in merchandise export earnings of selected least developed countries in South and South-West Asia, 1999-2002**

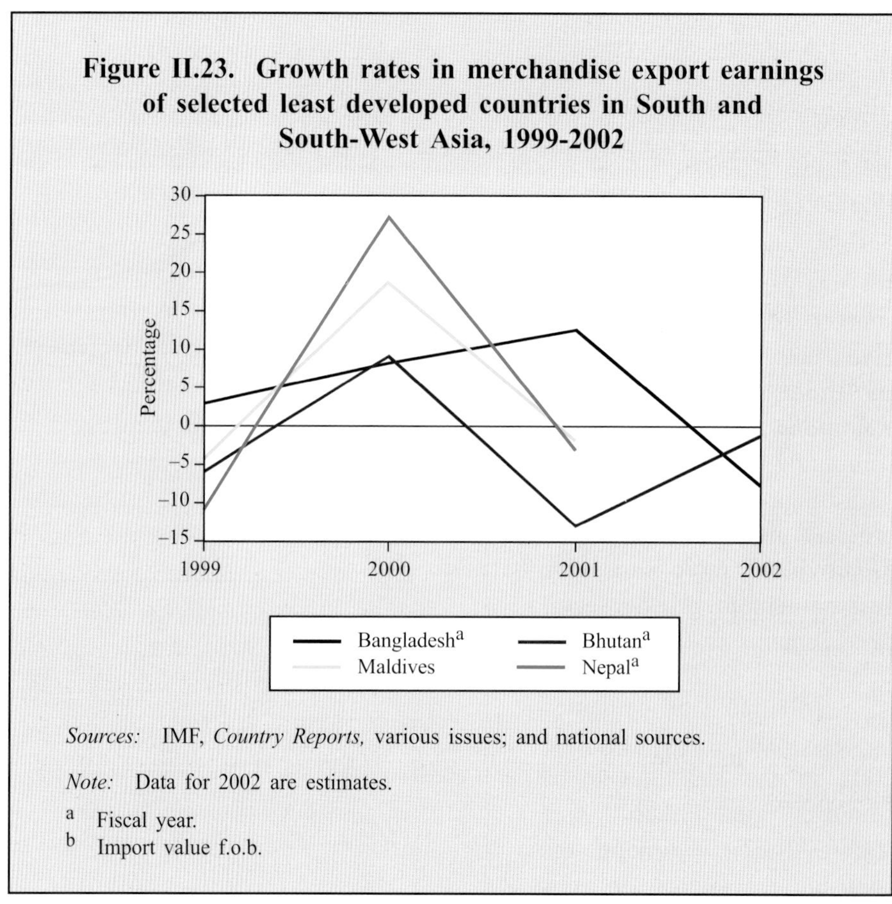


*Sources:* IMF, *Country Reports,* various issues; and national sources.

*Note:* Data for 2002 are estimates.

[a] Fiscal year.

[b] Import value f.o.b.

import cover in Bangladesh and Maldives to over 20 months in Bhutan. Their exchange rates came under some pressure in 2001-2002 and were either devalued, in the case of Bangladesh and Maldives, or depreciated in line with the Indian rupee, to which they are pegged, in the case of Bhutan and Nepal (figure II.25).

**Figure II.24. Growth rates in merchandise import spending of selected least developed countries in South and South-West Asia, 1999-2002**

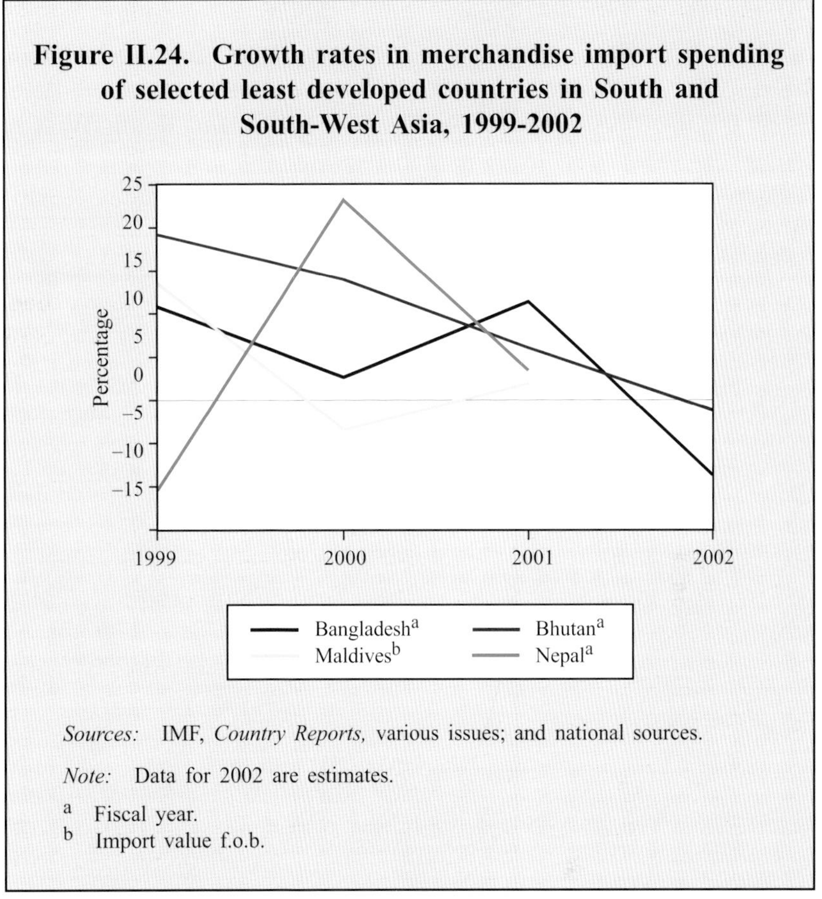


*Sources:* IMF, *Country Reports,* various issues; and national sources.

*Note:* Data for 2002 are estimates.

[a] Fiscal year.

[b] Import value f.o.b.

The South Asian least developed countries, among many others in the world, rely on a narrow base of products and markets in terms of both production and trade. In Bangladesh, for example, more than four fifths of the total exports are destined for North America and the EU. Some three fourths of total exports are garments, which will face open competition in all markets after the expiration of the Multifibre Arrangement on 1 January 2005. Electricity sales to India continue to be the single most important source of export revenue in Bhutan. Maldives' overwhelming reliance on export fisheries could result in difficulties in future as graduation from its status as a least developed country would entail loss of market access preferences.

***Diversification of export commodities and markets is essential***

The major policy issues to be managed by the least developed countries in South Asia are long-standing in nature: poverty reduction and the need for faster, pro-poor economic growth; better management of public finances and an enhanced process of domestic resource mobilization; greater private sector participation for sustained economic growth and employment generation; and strengthening of the financial sector in order to serve all members of society efficiently and adequately.

**Figure II.25. Index of exchange rates against the United States dollar in selected least developed countries in South and South-West Asia, 1996-2002**

*(1996 = 100)*

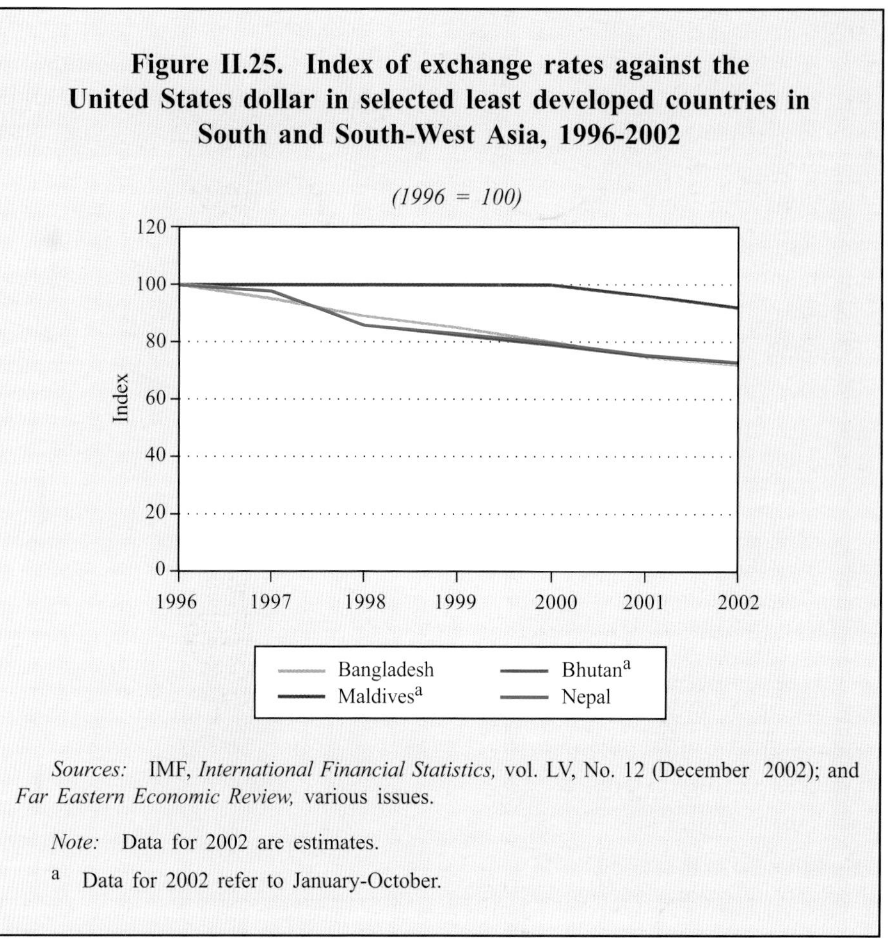


*Sources:* IMF, *International Financial Statistics,* vol. LV, No. 12 (December 2002); and *Far Eastern Economic Review,* various issues.

*Note:* Data for 2002 are estimates.

[a] Data for 2002 refer to January-October.

## *GDP growth performance*

***The global economic slowdown and fiscal and monetary tightening contributed to a marginal decline in GDP growth in Bangladesh***

Aggregate production in Bangladesh expanded by an annual average of 5.6 per cent in 2000-2001 and by a slightly lower rate of 4.8 per cent in 2002. This marginal decline was a result of falling exports, owing to the global economic slowdown, unfavourable weather conditions and some demand compression resulting from fiscal and monetary tightening for stabilization purposes (table II.25). There was slower growth in the agricultural sector, from 3.1 per cent in 2001 to 2.8 per cent in 2002, as rice production suffered from adverse weather conditions. Other crops and horticulture were also affected, but fisheries recovered strongly from a decline in 2001. The rate of manufacturing growth slowed from 6.5 per cent in 2001 to 4 per cent in the following year, contributing to the observed decline in industrial value added, from 7.4 per cent in 2001 to 6.1 per cent in 2002. Falling exports of garments caused the slowdown in manufacturing activities, with many manufacturing units ceasing operations. Construction was also experiencing a slight decline, growing by just under 8 per cent in 2002 compared with 8.6 per cent a year earlier,

**Table II.25. Selected least developed countries in South and South-West Asia: growth rates, 1999-2002**

*(Percentage)*

| | | Rates of growth | | | |
|---|---|---|---|---|---|
| | | *Gross domestic product* | *Agriculture* | *Industry* | *Services* |
| Bangladesh | 1999 | 4.9 | 4.7 | 4.9 | 4.9 |
| | 2000 | 5.9 | 7.4 | 6.2 | 5.2 |
| | 2001 | 5.3 | 3.1 | 7.4 | 5.3 |
| | 2002 | 4.8 | 2.8 | 6.1 | 5.1 |
| Bhutan[a] | 1999 | 7.4 | 5.3 | 11.6 | 5.2 |
| | 2000 | 5.7 | 4.7 | 4.0 | 9.1 |
| | 2001 | 6.6 | 3.2 | 13.4 | 6.6 |
| | 2002 | 5.7 | .. | .. | .. |
| Maldives | 1999 | 7.4 | 3.3 | 6.8 | 7.8 |
| | 2000 | 4.6 | −0.2 | −4.4 | 6.3 |
| | 2001 | 2.1 | 1.6 | 3.7 | 1.6 |
| | 2002 | 2.0 | 1.4 | .. | .. |
| Nepal | 1999 | 4.5 | 2.9 | 6.0 | 5.4 |
| | 2000 | 6.4 | 5.0 | 8.9 | 6.2 |
| | 2001 | 4.9 | 4.2 | 2.7 | 7.0 |
| | 2002 | 0.8 | 1.7 | 0.2[b] | .. |

*Sources:* ESCAP, based on ADB, *Key Indicators of Developing Asian and Pacific Countries 2002,* vol. XXXIII (ADB, 2002); Economist Intelligence Unit, *Country Reports* (London, 2002), various issues; and national sources.

*Notes:* Data for 2002 are estimates. Industry comprises mining and quarrying; manufacturing; electricity, gas and power; and construction.

[a] GDP at factor cost.
[b] Rate of growth of non-agriculture.

owing to the scaling-down of public sector spending. Signs of a recovery in manufacturing appeared towards the last quarter of 2002 following lower interest rates. Meanwhile, the service sector appeared to have retained its momentum, expanding by just over 5 per cent in 2002, as it had done on average between 1999 and 2001. Weakened external trade had some effect on transport, storage and communications, wholesale and retail trade and financial intermediation.

Both the domestic savings and investment ratios remained largely unchanged in Bangladesh in 2001-2002 (table II.26). The private sector component of investment increased to 16.1 per cent of GDP in 2002 from 15.9 per cent of GDP in the previous year, while the public sector component decreased slightly, to 7.1 per cent of GDP from 7.3 per cent

**Table II.26. Selected least developed countries in South and South-West Asia: ratios of gross domestic savings and investment to GDP, 1999-2002**

*(Percentage)*

| | *1999* | *2000* | *2001* | *2002* |
|---|---|---|---|---|
| **Savings as a percentage of GDP** | | | | |
| Bangladesh | 17.7 | 17.9 | 18.0 | 18.0 |
| Bhutan | 13.5 | 17.2 | 21.0 | 16.0 |
| Nepal | 13.6 | 15.0 | 14.7 | 13.1 |
| **Investment as a percentage of GDP** | | | | |
| Bangladesh | 22.2 | 23.0 | 23.1 | 23.2 |
| Bhutan | 43.1 | 43.8 | 45.7 | 44.0 |
| Nepal | 20.5 | 24.2 | 24.5 | 24.1 |

*Sources:* ESCAP, based on ADB, *Key Indicators of Developing Asian and Pacific Countries 2002,* vol. XXXIII (ADB, 2002) and *Asian Development Outlook 2002* (Oxford University Press, 2002); and national sources.

*Note:* Data for 2002 are estimates.

over the same period, as the implementation of development projects with lower priority was curtailed. This trend in the composition of investment is expected to continue: the medium-term macroeconomic framework shows an absolute increase in public investment but a gradual decline as a share of GDP.

***In Bhutan, hydropower generation remained a major source of economic growth***

In Bhutan, GDP growth was about 1 percentage point lower, 5.7 per cent in 2002 compared with 6.6 per cent in the previous year. Agricultural output, including from animal husbandry and forestry, had gone up by 3.2 per cent in 2001 and continued to be the main source of domestic employment, in addition to making a contribution of 34.3 per cent to GDP. However, the industrial sector had a relative GDP share of about 23 per cent and had expanded at a much faster rate than agriculture in recent years, reflecting the gradual transformation in the production structure of the Bhutanese economy. The electricity subsector alone contributed 12 per cent of GDP. With the commissioning of two hydropower projects in 2001, the power sector was expected to emerge as the most important sector in the economy; this was due not only to its own contribution but also to its linkages to other sectors. For example, the construction and transport sectors, with relative GDP shares of 15.1 and 8.7 per cent respectively, grew by over 21 per cent in 2001 as a result of hydropower development. Tourism is the most important service industry, in terms of both convertible currency earnings and a stimulus to the hotel and retail business. However, it had suffered a major setback in 2001, when tourist arrivals fell by 15.4 per cent.

*Maldives was economically vulnerable as a result of a narrow economic base*

Maldives has a GDP per capita of $2,200, about twice the maximum level of $1,035 set by the United Nations for least developed country status. However, it continues to be classified as one because of its high vulnerability to external economic and other shocks, given its small size and narrow economic base. Maldives is heavily dependent on the sustainable development of two environmentally sensitive activities, tourism and fishing. Overall production remained largely stagnant, gaining around 2 per cent each in both 2001 and 2002. This was due to lower tourism receipts and tourism-related construction activities (following the opening of 14 island resorts in 1999), and subdued seafood exports compounded by adverse terms of trade brought about by falling fish prices and rising oil prices. Agricultural output was also subdued, expanding by 1.4 per cent in 2002 from 1.6 per cent in the previous year as a result of negligible growth in fisheries, which accounted for more than three fifths of the output in that sector. Industrial growth was projected to decline as a result of slower growth in construction; manufacturing and mining were of relatively minor importance. Service sector growth has declined in recent years along with tourism receipts. The Maldives currency is pegged to the United States dollar, whose strength, prior to the recent devaluation of the rufiyaa, made the country a more expensive destination for tourists from Europe and Japan, its two main sources of visitors. Visitor arrivals dropped after the 11 September 2001 events and resort prices were also softening owing to increased competition from many newly opened tourist resorts in the country.

*The falling demand for garments, and civil unrest, contributed to the decline in manufacturing and tourism receipts in Nepal*

Economic growth in Nepal slowed considerably, from 4.9 per cent in 2001 to less than 1 per cent in 2002; the global economic slowdown and social instability contributed to lower export and tourism revenue. There was also a sharp decline in agriculture, which employs 80 per cent of the labour force, owing to the lower output of paddy, millet, jute and tobacco. The sector as a whole added 1.7 per cent to gross output in 2002, compared with just over 4 per cent in the previous year. Industrial growth was also subdued as a result of slowing manufactured exports, while the service sector suffered from the adverse effects of an estimated fall of one third in tourism receipts in 2002. Tourist arrivals declined from a high of 491,500 recorded in 1999 to 363,000 in 2001, even as hotel bed capacity continued to grow.

### Inflation

*A spurt in non-food prices contributed to a marginal increase in inflation in Bangladesh*

Annual inflation in Bangladesh had shown a sharp downward trend for a few years, falling from almost 9 per cent in 1999 to just 1.6 per cent in 2001 before picking up again to 2.4 per cent in 2002 (table II.27). Food prices rose by only 1.2 per cent as there was no major disruption in domestic production, but there was a sharper increase of 4.5 per cent in non-food prices, which was, due in part to fiscal and monetary tightening. Administered increases in gas, electricity and petroleum prices led to a rise in the fuel, lighting and transport components of the consumption basket, while higher regulatory duties and mandatory margin requirements on

**Table II.27. Selected least developed countries in South and South-West Asia: inflation and money supply growth (M2), 1999-2002**

*(Percentage)*

| | *1999* | *2000* | *2001* | *2002* |
|---|---|---|---|---|
| **Inflation**[a] | | | | |
| Bangladesh[b] | 8.9 | 3.9 | 1.6 | 2.4 |
| Bhutan[b] | 9.2 | 3.6 | 3.6 | 2.7 |
| Maldives | 3.0 | −1.2 | 0.7 | 2.5 |
| Nepal[b, c] | 11.4 | 3.5 | 2.4 | 2.9 |
| **Money supply growth (M2)** | | | | |
| Bangladesh | 15.5 | 19.3 | 14.7 | 13.7[d] |
| Bhutan | 32.0 | 17.4 | 7.9 | 19.9[e] |
| Maldives | 3.6 | 4.1 | 9.0 | 15.1[f] |
| Nepal | 20.8 | 21.8 | 15.3 | 11.5 |

*Sources:* ESCAP, based on ADB, *Key Indicators of Developing Asian and Pacific Countries 2002,* vol. XXXIII (ADB, 2002); IMF, *International Financial Statistics,* vol. LV, No. 11 (November 2002); Economist Intelligence Unit, *Country Reports* (London, 2002), various issues; and national sources.

*Note:* Data for 2002 are estimates.

[a] Changes in the consumer price index.
[b] Fiscal year.
[c] National urban consumer price index.
[d] January-July.
[e] January-June.
[f] January-September.

commercial imports also raised the prices of several goods and services. The general wage index rose by 4.2 per cent in 2002, well above the rate of inflation. However, only 19 per cent of the labour force was in formal employment and therefore the impact of the wage increase on prices was limited. Annual inflation of 3 per cent has been targeted for the period 2003-2005 in line with the Government's intention to contain price increases; however, some upward pressure on prices could be felt if there were adverse weather conditions leading to higher food prices, and a depreciation of the currency leading to higher prices on landed imports.

***The base lending rate was cut to sustain economic activities in Bangladesh***

In view of widening fiscal deficits and weakening exports in 2001, Bangladesh tightened its monetary policy in the following year; credit to the public sector, in particular, showed a notable decline. In the first seven months of 2002, the broad money supply (M2) expanded by 13.7 per cent, higher than the targeted 10 per cent, as a result of higher inward remittances, but 1 percentage point lower than the rate recorded in 2001. To counter the slowdown in private sector economic activities resulting from the slump in export demand, the Central Bank lowered its base lending rate from 7 to 6 per cent in 2002, thus underpinning the 14.4 per cent growth of private sector credit in 2002.

***Movements in consumer prices in Bhutan were linked to inflation in India***

The exchange rate peg at parity of the Bhutanese ngultrum to the Indian rupee provides an important anchor for the economy but limits the scope for an independent monetary policy. The first half of 2002 witnessed a significant increase in the broad money supply (M2), a rise of almost one fifth compared with less then 8 per cent in the previous year, owing to higher net foreign assets, reasonably strong economic activities and the ongoing monetization of the economy. Inflation in Bhutan is also linked to that in India because of the exchange rate peg and close trade relationships. Inflation stabilized at 3.6 per cent in both 2000 and 2001, well below the 20-year average of 8.6 per cent. It fell further to a record low of 2.7 per cent in 2002, reflecting improved food supply and availability; in particular, food price inflation was 3.5 per cent in 2002, compared with 8 per cent a year earlier. However, according to the Ninth Five-year Plan, the average annual rate of inflation is targeted to be higher in Bhutan over the period 2003-2007.

***Import prices and fish prices determined the rate of inflation in Maldives***

Maldives experienced an acceleration in inflation, although at 2.5 per cent in 2002 it was still relatively low; consumer prices were very stable, rising by only 0.7 per cent in 2001. The upturn in inflation reflected, in part, the effects of a currency devaluation in July 2001 on imported goods, which comprised nearly 60 per cent of the consumption basket. Fluctuations in the prices of domestically caught fish (important in the food component, which has a relative weight of almost 37 per cent of the consumption basket) and the prices of imported consumer goods, which are exogenously determined, largely determine movements in inflation in Maldives. Notably, in this connection, Maldives experienced deflation in 2000 as a result of currency appreciation in that year, while the low rate of inflation in 2001 was the net result of a 21 per cent drop in fish prices, which compensated for an increase of just over 10 per cent in the prices of other food items. The prices of staples such as rice, flour and sugar are under government control.

***Credit was provided to fund the budget deficit in Maldives***

In Maldives, monetary policy has been directed to supporting low-inflation growth and maintaining an external balance while, at the same time, financing a substantial part of the fiscal deficit. In mid-2001, several reforms aimed at eliminating direct monetary controls were introduced in order to increase policy reliance on market-based, indirect instruments. The broad money supply (M2) went up by 9 per cent in 2001 and net credit to the Government by an estimated 8 per cent; in comparison, private sector credit growth accelerated to almost 30 per cent from 8 per cent in 2000. The broad money supply rose more strongly, by over 15 per cent in the first three quarters of 2002.

Inflation in Nepal was held below 3 per cent in 2001-2002 as a result of weak domestic demand and generally stable prices in India. However, inflation was expected to creep upwards towards the end of the year along with an increase in Indian food prices. Consumer prices were projected to be higher by 4.5 per cent in 2003, in line with the expected inflation rate in India.

***Credit expansion to the public sector in Nepal was strong, while private sector loan demand remained weak***

In Nepal, as in Maldives, monetary policy continued to accommodate fiscal needs. Broad money supply (M2) growth slowed to 11.5 per cent in 2002 from 15 per cent a year earlier, as a result of the weaker economy. However, net claims on the Government expanded by 19 per cent. Meanwhile, liquidity shortages in some banks led the Central Bank to lower cash reserve requirements as well as refinancing rates. Interest rates on deposits and treasury bills declined to around 4 per cent in 2002, below the corresponding rates in India, partly as a result of weak loan demand reflecting, in turn, the limited investment opportunities in Nepal. The Central Bank also provided a refinancing facility at 3 per cent interest to encourage commercial banks to provide concessional loans to industries affected by the economic slowdown. Nevertheless, growth in private sector credit was lower at 8 per cent in 2002, down from 16 per cent in 2001, and was mainly directed at refinancing troubled loans.

### *Foreign trade and other external transactions*

#### *External trade*

***Although export growth in Bangladesh suffered from weak overseas demand, imports declined even more sharply, leading to a narrower trade deficit***

Merchandise exports had gone up by 12.6 per cent to reach $6.42 billion in 2001 in Bangladesh but declined by over 7.6 per cent in 2002 as a result of lower demand in overseas markets (table II.28). Although the volume of apparel exports increased by almost 14 per cent in 2002, falling prices were responsible for a drop of almost 6 per cent in their value. Exports of frozen foods, leather, raw jute and tea also experienced a fall-off in both volume and value terms; by contrast, the export volumes and values of jute goods and agricultural products were higher in 2002.

In the meantime, there was an absolute decline in import spending, by approximately 8.7 per cent, in 2002, as a result of lower imports of inputs for export processing activities as well as fiscal and monetary tightening (table II.29). The fall reversed a substantial expansion of over 11 per cent in import value during the previous year. In 2002, lower import expenditure on cotton, yarns and textiles led to a 13.4 per cent reduction in the value of imported intermediate goods and industrial inputs, which together constituted over two fifths of total imports. Petroleum imports were also lower, while import spending on rice, wheat and sugar went down as a result of increased domestic output; however, imports of edible oils increased considerably. Commercial imports of consumer durables and automobiles declined by over 10 per cent in 2002 after the imposition of margin requirements and supplementary duties had lowered demand. By contrast the continued positive investment outlook accounted for a modest rise in imported capital goods.

**Table II.28. Selected least developed countries in South and South-West Asia: merchandise exports and their rates of growth, 1999-2002**

| | Value (millions of US dollars) | Exports (f.o.b.) | | | |
|---|---|---|---|---|---|
| | | Annual rate of growth (percentage) | | | |
| | 2001 | 1999 | 2000 | 2001 | 2002 |
| Bangladesh[a] | 6 419 | 2.9 | 8.2 | 12.6 | −7.6 |
| Bhutan[a] | 99 | −5.9 | 9.1 | −12.9 | −1.2 |
| Maldives | 107 | −4.3 | 18.8 | −1.7 | .. |
| Nepal[a] | 941 | −10.9 | 27.3 | −3.1 | .. |

*Sources:* IMF, *Country Reports,* various issues; and national sources.

*Note:* Data for 2002 are estimates.

[a] Fiscal year.

Both exports and imports showed some recovery towards the end of the year and the medium-term macroeconomic framework projects a growth rate of 7.1 and 8.9 per cent for exports and imports respectively in 2003. The trade deficit narrowed in 2002 as a result of the steeper decline in imports than in exports and, together with a substantial increase in remittance receipts, contributed to narrowing of the current account deficit from 1 per cent of GDP in 2001 to 0.6 per cent in 2002 (table II.30).

**Table II.29. Selected least developed countries in South and South-West Asia: merchandise imports and their rates of growth, 1999-2002**

| | Value (millions of US dollars) | Imports (c.i.f.) | | | |
|---|---|---|---|---|---|
| | | Annual rate of growth (percentage) | | | |
| | 2001 | 1999 | 2000 | 2001 | 2002 |
| Bangladesh[a] | 8 430 | 10.9 | 2.7 | 11.4 | −8.7 |
| Bhutan[a] | 196 | 19.2 | 14.0 | 6.1 | −1.2 |
| Maldives[b] | 349 | 13.6 | −3.4 | 2.0 | .. |
| Nepal[a] | 1 773 | −10.4 | 23.2 | 3.5 | .. |

*Sources:* IMF, *Country Reports,* various issues; and national sources.

*Note:* Data for 2002 are estimates.

[a] Fiscal year

[b] Imports f.o.b.

**Table II.30. Selected least developed countries in South and South-West Asia: budget and current account balance as a percentage of GDP, 1999-2002**

*(Percentage)*

| | *1999* | *2000* | *2001* | *2002* |
|---|---|---|---|---|
| **Budget balance as a percentage of GDP** | | | | |
| Bangladesh[a] | −4.8 | −6.2 | −5.5 | −4.3 |
| Bhutan | −1.6 | −4.1 | −11.8 | −6.8 |
| Maldives | −4.2 | −4.9 | −5.3 | −7.6 |
| Nepal | −5.3 | −4.7 | −5.8 | .. |
| **Current account balance as a percentage of GDP** | | | | |
| Bangladesh | −0.8 | −0.7 | −1.0 | −0.6 |
| Bhutan | −22.5 | −26.8 | −23.4 | .. |
| Maldives | −14.6 | −9.5 | −10.7 | .. |
| Nepal | −5.1 | −5.6 | −6.2 | −6.0 |

*Sources:* ESCAP, based on ADB, *Key Indicators of Developing Asian and Pacific Countries 2002,* vol. XXXIII (ADB, 2002) and *Asian Development Outlook 2002* (Oxford University Press, 2002); IMF, *International Financial Statistics,* vol. LV, No. 11 (November 2002); Economist Intelligence Unit, *Country Reports* (London, 2002), various issues; and national sources.

*Note:* Data for 2002 are estimates.

[a] Excluding grants.

***Bhutan depended on India for nearly all of its merchandise exports and imports***

According to Bhutan's balance-of-payments estimates for 2002, both merchandise exports and imports declined only marginally, by approximately 1.2 per cent in each case. The country is heavily dependent on India for trade as a result of the Free Trade Agreement between the two countries as well as the free convertibility between the ngultrum and the Indian rupee. India was the source of over 83 per cent of Bhutan's imports and over 95 per cent of its exports in 2002; electricity sales alone accounted for half of the total merchandise exports to India. Further growth in energy sales is expected in the medium term.

Imports into Bhutan were dominated by chemical and mineral products, machinery, mechanical appliances and base metals; many of those imported items were mainly associated with the construction of hydroelectric projects. In recent years, vehicle imports from India have increased significantly; 600 out of the 740 cars imported in 2001 originated in India. Net receipts of income and current transfers helped to offset the large trade deficit in Bhutan to some extent, narrowing the current account deficit somewhat from the 26.8 per cent of GDP recorded in 2000; nevertheless, the deficit was still equivalent to 23.4 per cent of GDP in the following year.

***Maldives was heavily dependent on trade, principally on inward tourism, for its export earnings***

Maldives has a ratio of trade in goods and non-factor services to GDP of around 170 per cent. Earnings from tourism constituted about 70 per cent of total export receipts, which have suffered in recent years owing to the weakness in that sector. In particular, a reduction in tourist arrivals in 2001-2002, compounded by shorter stays and lower prices resulting from low occupancy rates, led to zero growth in earnings from tourism in 2001 and a contraction of 1.3 per cent in such receipts in 2002. Meanwhile, merchandise exports were heavily dominated by marine products; fresh and processed tuna, for example, accounted for almost three fifths of the merchandise export value in 2001.

About 70 per cent of imports were sourced from Asia and the value of merchandise imports was far in excess of that of exports, including re-exports, leading to a merchandise trade deficit equivalent to nearly 4 per cent of GDP in 2001. The share of re-exports, mainly jet fuel, rose from 21 per cent of merchandise exports in 1997 to 31 per cent in 2001. Manufactured products, intermediate inputs for the apparel industry, food and fuels dominated imports; transport and insurance were the most important service imports. Exports to Asian and European markets have declined in recent years, although this trend has been offset by higher exports, mainly of garments, to the United States. There has, however, been substantial year-to-year volatility in both the value and the volume of exports to most of the major markets. The current account deficit in Maldives widened from 9.5 per cent of GDP in 2000 to just under 11 per cent in 2001, as outward remittances increased by 7.5 per cent over the same period.

***Nepal's exports to countries other than India have fallen significantly***

Nepal's merchandise exports, excluding re-exports, were down by about 3 per cent, to $941 million, in 2001, after a substantial expansion of over 27 per cent a year earlier. Sales to countries other than India declined by more than two fifths, owing to lower garment, carpet and pashmina exports. Earnings on exports to India were slowing as well, as a revised bilateral treaty signed in March 2002 introduced some non-tariff barriers on exports from Nepal; vegetable ghee was the only commodity to have shown a significant increase in exports in 2002. Re-exports to India had also fallen steeply between 1998 and 2001. Generally, any noticeable recovery in overall merchandise exports is expected to be slow as garment exports face increasing international competition.

Merchandise imports were led by minerals, fuels and lubricants, manufactured goods, machinery and transport equipment; their value increased by 3.5 per cent, to $1.77 billion, in 2001. Despite increased migrant remittances, which grew by 8 per cent in 2002 to exceed merchandise exports in value, the current account deficit was around 6 per cent of GDP in 2002; shortfalls in the current account had remained at 5-6 per cent of GDP for several years. An improved balance in the current account is expected in the near term along with slowing import growth, a recovery in tourism receipts and a steady rise in inward remittances.

***A number of initiatives were launched to facilitate regional trade***

The establishment of the South Asian Association for Regional Cooperation (SAARC) Preferential Trading Arrangement (SAPTA) was expected to provide a framework for the gradual liberalization of intra-regional trade and the exchange of concessions on tariffs and quantitative barriers. India and Sri Lanka have become the main Asian trading partners of Maldives under SAARC preferences. To promote liberalized trade, Bhutan recently renewed the bilateral Free Trade Agreement with India up to 2005 and expanded product coverage under the existing Preferential Trade Arrangement with Bangladesh. Bhutan and Nepal, which are merely observers at present, are in the process of accession to WTO as members. Both countries intend to reduce qualitative and quantitative barriers to trade; Nepal is expected to restructure its import tariff bands from five to four, with a maximum rate of 35 per cent, and to convert the exceptional tariff rates on vehicles to excise taxes. Landlocked Bhutan expects the establishment of a dry port in Phuentsholing to reduce transport costs and improve trade documentation processes and procedures (see box II.4).

## Box II.4. Landlocked developing countries

Owing to their lack of territorial access to the sea, remoteness, isolation from world markets and high transit costs, landlocked developing countries are among the poorest within the developing region. Of the 30 landlocked developing countries in the world, 12 are in the ESCAP region: Afghanistan, Armenia, Azerbaijan, Bhutan, Kazakhstan, Kyrgyzstan, Lao People's Democratic Republic, Mongolia, Nepal, Tajikistan, Turkmenistan and Uzbekistan. Four of these, Afghanistan, Bhutan, the Lao People's Democratic Republic and Nepal, are also classified as least developed, while 9 are economies in transition, Armenia, Azerbaijan, Kazakhstan, Kyrgyzstan, the Lao People's Democratic Republic, Mongolia, Tajikistan, Turkmenistan and Uzbekistan.

Longer distances from international markets and time-consuming border-crossing and transit formalities increase the total costs as well as the transit time for the imports and exports of landlocked developing countries, thereby eroding their competitive edge. On the basis of IMF Balance-of-Payments Statistics, UNCTAD has estimated that in 1995 landlocked developing countries spent on average almost two times more of their export earnings for the payment of transport and insurance services than the average payment borne by developing countries, and three times more than that borne by developed economies.[a]

[a] "Specific actions related to the particular needs and problems of landlocked developing countries", note by the Secretary-General (A/56/427) (<http://www.un.org/documents/ga/docs/56/a56427.pdf>).

The geographical disadvantage of landlocked countries is often compounded by poor infrastructure and "missing links" in transit corridors. Efforts to develop these corridors, however, tend to be hampered by the fact that landlocked developing countries find it difficult to attract FDI for infrastructure development. In 2001, for example, landlocked developing countries in Asia were the destination for less than 2 per cent of global FDI flows to all developing economies, despite the fact that the Asian and Pacific region as a whole received close to half of such flows.[b] In that context, the availability of efficient infrastructure and transport systems is often a prerequisite to attracting FDI. The international community therefore has a critical role to play in assisting landlocked developing countries in improving their basic infrastructure and related services.

While there have been some improvements in transit transport systems across the world, the rate of progress is overshadowed by rapid changes in the organization and modalities for production and trade across the globe. The globalization of supply chains and the spread of "just-in-time" delivery, for example, mean that the ease with which parts and products can be imported and exported has become a major consideration for international firms in their decision to invest and relocate overseas. Several non-physical aspects of transit transport can thus become a major barrier to transport and hence to trade and investment flows. These aspects include, to name just a few, cumbersome documentation processes, different working hours at border-crossings, duplicative customs checks and, more generally, the absence of an institutional framework for transit transport. The alignment or standardization of trade documents and the automation of customs procedures are just two of the ways in which both landlocked and transit countries can take action to remove these barriers.

As part of their efforts to address the above issues, many landlocked and transit developing countries have entered into bilateral and subregional agreements on transit trade and transport which provide the legal basis for such operations. Some of these subregional agreements facilitate the movement of transit cargo, not only from landlocked countries to third countries but also through landlocked countries themselves. International conventions represent another type of legal instrument which can facilitate transit trade and transport. On 23 April 1992, the Commission adopted resolution 48/11 on road and rail transport modes in relation to facilitation measures, in which member countries were encouraged to accede to seven international transport conventions, including those on the transport of goods under cover of TIR carnets and on the harmonization of frontier control of goods. The International Convention on the Simplification and Harmonization of Customs Procedures, which was signed at Kyoto, Japan, in 1973 and revised in 1999, relates to trade facilitation. This Convention has served to reduce the delays and paperwork associated with customs procedures. As landlocked and transit developing countries accede to WTO, they will be called upon to provide adequate transport and related infrastructure as well as a conducive regulatory environment to support trade.

In order to create a global consensus on ways and means to address the challenges discussed above, the General Assembly decided to convene the International Ministerial Conference of Landlocked and Transit Developing Countries and Donor Countries and International Financial and Development Institutions on Transit Transport Cooperation, which will be held at Almaty on 28 and 29 August 2003. The Conference will review the current status of transit transport systems around the world and identify new or recurring problems. As part of the global preparatory process, the ESCAP secretariat is conducting a series of studies and subregional seminars on the transit transport systems of its landlocked member States. The outcome of these seminars will form the basis of a regional position paper which will be debated and endorsed by the ESCAP Special Body on Least Developed and Landlocked Developing Countries at its sixth session, to be held in April 2003. This process will involve the Governments, donors and the private sector of both landlocked and transit developing countries; its aim is to ensure that the concerns of all relevant stakeholders are considered when measures to improve transit transport processes are being developed.

---

[b] UNCTAD, *World Investment Report 2002.* United Nations publication, Sales No. E.02.II.D.4), table B.1. This figure excludes the Pacific island States.

*Capital flows and exchange rates*

***External debt and debt service were manageable in Bangladesh***

Net capital flows into Bangladesh declined significantly, from $580 million in fiscal 2001 to $312 million in 2002. Although total ODA receipts rose slightly, from $1.15 billion in 2001 to $ 1.23 billion in 2002, the amount of grant aid was slightly lower, from $432 million to $410 million, over the same period. Inward FDI was worth $174 million in 2001 but was down to $65 million in the following year; there was an outflow of foreign portfolio investment of $6 million. The Central Bank's foreign exchange reserves were adequate to cover 10 weeks of imports in October 2002 as a result of tightened fiscal and monetary policies, administrative measures to compress import demand, and higher remittances; this represented a notable improvement as the foreign reserve position, at $1.1 billion by October 2001, had covered less than six weeks of imports. Total official external debt, which is almost entirely on concessional terms, reached $16.6 billion (or just over 35 per cent of GDP) at the end of 2002. Debt-service obligations accounted for under 10 per cent of annual export earnings. The outstanding external debt of the private sector was estimated to be $1.1 billion as at December 2001. Given the relatively modest levels of the external debt and debt-service burden, Bangladesh is not included in the multilateral debt forgiveness arrangements under the World Bank's Heavily Indebted Poor Countries Initiative.

The transition to a market-based exchange rate regime, which is now under consideration in Bangladesh, will bring an additional variable for consideration in government efforts to stabilize prices. At present, the dealing banks anchor the taka exchange rate for customer and interbank transactions around a narrow band within which the Central Bank undertakes spot purchase and sale transactions. This exchange rate band was revised once in 2001 from Tk 54.00 per United States dollar to Tk 57.00 per dollar and again in 2002 to Tk 57.90 per dollar within a band of one taka.

***Much of Bhutan's external debt consists of concessional loans for hydropower development***

In Bhutan, ODA consists mainly of concessional loans for hydropower projects and the amount was estimated to have increased by around 20 per cent to $56.4 million in 2002. Bhutan also received $1.8 million in FDI, as selected sectors of the economy were opened for private investment of that type; a new FDI policy is in the final stages of approval. As a result of these developments, international reserves went up from $294.2 million at the end of 2001 to $316 million at the end of 2002; the latter sum was equivalent to 20 months of import cover. Total external debt rose by over 23 per cent at the end of 2002 to $289.6 million, or about 58 per cent of GDP; of that amount, 55 per cent was in Indian rupees for the financing of hydropower projects. Most loans in convertible currencies were on concessional terms and total debt-service payments amounted to $4.2 million in 2002, of which 31 per cent was for interest payments.

The ngultrum is pegged to the Indian rupee at parity and is freely convertible with the rupee. In line with the Indian rupee, the ngultrum depreciated by 4 per cent against the United States dollar in 2002.

***In Maldives, private capital inflows decreased along with the completion of new tourist resorts***

In recent years, ODA from bilateral and multilateral sources to Maldives has declined, but more of it has been on concessional terms. Official grants increased by about 10 per cent to $19.6 million in 2001, while private capital inflows were also down from almost $43 million to $24.3 million in 2001 as the construction of additional resorts was completed. External debt, of which 87 per cent was either long- or medium-term, decreased marginally from $211.6 million, or 37.7 per cent of GDP, in 2000 to $209.8 million, or just under 37 per cent of GDP, in 2001 owing to a substantial fall in the short-term foreign liabilities of commercial banks. External debt-servicing amounted to 4.3 per cent of merchandise and non-factor service exports. As a result of higher prices for imported fuel, the amortization of tourism sector debts and growing fiscal expenditure, international reserves went down from $124 million, or 3.8 months of import cover, in 2000 to $94.3 million, or 2.9 months of import cover, in the following year.

Maldives has maintained a de facto fixed exchange rate since 1994, with the rufiyaa anchored to the United States dollar. There are no exchange rate restrictions and the rufiyaa is fully convertible for current and capital account transactions. The strengthened dollar between 1995 and 2000 meant in effect an appreciation of the rufiyaa by about 30 per cent, thus affecting the international competitiveness of fishery exports and inward tourism adversely and discouraging new exports and economic diversification. The rufiyaa was subsequently devalued by 8.5 per cent to Rf 12.8 per dollar in 2001, contributing to some upward push on consumer prices in 2002 in an economy heavily reliant on imports.

***Declining ODA contributed to the overall balance-of-payments deficit in Nepal***

Nepal registered an overall deficit of $77 million in 2002, as compared with an overall balance-of-payments surplus of $38 million in 2001; however, the overall balance of payments was expected to be positive in 2003 as a result of improved aid disbursements. Meanwhile, gross official reserves stood at over $1 billion, covering 6.5 months of imports. The debt-service ratio remained at about 5 per cent of current account receipts as a result of the concessional nature of much of Nepal's debts as well as the high level of inward remittances. Although Nepal maintains an exchange rate system free of restrictions for current international transactions, there continue to be quantitative restrictions on the availability of foreign exchange for travel abroad. The pegging of the Nepalese rupee to the Indian currency at NRs 1.6 to Rs 1 since 1997 has provided a suitable nominal anchor, given the close economic ties with its neighbour. With the depreciation of the Indian currency, the Nepalese rupee weakened slightly against the dollar over the course of 2002. The real effective exchange rate was reported to be stable and the informal market premium was minimal.

### *Key policy issues*

***The modest levels of economic growth in Bangladesh and Nepal, where nearly half of the population live below the poverty line, posed problems for poverty reduction***

Most least developed countries in South and Suth-West Asia have managed to achieve positive GDP growth rates in recent years. Afghanistan, however, is facing a formidable challenge in economic rehabilitation and reconstruction, and in nation-building more generally (see box II.5). The trend rates of economic growth in some countries, such as Bangladesh and Nepal, were not adequate to ensure sustained poverty reduction. Despite domestic and international efforts over the years, it is estimated that some two fifths of the population of Nepal live in poverty as a result of slow growth in the agricultural sector and poor infrastructure and social service delivery. To achieve the goal of poverty reduction, sustained annual growth rates of 6 per cent or higher are necessary, with deliberate pro-poor targeting of public expenditure by choosing projects with high growth and poverty reduction impact; greater attention also needs to be focused on the maintenance of existing public facilities. Given the low levels of domestic income and savings in Bangladesh and Nepal, the higher growth rates necessary for rapid poverty alleviation are attainable only with continued investment inflows from external sources, both official and private.

Bhutan and Maldives, however, have achieved perceptible changes in terms of both income and social indicators. For example, in Bhutan, during the period of the Eighth Five-year Plan ending in 2002, per capita income increased from $545 to $713, primary education enrolment reached 89 per cent and access to piped potable water was available to almost four fifths of rural households. In Maldives, GDP per capita amounted to $2,200 and the country is almost in the top one third of "medium human development" countries.

***Better fiscal management continued to be an important preoccupation for least developed countries in South Asia***

Although Bangladesh maintained current budget surpluses during the period 1999-2002, those surpluses were insufficient to cover development expenditure of around 6 per cent of GDP; the financing gap was bridged by external grants and by external and domestic borrowings. In 2002, the curtailment of current and development expenditure and higher revenue narrowed the deficit to 4.3 per cent of GDP from 5.5 per cent in the previous year (table II.30). A decline in the overall deficit, excluding grants, to 3.9 per cent of GDP is projected for 2003. Net domestic financing is likely to decline somewhat, while increased inflows of external grants and loans after the finalization of the Poverty Reduction Strategy Paper are expected to cover a somewhat wider future financing gap.

***Bhutan narrowed its fiscal deficit by curtailing public expenditure***

In Bhutan, the budget shortfall narrowed to 6.8 per cent of GDP in 2002 from 11.8 per cent in the previous year as a result of declining government outlays. Tax revenue, generated through enterprise profit taxes and direct taxes on goods and services, was up by a quarter; it was equivalent to almost 44 per cent of total domestic revenue, with the

## Box II.5. Afghanistan: accomplishments and challenges

While so far the successes of the new regime with the assistance of donors are encouraging, the Government still faces daunting challenges. There are signs of economic recovery: in 2002, agricultural production grew by an estimated 82 per cent compared with 2001.[a] This large increase in agricultural production was helped by relatively improved weather conditions and the increased availability of key inputs, including seeds and fertilizer. The vast majority of the population live in rural areas and are dependent on agriculture, which is therefore the key to the revival of economic activity, enhancing food security and reducing poverty.

The Government introduced a new currency in October 2002, under which 1,000 old afghani were replaced by 1 new afghani. This should make transactions simpler and, more important, set the stage for monetary control by the Central Bank. After initial depreciation, the domestic currency recovered and was trading at 45 afghanis to the United States dollar in December 2002. A stable exchange rate is the key to promoting foreign trade. In order to expand exports, the Government has decided not to levy customs duties on them. In January 2003, the United States Government made Afghanistan a beneficiary of the generalized system of preferences, eliminating tariffs on approximately 5,700 Afghan products.

Programmes aimed at eradicating polio and vaccination against measles and tuberculosis have been launched successfully. The numbers of students and teachers returning to school have exceeded expectations, with 3 million students enrolled (including 1 million girls) and another 1.5 million looking for schooling opportunities.

Despite these successes, the challenges are enormous.[b] Most people in the country live in extreme poverty; only 23 per cent have access to safe water, 12 per cent to adequate sanitation and 6 per cent to electricity. The physical infrastructure needs to be rebuilt and most of the country's roads and more than 70 per cent of the schools need repair.

Other daunting challenges and tasks include drafting a constitution, developing a sound financial and banking system and a professional national security system and holding free and fair elections. With private sector-led growth, a central plank of its reconstruction strategy, the Government has been preparing an investment law and other laws and regulations to provide a sound enabling environment.[c]

Owing to a lack of revenue sources of its own, the Government is heavily dependent on foreign aid. About $1.9 billion in foreign aid had been promised for 2002; roughly two thirds of this was made available. A large part of the aid received was spent on such necessities as food and helping refugees through aid agencies. A small part of the funds went to the Government itself. At the International Donors Conference for Afghanistan held at Oslo in December 2002, President Hamid Karzai asked the donors to focus more on long-term infrastructure projects for economic recovery. He emphasized that his country needed help in building roads and infrastructure and restoring farming, as well as creating or rebuilding government structures and services. The donors at the Conference pledged about $1.7 billion in aid for 2003.[d]

---

[a] World Bank web page "Afghanistan country update" at <http://Inweb18.worldbank.org/SAR/sa.nsf/Attachments/afghupdatetextonly/$File/afghanistanupdatetextonly.pdf>, 6 January 2003.

[b] Some of these challenges were discussed in *Survey 2002,* box II.2, pp. 44-46.

[c] William Byrd, "Afghanistan's reconstruction, regional and country context: a discussion paper", available at <http://Inweb18.worldbank.org/SAR/sa.nsf/Attachments/1031/$File/Afghanistan+Reconstruction+Paper+1031-pdf >, 6 January 2003.

[d] The exact amount of the pledges made at the Conference was difficult to determine as a number of countries' fiscal budgets have yet to be approved by their parliaments and because the countries spread out their pledges over varying periods.

*(Continued overleaf)*

*(Continued from preceding page)*

Earlier, most of the aid had been coordinated by a loose organization called the Afghanistan Support Group. The Oslo Conference dissolved the Group and turned responsibility over to a streamlined Consultative Group based at Kabul and led by the Finance Minister of Afghanistan. This shift signals that the Afghans are taking responsibility for their own future. Allaying the fears of corruption, President Karzai promised transparency, accountability and efficiency in the use of funds.

Just as the conflict in Afghanistan affected the surrounding countries negatively, post-conflict reconstruction brings opportunities for regional development and greater integration.[e] On 27 December 2002, Afghanistan, Pakistan and Turkmenistan signed an agreement to build a natural gas pipeline estimated to cost $2.5 billion. The 1,400-kilometre line is designed to link the vast gas reserves of Turkmenistan, the world's third largest, with Pakistan and eventually India. The only way to open the South Asian market to Turkmenistan's reserves is across Afghanistan, and decades of instability there kept the project on the drawing board. The ADB feasibility study of the project is expected to be completed by July 2003, after which international companies will have a chance to form a consortium to build the pipeline. With Turkmenistan profiting from a new market and Pakistan from a new source of supply, Afghanistan stands to gain from transit fees. The project will facilitate the building of roads and improve communications in the country, which will increase economic cooperation in the region and help the security situation.

About 2 million refugees have returned to Afghanistan from neighbouring and other countries. The process of repatriation of refugees from neighbouring countries has slowed because of the lack of adequate economic activities for the returnees. It is important for the international community to target its assistance to the rural areas from which the refugees originated so as to ensure that those who returned home have a reason to stay. The returning refugees, whose numbers are virtually unprecedented in international experience, may be a cost burden in the short term but constitute a resource for the longer term.

Security and peace are the keys to Afghanistan's reconstruction and development. The International Security Assistance Force has helped to improve the security situation in Kabul considerably. In the short run, expanding the mandate of the Force to include other Afghan cities still suffering from unrest could enhance security. Moreover, it is also important to accelerate the formation of a national army and police force not tied to or staffed by existing armed factions or militias. International donors are helping to create a national army and police force, but it will be years before they can really control the country. The Government of Afghanistan has decided to create a 70,000-strong national army to be trained by United States and French personnel. A national army would save Afghanistan from dependence on factional forces for its protection. Economic recovery through rebuilding the country and creating ample employment opportunities can help to achieve peace and security.

On 22 December 2002, the Transitional Administration of Afghanistan and the Governments of China, the Islamic Republic of Iran, Pakistan, Tajikistan, Turkmenistan and Uzbekistan signed the Kabul Declaration on Good-Neighbourly Relations, in which those countries pledged never to interfere in the affairs of the war-ravaged country. The Declaration also emphasizes constructive and amicable relations, mutual respect for sovereignty and territorial integrity and a commitment to refrain from action that could jeopardize peace. Its aim is to improve regional relations and help both the consolidation of peace in Afghanistan and the big task of reconstruction.

---

[e] William Byrd, op cit.

remainder coming from non-tax revenue sources, mainly surplus transfers from State-owned enterprises. The introduction of a personal income tax in 2003 was expected to improve fiscal resource mobilization. Although foreign grants decreased by 11 per cent in 2002, they were estimated to contribute almost 38 per cent to total budgetary resources. The level of current expenditure remained modest, at around 19.4 per cent of GDP in

2002; of that total, 35 per cent was on the social sector. The ratio of capital expenditure to total expenditure, estimated at 55 per cent in 2002, was about 15 per cent lower than in the previous year. Nearly two thirds of the deficit in 2002 was financed from external loans and the remainder from internal sources.

***The budget deficit increased in Maldives owing to current expenditure overruns***

As a result of expansionary fiscal policies, budget deficits in Maldives have been on a rising trend, from 1.4 per cent of GDP in 1997 to 5.3 per cent in 2001 and further to 7.6 per cent in 2002; government expenditure, especially outlays on administration and social services, exceeded targets. Meanwhile, government revenue, including foreign grants and aid, was expected to rise, from 36 per cent of GDP in 2001 to nearly 39 per cent in 2002. The main sources of government revenue were tourism tax, import duty and bank profit tax, as well as non-tax revenue generated from resort leases and public enterprises. The revenue position was adversely affected by a number of commercially non-viable State-owned enterprises, despite the implicit government subsidies and monopoly powers given to them. In that connection, the role of the Public Enterprise Monitoring and Evaluation Board was expanded in 1999 to oversee their performance and remove subsidies, such as the provision of rent-free public land. Maldives is also overhauling the government accounting system and introducing "programme-oriented" budgeting to promote cost-effective public spending. Expenditure controls and financial discipline are being strengthened to curtail persistent budget overruns and ensure better prioritization of spending programmes based on a review of public expenditure.

***Nepal has implemented a number of measures to improve revenue collection***

Social instability in Nepal has led to higher spending on security while constraining tax collections. Partly as a result, capital spending was reduced sharply to contain the budget deficit and domestic borrowings were increased to compensate for lower financing from international sources. In 2002, there was a shortfall in revenue of 1.5 per cent of GDP as a result of weaker economic performance, and additional resources were mobilized through the introduction of a scheme for the voluntary disclosure of income and special revenue measures to fund spending on security. Such spending, at 3 per cent of GDP, was estimated to be 1 per cent higher than budgeted. Meanwhile, budgeted capital spending was reduced by 3 per cent of GDP, thus affecting foreign aid disbursements and financing. As part of public sector reforms, fiscal transparency has been much improved through greater coverage, timeliness and detail in budget reporting. At the end of fiscal 2002, the World Bank and ADB, with some bilateral donors, were considering the provision of budget support to encourage spending prioritization, the decentralization of social service provision and greater government accountability in Nepal. The fiscal 2003 budget focuses on channelling public spending towards achieving tangible improvements in basic infrastructure and social services as well as improving revenue mobilization.

***Alternative means to raise government revenue must be considered***

Despite efforts to raise government revenue in the least developed countries, there are still constraints on the widening and deepening of the domestic revenue base, including a small private sector, widely scattered population and subsistence farming as the primary occupation. A higher degree of reliance on direct taxes on income and profits was expected to lead to greater equity; such taxes did not exist in a number of least developed countries in South and South-West Asia, leading to a greater reliance on border taxes. In Maldives, there are no direct taxes, except for a bank profits tax, and no general consumption tax. Indirect taxes, such as import tariffs and a hotel bed tax of $6 per night levied on foreign tourists, accounted for 92 per cent of total government tax revenue in 2000. Bhutan also had no income tax until its introduction in 2003, and its impact on revenue-raising is expected to be modest. Given the highly inelastic tax base in Bhutan, most of the current revenue comes from profits from public enterprises and service fees from government agencies, while land-lease payments for tourist resorts surpassed the tourist bed tax in 1998 to become the second-largest single source of revenue after tariffs in Maldives. Although Nepal has a relatively efficient tax system based on low income tax rates and VAT, increased spending on security has contributed to the current fiscal deficit and higher domestic borrowing. The country was expected to raise revenue by 0.25 per cent of GDP, to reach 11.6 per cent of GDP, in 2003 through audits of large taxpayers and improved customs valuation.

***The essential role played by the private sector in achieving sustained economic growth has been recognized in the South and South-West Asian least developed countries***

The private sector in most of the least developed countries of the subregion faces a number of severe constraints, including a shortage of skilled labour, inadequate managerial and entrepreneurial capacity, high transport costs, limited credit facilities and a small domestic market with limited access to export markets. Countries have therefore focused on the provision of tax incentives, policy liberalization, human resources development and the creation of an enabling infrastructure. A number of legal instruments, such as the amended Companies Act, the Sales Tax, Customs and Excise Act, the Negotiable Instruments Act and the Bankruptcy Act were enacted in Bhutan to promote an appropriate enabling policy environment. In addition, several tax holiday schemes were introduced in July 2002 to encourage the establishment of new industries and business houses. In Maldives, the number of licensed shops and importing agencies has been increased in order to improve competition. Infrastructure limitations in ports, communications and utilities have constituted a bottleneck to business activities. These sectors are traditionally dominated by public sector entities and their restructuring requires the cooperation of all stakeholders. Transition to regulated but market-based pricing of gas and electricity could ease supply constraints by attracting additional investments and restoring the financial health of the service providers.

***The privatization of State-owned enterprises has increasingly been seen as a necessary step***

Recognizing the need to avoid engagement in manufacturing or commercial activities as part of its public investment strategies, Bangladesh closed a large publicly owned enterprise. In Bhutan, the privatization of public enterprises was reported as being nearly complete, with majority ownership and management of public sector enterprises transferred to the private sector. Although the privatization of State-owned enterprises was launched in Maldives in 1999, concerns about the anti-competitive effects of privatized firms in the small domestic market have impeded its progress. Efforts have instead been focused on improving the efficiency of State-owned enterprises through greater "commercialization" and the introduction of better management practices and performance monitoring. Seven State-owned enterprises have been opened to minority private participation, while greater public sector efficiency is also to be achieved by restricting the size of the public sector and limiting its role to the delivery of key services. In Nepal, restructuring and privatization efforts continued to be constrained by the fiscal liabilities of the 7 financial and 36 non-financial public enterprises, such as arrears in payments to employees and to banks and suppliers.

***An effective financial sector, especially in underserved markets, is essential to promote the private sector***

The least developed countries of South Asia have also recognized the need for better financial intermediation as a prerequisite to promoting greater participation and competitiveness in the private sector. Significant portions of the economically active population, particularly in rural areas, remain underserved in many least developed countries, as financial institutions focus attention on commercial and industrial activities in urban centres. In Bangladesh, only 12 per cent of domestic credit was directed to the agricultural sector, which contributed a quarter of GDP in 2002. In contrast, the term loan component alone comprised 17.6 per cent of domestic credit to the industrial sector, which contributes approximately the same share to GDP. Small-scale enterprises, which could create considerable employment and outputs in Bangladesh, received little credit from either microcredit organizations or formal financial institutions. Since banks are the major providers of finance, the high cost of bank credit has an adverse impact on the competitiveness of the private sector. Although interest rates on bank credit decreased marginally in 2002, to approximately 13.2 per cent, the real interest associated with bank borrowing is high, given the low level of inflation.

In Bhutan, development of the financial sector has been impeded by limitations on private sector development, inadequate legal and institutional infrastructure, and insufficient debt and capital markets and human resources development. However, improvements in the process of financial intermediation are expected with the establishment of specialized non-bank financial institutions to provide such services as leasing, housing finance and insurance, and policy efforts to ensure greater openness of the financial sector to foreign participation.

# South-East Asia

## A. Developing countries in the subregion

### *Subregional overview and prospects*

***Economic recovery supported by both domestic and external demand***

After the global slowdown that affected most countries in the subregion in 2001, economic growth recovered in South-East Asia in 2002, although the degree to which it was sustained through the year varied between countries (figure II.26). In Thailand and Malaysia, for example, economic activities were helped by rising consumer expenditure, accommodative fiscal and monetary policies, and a recovery in exports, mainly of electronics and electrical goods and primary commodities. In both countries, investment was also lifted to some extent in the second half of 2002. Strong domestic and external demand was also responsible for the continued vigorous growth in Viet Nam, where investment, in particular, increased strongly. However, the collapse of investment in Indonesia and reduced investment in the Philippines was a matter of concern, while weakened consumer spending and export demand offset the early gains in Singapore's growth somewhat. The return of global uncertainty, together with a slowdown in electronics, in the second half of 2002 added to doubts about future growth performance. The situation of the least developed countries of the subregion, Cambodia, the Lao People's Democratic Republic and Myanmar, is discussed later in this section.

**Figure II.26. Rates of GDP growth in selected South-East Asian economies, 1999-2002**

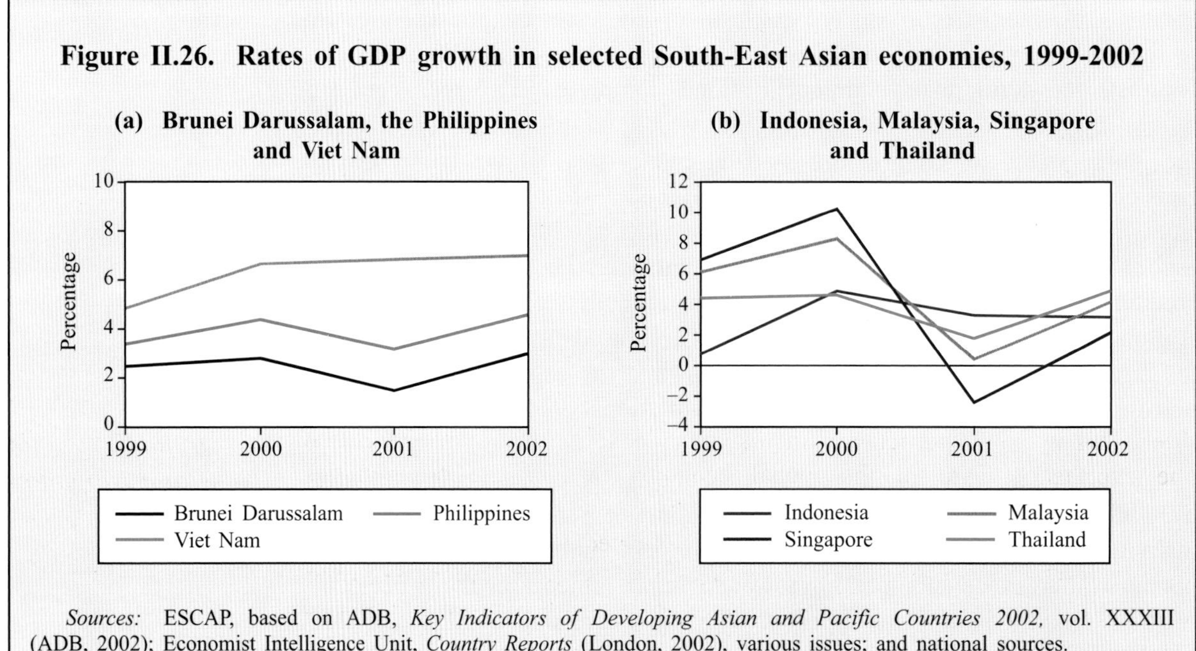


*Sources:* ESCAP, based on ADB, *Key Indicators of Developing Asian and Pacific Countries 2002,* vol. XXXIII (ADB, 2002); Economist Intelligence Unit, *Country Reports* (London, 2002), various issues; and national sources.

*Note:* Data for 2002 are estimates.

***The outlook for 2003 is less certain***

The outlook for economic growth in the subregion in the coming year depends on the prospective strength of both external and domestic demand. Global economic conditions suggest that export demand is likely to be subdued, at least until the second half of 2003, and competition is intensifying. Consumer expenditure is likely to remain strong in 2003 as long as incomes and interest rates hold steady, but is unlikely to grow as fast as in 2002, particularly as consumer debt levels are now relatively high. Firm commodity prices at least into 2003 will support rural incomes, and accommodative monetary policy can be expected to continue. However, the need for fiscal consolidation may dampen prospects for greater fiscal stimulus to offset weakness in demand. Some of the increase in private investment in 2002 reflected the revival of the property sector; how durable the increase is remains to be seen, given the relatively high margin of unutilized capacity and the weakness of FDI flows.

***Faster growth forecast in Malaysia and Thailand***

For 2003, Malaysia expects an increase in GDP growth to 6-6.5 per cent but the weakening global outlook and slowing exports may be a constraining factor. However, the planned expansion of oil palm acreage will lead to higher agricultural growth, supported by firm commodity prices. Although the number of applications for new investment from foreign investors increased in 2002, that of approvals of both foreign direct and domestic investment fell sharply; however, the Government has indicated that it is ready to provide additional pump-priming to sustain the growth momentum, notwithstanding its desire to initiate fiscal consolidation.

In Thailand, the Government has indicated that fiscal policy will be conditioned by the need to cap public debt at 55 per cent of GDP. Private consumption, while remaining strong, is unlikely to expand as rapidly in 2003 as previously, particularly as consumers are coping with higher levels of personal debt following major purchases of housing and vehicles in the current year. In addition, regulations on the issuance of credit cards have again been tightened after having been relaxed in 2002. However, the fiscal incentives that helped to revive the property sector in 2002 are to be extended for another year and additional incentives given for the construction of low-cost housing. The official forecast for GDP growth in 2003 is in the range of 3.5-4.5 per cent.

***The external outlook for Viet Nam and Singapore in 2003 is expected to be positive***

The Government expects the external environment to be better for Viet Nam in 2003, particularly in the second half of the year, along with the expected revival of the global economy and as the opportunities presented by the trade agreement reached with the United States in 2001 are exploited more fully. GDP growth is projected to accelerate to 7.5 per cent in 2003 owing to improved performance from all sectors. The export rebound expected in the second half of the year will also benefit Singapore, but private consumption expenditure is likely to remain subdued in 2003 until labour market conditions improve. Given the weakening of business confidence reported in the fourth quarter of 2002, a strong revival in private investment is still some way off. Reflecting these uncertainties, the Government expects GDP growth in 2003 to be around 2-5 per cent.

***The Philippines and Indonesia have revised their growth forecasts downwards***

Business confidence also turned down towards the end of 2002 in the Philippines, indicating that an early uplift in investment spending was not likely. Private consumption may remain subdued as rural incomes are likely to remain low, while public spending is constrained by the need to contain the burgeoning fiscal deficit. The Philippine Government's forecast range for GDP in 2003 was 5-5.5 per cent before the recent slowdown, but was revised marginally downwards to 4.2-5.2 per cent.

The Government of Indonesia also had to revise its forecast downwards for 2003, from 5 to 4-4.5 per cent, following the Bali bombing, but much depends on global developments as well as the state of consumer and business confidence. Although tourism employs around 10 million people in Indonesia, it accounts for a relatively small share of GDP and earns less in foreign exchange than such sectors as oil, gas and textiles. The Government announced a stimulus package of Rp 10.63 trillion after the bombing, with support from IMF and the Consultative Group for Indonesia. Donors have also pledged support for the post-conflict reconstruction of Aceh (box II.6). The agricultural sector benefits from firm commodity prices but the outlook for this sector is conditioned by the possibility of a drought following a mild El Niño event.

## Box II.6. Post-conflict reconstruction in Aceh

On 9 December 2002, following two years of negotiations, the Government of Indonesia and the Free Aceh Movement signed a framework agreement in Geneva on the cessation of hostilities in the troubled oil-rich province on the island of Sumatra. The agreement, which was facilitated by the Henri Dunant Centre for Humanitarian Dialogue with an advisory role played by a committee of three "wise men",[a] brought the current rebellion, which began in 1976 and in which many thousands have lost their lives, to an end. Under the terms of the agreement, a Joint Security Committee comprising representatives of both sides as well as officials from the Philippines and Thailand will formulate the process for implementing the agreement, oversee the security situation with the assistance of international monitors and define the process of demilitarization. The Committee will also designate "peace zones" that will become the focus of initial humanitarian, reconstruction and rehabilitation efforts if peace is established successfully. The Government, which has committed itself to granting Aceh a full measure of autonomy, is to engage in an all-inclusive dialogue within the province, which will be supported by the Free Aceh Movement, with a view to holding full and fair elections in 2004.

---

[a] The committee was made up of former United States Marine Corps General Anthony Zinni, the former Ambassador of Yugoslavia to Indonesia, H.E. Mr. Budamir Loncar, and H.E. Dr. Surin Pitsuwan, former Minister for Foreign Affairs of Thailand.

The conflict in Aceh has long historical antecedents and several issues, such as the Movement's demand for independence and finding the best method to deal with the human rights abuses committed by both sides, remain to be resolved. Although the peace agreement has drastically reduced the level of violence, sporadic fighting between soldiers and rebels continues. However, the cautious optimism with which the agreement was greeted and the belief that, unlike its predecessors, it is likely to work derive from some unique features: (a) it is the first time that a sovereign Government has negotiated with a separatist movement under the auspices of an international non-governmental organization; (b) international monitors will have an important role to play in the implementation process; and (c) the donor community has pledged support for the agreement. In fact, in anticipation of the signing of the agreement, the European Union, Japan, the United States of America and the World Bank co-sponsored the Preparatory Conference on Peace and Reconstruction in Aceh, held at Tokyo in December 2002, at which donors met representatives of both sides to see how best they could help. Five priority areas for donors were agreed in Tokyo: support to the peace process; short-term humanitarian assistance; community reconstruction; governance and public planning; and restoration of the social and physical infrastructure.

As a follow-up to the Conference, the four Co-chairman visited Aceh early in January 2003 to meet representatives of local government and the people of Aceh. Donors have agreed on a coordinated approach to support, focusing on quick-impact, community-based programmes that affect people's welfare directly and so lessen conflict. A participatory planning process involving all segments of society in Aceh, as well as major changes in the quality of governance, to reduce corruption, increase transparency and improve the administration of justice, were also identified as being necessary to restore confidence in development.

As outlined in a World Bank document[b] presented to the Consultative Group Meeting on Indonesia, held on 21 and 22 January 2003, the process of recovery and development in Aceh has short-, medium- and long-term aspects. The focus in the short term has to be on supporting the peace process and providing humanitarian assistance in the conflict areas of the province, where poverty rates are now high. Large numbers of refugees remain to be resettled (both those displaced within Aceh and those, generally of Javanese origin, who have moved out of the province). The local administration has identified the dominant social problem that it faces as being the welfare of the estimated 47,000 widows and 50,000 orphans left as a result of the conflict. Education, in particular, has suffered as many schools were burnt. Many houses that were destroyed or damaged in the conflict also have to be replaced or rehabilitated.

In the medium term, the focus has to shift to the delivery of social services throughout the province of Aceh and rebuilding the private sector through restoration of the investment climate. Although poverty rates in Aceh, with the exception of the conflict areas, are below the national average, the conflict disrupted both the quality and the coverage of public services, which now need to be restored. To improve the business climate, infrastructure will have to be repaired and security improved. Aceh is largely an agricultural province, and plantation and estate crop and forestry activities cannot be undertaken without peace and security and a functioning transport system. Similarly, multinational corporations active in the oil and gas sector, as well as in other resource-based operations, will need to see stability in the business environment before contemplating a return to the province. Power shortages, which were a problem even before the conflict, have become acute as a result of it. Governance issues, including corruption, remain constraints on investment. Small and medium-sized businesses will also need adequate credit and technical assistance to enable them to recommence or initiate activities.

Finally, in the long term, many of the issues facing the province regarding its economic and social development are similar to those faced by the rest of Indonesia. However, Aceh is also in a position to attempt to ensure that its development is sustainable by making judicious use of the high share it receives of the oil and gas revenues generated by its endowments, as these are likely to be depleted within the next 10 years.

---

[b] "Promoting peaceful development in Aceh", available at <http://lnweb18.worldbank.org/eap/eap.nsf/Attachments/012103-12CGI-Aceh/$File/CGI_Acehupdate.pdf>, 4 February 2003.

**Figure II.27. Inflation in selected South-East Asian economies, 1999-2002[a]**

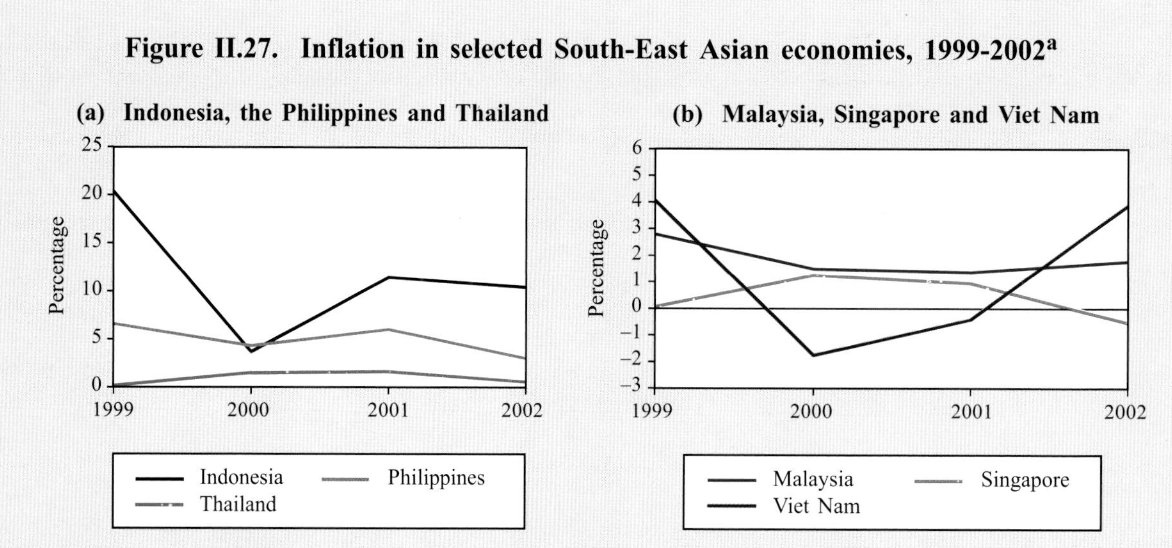


*Sources:* ESCAP, based on ADB, *Key Indicators of Developing Asian and Pacific Countries 2002,* vol. XXXIII (ADB, 2002) and *Asian Development Outlook 2002 Update* (ADB, 2002); IMF, *International Financial Statistics,* vol. LV, No. 11 (November 2002); Economist Intelligence Unit, *Country Reports* (London, 2002), various issues; and national sources.

*Note:* Data for 2002 are estimates.

[a] Changes in the consumer price index.

***Inflation slowed as demand and cost pressures were generally absent***

With the exception of Viet Nam and, to some extent, Malaysia, inflationary pressures moderated noticeably in South-East Asia in 2002 as demand pressures were not excessive and cost pressures remained manageable, the latter in part the result of currency appreciation (figure II.27). However, inflation remained in double digits in Indonesia. Although Singapore was the only country to record a small fall in prices, deflationary pressures were felt in other countries, such as Thailand, during parts of the year. Increases in administered prices, for fuel, utilities, transport and telephone charges, were responsible for some increases in inflation during the year in some countries, as were higher food prices following natural disasters. In the Philippines, concerted attempts were made to monitor and check price increases, including through liberalizing imports of food items and reducing administered prices for electricity. By and large, central banks pursued accommodative monetary policies with interest rates declining in most countries, reaching particularly low levels in Singapore and Thailand, as liquidity remained ample and loan demand generally weak.

Merchandise export earnings had declined in most countries in the subregion in 2001 owing to reduced demand in major export markets, such as the United States, the EU and Japan, as well as within the region itself. By contrast, exports returned to positive growth in some countries

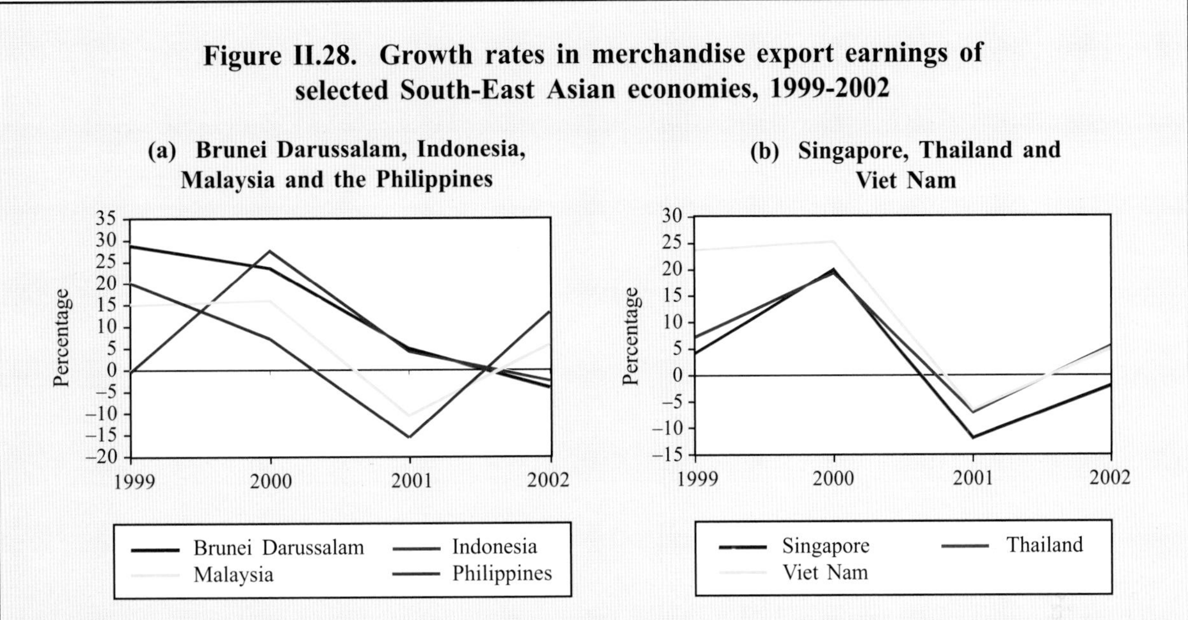


**Figure II.28. Growth rates in merchandise export earnings of selected South-East Asian economies, 1999-2002**

*Sources:* IMF, *Direction of Trade Statistics* (CD-ROM), January 2003; National Economic and Social Development Board of Thailand web site <http://www.nesdb.go.th>, 13 January 2003; and Bank Negara Malaysia web site <http://www.bnm.gov.my>, 27 February 2003.

*Note:* Figure for 2002 for Malaysia is for the whole year and for Thailand is a projection for the whole year; data for other countries refer to January-August.

***Merchandise exports made a modest recovery, while demand from traditional markets remained weak***

of South-East Asia in 2002, although the extent of the increase was modest in comparison with the strong increase recorded in 2000 (figure II.28). There were higher exports of primary commodities, from the energy and agricultural sectors in particular, as well as manufactured goods, such as electronics and electrical products and chemicals. Within the subregion, some countries with more favourable trade access, particularly to the United States, expanded garment and footwear exports, while others found it difficult to withstand competition in third markets from lower-cost producers such as China. Exports of services were mixed; tourism picked up in some countries at the expense of others after the shock of the Bali bombing. Traditional export markets remained soft after an initial revival in the first half of the year but demand from within the East Asian region picked up significantly, for both goods and services.

The performance of merchandise imports reflected a similar pattern and strength of economic growth in the different countries of the subregion (figure II.29). Increased imports of intermediate goods, together with consumer and capital goods in some cases, boosted imports in most countries. However, the continuing weakness in manufacturing saw imports contract in Singapore in 2002, as in 2001, and Indonesia, particularly sharply in the latter.

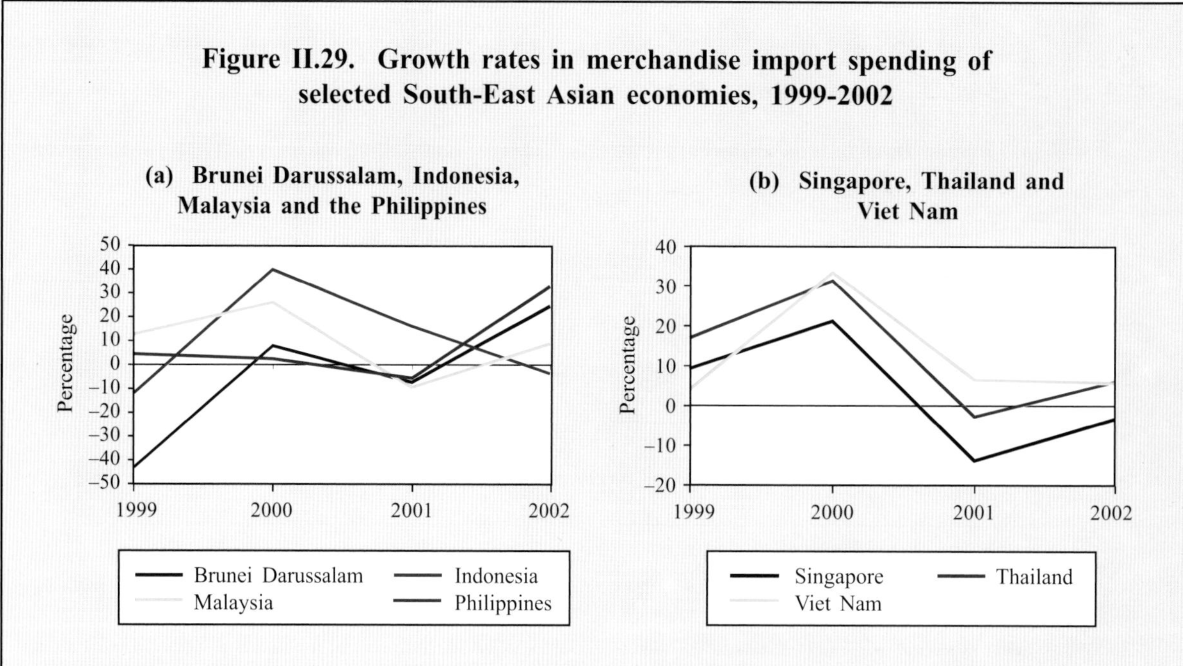


**Figure II.29. Growth rates in merchandise import spending of selected South-East Asian economies, 1999-2002**

*Sources:* IMF, *Direction of Trade Statistics* (CD-ROM), January 2003; National Economic and Social Development Board of Thailand web site <http://www.nesdb.go.th>, 13 January 2003; and Bank Negara Malaysia web site <http://www.bnm.gov.my>, 27 February 2003.

*Note:* Figure for 2002 for Malaysia is for the whole year and for Thailand is a projection for the whole year; data for other countries refer to January-August.

***The slowdown in FDI is a worrying development for the subregion***

A worrying feature of the capital account in most parts of the subregion in 2002 was the slowdown in FDI. Portfolio investment was more mixed, with some countries attracting significantly higher flows than in 2001. Official foreign exchange reserves increased in all countries, even though foreign debt was higher in several countries with external borrowing, Thailand being the notable exception. International confidence in the countries of South-East Asia has generally improved, although it remains low in Indonesia and the Philippines. The exchange rate performance was more variable (figure II.30). Malaysia and Brunei Darussalam maintain currency pegs, the former against the United States dollar and the latter against the Singapore dollar. Other countries in the subregion permitted exchange rates to move with market conditions. Most currencies appreciated against the United States dollar, although the Philippine peso and Vietnamese dong weakened.

Finally, the major policy issues confronting Governments in the subregion in 2002 were not radically different from those faced in previous years. Social concerns such as unemployment and the incidence of poverty continue to be at the top of the policy agenda. The recent lack

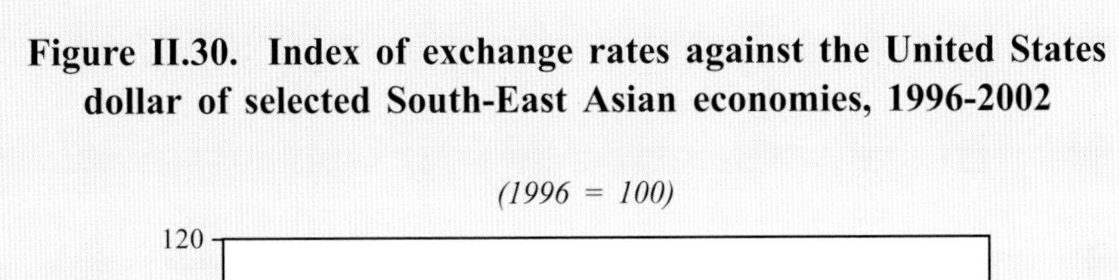

**Figure II.30. Index of exchange rates against the United States dollar of selected South-East Asian economies, 1996-2002**

*(1996 = 100)*

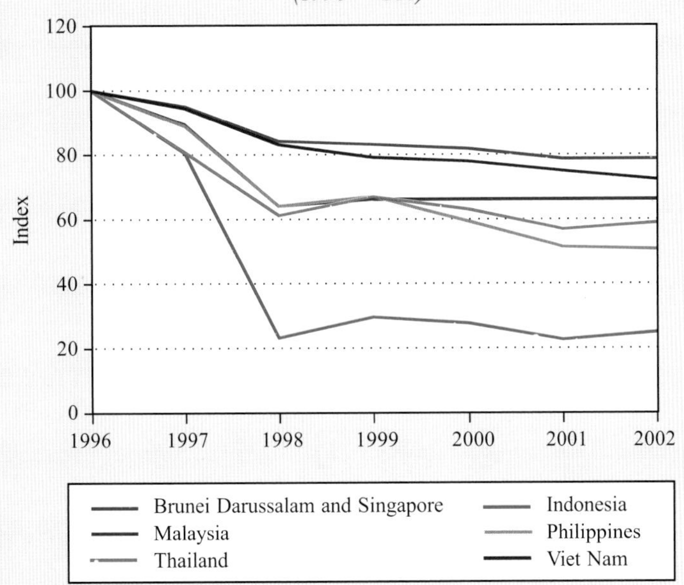


*Sources:* IMF, *International Financial Statistics,* vol. LV, No. 12 (December 2002); *Far Eastern Economic Review,* various issues; and ADB, *Key Indicators of Developing Asian and Pacific Countries 2002,* vol. XXXIII (ADB, 2002).

*Notes:* Data for 2002 are estimates. The currency of Brunei Darussalam is set at par with the Singapore dollar.

of investment in the subregion has focused attention on matters relating to the medium-term sustainability of growth and long-term competitiveness. Issues such as fiscal consolidation and financial restructuring, which have been on the agenda since the 1997-1998 financial crisis, have acquired greater urgency in some countries as a result of the relatively weaker economic performance in 2001-2002.

***Medium-term sustainability of growth and competitiveness have joined unemployment and poverty alleviation on the policy agenda***

## *GDP growth performance*

The economy of Thailand rebounded very strongly in 2002 from the low 1.8 per cent GDP growth of 2001, with growth accelerating in each quarter to reach 4.9 per cent for the full year, compared with the annual average of 4.5 per cent in 1999-2000 (table II.31). Private consumption expenditure, a major factor in this expansion, was underpinned by fiscal stimulus and easy monetary conditions, while rising farm incomes reflected stronger world prices for rubber, cassava and oil palm. Malaysia

***Expansionary policies supported consumption in Thailand and Malaysia as exports rebounded and investment revived***

**Table II.31. Selected South-East Asian economies: growth rates, 1999-2002**

*(Percentage)*

| | | Rates of growth | | | |
|---|---|---|---|---|---|
| | | *Gross domestic product* | *Agriculture* | *Industry* | *Services* |
| Brunei Darussalam | 1999 | 2.5 | –0.1 | 3.2 | 1.7 |
| | 2000 | 2.8 | .. | .. | .. |
| | 2001 | 1.5 | .. | .. | .. |
| | 2002 | 3.0 | .. | .. | .. |
| Indonesia | 1999 | 0.8 | 2.2 | 2.0 | –1.0 |
| | 2000 | 4.9 | 1.7 | 6.2 | 2.2 |
| | 2001 | 3.3 | 0.6 | 4.3 | 2.0 |
| | 2002 | 3.2 | 3.7 | 3.3 | 1.7 |
| Malaysia | 1999 | 6.1 | 0.5 | 8.8 | 4.9 |
| | 2000 | 8.3 | 2.0 | 14.4 | 3.8 |
| | 2001 | 0.4 | 1.8 | –3.2 | 5.7 |
| | 2002 | 4.2 | 0.3 | 4.0 | 4.5 |
| Philippines | 1999 | 3.4 | 6.5 | 0.9 | 4.0 |
| | 2000 | 4.4 | 3.4 | 4.9 | 4.4 |
| | 2001 | 3.2 | 3.7 | 1.3 | 4.4 |
| | 2002 | 4.6 | 3.5 | 4.1 | 5.4 |
| Singapore | 1999 | 6.9 | –1.1[a] | 7.1 | 6.8 |
| | 2000 | 10.3 | –5.7[a] | 10.8 | 10.0 |
| | 2001 | –2.4 | –4.9[a] | –9.2 | 2.0 |
| | 2002 | 2.2 | –1.5[a, b] | 4.0 | 1.5 |
| Thailand | 1999 | 4.4 | 2.1 | 9.6 | 0.3 |
| | 2000 | 4.6 | 4.8 | 5.2 | 4.0 |
| | 2001 | 1.8 | 3.3 | 1.3 | 2.3 |
| | 2002 | 4.9 | 4.4 | 3.3 | 6.6 |
| Viet Nam | 1999 | 4.9 | 5.2 | 7.9 | 2.3 |
| | 2000 | 6.7 | 4.0 | 9.8 | 5.6 |
| | 2001 | 6.8 | 2.7 | 10.4 | 6.1 |
| | 2002 | 7.0 | 5.0 | 14.4 | 6.2 |

*Sources:* ESCAP, based on ADB, *Key Indicators of Developing Asian and Pacific Countries 2002,* vol. XXXIII (ADB, 2002) and *Asian Development Outlook 2002 Update* (ADB, 2002); Economist Intelligence Unit, *Country Forecasts* (London, 2002), various issues; and national sources.

*Notes:* Data for 2002 are estimates. Industry comprises mining and quarrying; manufacturing; electricity, gas and power; and construction.

[a] Including quarrying.
[b] Estimate.

also benefited from strong domestic demand and rising exports, principally of semiconductors and crude palm oil, in 2002. However, growth eased as export demand became more muted towards the second half of the year. GDP growth at 4.2 per cent in 2002 was nevertheless well up on the out-turn of 0.4 per cent in 2001.

**Table II.32. Selected South-East Asian economies: ratios of gross domestic savings and investment to GDP, 1999-2002**

*(Percentage)*

| | *1999* | *2000* | *2001* | *2002* |
|---|---|---|---|---|
| **Savings as a percentage of GDP** | | | | |
| Indonesia | .. | 29.5 | 28.0 | 23.0 |
| Malaysia | 47.3 | 46.7 | 42.5 | 41.8 |
| Philippines | 14.3 | 16.1 | 16.8 | 17.4 |
| Singapore | 48.8 | 49.3 | 45.8 | 44.5 |
| Thailand | 32.9 | 32.9 | 30.0 | 28.7 |
| Viet Nam | 24.6 | 27.0 | 29.0 | 28.7 |
| **Investment as a percentage of GDP** | | | | |
| Indonesia | .. | 29.3 | 24.7 | 18.5 |
| Malaysia | 22.3 | 26.8 | 24.0 | 25.0 |
| Philippines | 18.8 | 18.4 | 17.6 | 17.8 |
| Singapore | 31.9 | 31.6 | 24.3 | 23.6 |
| Thailand | 20.5 | 22.7 | 24.0 | 24.2 |
| Viet Nam | 27.6 | 29.5 | 31.9 | 33.0 |

*Sources:* ESCAP, based on ADB, *Key Indicators of Developing Asian and Pacific Countries 2002,* vol. XXXIII (ADB, 2002) and *Asian Development Outlook 2002* (Oxford University Press, 2002); and national sources.

*Note:* Data for 2002 are estimates.

In both countries, consumer credit to purchase houses and motor vehicles expanded strongly as interest rates remained low and savings as a percentage of GDP continued to decline (table II.32). Improved consumer and business confidence were also responsible for the increasing momentum of private investment in Thailand, particularly in residential and commercial construction, as the effects of tax incentives and low interest rates were felt. An encouraging sign was the sharp increase in investment in machinery in the third quarter of 2002. In Malaysia, the growth rate in investment became positive in the third quarter of 2002, after declining from the middle of 2001, and accelerated strongly in the fourth. The investment-to-GDP ratio increased to 25 per cent in 2002 from 24 per cent in 2001. Inventory accumulation also increased in both countries.

***Thailand is a good case study of economic diversification***

In terms of production, Thailand is an illustration of the advantages of a diversified economy. Although paddy output was affected by drought in the second quarter and widespread flooding in the third, agricultural growth was driven by the higher production of sugar cane and rubber, as well as livestock and fisheries (despite the negative effects on prawn cultivation of health concerns in major export markets). In manufacturing, the output volumes of construction materials, electronics and electrical products and vehicles expanded very strongly. Average capacity utilization in all sectors improved to around 59 per cent in 2002 from 53 per cent in 2001. Mining output was also significantly higher as crude oil production was stepped up to meet increased domestic demand and more limestone was quarried for the cement industry. Growth in services was also very strong, particularly in financial intermediation and activities related to property. Tourism was affected somewhat following the Bali bombing but there were signs of a strong recovery towards the end of the year.

***Manufacturing expanded strongly in Malaysia***

Malaysian growth was driven primarily by manufacturing and services in the first half of 2002, but became more broadly based later in the year as the strong revival in commodity prices stimulated agricultural production in the second half of the year. Industrial output went up by 4 per cent in 2002, reversing a decline of 3.2 per cent in 2001, as value added in mining increased in line with higher oil and gas prices. There was also strong expansion in manufacturing activities, particularly electronics, off-estate processing and chemicals and chemical products. Growth in the construction sector declined somewhat following the mid-year expulsion of illegal migrant workers, which led to labour shortages. Growth in services at an annual rate of 5.7 per cent had been crucial in sustaining the rise in GDP in 2001, but it slowed to 4.5 per cent during 2002, owing to a sharp decline in intermediate services such as transport and financial services.

***Investment from new businesses is proving vital to Viet Nam***

Viet Nam was the only economy in the subregion with unabated growth in 2001, largely due to strong domestic demand. The country improved on its performance in 2002 as GDP went up by 7 per cent. Strong expansion in domestic demand was again the principal driver of growth, with retail sales returning to levels prevailing before the 1997-1998 crisis. Investment, particularly in the private sector, also boomed and was equivalent to one third of GDP in 2002, one full percentage point higher than the 2001 ratio (table II.32). The number of new businesses established in 2002 increased 17 per cent to 20,000 and investment by new SMEs in the formal economy was expected to reach $2.7 billion in 2002.

As in previous years, much of the impetus for growth in Viet Nam in 2002 came from the industrial sector, where output was 14.4 per cent higher in response to stronger demand for consumption-related products such as vehicles, particularly motorcycles, television sets, ceramic tiles and other building materials. Garment production also boomed as a result of the current quota-free access to the United States market. The private and foreign-invested sectors led growth, while expansion in the State sector was more modest. Drought in the Central Highlands, combined with lower world prices, resulted in decreased coffee production and severe flooding in the South affected the rice output. Nevertheless, growth in the agricultural sector improved to 5 per cent in 2002 owing to, among other things, higher production of black pepper and cassava. As in Thailand, the fisheries output (shrimp in particular) was affected by health concerns in export markets as well as a trade dispute with the United States regarding the alleged dumping of catfish. The service sector grew at a robust 6.2 per cent in 2002; inward tourism boomed, particularly in the last quarter as tourists looked for alternatives to destinations where the perceived terrorism risks were higher.

***The strong rebound in economic growth and exports proved to be short-lived in Singapore***

The severe economic contraction that began in Singapore in 2001 appeared to have bottomed out in the first half of 2002 following a spurt in global economic activity that stimulated export demand, including in the IT sector. However, the economic rebound was short-lived, and a W-shaped (rather than V-shaped) recovery appeared likely with GDP growth at 2.2 per cent in 2002. While much of the early recovery was driven by increased external demand, domestic consumption expenditure was also sustained by the effects of two fiscal stimulus packages adopted by the Government in 2001 (totalling 8.5 per cent of GDP), together with an expansionary budget for 2002 and monetary easing. However, private consumption contracted in the second half of 2002 as job insecurity worsened with continuing retrenchments, and the decline in private investment resumed as export demand softened and excess capacity persisted.

Recovery in Singapore in the first half of 2002 was strongly led by manufacturing, particularly electronics and chemicals, mainly pharmaceuticals, as the production of high value added intermediaries surged and new production facilities came on-stream. However, those trends were reversed later in the year and the lower production of pharmaceuticals accounted for most of the contraction in manufacturing output. Construction had been on a decline since the third quarter of 2001; it contracted even more sharply in 2002. Growth slowed in the service sector but was by and large similar to the pattern recorded in 2001 as improved entrepôt trade and transport and communications compensated somewhat for a slower expansion in retail sales, tourism and financial services.

***Strong private consumption compensated for investment weakness and restrained public spending in the Philippines***

The Philippines managed to sustain GDP growth at a healthy rate of 3.2 per cent in the face of the global slowdown in 2001, and saw this accelerate to 4.6 per cent in 2002. In terms of demand, the overall resilience of the Philippine economy was due largely to sustained personal consumption expenditure and increased government expenditure in the second half of 2002. However, capital formation was very weak; inventories in particular were run down noticeably during the year.

GDP expansion in the first half of the year was initially led by the strong performance of agriculture but the declining production of coconut, rice and corn led to a subsequent slowdown in that sector. Meanwhile, a rebound in export demand, along with sustained consumer spending, saw industry, particularly manufacturing, and services taking up the slack and growing strongly. A higher level of industrial activity was maintained by substantial increases in mining and quarrying, as the output of gas, copper and gold was stepped up, and in the demand for utilities. Within the manufacturing sector, food manufacturing and electrical machinery output faltered. The service sector witnessed strong expansion in the transport, communications and storage subsectors.

***Improved macroeconomic stability did not herald faster growth in Indonesia***

Economic growth in Indonesia slowed slightly to 3.2 per cent in 2002. Consumer sentiment improved with growing political and economic stability and this, together with rapid increases in formal sector wages and consumer credit, served to fuel expenditure growth. The impression is that the Bali bombing has not deterred consumers so far, but it may be too early for a full evaluation of the impact of that event. Capital investment, however, remained weak and this was a major reason why economic growth did not take off despite the much-improved macroeconomic stability. The investment ratio declined to 18.5 per cent of GDP in 2002 from almost a quarter in 2001. Investment approvals were also down, thus clouding the prospects for a major turnaround in the near future. Capacity utilization in manufacturing was reported to be averaging 60 per cent in the first half of 2002, down from 70 per cent in the same period in 2001. Inventories were also run down in 2001-2002, with a dampening effect on growth.

***The strengthening of commodity prices benefited the Indonesian economy, among others***

On the supply side, agriculture rebounded in Indonesia in 2002 despite extensive flooding in the first two months of the year. The country benefited from improved commodity prices during the year, in particular for crude palm oil, wood pulp and cocoa. In a bid to assist domestic rice farmers, the Government announced a 15 per cent increase in the floor price of unhusked rice and the imposition of a 75 per cent import tariff, but unresolved issues concerning land ownership hindered agricultural development. Forest fires and the consequent haze continued in 2002 as the use of slash-and-burn techniques to clear land, particularly by large corporations, eluded control. Industrial growth slowed in the first half of 2002, with a marked decline in manufacturing. The downturn in investment also slowed construction activities. Mining was affected by uncertainty following decentralization, as local governments sought to play a more prominent role. More generally, the outputs of oil and gas, leather and textiles and wood and wood products were on the decline, although exports to China were sharply up. Sales of automobiles, boosted by low interest rates, had also started falling by mid-year, although the demand for motorcycles remained strong.

***Revenues from the energy sector continue to sustain the economy of Brunei Darussalam***

Brunei Darussalam's economy continues to depend heavily on revenue from the oil and gas sector, and the return of higher energy prices coincided with the higher growth of 3 per cent recorded in 2002. Consumer spending was the main domestic driver of growth, particularly as the Government appears to have encountered some capacity constraints in implementing its long- and short-term fiscal stimulus measures.

A reduction in automotive tariffs to a flat 20 per cent (from 20 to 200 per cent) in November 2001 was partly responsible for the surge in consumer expenditure in 2002, along with low interest rates and easy credit.

In 2001, the contraction in construction, brought about in part by fiscal stringency, contributed to weaker economic growth, but the implementation of measures to stimulate the economy in 2002 led to a revival of this sector, with important multiplier effects on the rest of the economy. The performance of the agricultural sector was mixed, while output in the industrial sector, particularly manufacturing, appeared to have decreased after an initial surge in the production of garments was subsequently dampened by weaker export demand.

Finally, Timor-Leste is facing enormous challenges in nation building with the economy stagnating in 2002 after GDP growth averaging 16 per cent annually over 2000-2001 (see box II.7).

### *Inflation*

***Inflationary pressures were missing in most countries of South-East Asia, with the exception of administered price changes and some weather-related increases in food prices***

The slight acceleration in inflation in Malaysia in 2002, to 1.8 per cent from 1.4 per cent in 2001 (table II.33), was attributable to one-off changes in administered prices for transport and communications, particularly telephone charges. Monetary policy was largely accommodative, as the Central Bank attempted to keep interest rates stable in the face of increased consumer expenditure and the fiscal stimulus, and liquidity was ample. However, demand pressures on prices remained weak.

In Viet Nam, low inventories of rice pushed food prices up in 2002, as flooding increased price pressures, and by November they were approximately 8 per cent higher than in 2001. Inflation increased to 3.9 per cent in 2002 as nearly half of the consumption weight in the calculation of the consumer price index is given to food items. Higher prices of building materials also contributed to the more rapid rate of inflation. Meanwhile, inflation is projected to be at the level of 5 per cent in 2003 as depreciation of the dong, which slowed in 2002, picks up again. The growth of credit in the economy fell sharply from 38 per cent at the end of 2000 to 21.5 per cent at the end of 2001; the target for 2002 was 20.5 per cent. The broad money supply (M2) also expanded more slowly, from 35.4 per cent in 2000 to an estimated 14.6 per cent in the first nine months of 2002. The State Bank of Viet Nam lifted caps on lending rates for dong-denominated loans from June 2002, thus giving commercial banks more freedom to manage interest rate spreads and respond to the needs of the private sector. The average deposit rate was 6.39 per cent in the second quarter of 2002, up from 4.96 per cent in the same quarter of 2001, while the average lending rate fell to 8.75 per cent from 9.35 per cent over the same period.

## Box II.7. Timor-Leste: facing enormous challenges in nation-building[a]

Timor-Leste (formerly East Timor) became an independent country on 20 May 2002, making it the first new country of the new millennium. It joined the United Nations as the 191st Member State on 27 September 2002.

The United Nations played an important part in the creation of the new country. The General Assembly placed East Timor on the international agenda in 1960, when it added the territory to its list of Non-Self-Governing Territories, and had been actively involved since then by facilitating negotiations between the Indonesian and Portugese authorities on the future of East Timor. Similar to its role in the events leading up to the independence of Cambodia in 1992, the United Nations took an active part in the affairs of East Timor with the establishment of the United Nations Mission in East Timor (UNAMET) in June 1999 and the holding of the referendum on 30 August 1999 to begin a process leading towards political independence. This was followed by the establishment in October 1999 of the United Nations Transitional Administration in East Timor (UNTAET), which administered East Timor from that date up to the time of independence in May 2002.

UNTAET consisted of a governance and public administration component, a civilian police component of up to 1,640 persons and an armed United Nations peacekeeping force. In addition, humanitarian assistance and rehabilitation components were incorporated within the structure of the Transitional Administration. To finance the activities of UNTAET, the Donors' Meeting for East Timor, convened at Tokyo in December 1999, pledged more than $520 million.

UNTAET, with the assistance of multilateral and bilateral development agencies, had the enormous task of economic and social reconstruction in East Timor. Apart from the task of establishing the administrative structure for East Timor, it was also faced with the formidable task of rehabilitating essential infrastructure and transport networks, the provision of basic health care, the reopening of schools and, very importantly, the resumption of markets and economic activities which had been devastated by the civil unrest following the overwhelming vote by the Timorese for independence over autonomy within Indonesia.

The assistance from the international community has been very important in the rebuilding process of the new country. At the Tokyo Meeting in 1999, the international donor community set up the Trust Fund for East Timor (TFET) to provide assistance in rebuilding the country. ADB and the World Bank propose and manage projects financed under the Trust Fund. ADB is responsible for managing TFET-funded projects worth $52.8 million. Since 1999, ADB has also committed $8 million in technical assistance grants to help to prepare projects and capacity-building. An emerging infrastructure rehabilitation project which has been managed by ADB since April 2000 has helped to repair roads, expand port facilities and restore power supply. Up to 85 per cent of Timor-Leste's infrastructure was destroyed during the civil unrest. Some of the infrastructure damaged or destroyed has been rebuilt or upgraded under the water supply and sanitation rehabilitation project. Many development agencies have been helping the country to reopen schools, which had also been extensively destroyed. In some cases, UNICEF helped by paying for some building materials; the Government of Timor-Leste was paying teachers' salaries and providing equipment, while the school fees were paid voluntarily as most parents were unemployed. Oxfam,

**TIMOR-LESTE**

**Facts and figures**

- *Population:* 800,000
- *Capital:* Dili
- *Major languages:*
  Tetum
  Portuguese
  English
  Bahasa Indonesia
- *Major religion:*
  Christianity
  (Roman Catholic)
- *GDP growth*

1999 –34%
2000 15%
2001 18% (estimated)
2002 zero (projected)
2003 2% (projected)

- *Main economic activity:* agriculture
- *Major export:* coffee
- *Natural resources:*
  Offshore oil and gas reserves in the Timor Sea, being developed by Australia under the Timor Sea Treaty signed on 20 May 2002.
  Production is expected to begin in 2004 and gas deliveries are expected to begin late in 2005.

**Some important dates**

- **1999**

  *23 June* – Indonesia announces a plan to grant East Timor extensive autonomy

[a] This box is largely based on *ADB Review*, September-October 2002, pp. 4-11.

an international non-governmental organization, is helping to implement both the ADB and EU programmes in the country. The World Bank signed an agreement with UNTAET on 21 February 2001 for the disbursement of $21.5 million over two and a half years for community empowerment and local government projects. It also signed a $12.7 million grant on 7 June 2000 to help to revamp the country's health sector. On 23 June 2000, the donor community, at a meeting held at Lisbon, pledged its continued support for the reconstruction of Timor-Leste and for closing the financing gap of $16 million for financial year 2001.

There are many challenges facing the new country. One of the most urgent tasks of the Government is to establish not only a small, competent and transparent Government but one which is lean and cost-effective so as to keep aggregate expenditure aligned with the country's absorptive capacity. This will require, among other things, the development of the country's human resources to ensure effective public administration, transparency and accountability and, more important, better aid coordination and absorption at the national level. Domestic revenue sources are important to finance the country's recurrent budget. The maintenance of a good economic and regulatory environment conducive to efficient private sector activities is important in this context. Timor-Leste is well endowed on a per capita basis, with natural resources both onshore and offshore. The projected oil and gas revenues from the Timor Sea for the medium term are promising following the signing of the Timor Sea Treaty allowing Australia to develop Timor-Leste's offshore oil and gas reserves. Production is expected to begin in 2004 and gas deliveries late in 2005. Gas-based export income will be supplemented by earnings from marble, coffee and other agricultural produce, and tourism, since Timor-Leste has a comparative advantage in these activities.

As three quarters of the people are engaged in agriculture, Timor-Leste will need to strengthen the traditional agriculture by using appropriate technology inputs to increase crop yields. Adequate access to rural banking and microcredit facilities are also important to help to increase the sector's output growth and provide a sound basis for sustained economic growth and poverty alleviation through export-oriented primary activities. ADB is implementing a TFET-financed project, under which a microfinance institution has been established and is operating successfully in the country. With a small natural resource base and limited domestic financial resources, Timor-Leste needs to engage actively in trade if it is to achieve sustained economic growth to enable it fight unemployment and poverty effectively.

The United Nations will continue to maintain a presence in Timor-Leste in the post-independence period to ensure the security and stability of the new country. A successor mission, known as the United Nations Mission of Support in East Timor (UNMISET), will adopt a milestone-based approach to its gradual withdrawal from the country and will support the Timorese authorities in the areas of economic stability, democracy and justice, internal security and law enforcement, and external security and border control. For its part, the new Government will need to take bold initiatives, including steps towards good governance, so that it will continue to have the support and goodwill of the international community to assist it in its development efforts. Being a latecomer can also be a blessing in disguise for Timor-Leste as the authorities can learn from the mistakes made by other developing countries in their early stages of independence. In this connection, Timor-Leste could foster closer economic cooperation with countries in the ESCAP region, including those from the Pacific island subregion, and learn from their experience in development. Timor-Leste could, for example, seek the assistance of ESCAP through such modalities as economic and technical cooperation among developing countries, with the assistance of concerned member Governments.

*30 August* – In a referendum supervised by the United Nations, an overwhelming 78.5 per cent of voters choose independence over autonomy within Indonesia. In the violence that erupts after the vote, hundreds of people are killed, and hundreds of thousands are forced to flee their homes.

*26 October* – Indonesia officially yields authority over its former territory to UNTAET.

- **2001**

  *30 August* – East Timor elects a constitutional assembly.

- **2002**

  *22 March* – East Timor's Constituent Assembly signs into force the first constitution.

- *14 April* – East Timor elects Xanana Gusmão as the country's first president.

  *20 May* – UNTAET hands over authority to the elected Government of independent Timor-Leste.

  *27 September* – General Assembly admits Timor-Leste as its 191$^{st}$ Member State.

**Table II.33. Selected South-East Asian economies: inflation and money supply growth (M2), 1999-2002**

*(Percentage)*

| | *1999* | *2000* | *2001* | *2002* |
|---|---|---|---|---|
| **Inflation**[a] | | | | |
| Indonesia | 20.4 | 3.7 | 11.5 | 10.5 |
| Malaysia | 2.8 | 1.5 | 1.4 | 1.8 |
| Philippines | 6.7 | 4.4 | 6.1 | 3.1 |
| Singapore | 0.1 | 1.3 | 1.0 | –0.4 |
| Thailand | 0.2 | 1.6 | 1.7 | 0.7 |
| Viet Nam | 4.1 | –1.7 | –0.4 | 3.9 |
| **Money supply growth (M2)** | | | | |
| Indonesia | 11.9 | 15.6 | 13.0 | 6.6[b] |
| Malaysia | 13.7 | 5.2 | 2.2 | 5.8 |
| Philippines | 16.9 | 8.1 | 3.6 | 9.1[c] |
| Singapore | 8.5 | –2.0 | 5.9 | –0.7[b] |
| Thailand | 5.4 | 3.4 | 2.2 | 0.6[c] |
| Viet Nam | 66.4 | 35.4 | 27.3 | 14.6[d] |

*Sources:* ESCAP, based on ADB, *Key Indicators of Developing Asian and Pacific Countries 2002,* vol. XXXIII (ADB, 2002) and *Asian Development Outlook 2002* (Oxford University Press, 2002); IMF, *International Financial Statistics,* vol. LVI, No. 2 (February 2003); Economist Intelligence Unit, *Country Forecasts* (London, 2002), various issues; and national sources.

*Note:* Data for 2002 are estimates.

[a] Changes in the consumer price index.
[b] January-November.
[c] January-October.
[d] January-September.

***Inflation subsided with currency appreciation and monetary restraint in Indonesia but was still in double digits***

Inflation in Indonesia had peaked at 15 per cent in the second quarter of 2002, when administered prices for petroleum products, electricity and other utilities and transport were raised and flooding led to higher prices. It then went down to an average of 10.5 per cent, slightly above the Government's target range, for the year as a whole. Appreciation of the rupiah and slower growth in the money supply helped to stabilize prices. Nevertheless, the interest rate on short-term Bank Indonesia paper was a little above 13 per cent in December 2002, down from 17.6 per cent at the end of 2001. A lower rate of inflation, in the 8.5-9.5 per cent range, is targeted for 2003; the partial clawback of the second round of increases in administered prices in January 2003, together with appreciation of the rupiah, may enable this price goal to be achieved.

***Concerted action brought inflation down sharply in the Philippines***

In the Philippines, food prices have a 51 per cent weight in the consumer price index and were monitored by a specially formed task force. The prices were held down by stable supply conditions, helped in part by liberalized imports that offset the effects of a weaker peso. Food prices rose by 1.8 per cent in 2002, down from 3.9 per cent a year earlier. Electricity tariffs were reduced through a series of administrative measures. At the same time, excess capacity, coupled with weakening demand, limited the ability of producers to raise prices. The overall rate of inflation decelerated significantly to just over 3 per cent in 2002, from 6.1 per cent in 2001, well below the Government's 4-4.5 per cent target for the year. Inflation was expected to increase somewhat in 2003 owing to higher oil and food prices but to remain in the 4-5 per cent range. Interest rates were lower in 2002 compared with 2001. The Central Bank continued monetary easing into the first quarter before switching to a neutral stance, which was to remain in place provided that inflation was manageable. Market interest rates rose in the second half of the year, however, owing to concerns about rising fiscal deficits as well as global economic prospects and regional security. The yield on 91-day treasury bills was 5.3 per cent in December 2002, compared with 4.3 per cent in May; bank lending rates also drifted higher.

***There were worries about deflation in Thailand until inflation picked up late in the year***

Inflationary pressures in 2002 were very muted in Thailand, as demand pressures during the year were not excessive, and cost pressures were contained by the low capacity utilization, the absence of wage push and the appreciation of the baht. The inflation rate of 0.7 per cent for the full year was well below the 1.7 per cent rate of 2001, and there was some concern about deflation during the year. However, inflation picked up in December 2002, with consumer prices 1.6 per cent higher than the level prevailing in the same month a year earlier, owing to increased prices of food items (attributable, in turn, to adverse weather conditions), oil and some consumer goods. Inflation is expected to remain at 1.5 per cent in 2003, largely owing to higher prices for oil.

Monetary policy in Thailand was generally accommodative in 2002 but was also conditioned by the Bank of Thailand's desire to target the level and stability of the exchange rate. The benchmark 14-day repurchase rate was cut in December 2001 and again in January 2002 by a total of 50 basis points to 2 per cent. It was left at that level for much of the year to maintain a small premium over interest rates in the United States and thus discourage domestic banks from sending excess liquidity overseas. Continued global economic weakness, together with low domestic inflation and a declining fiscal stimulus, prompted the Bank of Thailand to make a further 25 basis point cut in November 2002, bringing the repurchase rate to 1.75 per cent.

***Deflation occurred in Singapore as wage growth was negligible in the slackening labour market***

Singapore experienced modest deflation of around –0.4 per cent in 2002. This reflected weak demand and restrained domestic costs, following the slack labour market conditions and negligible wage growth. In 2003, inflation is expected to pick up but remain comparatively low, at between 0.5 and 1.5 per cent, as the result of modest wage growth and the phasing-in of an increase in the Goods and Services Tax from 3 to 4 per cent. However, the sluggish economic recovery is likely to limit the ability of producers to pass the tax increase on to consumers. Domestic interest rates declined in 2002, in line with global interest rates and abundant liquidity in the domestic money market. The three-month interbank lending rate went down from 2.8 per cent at the end of 2000 to 1.3 per cent at the end of 2001 and further to 0.8 per cent at the end of 2002.

## *Foreign trade and other external transactions*

### *External trade*

***Merchandise exports and imports rebounded very strongly in the Philippines***

The Philippines experienced a sharp upswing in merchandise exports in 2002, albeit from a relatively low level in 2001 (table II.34). Increased shipments of electrical machinery and semiconductors accounted for the revival, particularly to markets in developing countries in East Asia; electronics expanded by almost 23 per cent. Garment exports were also up

**Table II.34. Selected South-East Asian economies: merchandise exports and their rates of growth, 1999-2002**

| | *Exports (f.o.b.)* | | | | |
|---|---|---|---|---|---|
| | *Value (millions of US dollars)* | *Annual rate of growth (percentage)* | | | |
| | *2001* | *1999* | *2000* | *2001* | *2002 Jan.-Aug.* |
| Brunei Darussalam | 3 318 | 28.9 | 23.7 | 5.1 | –3.9 |
| Indonesia | 64 840 | –0.4 | 27.6 | 4.4 | –2.4 |
| Malaysia[a] | 88 199 | 15.1 | 16.1 | –10.4 | 6.0 |
| Philippines | 32 140 | 20.3 | 7.3 | –15.6 | 13.4 |
| Singapore | 121 717 | 4.4 | 20.2 | –11.8 | –1.8 |
| Thailand[b] | 63 200 | 7.4 | 19.5 | –6.9 | 5.7 |
| Viet Nam | 13 569 | 24.0 | 25.5 | –6.3 | 5.2 |

*Sources:* IMF, *Direction of Trade Statistics* (CD-ROM), January 2003; National Economic and Social Development Board of Thailand web site <http://www.nesdb.go.th>, 13 January 2003; and Bank Negara Malaysia web site <http://www.bnm.gov.my>, 27 February 2003.

[a] Figure for 2002 is for the whole year.

[b] Figure for 2002 is a projection for the whole year.

**Table II.35. Selected South-East Asian economies: merchandise imports and their rates of growth, 1999-2002**

| | Imports (c.i.f.) | | | | |
|---|---|---|---|---|---|
| | Value (millions of US dollars) | Annual rate of growth (percentage) | | | |
| | 2001 | 1999 | 2000 | 2001 | 2002 Jan.-Aug. |
| Brunei Darussalam | 1 321 | –43.4 | 7.6 | –7.6 | 24.5 |
| Indonesia | 38 810 | –12.2 | 39.6 | 15.8 | –3.9 |
| Malaysia[a] | 73 857 | 12.3 | 25.5 | –10.0 | 8.3 |
| Philippines | 29 558 | 4.1 | 2.1 | –5.8 | 32.6 |
| Singapore | 116 018 | 9.3 | 21.2 | –13.8 | –3.3 |
| Thailand[b] | 60 700 | 16.9 | 31.3 | –2.8 | 6.0 |
| Viet Nam | 16 618 | 3.8 | 33.2 | 6.3 | 5.6 |

*Sources:* IMF, *Direction of Trade Statistics* (CD-ROM), January 2003; National Economic and Social Development Board of Thailand web site <http://www.nesdb.go.th>, 13 January 2003; and Bank Negara Malaysia web site <http://www.bnm.gov.my>, 27 February 2003.

[a] Figure for 2002 is for the whole year.
[b] Figure for 2002 is a projection for the whole year.

sharply in the second half of 2002, reversing four consecutive quarters of decline. Boosted by demand for intermediate inputs, merchandise imports also grew strongly, reducing the trade surplus (table II.35). Significant expansion was recorded in imported materials and accessories for the manufacture of electronics products, and in capital goods imports. The deficit on the service account narrowed, mainly owing to higher net receipts from travel; fewer residents travelled overseas because of the weaker peso and a government campaign to attract domestic as well as foreign tourists was a success. Helped also by robust growth in migrant workers' remittances, the surplus on the external current account increased to 6.8 per cent of GDP in 2002 from 6.3 per cent in 2001 (table II.36).

***Increased revenues from exports of agricultural commodities strengthened the trade accounts of many countries in the subregion***

Export growth in Thailand in 2002 was estimated at 5.7 per cent for the full year and import growth at 6 per cent. Agricultural items, electronic products, electrical appliances, plastic goods and vehicles and parts all contributed to the export growth, while there was a decline in earnings on exported fishery products and garments. Durable consumer goods, computers and intermediate goods for the electronics and vehicle industries led import growth. As a result of the positive balance on the trade and services and transfer accounts, the current account surplus rose to 4.8 per cent of GDP in 2002.

**Table II.36. Selected South-East Asian economies: budget and current account balance as a percentage of GDP, 1999-2002**

*(Percentage)*

| | *1999* | *2000* | *2001* | *2002* |
|---|---|---|---|---|
| **Budget balance[a] as a percentage of GDP** | | | | |
| Indonesia | −2.5 | −1.2 | −2.7 | −2.5 |
| Malaysia | −3.2 | −5.8 | −5.5 | −4.7 |
| Philippines | −3.8 | −4.1 | −4.0 | −5.6 |
| Singapore | 2.6 | 3.5 | 1.9 | 0.1 |
| Thailand | −3.3 | −2.2 | −2.4 | −2.2 |
| Viet Nam[b] | −1.0 | −3.0 | −3.5 | −4.0 |
| **Current account balance as a percentage of GDP** | | | | |
| Indonesia | 4.1 | 5.3 | 4.5 | 2.3 |
| Malaysia | 15.9 | 9.4 | 8.0 | 6.8 |
| Philippines | 10.4 | 11.3 | 6.3 | 6.8 |
| Singapore | 20.0 | 17.2 | 20.9 | 21.0 |
| Thailand | 10.2 | 7.6 | 5.4 | 4.8 |
| Viet Nam | 4.1 | 3.5 | 2.4 | −1.2 |

*Sources:* ESCAP, based on ADB, *Key Indicators of Developing Asian and Pacific Countries 2002,* vol. XXXIII (ADB, 2002) and *Asian Development Outlook 2002* (Oxford University Press, 2002); IMF, *International Financial Statistics,* vol. LV, No. 11 (November 2002); and Economist Intelligence Unit, *Country Forecasts* (London, 2002), various issues.

*Note:* Data for 2002 are estimates.

[a] Excluding grants.
[b] Excluding grants and on-lending.

Viet Nam suffered a sharp fall in export earnings in 2001. Exports continued to display a weak performance into the first half of 2002 but a significant turnaround occurred in the third quarter and export revenues were up by 5.2 per cent year on year in the first eight months of 2002. The underlying strengths were improved commodity prices and a substantial increase in sales to the United States. Exports of rubber, handicrafts and fine art products and garments and textiles went up by rates in excess of 30 per cent, while double-digit growth of exports was recorded for rice, footwear and seafood. Export earnings from vegetables and fruit, fell sharply, however, as did those from coffee and computers and other electronic products. Crude oil exports were also down, owing to capacity constraints. In the first 10 months of 2002, 55 per cent of Viet Nam's exports went to countries in Asia; about 19 per cent went to other ASEAN countries and just over 36 per cent to non-ASEAN countries, of which 14 per cent went to Japan and 9 per cent to China. However, exports to the United States more than doubled between 2001 and 2002, passing the $2 billion mark, with exports of garments alone expanding 18-fold.

The growth in the value of imports, which also declined very sharply in 2001, outpaced that in export revenues somewhat in 2002. The fastest expansion was in imported machinery and equipment, refined oil, materials for the garment and textile industries, computers and electronic components. By contrast, import spending on motorcycle assembly kits declined by nearly one half following a reduction in quotas. As a result of these developments, both the trade and current accounts were expected to be in deficit in 2002. As a percentage of GDP, the current account surplus decreased in recent years, from 4.1 per cent in 1999 to a deficit of 1.2 per cent in 2002.

***China and other countries in East Asia, as well as countries in the subregion, are emerging as important markets for some countries in South-East Asia***

The decline in exports from Malaysia in 2001 bottomed out in the first quarter of 2002 and export earnings staged a sharp recovery that was generally broad-based. The upsurge was particularly marked for agriculture, in response to stronger commodity prices, followed by manufacturing, mainly electronics and electrical products, chemical products and wood products, including furniture. Signs were emerging, however, of some loss of momentum in exported electronics and electrical goods following weakening demand in major markets. On a brighter note, China and other countries in ASEAN are emerging as important markets for Malaysia; exports to China went up by almost 44 per cent and to ASEAN, by just under 19 per cent year on year in the third quarter of 2002.

Meanwhile, strong growth was registered by all categories of imports, capital, intermediate and consumer goods. In fact, the rate of import expansion outpaced that of exports, causing a narrower trade surplus. However, lower deficits on the services and income accounts, which reflected payments for transport services on the one hand and investment income on the other, contributed to containing the reduction in the surplus in the current account. As a percentage of GDP, the surplus declined from 8 per cent in 2001 to 6.8 per cent in 2002.

***Imports contracted sharply in Singapore for the second year in a row owing to continued weakness in manufacturing***

In the first eight months of 2002, merchandise exports in Singapore contracted by 1.8 per cent, considerably less than the decline of almost 12 per cent experienced during the previous year. The improved performance was due to both non-oil domestic exports, mainly pharmaceuticals, petrochemicals and disc media products, and re-exports, principally of electronics products. Although markets in the EU and Japan remained weak, there were signs of recovery in the United States market, while China and Hong Kong, China, have emerged as major export destinations. Other economies in the region, such as the Philippines, the Republic of Korea and Thailand, have also increased in relative importance as a source of export demand for Singapore.

Meanwhile, import spending fell by 3.3 per cent in January-August 2002, following a contraction of almost 14 per cent in 2001, with intermediate electronics and pharmaceutical imports showing faster growth later in the year. As a result of the sharper contraction in imports than in exports, the trade surplus widened and there was also a significant improvement in the services balance. Nevertheless, the current account balance at 21 per cent of GDP in 2002 was substantially unchanged from the previous year's level.

***Large wage increases and currency appreciation are eroding Indonesia's competitiveness***

Merchandise exports from Indonesia declined in the first eight months of 2002, with earnings from non-oil and gas exports falling particularly sharply, although there were some signs of a recovery in exported machines and electrical products. Large wage increases and the appreciation of the rupiah eroded somewhat the competitiveness of the Indonesian textile industry, where exports were stagnant, particularly to traditional markets such as the United States, the EU and Singapore. China's importance as an export destination has increased rapidly; exports to that country rose by nearly two fifths in the first nine months of 2002 as compared with a year earlier. However, the competitive strength of China is being felt by Indonesia, among others, in third-country markets, where prices were increasingly coming under pressure.

Non-oil and gas imports fell sharply in Indonesia in 2002, continuing the negative trend that had started in 2001. The decline was observed across the board but was particularly marked for capital goods and raw material inputs for manufacturing. The current account balance remained higher than expected in 2000-2002, mainly owing to the reduction in imports but also because of higher commodity prices, particularly of oil.

*Capital flows and exchange rates*

***The ringgit peg to the United States dollar has proved to be an anchor of stability***

Capital flows, which had been somewhat volatile in Malaysia in recent years, stabilized from mid-2001 in response to the improved macroeconomic fundamentals and the interest rate differential in favour of Malaysia. At the same time, the decline in capital outflows enabled the Central Bank to build up international reserves to $34.6 billion at the end of 2002 (adequate to finance 5.4 months of retained imports and 5.1 times short-term external debt). Net portfolio investment turned negative from the second quarter of 2002 as stock markets softened worldwide. Net FDI, which had amounted to only $0.3 billion in 2001, picked up significantly in 2002, reaching $1.5 billion in the first half of the year as production facilities were relocated to Malaysia from neighbouring countries. The ringgit remained pegged at M$ 3.80 to the United States dollar and there was little pressure for this to change. In the view of IMF, the improved macroeconomic situation in Malaysia was supportive of the exchange rate peg as a "stability anchor", and the value of the currency did not appear to be misaligned. In line with the dollar exchange rate, the ringgit generally depreciated against most other major and regional currencies from the end of 2001 to the end of 2002, thus giving some relief to the country's exporters.

***FDI slowed in Thailand, as in many other countries of the subregion***

The net outflow on the capital account in Thailand of $2.6 billion in the first nine months of 2002 was appreciably lower than the $4.1 billion outflow in the same period in 2001. The causal factors for this improvement included higher net portfolio investment and a reduction in commercial banks' foreign assets. However, public debt repayments were higher, as were outflows from non-resident baht accounts. In addition, FDI appeared to have slowed considerably. The overall surplus on the balance of payments in the first nine months of 2002 amounted to $3.1 billion, up from a deficit of $0.1 billion in the same period in 2001. International reserves were estimated to have risen to $38.4 billion by December 2002. The baht appreciated against the United States dollar in the first half of the year, but the uncertain global economic outlook led to a reversal of this trend in the second half before the appreciation resumed. The currency traded in a range between 40 and 44 baht to the dollar in 2002, in line with market conditions and regional trends; it is expected to continue doing so in 2003, with Bank of Thailand intervention likely to maintain stability.

***Disbursements of official capital to Indonesia revived after the Bali bombing***

Lower debt repayments in 2002 served to slow private capital outflows from Indonesia, while inflows picked up as a result of asset disposals by the Indonesian Bank Restructuring Agency and the privatization programme. Portfolio investors have also been returning to Indonesia, although FDI fell 35 per cent in terms of value and 15 per cent in terms of the number of projects in 2002. Disbursements of official capital revived after the Bali bombing, conditional on the implementation of reforms and action to fight poverty, and by the end of 2002 Bank Indonesia's foreign exchange reserves had risen to $31.7 billion. The rupiah strengthened throughout the year, with the exception of a surprisingly brief period of weakness in the immediate aftermath of the Bali bombing; from Rp 10,320 to the dollar at the end of 2001, it reached Rp 8,965 at the beginning of December 2002. The currency's strength was partly a reflection of general currency strength in the region and partly of the weakness of the United States dollar, but it also reflects the greater political and macroeconomic stability achieved by the country.

***Increased remittances and portfolio investment mitigated the weakness of the Philippine peso***

The deficit on the capital and financial accounts increased in the Philippines in the first half of 2002 owing to higher net outflows of direct investments as well as higher outflows of "other" investments. Direct investments declined because of lower equity investments by non-residents and repayment of intercompany loans. Higher residents' investment in equity capital abroad also contributed to the increase in outflows. The net outflow of "other" investments reflected higher net deposits abroad by resident banks. Meanwhile, net portfolio investments rose sharply owing to non-residents' investment in government-issued medium-term bonds. In the first nine months of 2002, the overall surplus on the balance of payments was only $0.5 billion, which was nevertheless an improvement over the deficit of $1.3 billion recorded in the same period in 2001. Gross international reserves stood at $16 billion at the end of September 2002, a marginal improvement from $15.7 billion at the end of 2001 and enough to cover 9.3 months of imports. Increased inflows of foreign portfolio investment as well as remittances, together with the general strengthening of regional currencies against the dollar, supported the peso exchange rate in the first half of 2002. However, deteriorating market sentiment, influenced in part by the burgeoning fiscal deficit, drove the peso lower in the second half of the year and the exchange rate hovered in the range of 53-53.5 pesos to the dollar towards the end of the year.

***FDI flows are increasingly directed to small and medium-sized projects in Viet Nam***

Remittances are also gaining in importance in Viet Nam following the Government's adoption of measures to attract them in 1999. Remittances were estimated to have reached $1.9 billion in 2001 and to exceed $2 billion in 2002. Inward FDI was relatively stable in 2000-2002 in terms of disbursements, at around $2.1 billion a year. Although commitments were lower in 2002, they covered a larger number of projects, thus indicating a shift towards small and medium-sized projects. There have been substantial inflows of ODA to Viet Nam in recent years. Of a total of $5.82 billion committed between 2000 and 2002, some $5.25 billion was disbursed. Official reserves increased from $3.4 billion in 2000 to approximately $4 billion in 2002. The dong has been depreciating against the United States dollar since 1997, although the rate of depreciation slowed in 2002 to 2.1 per cent, or just over half of the 3.9 per cent depreciation in 2001. However, given the weakness of the United States dollar against most other currencies in 2002, the effective depreciation of the dong was much greater. The dong was trading at 15,400 to the dollar in December 2002.

***Gross official reserves increased significantly in Singapore in spite of the deficit on the capital and financial accounts***

The shortfall in the capital and financial accounts in Singapore widened in the third quarter of 2002, after narrowing in the first half, because of higher net outflows of portfolio and direct investment. Nevertheless, gross official reserves were expected to increase to $83.3 billion by the end of 2002. From the beginning of July 2001, the Monetary Authority of Singapore has maintained a neutral policy stance, targeting a zero appreciation in the trade-weighted nominal effective exchange rate for the Singapore dollar, which fluctuated in the upper band of its target range for much of 2002. The Singapore dollar appreciated against the United States dollar in 2002, ending the year at S$ 1.74 to the United States dollar. On the exchange markets, the Brunei dollar has followed the Singapore dollar, to which it is linked by a currency peg.

*External debt*

***External debt was down in Indonesia but much of it remains short-term in nature***

At the end of July 2002, total external debt in Indonesia amounted to just over 90 per cent of GDP, down from 91.3 in 2001, the Government's portion of foreign debt being 57 per cent of the total. Although external debt has been on the decline, and is well down from the peak of 157 per cent of GDP in 1998, much of it remains short-term. The World Bank has estimated that debt due within one year constituted 70 per cent of gross reserves in 2002, 10 per cent lower than the 2001 figure but nevertheless much higher than comparable figures for the other countries hit by the 1997-1998 financial crisis. Rescheduling agreements were reached for debt-service payments with the Paris Club in April 2002 and with the London Club in June 2002, easing considerably the burden of short-term debt obligations on the government budget and on official reserves. Indonesia's foreign currency sovereign debt ratings are currently CCC+/B3 with a stable or positive debt outlook; although these ratings have improved, they are still below those for comparable economies in the subregion.

***Aggressive borrowing on international capital markets to finance the Philippine Government's fiscal deficit has eroded confidence somewhat***

External debt was on a rising trend in the Philippines as the Government was financing its deficit by borrowing aggressively in international capital markets, in part to take advantage of lower interest rates. By the end of June 2002, the total government debt amounted to 67 per cent of GDP, a comparatively high value for the subregion; of this amount, 47 per cent was external debt. From just over $46 billion in 2000-2001, it had ballooned to almost $55 billion by mid-2002. External debt declined in the third quarter to $53.6 billion, of which the public sector share was 65 per cent. However, the unexpected widening of the fiscal deficit led the Government to resort to additional external borrowing. Although major ratings agencies have maintained current ratings for foreign currency sovereign debt at BB+/Ba1, the debt outlook was downgraded to negative from stable by some agencies following those developments.

***The Government's external debt has also been rising in Malaysia but market sentiment remains favourable***

Total external debt as a percentage of GDP has also been on a rising trend in Malaysia since 2000, when it amounted to 46.7 per cent of GDP; the ratio reached 51.8 per cent in 2001 and an estimated 53.3 per cent of GDP by September 2002. The share of the public sector external debt of a medium- and long-term nature also rose, accounting for 64.8 per cent in the third quarter of 2002 as compared with 61.3 per cent in the first quarter of 2001. While the Government was initially keen to limit borrowing overseas, its current priority is to maintain the fiscal stimulus in the face of a weakening global economy, while at the same time limiting the impact of public spending on domestic interest rates. Market sentiment as regards Malaysia appears to be favourable: credit rating agencies upgraded the country's foreign currency sovereign debt to BBB+/Baa1 in the third quarter of 2002, and new placements of sovereign bonds in April and June 2002 were oversubscribed.

***The increase in official reserves has led Thailand to repay the outstanding balance of the loan from IMF two years ahead of schedule***

Thailand's external solvency has improved greatly in recent years. Total external debt at the end of August 2002 was in the region of $64.4 billion, roughly 55 per cent of GDP, well below the 93 per cent of GDP prevailing at the end of 1998. Approximately 79 per cent of this debt was long-term, and the share of the public sector in total external debt was around 41.3 per cent. The high level of international reserves will permit the earlier repayment of the $4.8 billion outstanding from the IMF loan following the financial crisis of 1997-1998 within a six-month period beginning February 2003, two years ahead of schedule, thus saving $126 million in interest payments. International ratings agencies, while maintaining Thailand's ratings for sovereign foreign currency debt at BBB-/Baa3, raised the debt outlook to positive from stable.

Viet Nam's stock of external debt outstanding was expected to reach $13.3 billion by the end of 2002, up from $12.1 billion at the end of 2001. This represents 37 per cent of GDP and 84 per cent of exports. Most of this debt is on concessional terms and carries very low interest rates. The external debt-service ratio, which was just under 23 per cent of export earnings in 1997, fell very sharply to 9.4 per cent in 2001 and further to 7.9 per cent in 2002. This is judged to be a sustainable level and Viet Nam is not likely to qualify for debt relief under the Highly Indebted Poor Countries Initiative. International ratings agencies raised Viet Nam's sovereign foreign currency debt ratings in 2002 to BB-/B1, with a stable or positive debt outlook.

### *Key policy issues*

***Unemployment and poverty alleviation continue to head the policy agenda of most countries in the subregion***

Issues related to poverty and unemployment continued to head the policy agenda in many countries in the subregion. Although the officially-defined poverty headcount index in Indonesia declined from the 27 per cent value it had reached in 1999 after the financial crisis to 13.2 per cent early in 2001, it has since drifted upwards as a result of modest economic growth. The index, which stood at 17 per cent at the end of 2002, was to be lowered to 15 per cent in 2003, but recent price increases for products such as kerosene, after fuel subsidies were cut as part of the IMF-mandated reform programme, and rice, following increases in the paddy support price and import tariffs, may make it more difficult to attain this goal. The latest round of fuel price increases was greeted with extensive demonstrations, prompting the Government to change its policy and cut subsidies gradually. This action may have clouded prospects for the disbursement of much-needed official aid somewhat, but the response of donors so far has been sympathetic. The Bali bombing is also likely to increase the incidence of poverty in the short to medium terms; according to World Bank estimates, another 2-3 million people will fall below the poverty line as a result of the adverse impact of the bombing on economic growth.

***Growth remains insufficient to absorb the unemployed in Indonesia***

Per capita incomes in urban areas of Indonesia appear to have returned to pre-financial crisis levels as a result of the steep rise in minimum wages across the country, by 30 per cent on average in 2002, and in government wages, by 15-20 per cent in the same year. Real wages in agriculture and in the informal sector and among SMEs, however, remain well below pre-crisis levels because of increased competition for the available jobs from the large number of displaced formal sector workers. The volume of unemployment is thought to be considerably larger than the official estimate of 8.4 million in 2002 and is likely to rise further as a result of higher minimum wages. A large number of illegal migrant workers have also been repatriated from Malaysia; a much faster rate of economic growth, around 6-7 per cent annually, is thought to be necessary to absorb these workers along with the 2.5 million new entrants to the labour force each year.

***The lack of new jobs in industry is largely responsible for the slow growth of employment in the Philippines***

The unemployment rate in the Philippines rose to 10.2 per cent in October 2002 (up from 9.8 per cent in October 2001). Based on a labour force survey in July 2002, the number of employed persons increased by 2.8 per cent, while the labour force expanded by 4.1 per cent year on year. Jobs generated in services and agriculture were the main cause of the expansion in employment, as the number of jobs in industry shrank. Meanwhile, the number of workers seeking employment overseas went up by 2.2 per cent in the same period. In addition, the volume of underemployment amounted to 15.3 per cent of those currently in employment. Nominal wages in the agricultural and non-agricultural sectors went up by just over 14 and 12 per cent respectively in the second quarter of 2002, compared with the same quarter a year earlier; real wages gained 10 and 8 per cent respectively in the same period.

***Early gains in poverty reduction in the Philippines have been reversed recently and vulnerability remains high***

Poverty in the Philippines fell very substantially from 34 per cent in 1991 to a little over 25 per cent in 1997, based on the officially-defined poverty headcount index. The latest index value available shows that in 2000 poverty had increased to 27.5 per cent nationally. The rural poverty rate, at slightly over 41 per cent, was more than three times the urban rate of 13.2 per cent. There are also many near-poor: the World Bank estimates that while the percentage of the population living on less than $1 per day was 12.7 in 2000, the percentage living on less than $2 per day was 45.7. Poverty is likely to have decreased in 2001 but the recent increase in unemployment suggests that it may have risen again in 2002. The Medium-term Philippine Development Plan, 1999-2004, targets a decrease in poverty incidence to 18.8 per cent in 2004 and 11.6 per cent in 2010 in order to meet the millennium development goal on poverty reduction, but more robust economic growth will be needed if these targets are to be met.

***Thailand has made considerable progress in reducing unemployment and the incidence of poverty, but poverty levels remain above those prevailing before the 1997-1998 crisis***

The labour market has improved noticeably in Thailand, with the official unemployment rate falling to its lowest level in five years, to 1.8 per cent in August 2002 compared with 2.1 per cent in August 2001. Employment increased markedly in construction and manufacturing; it increased less sharply in services and remained essentially stable in agriculture. The estimated volume of underemployment also declined, from 1.8 per cent in August 2001 to 1.4 per cent in the same month in 2002. Indications are that by the end of 2002, GDP per capita had returned to the level prevailing in 1996.

Progress has also been made in poverty reduction: the percentage of the population living on less than $2 per day fell to 32.3 per cent in 2002 from 35.6 per cent in 2000. According to World Bank estimates, however, the incidence of poverty remains above pre-crisis levels. In addition, while it appears to have declined faster in rural areas, it remains much higher there than in urban areas. The Government has implemented a number of measures to target low-income groups for further poverty reduction as well as to generate more employment opportunities, such as the village fund and debt suspension for farmers. There are, moreover, other schemes to raise the amount of credit available for SMEs as well as the universal health-care scheme of 30 baht per health-care visit. More recently, measures were also announced to encourage the construction of one million units of low-cost housing for low-income groups.

***Poverty remains largely a rural phenomenon in Viet Nam, where income inequality is also rising***

An employment survey conducted in Viet Nam in July 2002 found that the labour force had expanded by 2.9 per cent from the previous year, faster than the current growth rate of 1.5 per cent in the population but reflecting the more rapid rates of population growth of some years before. At the same time, the urban unemployment rate declined to 6 per cent from 6.3 per cent in 2001. In rural areas, open unemployment, estimated at 1 per cent of the labour force, was low but seasonal underemployment could be considerably higher. The survey found that in rural areas the amount of time spent working increased to 75 per cent of potential working hours in 2002 from 74 per cent in 2001.

Viet Nam has also made good progress in poverty reduction. According to World Bank estimates, the percentage of the population living on less than $1 per day declined from 15.2 per cent in 2000 to 10.4 per cent in 2002. However, vulnerability remains high as the percentage of the population living on less than $2 per day in 2002 was high, at 57.6 per cent (down from 64.7 per cent in 2000). Ninety per cent of the poor live in rural areas, where the poverty gap is wider and natural disasters are more frequent. Furthermore, there have been some signs that inequality may be widening in recent years after a decade of rapid growth and reform. Incomes of people in the top 10 per cent of the income scale were 10.6 times the incomes of those in the bottom 10 per cent in 1996. This figure rose to 12 times in 1999 and further to 12.5 times in 2002. In May 2002, Viet Nam embarked on a Comprehensive Poverty Reduction and Growth Strategy, which was strongly endorsed by international donors and multilateral agencies. The programme is due to last three years, at a total cost of $70 billion, with the bulk of the funds coming from the State budget.

***Pockets of poverty persist in Brunei Darussalam in communities of migrants***

In Brunei Darussalam, the official unemployment rate (based on those registered with the Government as seeking jobs) was 4.7 per cent in 2001, but the true figure is likely to be considerably higher. It has been estimated, for example, that one quarter of school-leavers might be unable to find work straight away. Close family networks and some welfare organizations provide a safety net for the unemployed, and the Government is looking for ways to ease youth unemployment in particular. Some pockets of absolute as well as relative poverty persist, particularly among communities of migrants who have been settled in the country for many generations. There is scope for enhanced intersectoral and inter-agency collaboration for more effective poverty alleviation.

***Lack of investment is primarily responsible for limited employment opportunities in Indonesia, where many businesses are closing***

Investment to generate job opportunities and maintain competitiveness was another important policy issue in 2002. The lack of adequate investment in the Indonesian economy is of concern. In particular, foreign investment approvals fell 40 per cent and domestic investment over 70 per cent in the first half of 2002, as compared with the same period in 2001. Four causal factors were cited: the weak legal system, increasing labour unrest, new regional autonomy laws and security concerns. In a recent UNCTAD study,[4] the country was ranked 138$^{th}$ out of 140 in its ability to attract FDI, relative to its size. Many large and medium-sized firms have been closed down and several others downsized or merged (a total of 1,323 in 2001, up from 1,149 in 2000). Labour-intensive sectors such as textiles and garments, leather and footwear seem to be the most affected, although Sony announced the closure of its audio equipment plant in March 2003, affecting approximately 1,000 employees. A number of multinationals such as Nike and Reebok have shifted purchase contracts to China and Viet Nam. Many companies in which firms from Japan and the Republic of Korea have invested have also threatened to close some factories and relocate others in response to labour unrest and high wage demands. In 2002, Indonesian manufacturers were actively seeking postponement of the full implementation of the ASEAN Free Trade Area for the textile and shoe industries as well as for chemicals and sugar.

---

4 UNCTAD, *World Investment Report 2002: Transnational Corporations and Export Competitiveness* (United Nations publication, Sales No. E.02.II.D.4).

***Weak investment in Philippine industry is also a reflection of low savings and investment ratios and limited FDI***

The slow rate of job creation in Philippine industry is also a reflection of insufficient investment in that sector. Unfortunately, both the savings and investment rates of the Philippines are low by subregional standards, and FDI inflows have also been less buoyant. In addition, business confidence on the part of both domestic and foreign investors was seriously affected by the Government's perceived lack of credibility in tackling the rising fiscal deficit.

***To reduce reliance on foreign trade and investment, the Malaysian Government is looking to SMEs, particularly in services and agriculture***

Malaysia is also faced with the challenge of sustaining medium-term growth through a return of private sector investment to the levels prevailing prior to the 1997-1998 crisis, given in particular the Government's declared aim of lowering dependence on foreign investment and trade. To this end, the 2003 budget introduced targeted tax cuts and tax incentives aimed at SMEs and at bolstering investment in services and agriculture. New initiatives were launched in 2002 to enable SMEs to adopt information and communication technologies to improve the management of resources, enhance design capabilities and integrate more closely with international supply chains.

***Improving total factor productivity will require a sustained effort to raise educational quality in Malaysia***

Malaysia is also seeking to transform itself into a knowledge- and service-based economy as it faces intensifying competition in third markets. Science and mathematics are to be taught in English in all schools to improve the competitiveness of the labour force and university admissions are to be based on merit and not race. In the Seventh Malaysia Plan, 1996-2000, total factor productivity contributed just under a quarter to economic growth, as compared with the relative shares of labour and capital, which were 25 per cent and just over 50 per cent respectively. In the Eighth Malaysia Plan, 2001-2005, total factor productivity is expected to contribute over 37 per cent to growth, while the relative shares of labour and capital are 21.5 and 41.3 per cent. Over the decade of 2001-2010, it is expected that the contribution of total factor productivity to overall growth will be raised to 42.5 per cent, a share much larger than the individual contributions of both labour (20.9 per cent) and capital (36.6 per cent). Much remains to be done, however, to upgrade educational quality and improve total factor productivity if Malaysia is to achieve its goal of developed country status by 2020. Education and vocational training continued to be accorded priority in the 2003 budget, as in the previous year.

***Singapore is also faced with the challenge of intensifying ...***

In Singapore, unemployment has been on a rising trend for some years, from an average of 1.8 per cent of the labour force in 1997 to a 15-year peak of 4.8 per cent (seasonally adjusted) in the third quarter of 2002. Although job losses have been concentrated in manufacturing and construction, there was also a contraction of employment in services.

*... international competition and the need to reduce vulnerability to external shocks*

While some of the increase in unemployment is no doubt cyclical, it is clear that Singapore is faced with the need to restructure and develop new industries as competitive pressures from other economies in the region intensify and global consolidation continues in such key sectors as financial services. Nevertheless, the country has maintained its ranking as the fourth most competitive economy in the world according to the World Economic Forum.

Singapore is also highly vulnerable to swings in external demand, given its significant reliance on trade. Since 1995, the country has experienced several external shocks: a downturn in the electronics industry in 1996-1997, the Asian financial crisis of 1997-1998 and another downturn in electronics in 2001. In response, the Government has maintained its medium-term focus by using fiscal measures not only to offset decreases in demand but also to influence supply-side variables, such as corporate taxation, so as to lower business costs. It has also adopted policies to promote labour market flexibility and reduce the burden of pension contributions on wages.

*Attracting highly qualified individuals and SMEs to relocate to Singapore is an important aspect of the Government's strategy*

Singapore has sought to diversify its economic activities by promoting services and chemicals, particularly pharmaceuticals, and high-end, niche products such as biomedicines. Education and training have received considerable investment. Encouraging entrepreneurship remains problematic in an economy with such a large government-linked sector, but the Government is now seeking to attract both highly qualified individuals and SMEs, particularly high-tech start-ups, to relocate to Singapore. An International SME Business Centre has been established to enable foreign SMEs to find inexpensive facilities, and the PartnerSingapore programme has also been designed to enable those firms to form partnerships with local SMEs. Attracting multinational corporations continues to be an important aim, but by broadening the focus to include SMEs the Government hopes to reduce some of the "footloose" nature of multinational investment.

*Free trade agreements are another important aspect of Singapore's strategy*

Singapore, which is a member of AFTA, has also moved aggressively to sign FTAs with other countries, not only as a means of stimulating Singaporean firms to be more competitive but also to improve the country's attractiveness as a business location. FTAs have been concluded with Australia, the European Free Trade Association, Japan and New Zealand, and the agreement with the United States is on the verge of conclusion. Singapore is also discussing FTAs with Canada, Mexico and the Republic of Korea. In 2002, ASEAN agreed to work towards establishing an FTA with China and tariffs will be eliminated for the more developed members of the grouping by 2010 (box II.8).

## Box II.8. Closer economic cooperation between ASEAN and China

At the Fourth ASEAN Informal Summit, held in Singapore in November 2000, the leaders of ASEAN and China agreed to look at measures to enhance economic cooperation and integration between them, with a view to establishing a free trade area. The imminent accession of China to the WTO and the rapid growth in trade and investment between both sides provided the spur to those discussions. ASEAN had additional reasons to search for major partners for its free trade area (AFTA). Its "flying geese" model of development, with Japan providing demand traction as well as enhanced supply potential through its FDI in ASEAN, had lost momentum with the slowdown in the Japanese economy that began in the early 1990s. The United States and the EU had provided alternative markets until the 1997-1998 financial crisis shook the confidence of their investors in the subregion. China's adoption of market-oriented development and its subsequent formidable growth have placed it in a position to play an important locomotive role for the subregion. The potential for this was demonstrated in 2002 when China was an important source of demand for the exports of goods and services from members of ASEAN.

The slow progress of multilateral negotiations on trade liberalization under WTO and the proliferation of regional and bilateral trading agreements have provided additional incentives for East Asian nations to move towards similar agreements among themselves. However, the strong commitment of Japan and the Republic of Korea to multilateral trade liberalization, as well as other issues such as trade in agriculture, have tended to slow their participation in regional trading arrangements.

Total trade between China and ASEAN grew at an average annual rate of 20.4 per cent from 1991, when total trade amounted to only $7.9 billion, to reach $39.5 billion in 2000, when ASEAN became China's fifth-largest trading partner.[a] This does not take into account the important but largely undocumented border trade between China and the new ASEAN-4, Cambodia, the Lao People's Democratic Republic, Myanmar and Viet Nam. While ASEAN's imports from China have tended to concentrate on machinery and electrical equipment, China's imports from ASEAN are moving away from resource-based products towards manufactures. In fact, the strongest rate of growth in trade between both sides is in manufactured products, with trade in machinery and electrical equipment, including electronics, growing the fastest. This suggests considerable potential for intra-industry trade between ASEAN and China, with its attendant benefits through greater product differentiation and economies of scale. Trade in services is also likely to increase sharply, including through the potentially large market in two-way tourism. Finally, the volume of direct FDI flows between China and ASEAN is still relatively small. Nevertheless, the importance of foreign-invested enterprises in exports from both sides suggests that increasing trade between them is likely to generate more investment, including from multinational corporations.

Against this background, the leaders of China and ASEAN took a decision at the summit held at Bandar Seri Begawan in November 2001 to launch negotiations for the creation of a free trade arrangement (FTA) within 10 years, and a Framework Agreement on Comprehensive Economic Cooperation between the Association of Southeast Asian Nations and the People's Republic of China was signed at the summit held at Phnom Penh in November 2002.[b] The objectives of the Agreement, which will come into force on 1 July 2003, are to strengthen and enhance economic, trade and investment cooperation, progressively liberalize trade in goods and services as well as facilitate investment, explore closer economic cooperation and facilitate the economic integration of the newer member States of ASEAN. To this end, an ASEAN-China FTA will be created, with tariffs being eliminated or reduced by China and the ASEAN-6, Brunei Darussalam, Indonesia, Malaysia, the Philippines, Singapore and Thailand, by 2010, when AFTA will be fully implemented, and by the new ASEAN-4 countries by 2015. A particular feature of the Agreement is the Early Harvest Programme of accelerated tariff reductions mainly on agricultural products. China has also committed itself to according most-favoured-nation treatment consistent with WTO rules and disciplines to all members of ASEAN that are not members of WTO. Negotiations are to begin early in 2003 on the agreement for

---

[a] After Japan, the United States, the EU and Hong Kong, China. See "Forging closer ASEAN-China economic relations in the twenty-first century", report submitted by the ASEAN-China Expert Group on Economic Cooperation, pp. 7-10, <http://www.aseansec.org/newdata/asean_chi.pdf>, 15 February 2003.

[b] See <http://www.aseansec.org/13196.htm>, 15 February 2003.

tariff reduction or elimination in order to implement the FTA by the agreed dates, and on trade in services and investments. The parties to the Framework Agreement have also agreed to strengthen cooperation in five priority areas, agriculture, ICT, human resources development, investment and development of the Mekong River basin. Particular regard will be given to capacity-building programmes and technical assistance for the newer members of ASEAN. Within a year of the entry into force of the Agreement, appropriate formal dispute settlement mechanisms and procedures will be established.

The ASEAN-China FTA will create a market of 1.7 billion consumers with a combined GDP estimated at over $2 trillion. For ASEAN, this is a major initiative, enabling it to leverage its privileged access to the Chinese market to position itself as a "hub" for future FTA "spokes", with Japan, the Republic of Korea, the United States and India, and possibly Australia and New Zealand.[c] It can also hope to retain its attractiveness as a destination for multinational FDI for the same reason. Furthermore, as Chinese companies are becoming major investors in foreign markets, ASEAN will be first in line for consideration as an investment location. The competitive pressure exerted on ASEAN by China, in terms of both exports of light manufactures, such as textiles, garments, footwear and leather products, to third-country markets, and attracting FDI flows, intensified during the 1990s. However, an examination of more recent data suggests that changing trade and FDI patterns in China, with a rising trend in the electronics sector, point to the emergence of a more complementary relationship between China and ASEAN.[d] Unlike light manufactures, where the scope for intra-industry and intra-firm trade is limited, trade in electronics is driven by multinational corporations that split the value added chain among several production locations in search of greater efficiency, lower costs and higher profitability. Thus, ASEAN can hope that greater integration with China will help it to stay in the picture if the subregion can maintain and enhance its own competitiveness.[e]

A potential problem exists, however, in the emergence of a "two-speed" ASEAN.[f] While more developed countries in ASEAN could benefit from China's growth through greater linkages with its high-tech industries, the less developed member countries (such as the new ASEAN-4 and possibly some "older" members as well) could find themselves being squeezed out of light manufacturing without the possibility of becoming part of the emerging regional production networks. Thus, there is a clear need to ensure that the development gap does not become insuperable in the process of promoting regional cooperation and enhancing regional integration.

The development of China is likely to open up unprecedented market opportunities for ASEAN. According to a recent study,[g] China will become East Asia's largest trading nation in 2020, its largest exporter in 2010 and its largest importer in 2005. It is projected to develop a structural trade surplus with Western economies but a structural trade deficit of the same magnitude with East Asia. Trade liberalization will ensure that the ASEAN economies will be in a position to take advantage of the net benefits of China's export success, even though there will be an inevitable process of adjustment as countries seek to strengthen and develop areas of comparative advantage.[h]

---

[c] Robert Scollay, "Economic impact of RTAs in Asia and the Pacific region", paper presented at the Expert Group Meeting on Regional Trade Arrangements in Asia and the Pacific, held at Bangkok on 30 and 31 January 2003.

[d] Kong-Yam Tan, "Comments on PRC's WTO entry: impact on rest of the region", paper presented at the ADB Fourth Asia Development Forum: Trade and Poverty Reduction, held at Seoul from 3 to 5 November 2002, <http://www.adb.org/Documents/Events/2002/ADF/tan_paper.pdf>, 15 February 2003.

[e] Simulations presented in Scollay, op.cit., suggest that ASEAN will be the principal beneficiary in terms of welfare of the ASEAN-China FTA, with the gain to China being negligible. An FTA that included Japan and the Republic of Korea, however, would provide greater welfare gains to both China and ASEAN.

[f] Kong-Yam Tan, op.cit., and Thitapha Wattanapruttipaisan, "ASEAN-China FTA: advantages, challenges and implications for the newer ASEAN member countries", forthcoming in *ASEAN Economic Bulletin*, April 2003.

[g] David Roland-Holst, "An overview of PRC's emergence and East Asian trade patterns to 2020", ADB Institute Research Paper 44 (Manila, October 2002), <http://www.adbi.org/PDF/wp/rp44.pdf>.

[h] The study points out, however, that although the ASEAN-China FTA will benefit most member countries, it will do so to a lesser extent than global trade liberalization. Furthermore, it will entail significant trade diversion from Japan, the Republic of Korea and Taiwan Province of China. See Roland-Holst, op. cit., and also Scollay, op. cit..

The structural problems of the labour market in Brunei Darussalam also remain to be resolved and may impinge on its ability to attract foreign investors; in the UNCTAD study referred to earlier, the country was ranked 128th out of 140 in its ability to attract FDI relative to its economic size. Many businesses are hard-pressed to find skilled workers and obtain manual labour to work on construction projects. There have also been delays in securing labour permits for migrant workers. However, many professionals are reported to be seeking jobs overseas owing to the lack of opportunities at home and government training programmes seem to attract limited interest.

***Progress in market-oriented reforms has been uneven in Viet Nam***

Viet Nam has embarked on a number of market-oriented reforms, including in the area of trade policy, where progress has been very rapid. Quantitative restrictions are being removed, tariffs reduced and other trade barriers lifted in accordance with a five-year timetable that was announced in April 2001. However, some recent backtracking has occurred with regard to motorcycles and passenger vehicles as protection continues for the domestic motorcycle and vehicle assembly and parts industries. At the same time, Viet Nam is moving ahead with commitments made under AFTA and the bilateral trade agreement with the United States. Viet Nam is also proceeding with a series of bilateral negotiations with a number of countries as it is seeking membership in WTO. Reform of State-owned enterprises has been viewed as a necessary complement to trade and banking reforms, but progress has not been as fast as expected, largely because of management and employee resistance and the heavy debt burden of those enterprises; the debt consists mainly of loans from State-owned commercial banks. The Government is seeking to revitalize the process by setting annual targets for the reform of State-owned enterprises, and 1,400 of these firms are to be equitized by mid-2004.

***The limited economic recovery in 2002 opened up the possibility of initiating fiscal consolidation in some countries in the subregion***

Fiscal consolidation has been a major preoccupation in some countries, such as Indonesia, which has little discretion on either the fiscal or monetary policy fronts. Economic policy is being formulated under an IMF progrmme due to expire in December 2003. Considerable progress has been made in reducing the Government's deficit through cuts in fuel subsidies, falling interest rates and some increases in tax revenue (table II.36). The actual deficit in 2001 was 2.7 per cent of GDP, below the planned 3.7 per cent, as the inability to meet reform commitments delayed disbursement of foreign financing. For 2002, the deficit target of 2.5 per cent of GDP is likely to be met. A more substantial reduction in the deficit, to 1.3 per cent of GDP, was planned for 2003 but this was revised upwards to 1.8 per cent after the Bali bombing. The Government-debt-to GDP ratio declined more rapidly than expected, from 98 per cent in 2000 to 80 per cent in mid-2002, but around 40 per cent of the State budget is currently allotted to servicing both foreign and domestic debts. Legislation adopted on 24 September 2002 established treasury bills as a new asset class, allowing the Government to issue those bills with maturities of 6-12 months to refinance bank recapitalization bonds as they come due. Previously, the bond market consisted of only short-term Bank Indonesia certificates and long-term recapitalization bonds, and the addition of these bills will increase liquidity and permit greater flexibility in financing.

***The fiscal deficit target was overshot by a very wide margin in the Philippines, where tax administration is in need of urgent reform***

In the Philippines, the fiscal balance went from a surplus of 0.1 per cent of GDP in 1997 to a deficit of 4 per cent in 2001, and a lower shortfall of 3.3 per cent of GDP was targeted in 2002. It now appears that the deficit for 2002 will be 5.6 per cent of GDP and targeted shortfalls for 2003 and following years will have to be reviewed. Interest payments consumed around one third of government revenues in 2002. A reduction in the fiscal shortfall appears to be mainly dependent on raising more revenue, as there is little room for further expenditure cuts if essential spending on the social sectors is not to be jeopardized. While there may be some room for increasing tax effort, tax administration appears to be the area most in need of reform, and the Government has introduced several measures to improve tax collection. A bill was also introduced in Congress to create an Internal Revenue Management Authority to strengthen the performance and accountability of the Bureau of Internal Revenue.

The concern on the part of investors is that, as the sovereign ratings of the Philippines slip, the cost of loans in foreign currency on which the Government has been relying will rise, forcing it to turn to domestic sources of funds. Capital markets are underdeveloped in the Philippines, as in other countries in the subregion, the principal type of financing for companies being short-term lending from domestic banks. While loan demand has been subdued, the banks have been more than willing to purchase government paper, but if demand from private investors were to rise, they could find themselves being "crowded out" by the public sector. Since companies in the Philippines tend to rely on retained earnings to finance investment much more than do other countries of the region, this effect could be mitigated somewhat but heavy public sector borrowing could still stand in the way of capital market development.

In Viet Nam, the 2001 fiscal deficit, widened to 3.5 per cent of GDP, from 3 per cent in 2000, as the Government had to incur additional capital expenditure to repair infrastructure damaged by flooding. For 2002, a further widening of the deficit, to 4 per cent of GDP, is expected as more resources are needed for poverty reduction and reforms.

***Fiscal consolidation in Viet Nam will require a major effort to develop non-oil sources of government revenue***

The Government is also hoping to stabilize the level of public debt in the medium term and the deficit is set to decline gradually to 2 per cent of GDP by 2007. However, the augmented deficit, including on-lending and the capital cost of reforms, will peak at 10 per cent of GDP in 2003. Total public sector debt, including the portion pertaining to State-owned enterprises, was approximately 70 per cent of GDP in 2001; it is expected to peak at 76 per cent in 2004 before a subsequent gradual decline. Achieving fiscal consolidation will require a major effort to increase non-oil revenue, apart from containing the public sector wage bill and the expenditure of State-owned enterprises. It is estimated that almost one third of government revenue came from oil in 2002, but this figure is likely to drop in the future because of capacity constraints and possibly softer international prices. Rapid economic growth and measures to improve tax administration and combat tax fraud, particularly in VAT, may help to raise tax collections. However, a further strain on the budget can be expected from lower import tariffs resulting from commitments made under AFTA and the bilateral trade agreement with the United States, as well as from the provision of such tax incentives as the agricultural tax exemption for poor farmers.

***Malaysia and Thailand have initiated the process of deficit reduction but much will depend on their economic performance in the immediate future***

With the 2002 budget, Malaysia aimed to initiate the process of fiscal consolidation while at the same time attempting to support growth. The target for the shortfall was 5.1 per cent, down from 5.5 per cent in 2001, and strong revenue performance during the year led to a downward revision of the deficit to approximately 4.7 per cent. The 2003 budget seeks a further reduction to 3.9 per cent of GDP, but it was formulated when growth prospects appeared brighter and the deficit target may have to be reconsidered if the global economy weakens significantly. Strong revenue performance also led to a downward revision of Thailand's actual budget deficit in 2002 to 2.2 per cent, below the programmed 3.7 per cent as well as the actual shortfall of 2.4 per cent in 2001. Government debt, however, increased from 14.5 per cent of GDP in 1996 to approximately 59 per cent of GDP in 2001, with two thirds of the increase related to the costs of financial restructuring. The government focus is increasingly on fiscal consolidation, and the deficit programmed for 2003 is 3.1 per cent of GDP; it is hoped to return to a balanced budget by 2007. The target ratio of government debt to GDP was lowered from 60 to 55 per cent of GDP.

***Indonesia has made reasonable progress in financial restructuring***

Financial restructuring continues to be an important preoccupation in some South-East Asian countries. In Indonesia, the Indonesian Bank Restructuring Agency is likely to achieve its revenue target for 2002, having disposed of NPLs worth Rp 81.6 trillion at an average recovery rate of 28.3 per cent. The revenue target for 2003 was raised following revision of the State budget after the Bali bombing, but the Agency is still confident of meeting the higher target level. NPLs in the banking system amounted to 12.1 per cent in July 2002, as against 15.8 per cent in July 2001. After the Bali incident, Bank Indonesia postponed the requirement for banks to reduce NPLs to 5 per cent of outstanding loans by the end of 2003. It has also indicated that it will not be rigid about enforcing a 12 per cent capital adequacy ratio in line with Basel requirements. Although the average capital adequacy ratio in mid-2002 was quite high, at 23.4 per cent, this could reflect continuing bank reluctance to lend and weak loan demand. Blanket government guarantees on bank deposits, introduced at the height of the financial crisis of 1997-1998, are to be phased out in 2003. The Jakarta Initiative Task Force, which was founded in 1998, has finalized debt-restructuring deals for about 60 per cent of its $29 billion portfolio. Its mandate was extended from 2001 to expire at the end of 2003, and companies are still seeking its assistance. However, its work has been hampered by continuing weak economic growth and inadequate bankruptcy legislation.

***The financial sector remains strong in Malaysia, where considerable progress has also been made in corporate governance***

Financial and corporate restructuring has been largely completed in Malaysia. The banking sector remains sound, with the risk-weighted capital adequacy ratio reaching 13.3 per cent and the net NPL ratio declining to 7.7 per cent in the third quarter of 2002. Danaharta has restructured all its NPL holdings, with an average expected recovery rate of 57 per cent. The Corporate Debt Restructuring Committee closed down its operations as scheduled in August 2002, completing all but one of its 48 debt-restructuring cases; the remaining case was resolved in September. Considerable progress has also been made in corporate governance: minority shareholders' rights were strengthened; a new accounting standard was issued so as to improve the timeliness and reliability of financial disclosures; code of conduct guidelines were developed; and laws governing listing on the Kuala Lumpur Stock Exchange were amended.

***The health of banks in Thailand has improved but private banks still need help with NPLs***

The Thai Asset Management Corporation, which was established to clear up the NPLs of financial institutions, expects to meet its restructuring target of B 500 billion for 2002 and to complete restructuring of the remaining B 280 billion in its portfolio by the end of 2003. By mid-December 2002, it had restructured B 482 billion in NPLs, with an average recovery rate of 45 per cent. In 2003, the Corporation will focus on smaller NPLs (below 20 million baht) of State-owned financial institutions and will take over the debts of the Industrial Finance Corporation of Thailand. Most of the loans in the Corporation's portfolio came from State-owned banks, where the NPL ratio was 5.3 per cent at the end of November 2002. Private banks continue to be burdened with bad loans and the NPL ratio for those banks was around 13.7 per cent at the end of November 2002. Banks are still reluctant to lend to businesses, preferring to expand credit card operations and home mortgages. This may be one factor holding back private investment, in addition to the opportunity to buy assets cheaply during restructuring. The Bank of Thailand has announced that it intends to assist commercial banks by acting as a mediator between banks and their debtors to clear up around B 840 billion in bad loans by the end of 2004. In other respects, the financial health of banks remains good and the risk-weighted capital adequacy ratio of all commercial banks was around 14.3 per cent in October 2002, well above the 8 per cent Basel minimum requirement.

***The NPL ratio in the Philippines is now higher than in the countries directly affected by the 1997-1998 financial crisis***

The Philippines was not as severely affected by the 1997-1998 financial crisis as other countries in the region, but the number of NPLs has been increasing in recent years. The NPL ratio went up from 4.7 per cent at the end of 1997 to 16.5 per cent in September 2002. At this level, the ratio is now higher than that prevailing in the countries most severely hit by the financial crisis (Indonesia, Malaysia, the Republic of Korea and Thailand). No centralized asset management corporation has been set up so far, but the Government is working on legislation (the Special Purpose Asset Vehicle bill) that will permit banks to sell non-performing assets to specially designed asset management corporations. However, progress in the passage of this bill has been slow.

***The Philippines is working to be removed from the Financial Action Task Force's list of non-cooperative countries***

The country is moving ahead to strengthen its banking system and introduced a new risk-based capital adequacy ratio for banks effective July 2001. At the end of March 2002, the ratio reached 16.7 per cent, well above the Basel minimum. Following the passage of the Anti-Money Laundering Act in September 2001, the Central Bank issued a manual for banks and other financial institutions to promote compliance. However, the Philippines remains on the Financial Action Task Force on Money Laundering's list of non-cooperative countries and the central banking authorities are working with other government agencies on drafting a bill to amend the Act to address outstanding concerns.

***Viet Nam has a long way to go before its banking sector can meet the challenge of multinational financial services corporations***

The opening of the service sector in Viet Nam, as envisaged in the bilateral agreement with the United States, will have a major impact on the banking industry, where reforms have also been progressing. The ratio of NPLs to the total loans of the banking system dropped from 12.7 per cent at the end of 2000 to 4.8 per cent at the end of 2002, and banks have had to absorb losses amounting to 57 per cent of the face value of NPLs. At the beginning of 2002, the four major State-owned banks had a capital adequacy ratio of 2.8 per cent, well below the Basel minimum. The first phase of recapitalization took place in 2002, and by 2004 the ratio will have reached 5 per cent.

## B. Least developed countries in the subregion

### *Overview and prospects*

***The fall in overall economic growth in Cambodia and the Lao People's Democratic Republic in 2002 was expected to be reversed in 2003***

The three least developed countries in South-East Asia, Cambodia, the Lao People's Democratic Republic and Myanmar, showed a varied economic performance in 2001-2002 (figure II.31). Notwithstanding the global and regional slowdown, the Lao People's Democratic Republic managed to sustain growth in all sectors; construction and the garment industry were the stimuli for the expansion in industrial output. By contrast, economic growth in Cambodia was softened by the decrease in garment exports and hence manufacturing output. However, with the opening of direct air routes to Siem Reap, tourism has become an important source of foreign exchange earnings. Following the double-digit growth officially recorded in recent years, GDP growth in Myanmar slowed considerably, despite the promise shown in agricultural output, oil and gas production and inward tourism. Adverse weather conditions in 2002 affected agricultural output in all three least developed countries in the subregion.

However, faster economic growth is expected in these countries in 2003. The Government of Cambodia is aiming at an increase of more than 6 per cent in aggregate output, although the civil unrest targeted at foreign interests late in January 2003 could have a dampening ripple effect. GDP is projected to rise by 6 per cent in the Lao People's Democratic Republic in 2003, industry and the service sector being the main stimuli; these two sectors account for just under half of domestic production. The Government of Myanmar is also aiming at an annual 6 per cent rate of expansion in GDP in the period 2003-2005, slightly higher than in 2002.

**Figure II.31. Rates of GDP growth in the least developed countries in South-East Asia, 1999-2002**

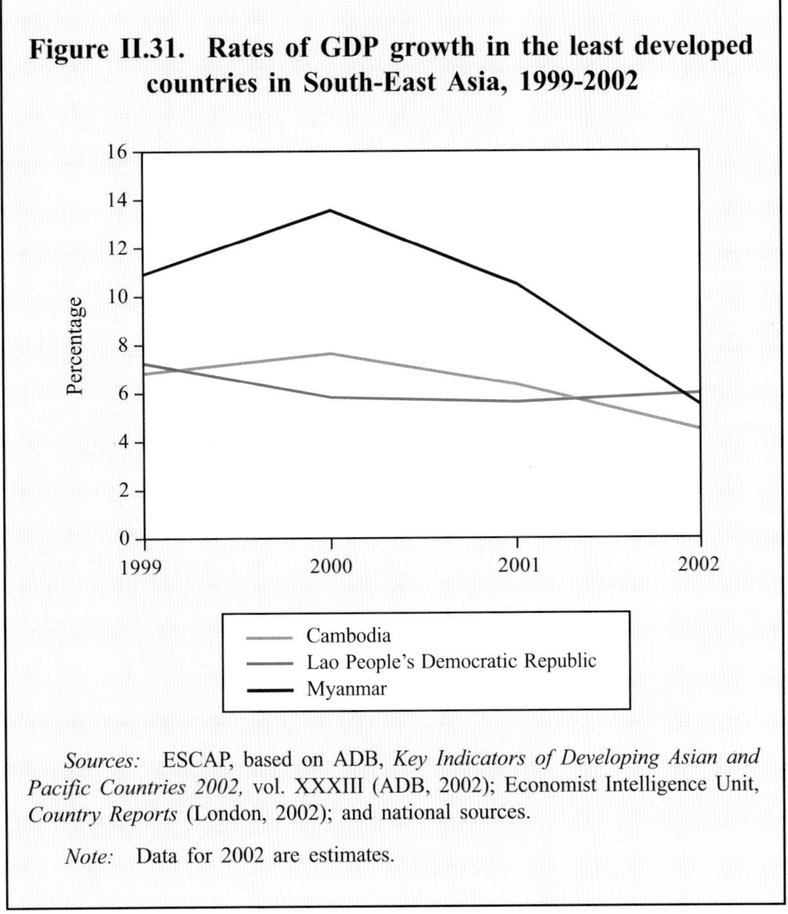


*Sources:* ESCAP, based on ADB, *Key Indicators of Developing Asian and Pacific Countries 2002,* vol. XXXIII (ADB, 2002); Economist Intelligence Unit, *Country Reports* (London, 2002); and national sources.

*Note:* Data for 2002 are estimates.

***There was a mixed picture in consumer price movements***

Both Cambodia and the Lao People's Democratic Republic managed to retain single-digit inflation rates in 2002 as they curtailed Central Bank financing of the fiscal deficit (figure II.32). Those countries were also able to sustain exchange rate stability while reaffirming their commitment to flexible exchange rate regimes, as evidenced by the narrow margin between official and market exchange rates. Central Bank financing of public expenditure in Myanmar, however, has led to spiralling inflation and depreciation of the kyat.

**Figure II.32. Inflation in the least developed countries in South-East Asia, 1999-2002[a]**

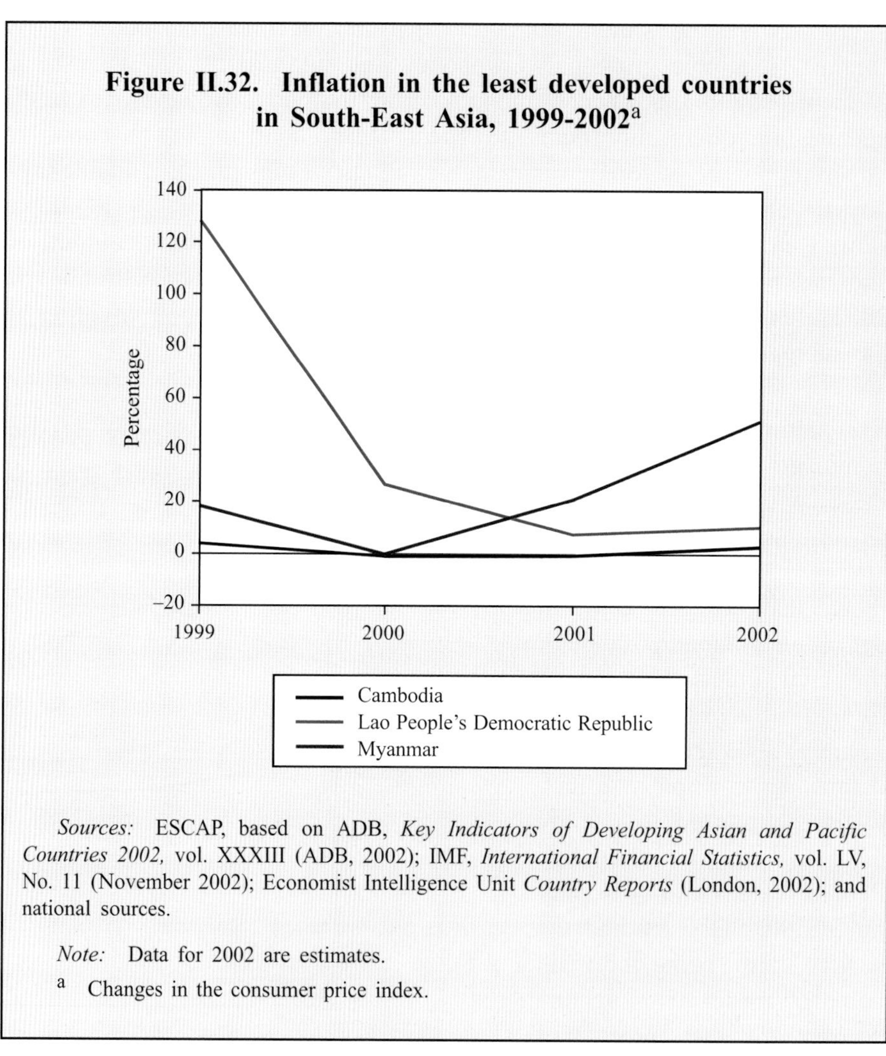


*Sources:* ESCAP, based on ADB, *Key Indicators of Developing Asian and Pacific Countries 2002,* vol. XXXIII (ADB, 2002); IMF, *International Financial Statistics,* vol. LV, No. 11 (November 2002); Economist Intelligence Unit *Country Reports* (London, 2002); and national sources.

*Note:* Data for 2002 are estimates.

[a] Changes in the consumer price index.

***Improved outcome in the external accounts***

Although export earnings continued to rise in all three countries, growth in a number of key sectors, such as garments in Cambodia and gas in Myanmar, was expected to slow in the coming year as demand from importing countries stabilized (figure II.33). Import spending was expected to grow more slowly than exports in the Lao People's Democratic Republic and to decline in Myanmar, leading to a slight

**Figure II.33. Growth rates in merchandise export earnings of the least developed countries in South-East Asia, 1999-2002**

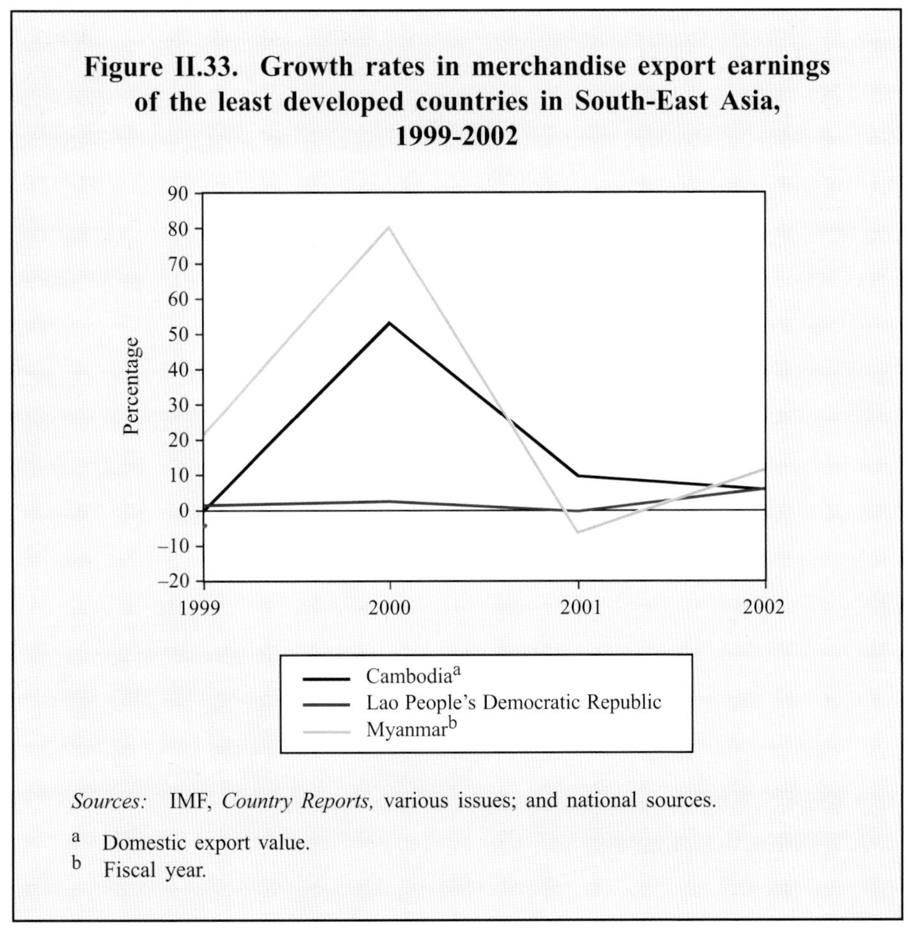


*Sources:* IMF, *Country Reports,* various issues; and national sources.

[a] Domestic export value.

[b] Fiscal year.

improvement in their external current accounts in 2002 (figure II.34). All three countries experienced an increase in official reserves in 2002, although the rise was rather small in Myanmar. The exchange rate performance was much improved in Cambodia, where the riel was essentially stable, and in the Lao People's Democratic Republic, where the depreciation of the kip slowed considerably (figure II.35).

## *GDP growth performance*

***Real GDP growth in Cambodia was adversely affected by reduced garment exports and tourism receipts***

Cambodia recorded a marginal decline in GDP growth, from 5.5 per cent in 2001 to an estimated 4.5 per cent in 2002, owing mainly to the declining growth in garment exports and tourism receipts (table II.37). A drought in 2002, followed by flooding in some areas, also depressed agricultural production, which comprises almost two fifths of current-price GDP, with knock-on effects on consumer demand Although garment export volumes were maintained, the prices of new orders were reported to have fallen by more than 10 per cent. Restructured concession agreements for forestry were not completed on schedule in 2001,

**Figure II.34. Growth rates in merchandise import spending of the least developed countries in South-East Asia, 1999-2002**

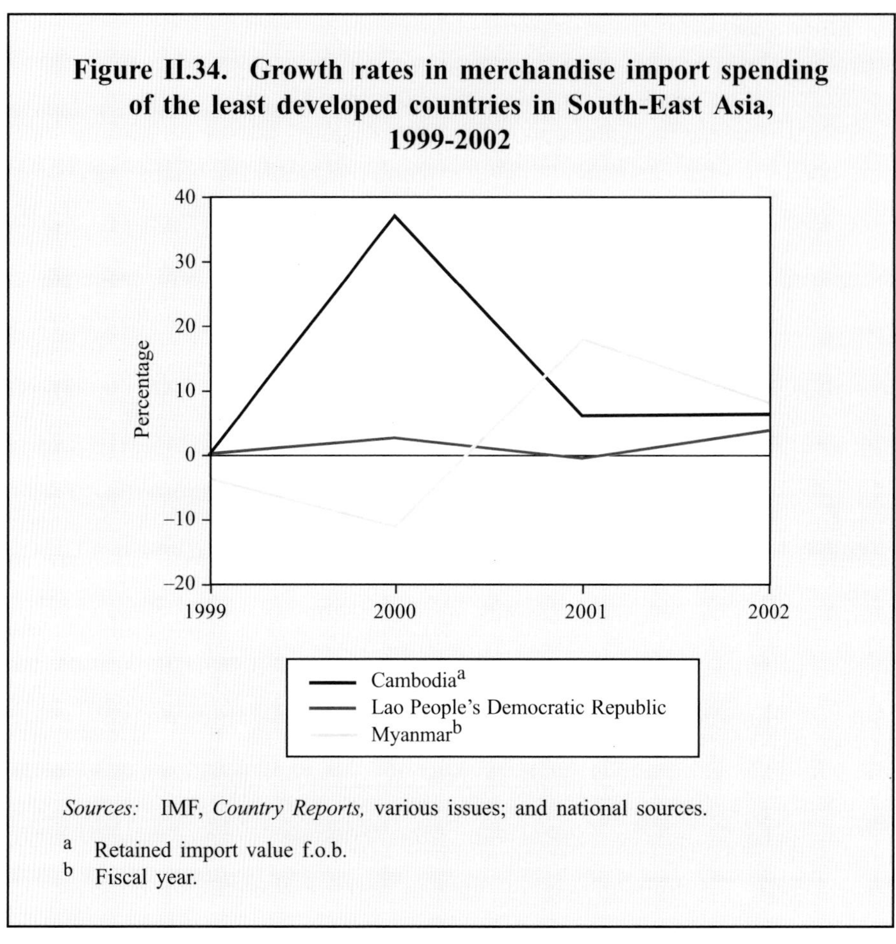


*Sources:* IMF, *Country Reports,* various issues; and national sources.

[a] Retained import value f.o.b.
[b] Fiscal year.

thereby affecting logging operations. However, foreign airlines were allowed to fly directly to Siem Reap, which is located near the Angkor Wat temple complex; as a result, visitor arrivals by air went up by over 70 per cent year on year in 2001 and by another 12 per cent year on year in 2002. Tourist arrivals from within the Asian region offset the decline in arrivals from outside Asia, particularly after the Bali bombing, but the decline at the higher end of the market affected overall tourism receipts.

***A rise in regional economic activity, new construction and other investments sustained growth in the Lao People's Democratic Republic in 2002***

A rise in regional economic activity, new construction and a number of large and medium-sized investments sustained a strong growth rate of 5.8 per cent in the Lao People's Democratic Republic in 2002. Progress in reforms, including streamlined approval procedures, has stimulated investment in the second mobile telephone network, manufacturing, mining and aviation. Investment in telecommunication and transport infrastructure was expected to further stimulate the tourism sector. Flooding in several provinces in 2002, however, could lead to lower output in the agricultural sector and affect overall economic growth in 2003 adversely.

**Figure II.35. Index of exchange rates against the United States dollar in the least developed countries in South-East Asia, 1996-2002**

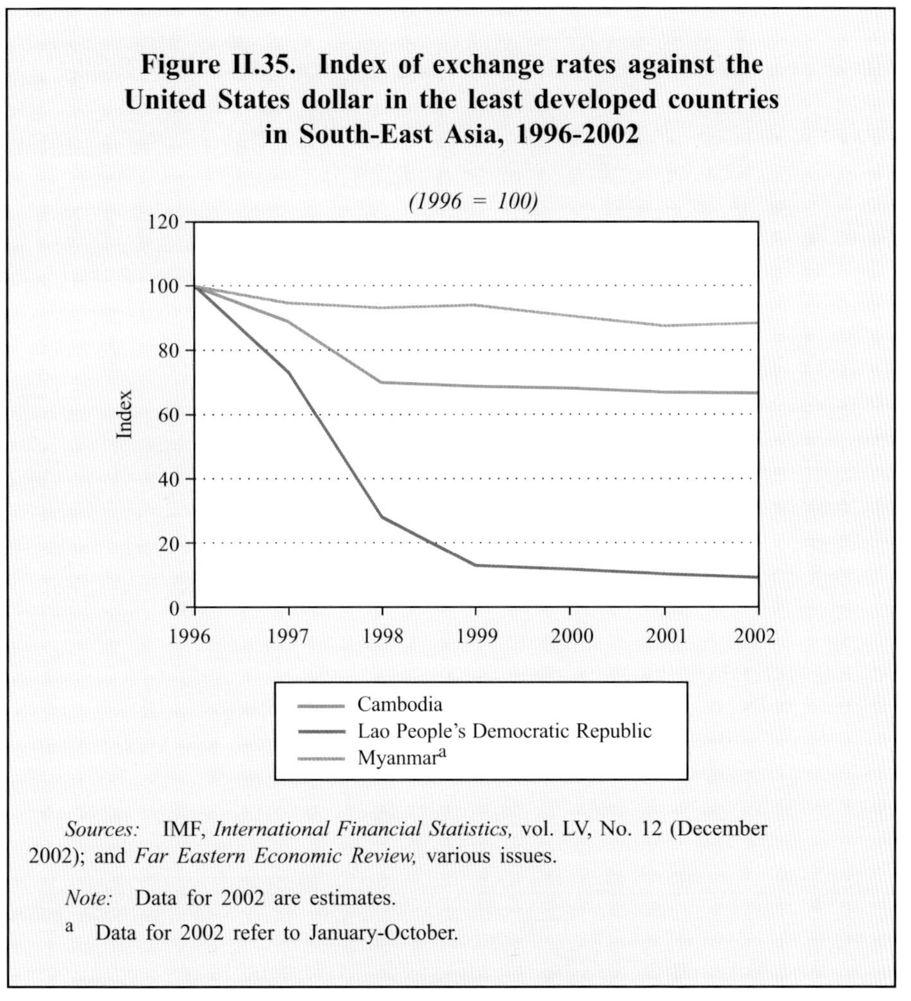


*Sources:* IMF, *International Financial Statistics,* vol. LV, No. 12 (December 2002); and *Far Eastern Economic Review,* various issues.

*Note:* Data for 2002 are estimates.

[a] Data for 2002 refer to January-October.

***Agriculture, oil and gas, as well as tourism, hold promise for future economic growth in Myanmar***

According to official figures, GDP in Myanmar went up by 10.5 per cent in 2001; economic growth was driven primarily by the agricultural sector, which performed well owing to the absence of flooding and drought. The expansion of primary production contributed, in turn, to growth in agro-processing, services and trade. A glut in the domestic rice market led to low rice prices, affecting farmers adversely. Other economic indicators, however, showed less positive signs. Domestic production and imports of fertilizer declined by more than half in 2001. Yields of rice crops also declined in 2001 owing to such factors as the current rice procurement system and a shortage of fertilizer as a result of foreign exchange constraints. Although cement production declined by almost 10 per cent over the period, power generation was reported to have increased by 10 per cent. GDP growth in Myanmar in 2002 slowed noticeably to 5.5 per cent, as floods affected agricultural output and industrial production remained sluggish. Weak domestic and international demand, reduced foreign investment and continuing power shortages constrained growth, although construction showed signs of recovery.

**Table II.37. Least developed countries in South-East Asia: growth rates, 1999-2002**

*(Percentage)*

| | | Rates of growth | | | |
|---|---|---|---|---|---|
| | | Gross domestic product | Agriculture | Industry | Services |
| Cambodia | 1999 | 6.9 | 0.0 | 13.2 | 7.1 |
| | 2000 | 7.7 | –0.3 | 34.6 | 5.8 |
| | 2001 | 5.5 | 3.9 | 15.5 | 2.9 |
| | 2002 | 4.5 | 0.9 | 11.8 | 3.9 |
| Lao People's Democratic Republic | 1999 | 7.3 | 8.2 | 8.0 | 6.7 |
| | 2000 | 5.8 | 4.1 | 9.4 | 5.5 |
| | 2001 | 5.7 | 4.0 | 7.0 | 7.7 |
| | 2002 | 5.8 | 4.0 | 9.8 | 5.8 |
| Myanmar | 1999 | 10.9 | 11.5 | 13.8 | 9.2 |
| | 2000 | 13.7 | 12.4 | 18.0 | 13.4 |
| | 2001 | 10.5 | 7.2 | 17.2 | 14.0 |
| | 2002 | 5.5 | .. | .. | .. |

*Sources:* ESCAP, based on ADB, *Key Indicators of Developing Asian and Pacific Countries 2002,* vol. XXXIII (ADB, 2002); Economist Intelligence Unit, *Country Reports* (London, 2002), various issues; and national sources.

*Note:* Data for 2002 are estimates. Industry comprises mining and quarrying; manufacturing; electricity, gas and power; and construction.

An examination of the savings and investment ratios of the least developed countries of South-East Asia indicates that these ratios are low and have declined in many cases (table II.38). In Cambodia, the sharp rise in the investment ratio in 2001 was not sustained, and the ratio fell by 1.7 percentage points in 2002; the savings ratio has declined moderately every year since 2000. By contrast, in the Lao People's Democratic Republic the investment ratio has improved gradually since 2000 but the fall in the savings ratio has been quite marked.

### *Inflation*

***After experiencing deflation through most of 2001, consumer prices were on the rise in Cambodia in 2002***

In Cambodia, there was slight deflation over 2000-2001 but inflation of around 3 per cent in 2002 (table II.39). Among the causal factors were drought-induced damage to the rice crop, which contributed to higher rice prices, and increased prices for housing and utilities. Inflationary pressures from higher food prices are likely to continue in 2003, and the Government has set an annual consumer price inflation target of 3.5 to 4 per cent for the period 2001-2005; this represents an upward revision of an earlier target of "close to zero".

**Table II.38. Least developed countries in South-East Asia: ratios of gross domestic savings and investment to GDP, 1999-2002**

*(Percentage)*

| | *1999* | *2000* | *2001* | *2002* |
|---|---|---|---|---|
| **Savings as a percentage of GDP** | | | | |
| Cambodia | .. | 10.7 | 10.2 | 10.0 |
| Lao People's Democratic Republic | 16.4 | 15.1 | 15.4 | 13.7 |
| Myanmar | 13.1 | 12.3 | .. | .. |
| **Investment as a percentage of GDP** | | | | |
| Cambodia | 15.9 | 13.5 | 17.9 | 16.2 |
| Lao People's Democratic Republic | 22.7 | 20.5 | 21.0 | 21.2 |
| Myanmar | 13.4 | 12.4 | 11.3 | .. |

*Sources:* ESCAP, based on ADB, *Key Indicators of Developing Asian and Pacific Countries 2002,* vol. XXXIII (ADB, 2002) and *Asian Development Outlook 2002* (Oxford University Press, 2002); and national sources.

*Note:* Data for 2002 are estimates.

Cambodia has a highly dollarized economy, and it has been estimated that foreign currency deposits accounted for just under 70 per cent of broad money supply (M2) in 2002. This, together with the weakness of the financial system, makes monetary policy largely ineffectual. Money supply growth accelerated sharply in 2000 to an annual rate of almost 27 per cent, but slowed subsequently as the National Bank of Cambodia has been avoiding bank financing of fiscal deficits; the growth rate was 22 per cent in 2002, slightly up on the previous year (table II.39). Meanwhile, more room has been created for the expansion of credit to the domestic private sector.

***Inflation in the Lao People's Democratic Republic remained stabilized, although at the double-digit level***

Macroeconomic stability has improved remarkably in the Lao People's Democratic Republic as a result of a variety of factors. Expenditure restraint and an increase in the number of auctions of government securities have eliminated the need for Central Bank financing of the budget. Consequently, money supply (M2) growth of 20 per cent in 2002 was largely unchanged from the previous year but significantly below the very high rates prevailing in 1999-2000. The rate of inflation, which had been in triple digits in 1999, has slowed substantially since then, reaching 7.8 per cent in 2001 before picking up somewhat to 10.6 per cent in 2002. This upturn was largely due to seasonal pressures and the introduction of large-denomination bank notes, which led to higher prices in the last quarter of the fiscal year. However, ongoing stabilization policies are expected to reduce inflation to 5 per cent by 2004.

**Table II.39. Least developed countries in South-East Asia: inflation and money supply growth (M2), 1999-2002**

*(Percentage)*

| | *1999* | *2000* | *2001* | *2002* |
|---|---|---|---|---|
| **Inflation**[a] | | | | |
| Cambodia | 4.0 | –0.8 | –0.5 | 3.0 |
| Lao People's Democratic Republic | 128.5 | 27.1 | 7.8 | 10.6 |
| Myanmar | 18.4 | –0.1 | 21.1 | 51.3 |
| **Money supply growth (M2)** | | | | |
| Cambodia | 17.3 | 26.9 | 20.4 | 22.0 |
| Lao People's Democratic Republic | 78.4 | 45.5 | 20.2 | 20.0 |
| Myanmar | 29.7 | 42.4 | 43.9 | 40.6[b] |

*Sources:* ESCAP, based on ADB, *Key Indicators of Developing Asian and Pacific Countries 2002,* vol XXXIII (ADB, 2002); IMF, *International Financial Statistics,* vol. LV, No. 11 (November 2002); Economist Intelligence Unit, *Country Reports* (London, 2002); and national sources.

*Note:* Data for 2002 are estimates.

a Changes in the consumer price index.
b January-April.

***Central Bank financing of public expenditure in Myanmar led to higher inflation and depreciation of the kyat***

In Myanmar, the annual growth rate in the money supply (M2) was over 40 per cent in the period 2000-2002. The financing requirements of the public sector and the continued low interest policy led to domestic credit growth of almost 37 per cent in 2001; private sector credit, primarily to the manufacturing and trade sectors, was also up by 57 per cent year on year over the same period. Consumer prices went up sharply, from virtually no inflation in 2000 to 21 per cent in the following year, with steep rises in the prices of essential commodities. In 2002, inflation went up further to a rate in excess of 50 per cent. Much of this acceleration could be traced to an increase in public sector wages that was financed by Central Bank lending to the Government. In addition, the rise in food prices, particularly of rice, in the wake of heavy flooding, was compounded by higher prices for imported goods following a steep depreciation of the free-market exchange rate and periods of border closure. Although the Government is expected to act to restrain prices in the near future, accommodative monetary policy and higher prices for imported goods are likely to generate domestic inflationary pressures.

## *Foreign trade and other external transactions*

### *External trade*

In Cambodia, domestic exports (excluding re-exports), at $1.3 billion in 2001, were expected to increase by only 6 per cent in 2002, compared with almost 10 per cent in 2001 (table II.40). Much of the slowdown reflected difficult market conditions in the United States for garment exports, which accounted for approximately 70 per cent of the value of merchandise exports in 2000. Although garment export quotas to the United States for Cambodia were raised by 15 per cent in 2002, non-quota exports slowed as demand remained weak and competition intensified. Cambodia benefited from firmer international rubber prices, but the volatile international prices of other commodities, such as black pepper and chillies, affected export earnings as traders switched sourcing.

***A marginal rise in Cambodia's external current account deficit resulted as a low rate of import spending did not offset slower export growth entirely***

**Table II.40. Least developed countries in South-East Asia: merchandise exports and their rates of growth, 1999-2002**

| | Exports (f.o.b.) | | | | |
|---|---|---|---|---|---|
| | *Value (millions of US dollars)* | *Annual rate of growth (percentage)* | | | |
| | *2001* | *1999* | *2000* | *2001* | *2002* |
| Cambodia[a] | 1 288 | .. | 53.2 | 9.8 | 6.0 |
| Lao People's Democratic Republic | 350 | 1.5 | 2.6 | −0.3 | 6.2 |
| Myanmar[b] | 2 293 | 21.6 | 80.6 | −6.1 | 11.6 |

*Sources:* IMF, *Country Reports,* various issues; and national sources.

[a] Domestic exports.
[b] Fiscal year.

Retained imports, which amounted to $1.6 billion in 2001, grew by 6.5 per cent in 2002, a rate marginally faster than that of exports but largely similar to that of import spending in the previous year (table II.41). As a result, the merchandise trade deficit widened in Cambodia in 2002. The slower growth in imports of the inputs needed for export-oriented industries was offset to some extent by higher import prices for oil. Inward tourism, which had expanded strongly in 2001, notwithstanding the events of 11 September 2001, did not grow as quickly in 2002 as the global economy weakened; the Bali incident also contributed to the slowdown in the number of visitors from outside the region. Consequently, the service balance weakened, and Cambodia's external current account deficit worsened, from 6.3 per cent of GDP in 2001 to

**Table II.41. Least developed countries in South-East Asia: merchandise imports and their rates of growth, 1999-2002**

| | *Value (millions of US dollars)* | *Imports (c.i.f.) Annual rate of growth (percentage)* | | | |
|---|---|---|---|---|---|
| | *2001* | *1999* | *2000* | *2001* | *2002* |
| Cambodia[a] | 1 647 | .. | 37.1 | 6.2 | 6.5 |
| Lao People's Democratic Republic | 567 | 0.3 | 2.7 | –0.4 | 3.9 |
| Myanmar[b] | 2 736 | –3.6 | –11.0 | 18.0 | 8.1 |

*Sources:* IMF, *Country Reports,* various issues; and national sources.

[a] Retained imports f.o.b.
[b] Fiscal year.

over 8 per cent in 2002 (table II.42). As one of the three pilot countries in the Integrated Framework for Trade-related Technical Assistance to Least Developed Countries, Cambodia has designated trade policy and facilitation as one of the pillars of its National Poverty Reduction Strategy and has expressed its commitment to the WTO accession process.

**Table II.42. Least developed countries in South-East Asia: budget and current account balance as a percentage of GDP, 1999-2002**

*(Percentage)*

| | *1999* | *2000* | *2001* | *2002* |
|---|---|---|---|---|
| **Budget balance as a percentage of GDP** | | | | |
| Cambodia[a] | –4.0 | –5.3 | –6.0 | –5.9 |
| Lao People's Democratic Republic[a] | –10.5 | –8.3 | –7.5 | –8.3 |
| Myanmar[b] | –4.5 | –8.3 | –4.6 | –4.9 |
| **Current account balance as a percentage of GDP** | | | | |
| Cambodia[c] | –8.4 | –7.6 | –6.3 | –8.1 |
| Lao People's Democratic Republic[c] | .. | –8.3 | –6.9 | –8.0 |
| Myanmar[a,d] | –0.2 | 0.0 | –0.1 | .. |

*Sources:* ESCAP, based on ADB, *Key Indicators of Developing Asian and Pacific Countries 2002,* vol. XXXIII (ADB, 2002) and *Asian Development Outlook 2002* (Oxford University Press, 2002); IMF, *International Financial Statistics,* vol. LV, No. 11 (November 2002); Economist Intelligence Unit, *Country Reports* (London, 2002); and national sources.

*Note:* Data for 2002 are estimates.

[a] Excluding grants.
[b] Refers to the consolidated public sector, including the Government and non-financial State enterprises.
[c] Excluding transfers.
[d] At official exchange rates.

*The removal of structural impediments is necessary to improve the long-term export competitiveness of the Lao People's Democratic Republic*

After contracting in 2001, both merchandise exports and imports returned to positive growth in the Lao People's Democratic Republic in 2002; export earnings went up by 6.2 per cent easily outpacing the import growth of just under 4 per cent. However, the deficit on the trade account rose from $217 million in 2001 to $285 million in 2002. Exports were dominated by electricity from hydropower plants, garments and wood products. The sluggish growth in imports reflected weak demand for the inputs needed for the export industries as well as slower domestic demand, although these compressing factors on import expenditure were somewhat offset by a higher bill for imported fuel. The deficit on the external current account, which had narrowed to 6.9 per cent of GDP in 2001, widened again to 8 per cent in 2002.

In August 2002, following the conclusion of an agreement to facilitate trade, Viet Nam lowered tariffs by around 50 per cent on 27 items commonly imported from the Lao People's Democratic Republic, among which were agricultural and wood products, industrial goods and handicrafts. Given the level of dollarization in the economy of the Lao People's Democratic Republic, the removal of structural impediments would be necessary in order to improve export competitiveness. Lack of access to the United States market in the absence of normal trading relations status is another problem limiting export potential. Import controls have been partially liberalized in line with international practices and commitments made under AFTA, with the lifting of quantitative restrictions on two out of six product groups before the end of 2002. However, in October 2002, customs officials began imposing a 20 per cent tariff on a wide range of imports from Thailand (with a value of B500 and above per item) brought in through the main border-crossing between the two countries.

*Priority import lists to maintain foreign exchange control in Myanmar have constrained the implementation of tariff reforms*

In Myanmar, the external current account (measured at the official exchange rate) deteriorated slightly, from an approximate balance in 2000 to a deficit of 0.1 per cent of GDP in 2001, as the merchandise trade balance declined. However, a better outcome was likely in 2002 as exports, led by gas and agricultural commodities, increased sharply by almost 12 per cent. Natural gas was the largest single export item and rice exports also showed notable gains following a series of good harvests. Exports of pulses and beans, mainly to Bangladesh and India, accounted for 18 per cent of non-gas exports in 2001. The suspension of the issuance of export licences to foreign traders in 2002, however, was expected to reduce such exports. Exports of seafood and hardwoods also performed well, but tourism receipts and private remittances were lower. State-owned enterprises, which accounted for 21 per cent of the aggregate output in Myanmar in 2000, handled the export of rice, petroleum, natural gas, precious stones and metals. The public sector's share of total exports rose to 47 per cent in 2001 from 30 per cent in the previous year.

Receipts from gas exports in 2000 financed public sector imports, contributing to a higher share of imports going to that sector: 35 per cent in 2001 compared with 28 per cent in previous years.

Imports into Myanmar expanded very sharply in 2001, by approximately 18 per cent, before slowing to a growth rate of 8 per cent in the following year. Imports of both capital and consumer goods fell, as investment remained depressed and the sharp depreciation in the free market exchange rate limited consumer demand. Although the country has implemented tariff reforms in line with the AFTA Common Effective Preferential Tariff Scheme, the continuation of priority import lists to maintain foreign exchange control exerted a restraining influence on external trade.

*Capital flows and exchange rates*

***International reserves increased in Cambodia, while external debt declined***

Cambodia's international reserves, which had amounted to $548 million (equivalent to three months of imports) by the end of 2001, reached $754 million in September 2002. Official transfers of $280 million and concessional lending of $131 million were expected in 2002. FDI inflows, however, were much lower, at an estimated $60 million for 2002. External debt had reached $2.1 billion (or 66.3 per cent of GDP) in 2001 but was expected to decline sharply to $1.5 billion in 2002; in consequence, the debt-service burden was expected to fall from 3.3 per cent of domestic exports in 2001 to just under 2 per cent in 2002. Debt-rescheduling was discussed with the Russian Federation and the United States, while the Paris Club of creditors expressed willingness to give assurances on a concessional basis (Naples terms) to cover the financing gap in 2002. The riel was essentially stable in 2002. At present, Cambodia has no restrictions on current international transactions and does not engage in discriminatory exchange rate practices. The difference between the official and market exchange rates remained stable at below 1 per cent in 2002.

***Official reserves were also up in the Lao People's Democratic Republic but debt service remained high***

The improved investment climate in the Lao People's Democratic Republic attracted considerable interest from foreign investors and the number of new projects involving FDI increased in 2001. Reflecting higher inflows of foreign exchange, gross international reserves in the country, at $178 million by the end of August 2002, were sufficient to cover just under four months of imports. Given the limited capacity to service debt, ODA flows were expected to cover the Government's projected financing gap in 2003 and 2004. However, there was a notable shift in favour of concessional loans (instead of grants); ODA inflows were expected to rise from $378.3 million (with about two thirds in grants) to $438.7 million (with just under one half in grants) in 2002-2003.

The Lao People's Democratic Republic, classified as a heavily indebted poor country (HIPC), has chosen not to take part in the HIPC initiative. Total debt service, including commercial borrowing by private hydroelectricity exporters, was equivalent to 15.5 per cent of merchandise export earnings in 2001. Public debt service was roughly one half of this amount but was expected to rise to almost 10 per cent of exports in 2003 because of the repayment of public commercial debt in the near term. In 2001, bank financing of the budget deficit in the Lao People's Democratic Republic contributed to a 10 per cent depreciation of the kip in the second quarter of 2001. The rate of depreciation slowed in 2002 and the margin between the official exchange rate and the parallel exchange rate remained at less than 2 per cent, in line with the Government's commitment to maintaining a flexible exchange rate regime.

***Private and public capital inflows into Myanmar virtually ceased but official reserves were somewhat higher***

International sanctions and the lack of private sector confidence contributed to a virtual stoppage of private and public capital flows into Myanmar. However, gross international reserves went up slightly, adequate to cover 2.5 months of imports, as a result of the $200 million swap arrangement with Malaysia. In 2001, total external debt amounted to more than $6 billion, almost four fifths of GDP, and external debt arrears exceeded $2.5 billion. The annual budget deficit was estimated at around 5 per cent of GDP in 2001-2002, and measures to enhance the budgetary control processes and reduce the shortfall could include replacing implicit taxes and subsidies with more explicit fiscal instruments. Meanwhile, the officially sanctioned foreign exchange certificate rate in the parallel market depreciated sharply to reach K 906 to the United States dollar in August 2002 (compared with the official exchange rate pegged at K 6.16 to the dollar). As a result of inflation and exchange rate depreciation, kyat-denominated financial assets were converted into gold and hard currency and into physical assets such as land and property. In response, the Government prohibited the acceptance of gold by banks as collateral for personal loans and suspended the issuance of export licences to foreign traders in 2002.

### *Key policy issues*

***Higher fiscal revenue was expected in Cambodia and the Lao People's Democratic Republic in 2002***

Sound macroeconomic management is a major challenge to the least developed countries of South-East Asia, particularly in the area of public finance. Cambodia's revenues were budgeted to increase from 12.5 per cent of GDP in 2001 to 13.5 per cent in 2002. Although tax revenues from domestic sources were in line with projections for 2001, customs revenues fell short as import volumes declined, leading to a slight shortfall in the overall amount of fiscal receipts. Since total expenditure was also held below target, the overall deficit, excluding grants, of 6.0 per cent of

GDP was fully financed from external concessional sources in 2001 (table II.42). The Government has committed itself to maintaining fiscal stability in the coming years, with a cap on the fiscal shortfall of around 6 per cent of GDP. Government revenues in the first quarter of 2002 reached $107 million, an increase in nominal terms of 16 per cent year on year following the launch of the fiscal reform programme and the introduction of new tax collection measures.

As in previous years, Cambodia has been focusing on improving revenue mobilization and redirecting expenditure from defence and security to the social sectors. The lowering of tariffs in compliance with AFTA commitments will present the country with further challenges. A unit focusing on large taxpayers and work plans for improving tax administration were introduced in 2001, while the capabilities of the Customs and Excise Department and the pre-shipment inspection services for imports were expected to be strengthened in 2002. In addition, the military was demobilized by 11.5 per cent and the civil service workforce reduced by 6 per cent through the computerization of the civil service payroll late in 2001.

***The Lao People's Democratic Republic experienced difficulty in reaching its revenue targets***

As a result of poor collections from large taxpayers, optimistic revenue targets for some provinces following fiscal decentralization and the continued weak performance of State-owned enterprises, government revenues in the Lao People's Democratic Republic reached only 37 per cent of the annual programme target during the first half of 2002; however, revenue collections were expected to pick up in the second half of the year. Domestically financed capital spending was consequently curtailed to 27 per cent of the programme target over the same period, while current expenditure was in line with the target. The overall fiscal deficit was 8.3 per cent of GDP in 2002, up from 7.5 per cent in 2001. Over the medium term, the Government intends to keep the budget deficit, including grants, to less than 5 per cent of GDP, with bank financing of the shortfall limited to 0.5 per cent of GDP. In view of the weak central tax administration, the Tax Department was reorganized to focus on revenue collection, monitoring and auditing, and progress was also made in developing a national customs service.

***Defence spending and weak performance by State-owned enterprises contributed to Myanmar's fiscal deficit***

Owing to declines in both capital and current expenditure, Myanmar's fiscal deficit has fallen significantly from the peak of 8.3 per cent of GDP reached in 2000. Nevertheless, it still amounted to almost 5 per cent of GDP in 2002, or more than twice the original target of 2 per cent in 2001. Revenues also declined from 7.8 per cent of GDP in fiscal 1997 to 4.2 per cent in 2001. However, total expenditure exhibited a sharp decrease, from 13.6 per cent of GDP in 2000 to 9.1 per cent in 2001. Meanwhile, the fiscal balance continued to be adversely affected by defence spending, which absorbed about a quarter of the government budget, a fivefold increase in public sector wages since 2000, persistent weak performance by State-owned enterprises and capital expenditure overruns. Total public sector debt is estimated to have reached 95 per cent of GDP by the end of 2001.

***Banking reform continued in Cambodia***

Strengthening the financial sector and improving monetary control is another area of policy concern in the least developed countries of the subregion. Cambodia embarked on the reform of its banking sector in the early 1990s and the process was given added impetus with the adoption of the law on Banking and Financial Institutions in 1999. Under a relicensing programme undertaken in 2001 and 2002, 12 private commercial banks that failed to meet the provisions of the Law were closed, while 13 others were operating under conditional licences. In preparation for the privatization of the State-owned Foreign Trade Bank, external management assistance to implement a reorganization plan, the issuance of bonds by the Ministry of Economy and Finance to replace the National Bank of Cambodia as the major shareholder and an unqualified external audit were expected to be completed in 2002. To improve bank supervision, all banks were required to use a new set of accounts starting in 2003.

***Financial sector reform is a priority of the Government of the Lao People's Democratic Republic***

The cessation by the Central Bank in the Lao People's Democratic Republic of its financing of the fiscal deficit has permitted it to focus on controlling inflation and stabilizing the exchange rate. As in Cambodia, the country is engaged in ongoing reform of the banking sector. Although there are some privately owned banks, the financial system is dominated by three State-owned commercial banks and a bank focusing on the agricultural sector. Much of the lending of the State-owned banks is to State-owned enterprises, and these loans often become non-performing. Two State-owned commercial banks are to be merged, and measures have been implemented to lower the volume of NPLs. At the same time, the Central Bank is expected to strengthen the enforcement of prudential regulations. It also initiated a review of the operations and credit decisions of the State-owned commercial banks in view of the excessive growth in their net domestic assets, which reflected, in turn, defaults on letters of credit and irregular lending, among other factors.

***NPL ratios were relatively modest in Myanmar's private sector banks***

In Myanmar, the NPL ratio for private banks fluctuated between 3 and 5 per cent; the ratio for the banking sector as a whole remained at 14 per cent, reflecting the weak position of the State-owned banks. The Control of Money Laundering Law was adopted in 2002.

The least developed countries of South-East Asia are under severe constraints with regard to institutional capacity and financing resources, which often serve to limit the extent of reforms or delay the adjustments

***Cambodia, the Lao People's Democratic Republic and Myanmar have recognized the need for economic growth led by the private sector***

necessary for long-term macroeconomic stability. However, a number of incremental measures, which take into consideration the constraints faced by these countries, could be taken over the medium term. In the Lao People's Democratic Republic, the implementation of streamlined regulations under the Foreign and Domestic Investment Promotion Laws seems to have spurred recent private sector investment in medium-scale projects. As noted earlier, the country has also initiated the restructuring of State-owned commercial banks. Tariffs for electricity, domestic airfares and water were adjusted in 2002 as the first step toward restructuring the State-owned enterprises concerned. As part of the National Poverty Eradication Programme, such reforms were expected to improve efficiency, attract domestic and foreign investment and develop both infrastructure and human resources. In Myanmar, a more stable macroeconomic environment could emerge from the gradual shift in the operations of the State-owned enterprises to the parallel foreign exchange market, the removal of restrictions on private exports of higher-quality rice, enhanced efforts towards revenue collection within the existing tax structure and the replacement of implicit taxes and subsidies with more explicit fiscal measures.

***The incidence of poverty remained high in the least developed countries of South-East Asia***

In Cambodia, an estimated 36 per cent of the population was living below the poverty line in 1997, nine tenths of these in rural areas. The Government embarked on a National Poverty Reduction Strategy in 2002 and hopes to eradicate poverty by 2015. In the Lao People's Democratic Republic, the incidence of such poverty was approximately 39 per cent in 1998 and again, poverty is widespread in rural areas, where 90 per cent of the poor live. In both countries, the lack of food security, particularly of the main staple, rice, is an important dimension of poverty. Although economic growth has helped to reduce poverty, there are some indications of growing income inequality. The Lao People's Democratic Republic is in the process of formulating a National Poverty Eradication Programme which is due to be completed in 2003.

***The negative impact of reform measures on low-income households needs to be addressed***

The restructuring processes being conducted in these least developed countries have generated some negative ripple effects on low-income households. In the Lao People's Democratic Republic, for example, tariffs on electricity and water were adjusted so that the increases were lower for small users. A social safety net was included in banking and enterprise reforms and a social fund will support community-based projects. To address poverty over the long term, both Cambodia and the Lao People's Democratic Republic are channelling a greater share of government expenditure to education and health. As a result, spending on education and health in Cambodia rose from 1 and 0.4 per cent of GDP respectively, in 1998 to 2.1 and 1.2 per cent of GDP in 2002. This compares with the continuing fall in spending on basic education to 0.3 per cent of GDP and on public health to 0.2 per cent of GDP in Myanmar in 1999.

# DEVELOPED COUNTRIES OF THE REGION

## Australia, Japan and New Zealand

### *Overview and prospects*

***Japanese economy contracts again while Australia and New Zealand show stronger growth in 2002***

In 2001, Japan experienced its third and most severe recession of the last decade. Its economy had shown unexpected strength and appeared to have turned the corner into positive growth in the first quarter of 2002. However, the pace could not be sustained as growth was narrowly based on net exports and public spending amid continuing weak domestic demand. Along with the deterioration in the external environment after the first quarter, particularly in the United States of America, Japan's GDP growth slowed markedly among the course of 2002, when the country once again experienced a contraction in output, as in 2001. In sharp contrast, following a slowdown in 2001, the Australian and New Zealand economies bounced back smartly in the first half of 2002, only for growth to lose some momentum in the latter part of 2002 as the external environment deteriorated. In Australia, drought was also a negative factor in the overall economic performance in 2002. However, largely on the basis of continued buoyancy in domestic demand, both countries were able to raise their total output in 2002 in line with their recent trend rate of 3 to 4 per cent a year (figure II.36).

With regard to consumer prices, Japan experienced its fourth year of deflation and the rate of price decline in fact intensified somewhat in 2002. In Australia, inflation came down sharply, from 4.4 per cent in 2001 to 2.5 per cent in 2002, while New Zealand saw a nominal decline in the inflation rate from 2.7 to 2.6 per cent in the same years (figure II.37). The benign infla-

**Figure II.36. Rates of GDP growth in developed countries in the ESCAP region, 1999-2002**

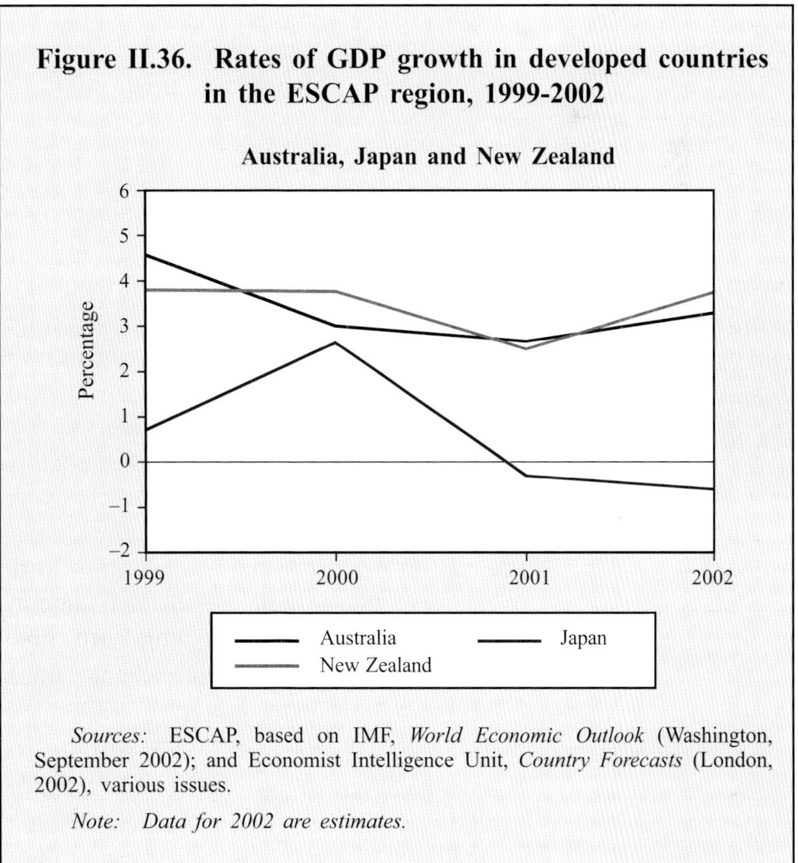


*Sources:* ESCAP, based on IMF, *World Economic Outlook* (Washington, September 2002); and Economist Intelligence Unit, *Country Forecasts* (London, 2002), various issues.

*Note: Data for 2002 are estimates.*

**Figure II.37. Inflation in developed countries in the ESCAP region, 1999-2002[a]**

**Australia, Japan and New Zealand**

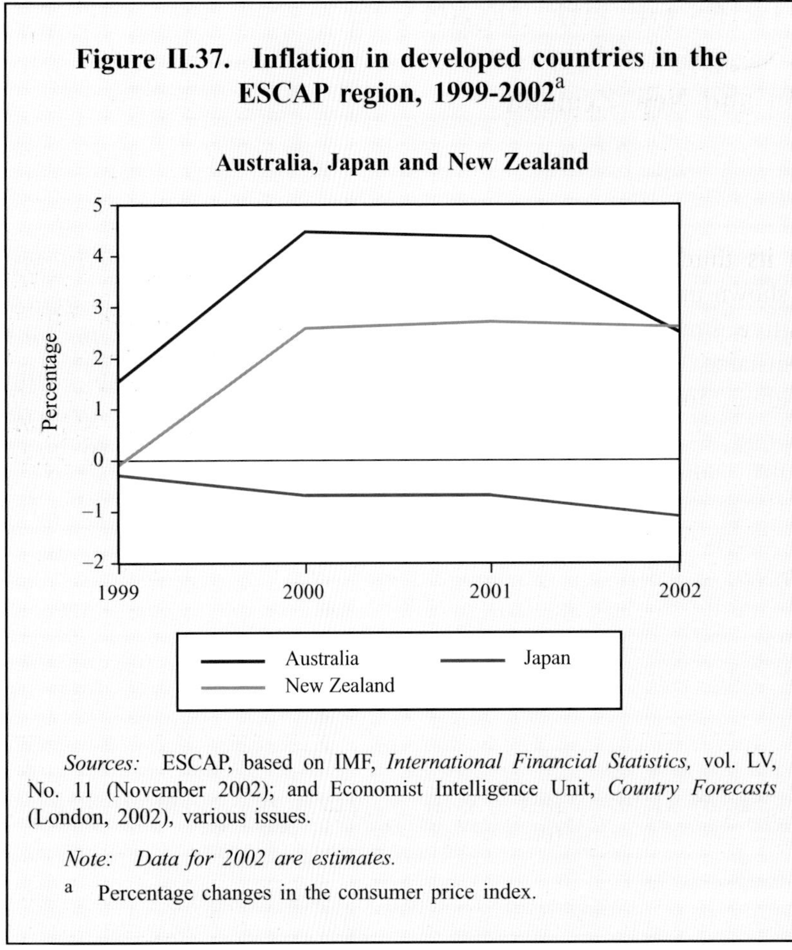


*Sources:* ESCAP, based on IMF, *International Financial Statistics,* vol. LV, No. 11 (November 2002); and Economist Intelligence Unit, *Country Forecasts* (London, 2002), various issues.

*Note: Data for 2002 are estimates.*

[a] Percentage changes in the consumer price index.

tionary environment facilitated the maintenance of a liberal monetary environment, notwithstanding some minor fluctuations in interest rates between late 2001 and mid-2002. In both Australia and New Zealand, for example, monetary policy was eased following the events of 11 September 2001 (table II.43). At the beginning of 2002, however, the easing was partially reversed as growth appeared to be more robust than had initially been forecast. Interest rates resumed their downward path subsequently as the external environment weakened perceptibly and by mid-2002 the rates stood at the same level as in the last quarter of 2001. Easier monetary conditions in Australia resulted in a rise in the investment-to-GDP ratio of 0.7 percentage points in 2002. In Japan, despite unchanged interest rates in nominal terms, deflation means that real interest rates are significantly positive (the typical lending rate of interest being close to 2 per cent) with deleterious consequences for the burden of debt service on both corporations and households. As interest rates cannot be reduced to below zero, this debt-service burden can be eased in part through a rise in the price level that increases corporate cash flows.

***Inflation remains benign in Australia and New Zealand; Japan experiences the fourth year of deflation***

In Japan, despite appreciation in the trade-weighted exchange rate of the yen, the current account balance-of-payments surplus widened, while in Australia and New Zealand the deficits widened with broadly unchanged trade-weighted exchange rates.

The consensus view is that the Japanese economy appears to have bottomed out at last and could therefore grow by around 1 per cent in 2003 should the external environment improve. However, as in 2001 and 2002, there are significant impediments to sustained economic

**Table II.43. Developed countries of the ESCAP region: short-term interest rates and money supply growth (M2), 1999-2002**

*(Percentage)*

| | *1999* | *2000* | *2001* | *2002[a]* |
|---|---|---|---|---|
| **Short-term interest rates** | | | | |
| Australia | 5.0 | 6.2 | 4.9 | 4.8 |
| Japan | 0.2 | 0.2 | 0.1 | 0.1 |
| New Zealand | 4.8 | 6.5 | 5.7 | 5.7 |
| **Money supply growth (M2)** | | | | |
| Australia | 11.7 | 3.8 | 13.2 | 11.9[b] |
| Japan | 3.4 | 1.1 | 2.2 | 5.2[c] |
| New Zealand | 8.2 | 0.9 | 14.7 | 5.2[c] |

*Sources:* ESCAP, based on IMF, *International Financial Statistics,* vol. LV, No. 11 (November 2002); and *OECD Economic Outlook,* No. 72 (December 2002).

[a] Estimates.
[b] January-March.
[c] January-August.

***The Japanese economy has bottomed out; prospects for Australia and New Zealand for 2003 are positive***

growth, including weak private consumption, weak corporate investment, persistent deflationary pressures and the still unfinished agenda of financial and corporate sector reform. Most observers agree that, for Japan, the medium-term growth path depends less on the external environment and more upon radical measures that address the long-standing problems of falling prices and bank and corporate sector reform. There is also the newer, and serious, issue of rising public debt. Progress in dealing with these problems would have a favourable impact on business and consumer confidence in the economy, stimulate higher corporate and household expenditure and provide a fillip to the momentum of growth in the economy in the coming years. Urgent action is needed, particularly in dealing with Japan's massive public debt, which, after several years of spending in excess of revenues, is projected to reach 160 per cent of GDP in 2003.

In Australia and New Zealand, the overall prospects for 2003 are, on balance, considered broadly positive. Domestic demand in the two economies is sufficiently strong to counteract the negative influences of an external environment beset by significant geopolitical and economic uncertainties and higher global downside risks (see chapter I). In the short term, a consistent policy approach based upon prudent macroeconomic policies should preserve the current momentum of growth.

## *GDP performance*

As is well known, the Japanese economy has been in the throes of a decade-long period of lacklustre growth following the collapse of the "bubble economy" in the early 1990s. This has been countered, though with little success, with a series of spending packages by the Government, raising public debt to a very high level. But higher public spending has been offset by lower private spending so that whatever growth was achieved between 1998 and 2002 came largely from net exports. The economy was therefore affected by the sharp downturn in the ICT sector in the United States, for which several Japanese companies are suppliers of components. In many quarters it was felt that the 2001 recession had ended with the resumption of growth in the first quarter of 2002. However, in hindsight, this expansion was essentially driven by a temporary surge in net exports to the United States, with a heavy preponderance of ICT and related products. External demand, especially from the United States, weakened sharply from the second quarter of 2002 onwards and, although this was offset to some extent by higher demand from within the region, the Japanese economy is estimated to have contracted by 0.6 per cent in 2002 as a whole (table II.44). This outcome is, however, an improvement over expectations at the beginning of 2002, when it had been predicted that the economy would contract by 1.2 per cent in that year.

As in the last few years, specifically from 1997 onwards though briefly interrupted in 2000, the principal drag on Japan's economic performance has been weak domestic demand, notwithstanding the many

**Table II.44. Developed countries of the ESCAP region: rates of economic growth and inflation, 1999-2002**

*(Percentage)*

| | *1999* | *2000* | *2001* | *2002*[a] |
|---|---|---|---|---|
| **GDP growth rates** | | | | |
| Australia | 4.6 | 3.0 | 2.7 | 3.3 |
| Japan | 0.8 | 2.6 | −0.3 | −0.6 |
| New Zealand | 3.8 | 3.8 | 2.5 | 3.8 |
| **Inflation**[b] | | | | |
| Australia | 1.5 | 4.5 | 4.4 | 2.5 |
| Japan | −0.3 | −0.7 | −0.7 | −1.1 |
| New Zealand | −0.1 | 2.6 | 2.7 | 2.6 |

*Sources:* ESCAP, based on IMF, *International Financial Statistics,* vol. LV, No. 11 (November 2002) and *World Economic Outlook* (Washington, September 2002); and Economist Intelligence Unit, *Country Forecasts* (London, 2002), various issues; and national sources.

[a] Estimates.

[b] Percentage changes in the consumer price index.

***Weak domestic demand remains the main drag on Japan's economic performance***

fiscal measures taken by the Government. Weak domestic demand, as stated earlier, had its origins in the collapse of the bubble economy in the early 1990s. It was driven by low consumer confidence compounded by the deflationary pressures that began in 1999; together these have undermined consumer spending and aggravated the burden of real debt. Furthermore, in the face of sluggish retail sales, high levels of excess capacity have built up in the Japanese economy. As the present Government has initiated some tentative steps towards fiscal consolidation with the 2002 budget (bond issues having been limited to 30 trillion yen), the problem of excess capacity could actually worsen in the next few years if growth and consumer confidence do not revive.

Excess capacity implies that corporate debt burdens have either remained largely unchanged or risen relative to equity in corporate balance sheets in the last few years; the latter had a direct impact on the financial sector in the form of NPLs. At the same time, wealth reduction has continued with falling equity and land prices. On the plus side, however, the pace of decline in fixed investment by corporations appears to be moderating and the profits of major corporations are beginning to show an improvement. More significantly perhaps, unemployment has stabilized at around 5.5 per cent, at least for the present. These are mildly encouraging signs but much more remains to be done, as is discussed in the section on policy issues.

***Strong private consumption drives growth in Australia and New Zealand***

In Australia, growth was primarily driven by private consumption in 2001 and 2002, with net exports playing a supporting role. Strong private consumption demand translated into a major spurt in gross fixed investment in 2002, mainly, but not exclusively, in private housing. There was considerable new investment in major resource projects. Although adversely affected by drought in 2003, Australia achieved one of the highest GDP growth rates, 3.2 per cent, among the major OECD economies. It should be stressed that domestic demand will need to grow further if the present momentum is to be sustained in the face of a weaker external environment in 2003. There is an expectation that such growth might not be forthcoming on both the investment and consumption sides; investment growth is likely to moderate as weaker equity markets dent business confidence and there is a cooling-off in the booming housing sector. Household consumption may experience a similar fate as consumers seek to reduce the household debt built up over several years of high spending. A further question mark hangs over the unemployment situation, which appears to have stabilized at the rather high level of 6 per cent or more despite several years of robust growth.

In New Zealand, the GDP growth rate rose by more than one percentage point in 2002. As in Australia, this was the result of buoyant growth in private consumption, chiefly in housing, aided by an increase in exports. New Zealand, as a small and open economy, was even more exposed to the state of the global economy in 2002, especially the sharp slowdown in the United States after the first quarter and the generally poorer sentiment in capital markets around the world. In the near term, this was mainly reflected in a flattening of investment expenditure in the second half of 2002 as New Zealand imports capital to finance its current account deficit. With a slightly less favourable year for some agricultural exports and some appreciation of the New Zealand dollar exchange rate, the current account deficit widened in 2002. However, it is estimated that overall GDP growth would have eased to a more sustainable level towards the end of 2002 and therefore the increase in the current account deficit is regarded as a temporary phenomenon that should pose no significant policy issues for the time being.

New Zealand's strong economic performance over the last few years is reflected in the low rate of unemployment, which is at a 14-year low; participation rates are also very high and labour shortages are becoming serious in certain skill categories. Even so, pressure from an upward drift in wage rates has essentially remained subdued and inflationary pressures are moderate.

### *Foreign trade and other international transactions*

***The yen appreciates in the face of strong fundamentals***

Following an increase of over 14 per cent in exports and over 22 per cent in imports in 2000, Japan's trade surplus narrowed substantially; the surplus on the external current account narrowed slightly from 2.6 to 2.5 per cent of GDP (figures II.38 and II.39). These trends intensified

**Figure II.38. Growth rates in merchandise export earnings of developed countries in the ESCAP region, 1999-2002**

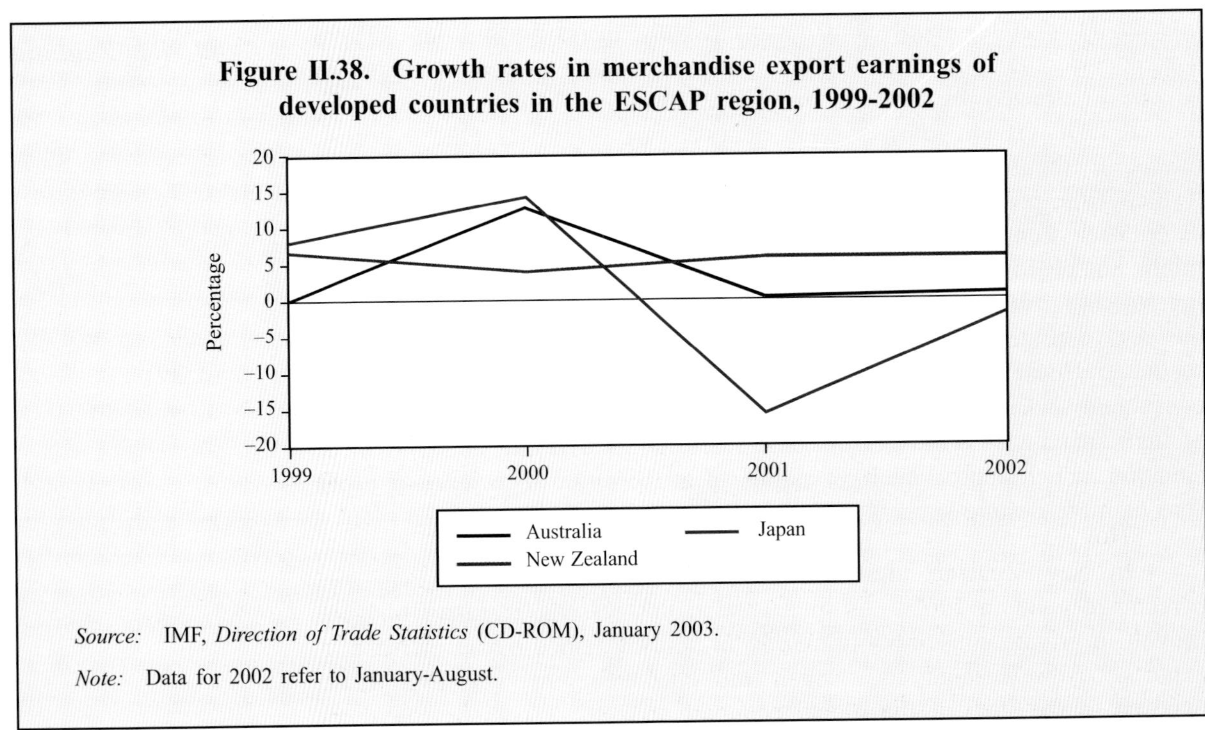


*Source:* IMF, *Direction of Trade Statistics* (CD-ROM), January 2003.

*Note:* Data for 2002 refer to January-August.

**Figure II.39. Growth rates in merchandise import spending of developed countries in the ESCAP region, 1999-2002**

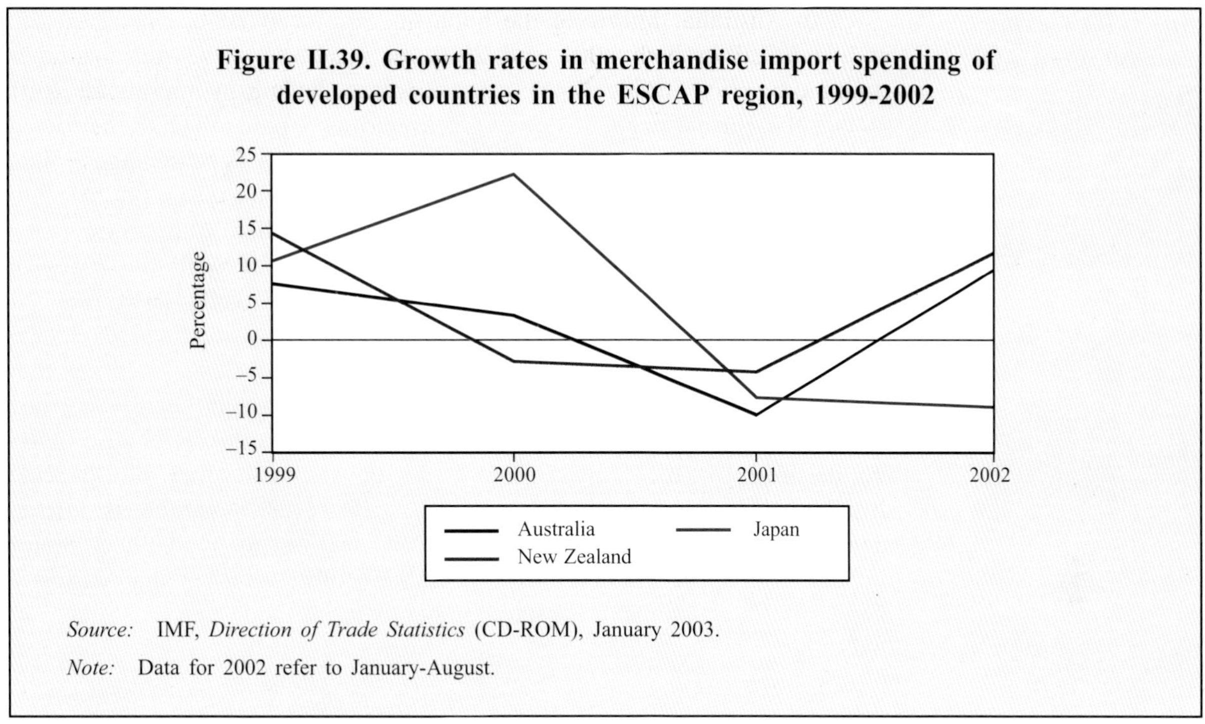


*Source:* IMF, *Direction of Trade Statistics* (CD-ROM), January 2003.

*Note:* Data for 2002 refer to January-August.

subsequently and the surplus narrowed further to 2.1 per cent in 2001. Exports, mainly of ICT components, were once again lower in 2002, but imports declined at an even faster pace as the economy contracted; as a result, the current account surplus widened to 2.8 per cent of GDP. Consequently, by July 2002 Japan's foreign exchange reserves had reached the staggering level of $446 billion. The upward trend in surplus accumulation has a clear bearing on the yen exchange rate, tending to push it upwards. The weak yen policy favoured by some as a means to revive growth through higher net exports is thus constrained by the relevant economic fundamentals, irrespective of Japan's sovereign credit rating or the credit rating of Japanese corporations. It is no surprise, therefore, that, instead of depreciating, the yen's trade-weighted exchange rate actually appreciated by around 4 per cent in 2002.

Such has been the weakness of the Japanese domestic economy that the appreciation of the yen exchange rate on a trade-weighted basis was paradoxically accompanied by a decline in overall Japanese imports in 2001 and 2002. The Japanese economy has provided little stimulus to global growth in the last two years through increased imports. This was in sharp contrast to its performance in 1999 and 2000, when, taking the two years together, imports went up by a third. The weak overall import demand from Japan has major implications for the region. All the subregions experienced reductions in exports to Japan in 2001 and 2002. However, some individual economies, such as China and Thailand, nonetheless managed to increase their exports to Japan.

***Australia's export growth slows in 2002***

In Australia, following the boom in exports in 2000, export growth was marginal in both 2001 and 2002 on the back of weaker or flatter commodity prices (table II.45). There was a decline in imports in 2001 so that the current account deficit, measured as a ratio of GDP, narrowed considerably compared with the previous year by 1.6 percentage points (table II.46). In 2002, however, the strong growth in consumption led to higher import growth, which, combined with weaker tourism receipts, widened the current account deficit to 3.8 per cent of GDP (table II.47). Australia's foreign exchange reserve position since 2000 has remained broadly constant at around $20 billion, and the trade-weighted exchange rate barely moved over the 12 months to December 2002. During that period, however, the Australian dollar appreciated significantly against the United States dollar. As roughly 10 per cent of Australian exports are destined for the United States, this development does not presage difficulties on the export front per se. However, Australia is also a significant exporter of commodities that are priced in United States dollars. An appreciation of the Australian dollar vis-à-vis that currency could indicate problems with competitiveness and market share in 2003.

**Table II.45. Developed countries of the ESCAP region: merchandise exports and their rates of growth, 1999-2002**

| | *Exports (f.o.b.)* | | | | |
|---|---|---|---|---|---|
| | *Value (millions of US dollars)* | *Annual rate of growth (percentage)* | | | |
| | *2001* | *1999* | *2000* | *2001* | *2002 Jan.-Aug.* |
| Australia | 63 357 | 0.1 | 12.7 | 0.4 | 0.9 |
| Japan | 403 383 | 8.1 | 14.1 | −15.6 | −1.9 |
| New Zealand | 13 456 | 6.6 | 4.0 | 5.8 | 5.9 |

*Source:* IMF, *Direction of Trade Statistics* (CD-ROM), January 2003.

Australia's external deficit has, on the whole, been comfortably financed by capital inflows given the traditional interest rate differential favouring the Australian dollar. Moreover, the Australian stock market declined much less than other markets in 2002 (by only 2.6 per cent in terms of the United States dollar compared with 16.8 per cent for the Dow Jones and 31.5 per cent for NASDAQ in the United States). At the same time, however, the relatively thinly traded nature of the currency, the

**Table II.46. Developed countries of the ESCAP region: merchandise imports and their rates of growth, 1999-2002**

| | Value (millions of US dollars) | Imports (c.i.f.) Annual rate of growth (percentage) | | | |
|---|---|---|---|---|---|
| | 2001 | 1999 | 2000 | 2001 | 2002 Jan.-Aug. |
| Australia | 66 851 | 7.6 | 3.3 | –10.0 | 9.4 |
| Japan | 349 056 | 10.5 | 22.1 | –8.0 | –9.3 |
| New Zealand | 13 353 | 14.3 | –2.9 | –4.3 | 11.7 |

*Source:* IMF, *Direction of Trade Statistics* (CD-ROM), January 2003.

fluctuations in commodity prices and shifts in global financial market sentiment make the Australian dollar vulnerable to bouts of volatility; such volatility could become a source of uncertainty and disruption in business planning and longer-term investment decision-making.

***Current account deficit widens in New Zealand***

New Zealand missed out on some of the buoyancy displayed by world trade growth in 2000. However, exports grew by around 6 per cent in 2001 and by the same amount in 2002, in sharp contrast to the

**Table II.47. Developed countries of the ESCAP region: consumption and investment as a percentage of GDP, 1999-2002**

*(Percentage)*

| | 1999 | 2000 | 2001 | 2002[a] |
|---|---|---|---|---|
| **Consumption as a percentage of GDP** | | | | |
| Australia | 78.4 | 78.2 | 78.3 | 78.5 |
| Japan | 72.6 | 72.5 | 74.2 | 75.2 |
| New Zealand | 80.6 | 78.3 | 76.7 | 76.8 |
| **Investment as a percentage of GDP** | | | | |
| Australia | 23.5 | 22.5 | 21.3 | 22.0 |
| Japan | 26.2 | 26.4 | 25.8 | 24.2 |
| New Zealand | 20.4 | 20.7 | 20.1 | 20.3 |

*Sources:* ESCAP, based on United Nations, "Project LINK Global Economic Outlook Forecast Tables" (October 2002); and Economist Intelligence Unit, *Country Forecasts* (London, 2002), various issues.

[a] Estimates.

experience of Australia during that period. As New Zealand's imports declined in 2001, the external current account deficit narrowed by a substantial 2.5 percentage points of GDP (table II.48). However, import growth and outgoings on services outpaced export growth in 2002 and the current account deficit widened to 3.5 per cent of GDP in 2002. New Zealand actually runs a modest surplus in merchandise trade; it is its deficit in services and a large gap in income from investments that contribute to the overall deficit. New Zealand's external position deteriorated to some extent in 2002 with the appreciation of its currency, which made imports more attractive.

**Table II.48. Developed countries of the ESCAP region: budget and current account balance as a percentage of GDP, 1999-2002**

*(Percentage)*

| | *1999* | *2000* | *2001* | *2002*[a] |
|---|---|---|---|---|
| **Budget balance[b] as a percentage of GDP** | | | | |
| Australia[c] | 0.9 | 0.9 | 0.2 | 0.1 |
| Japan | –7.0 | –7.3 | –7.1 | –7.2 |
| New Zealand | 0.4 | 0.8 | 1.4 | 1.5 |
| **Current account balance as a percentage of GDP** | | | | |
| Australia | –5.9 | –4.1 | –2.5 | –3.8 |
| Japan | 2.6 | 2.5 | 2.1 | 2.8 |
| New Zealand | –6.3 | –5.3 | –2.8 | –3.5 |

*Sources:* ESCAP, based on IMF, *International Financial Statistics,* vol. LV, No. 11 (November 2002) and *World Economic Outlook* (Washington, September 2002); and Economist Intelligence Unit, *Country Forecasts* (London, 2002), various issues.

[a] Estimates.
[b] General government fiscal balance.
[c] Data exclude net advances (primarily privatization receipts and net policy-related lending).

However, as in Australia, the external deficit is not a major policy issue. The interest rate differential makes it easy to finance the deficit and over the years New Zealand has succeeded in denominating the majority of its external liabilities in its own currency, thus removing the exchange rate risk. The exchange rate therefore has only a marginal bearing on the management of the external debt. The appreciation of the New Zealand dollar against the United States dollar in 2002 is considered to be temporary and a reflection of United States dollar weakness rather than any inherent upside potential in the New Zealand currency. Nevertheless, the exchange rate could be a source of uncertainty in the months ahead with some negative implications for investment expenditure (figure II.40).

**Figure II.40. Index of exchange rates against the United States dollar of developed countries in the ESCAP region, 1996-2002**

*(1996 = 100)*

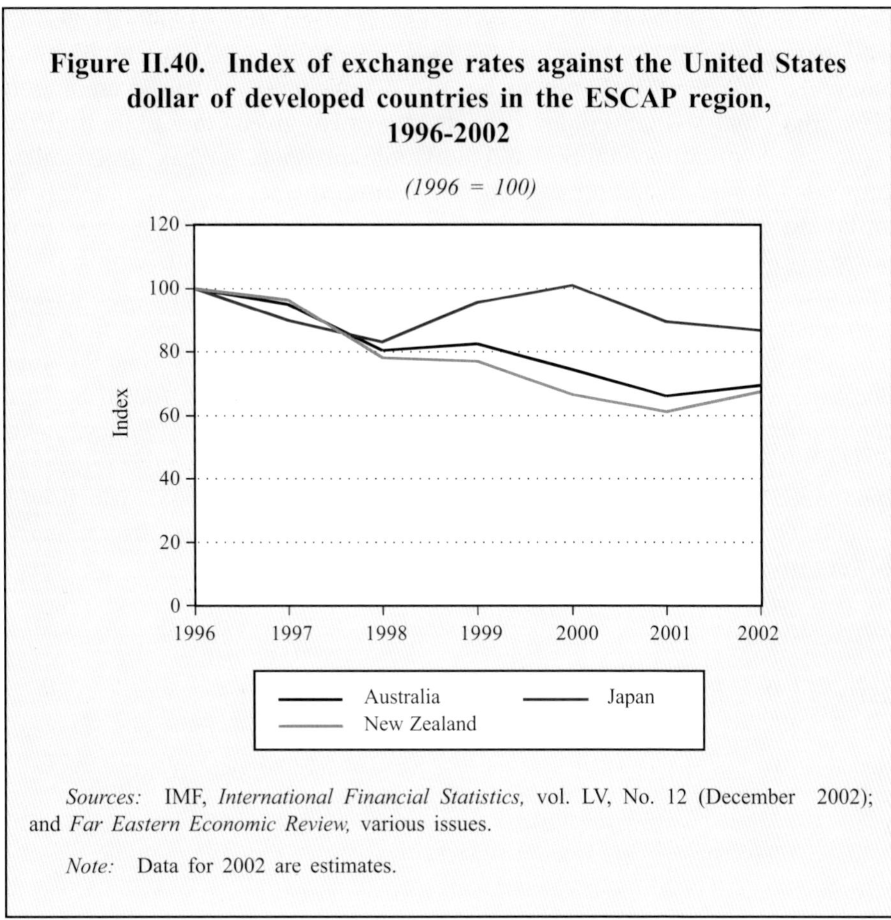


*Sources:* IMF, *International Financial Statistics,* vol. LV, No. 12 (December 2002); and *Far Eastern Economic Review,* various issues.

*Note:* Data for 2002 are estimates.

## *Key policy issues*

***Banking reform, deflation, fiscal consolidation and corporate sector restructuring remain key policy issues for Japan***

As the second largest economy in the world and the largest in the region, Japan exercises a major influence on developments in its trading partners. Therefore, the need for Japan to address its decade-long slump is of vital importance from both Japan's own national perspective and international and regional perspectives. The present Government has recognized the need to take radical action in the areas of banking reform, deflation, fiscal consolidation and other structural issues in the corporate sector. However, implementation has been slower than initially expected or, indeed, hoped for. Broadly speaking, there are four interrelated policy issues that the Japanese authorities have to tackle and in the following paragraphs an attempt is made to highlight the complexities involved in dealing with the underlying dilemmas.

Without meaningful progress in dealing with the chronic problems of the financial sector, the credit crunch in Japan will continue to deprive productive companies of access to financial resources that would enable them to restructure and grow. Despite loan write-offs equivalent to 16 per cent of GDP in the last 10 years, NPLs remain stubbornly high.

From official estimates, Japanese banks carry on their books some 47 trillion yen of NPLs, or roughly 8 per cent of GDP, although some observers consider this figure to be an underestimate. In fact, there is a clear risk that NPLs could rise dramatically given the extraordinary combination of falling output and deflation in Japan. Weak profitability constrains the provisioning capacity of banks, so that there would appear to be no respite available to them were they to be left to their own devices to tackle their balance-sheet problems. Japan's strategy for the financial sector has consisted of stricter loan classification, accelerated loan disposals through the Resolution and Collection Corporation and reduction of exposure to equity price risk through the Bank Shareholding Purchase Corporation. The strategy was given sharper focus by the appointment of a new head of the Financial Services Agency, who assembled a task force to propose a reform package. The task force has announced a plan that calls for halving NPLs by March 2005. Much will depend on how aggressively the Agency can exercise its discretionary powers in implementing this plan (see box II.9).

## Box II.9. Banking reform in Japan

Despite write-offs amounting to 16 per cent of GDP over the last decade,[a] the lingering NPL problem in the Japanese financial sector continues to be aggravated by asset-price deflation and contracting GDP. The recent deterioration in economic conditions in Japan further increases the risk that more loans could turn into NPLs. Arguably, a resolution of the NPL problem holds the key to renewed and durable economic growth in Japan.

The NPLs of all deposit-taking institutions amounted to ¥43.2 trillion ($355 billion) as at the end of March 2002, an increase by ¥9.6 trillion, or 28 per cent, from a year earlier. While the increase is partly due to the application of stricter criteria for the classification of NPLs, it primarily reflects steady deterioration in the business conditions of borrowers, despite the removal of ¥9.2 trillion from the balance sheets of banks.

To halt this vicious cycle, at the end of 2002 the Japanese Government announced a reconstruction programme called the Programme for Financial Revival, including a schedule for action plans designed to resolve the NPL problem through halving bad loans by March 2005.

### *Framework for a new financial system*

The framework has several elements. Its overall objective is to channel resources to productive companies and develop a viable and robust financial system within a realistic time frame. To maintain public confidence, the framework proposes postponement of the complete abolition of the blanket deposit guarantee scheme to the end of March 2005. In the interim, a task force on financial issues will be established to monitor the status of NPLs with a view to resolving the problem by the end of fiscal year 2004, that is, early 2005.

The NPL problem manifests itself in its starkest form in the parlous financial condition of SMEs. Here, high levels of borrowing have come up against declining collateral values, low demand and falling prices. As one of the measures to provide a safety net for SMEs, the framework suggests encouraging the entry of new lenders into the market who can better assess and cater for their financial needs, participate in their long-term rehabilitation and strengthen the monitoring of their operations in the future.

---

[a] *Japan: Staff Report for the 2002 Article IV Consultation; Staff Statement and Public Information Notice on the Executive Board Discussion* (IMF Country Report No. 02/175).

Above all, to halve the volume of NPLs by March 2005, the framework proposes a support system for troubled financial institutions which includes the provision of additional liquidity through special loans by the Bank of Japan, the injection of public funds based on the current Deposit Insurance Law and the assignment of resident inspectors to sit on the boards of troubled financial institutions. Through the latter, pressure for reform would be given a boost in financial institutions under the special support scheme. The framework also suggests establishing a new public funds scheme whereby the Government would inject funds into a troubled financial institution more promptly and thus ensure the stable functioning of the financial system.

### New framework for corporate rehabilitation

A key element of the plan is the enhanced role of the Financial Services Agency. The Agency is expected to promote and carry out structural reform, in particular in those financial institutions that come under the ambit of the special support scheme. It includes sales of bad loans to the Resolution and Collection Corporation and the injection of corporate reconstruction funds, plus others measures, such as the possible introduction of a credit guarantee system for Debtor-in-Possession finance. It also suggests strengthening the role of the Resolution and Collection Corporation in the rehabilitation of troubled institutions, enhancing cooperation with corporate reconstruction funds and developing a debt market involving the greater securitization of loans.

In order to facilitate structural reform by the Financial Services Agency, the planned framework proposes a stricter assessment of banking assets, improved capital adequacy and strengthened governance. In particular, it suggests tighter criteria for the classification of assets; such criteria should be more consistent with the market valuation of the assets. In this connection, the market valuation system is to include the use of discounted cash flow methods for calculating asset values and likely future provisions and a review of the period within which weak banks have to improve their capital-adequacy ratios. These measures are broadly in line with what constitutes international best practice as laid down by the Bank for International Settlements.

More fundamentally, a tax reform proposal for the improvement of capital adequacy includes a new scheme to recognize the provisions as tax losses, the removal of a freeze on the refund carry-back system and consideration of the extension of the carry-over period for tax liabilities. Finally, it suggests a strengthened role for external auditors in the assessment of the condition of troubled institutions, the conversion of preferred stock held by the Government into common stock in accordance with operational guidelines and enhancing the effectiveness of an early warning system through the careful monitoring of indicators such as overall profitability and liquidity in the banking system as a whole.

### Market response

By and large, the plan has been received with some disappointment by market participants. There was an expectation that the Government would undertake a more aggressive restructuring programme in the financial system and deal more decisively with the NPL problem. In particular, it is felt that the Government has failed to set a target for the amount of deferred tax assets that the banks can include in their Tier 1 capital.[b] Markets had seen this as one of the more effective measures for compelling banks to make new capital injections and maintain their capital-assets ratio at the required level.

In addition, the reform plan includes measures that will initially lead to an increase in NPLs and consequently impair the banks' capital-adequacy ratios, for example, through the proposal to adopt the discounted cash flow system for the evaluation of NPLs. There are also to be special inspections of the banks by the Financial Services Agency and such inspections would, in all probability, reveal additional impaired assets. The successful implementation of these policies is thus likely to be a major challenge for the Government and markets, hence the fear of some policy slippage. Finally, there is scepticism about the significance of the reform plan as it focuses primarily on the NPLs of major banks. This leaves aside a far larger amount of "grey" liabilities held in the non-banking financial sector.

---

[b] Banks set aside reserves to offset potentially bad loans but the reduction in taxable income occurs only when the borrower becomes insolvent. Currently, the expected future reduction in taxable income can be recognized in the profit and loss account as an expected refund and included in core capital, significantly boosting the banks' capital-adequacy ratios.

There is general agreement that deflation poses a critical threat to sustained improvement in GDP growth over the medium term. Thus far, the Bank of Japan has concentrated on expanding liquidity in the economy and the base money had increased, on a year-on-year basis, by 30 per cent by mid-2002. However, this policy has not yet succeeded in ending deflationary pressures in the economy. There is growing acceptance that the Bank has to take more innovative action and not rely on monetary policy alone to counter deflation. Since deflationary expectations can be as difficult to shift as inflationary expectations, one suggested approach is to alter the public's expectations in this regard by, say, announcing a commitment to end deflation within 12-18 months. Whether this would produce the desired effect is subject to some doubt.

While there is no formal fiscal consolidation programme, the present Government has initiated a move in that direction by putting a limit of 30 trillion yen on bond issuance in the current fiscal year. The twin problems of the public debt and fiscal consolidation reveal the dilemmas that the Japanese Government is facing in this area of policy. On the one hand, given the weakness in growth, it would be inappropriate to push too aggressively with fiscal consolidation in the near term; on the other, the ballooning public debt cannot be left adrift without some official commitment to end it over a credible time frame. Some degree of consolidation is needed to stabilize the debt, say, by 2007 and further measures will be needed thereafter to reduce it if Japan is to make public debt manageable at some point in the future. Given the lack of growth in the economy, this would be a very tall order. However, the Government could set broad objectives for its tax, expenditure and social security policies and initiate a public debate on the subject as a way of building consensus in society on this critically important issue.

Corporate restructuring has to be pursued to reduce the excessive leveraging of most companies, particularly SMEs. It is also necessary to enhance labour mobility and "sunk" capital needs to be salvaged from non-viable enterprises and reallocated to companies where the chances of long-term survival are better. In this context, the banking system has to deal with the problem of company debt, how it might be restructured and/or converted into securities, how sales of impaired assets to third parties might be financed and how the quality of decision-making might be improved in the banking system as a whole. Significant reform of the regulatory regime governing corporate enterprise is also needed and a more strategic approach is necessary in this regard. Entry barriers are still rather high in some sectors, notably telecommunications and electricity, and business start-ups are hampered by a complex process of official approvals. Accelerated disposal of property used as collateral is another area needing reform.

***Australia and New Zealand face broadly similar policy challenges: tax reform, welfare spending and incentives for production and employment***

In comparison with Japan, both Australia and New Zealand face essentially straightforward policy issues, namely, managing relatively sophisticated economies in a rapidly changing global environment, preserving competitiveness and the momentum of growth in a framework of macroeconomic stability and managing the trade-offs between taxation, welfare spending and incentives for production and employment. Notwithstanding signs of reform fatigue in Australia, as reported in the *Survey 2002,* the Government is examining afresh the matrix of taxation, labour market reforms, media laws, competition policy and welfare. The present Government has stated that it does not favour budget deficits; this constrains it in its desire to lower taxes over the long term. Indeed, the currently weaker international economy could reduce the projected fiscal surplus in fiscal year 2002/03. The Government has also put on hold plans to dispose of its remaining stake in Telstra. This suggests perhaps that more radical reforms of taxation might be deferred for now, that is, until the overall resource situation improves, the global environment stabilizes and the higher spending on defence, security and border protection, to which the Government recently committed itself, can be assessed as either temporary or permanent.

In New Zealand, similar tightening of the budget situation is on the cards despite the recent run of fiscal surpluses. Lowering the tax-to-GDP ratio in the near term appears problematic, however, given the unfunded liabilities in the New Zealand Superannuation Fund and the Accident Compensation Corporation and political commitment to boost spending on health, social security, public housing and education. The Government's preference is to allow some deterioration in the fiscal situation in the short term and maintain spending on key strategic priorities, so as not to disturb the current high momentum of growth. A longer-term issue facing the country is its relative underperformance compared with Australia since the mid-1980s. This comparison raises a host of difficult issues related to levels of capital intensity in the two economies and the negative impact of large net outward migration from New Zealand in recent years. New Zealand's small size and physical distance from its trading partners provide some explanation for its inability to reap economies of scale. However, this also suggests that any policy interventions would pose major problems.

# THE ROLE OF PUBLIC EXPENDITURE IN THE PROVISION OF EDUCATION AND HEALTH

## INTRODUCTION AND OVERVIEW

*Positive impacts of education and health are enormous*

Improving the education and health of people is not only a goal in itself for a better quality of life but also its positive impact on the economic development of a country is far-reaching. The provision of education and health is a key element of a policy to promote broad-based economic growth. The main asset of the poor is clearly their labour and both education and health services improve the productivity and earnings of workers. Education is considered a major remedy for many problems faced by developing countries. For example, high fertility rates are adding to population pressures in several countries. It is widely accepted that female education helps to lower fertility rates. Moreover, educated parents are in a better position to look after the education and health needs of their children. Similarly, the linkages of health to poverty eradication and long-term economic growth are strong. The burden of diseases such as HIV/AIDS can slow the economic growth of developing countries. Education and health are important tools to empower poor people and overcome exclusion based on gender, location and other correlates of poverty.

*Achievement of most millennium development goals is linked to education and health*

A number of millennium development goals are directly related to education and health. These are to (a) achieve universal primary education, (b) reduce child mortality, (c) improve maternal health and (d) combat HIV/AIDS, malaria and other diseases. Most other millennium development goals have strong linkages to education and health. The overarching goal is the eradication of extreme poverty, for which the development of human resources through education and health is key. By endorsing the goals, countries essentially recognize education and health as priority areas for action.

The public sector is still a major provider of education and health in developing countries of the ESCAP region. The objective of the present chapter is to evaluate the role of public expenditure in the provision of education and health in these countries. Not only are additional resources needed for education and health but also their effective utilization to maximize their positive impact, particularly on marginalized groups, is important. Therefore, key policy issues relevant to expanding resources for education and health and improving their effectiveness and efficiency are discussed. The main policy-oriented messages of the chapter are highlighted below.

***The State should continue to be the lead actor in financing basic education and primary health care***

- The public provision of education and health care may be considered using rights-based and needs-based approaches. Owing to the limited resources of Governments in developing countries, the universal provision of education and health care is almost impossible. However, basic education and primary health care command general support under a rights-based approach. The public provision (free or subsidized) of other education and health services should respond to the needs of marginalized and disadvantaged groups.

***Multiple channels of financing for education and health are needed***

- Huge financial resources are needed in most countries of the region to expand education and health services and improve their quality. Shifting resources from low-productivity sectors, such as defence and general administration, to education and health can go some way towards meeting the need. Multiple channels of financing will also be required to raise sufficient resources, including both public and private sources, communities, non-governmental organizations, bilateral donors and multilateral organizations. An integrative approach using multiple sources is recommended for the provision of education and health services.[1]

- The most reliable and sustainable public source is tax revenue. Countries in the region have been reforming their tax systems and many of them have introduced VAT. Improving tax administration and expanding the tax base will generate more revenue.

- Generally, the education and health services provided by the public sector are either free of charge or carry a nominal fee. Modest user charges for improved quality of services can be introduced. For reasons of equity, however, mechanisms are needed to ensure that the poor are not barred from using the services for lack of income.

- The active involvement of communities and non-governmental organizations can augment resources for education and health. Communities can make contributions in kind and/or cash. Non-governmental organizations have long been active in both the education and health sectors. They can mobilize internal and external resources and also provide leadership for advocacy.

- Private sector participation raises the quality, efficiency and supply of services, which allows the enhanced allocation of public resources to rural and remote areas as well as slums in urban areas

---

[1] "Introduction: context and scope", in G. Mwabu, C. Ugaz and G. White, eds., *Social Provision in Low-income Countries: New Patterns and Emerging Trends* (Oxford, Oxford University Press, 2001).

where they are most needed. Therefore, the participation of the private sector should be encouraged. At the same time, Governments should have proper regulatory regimes in place to maintain education and health service standards.

- Governments of many developing countries have borrowed heavily in the past and a major part of their revenue is spent on debt-servicing, including foreign debt. Rich countries can therefore assist developing countries in the provision of education and health services through debt reduction and enhanced development aid. At the same time, the effective utilization of aid in developing countries will encourage people and Governments in donor countries to be more supportive of increased funding.

***Effective utilization of resources to achieve better results***

- Utilizing resources more effectively and efficiently will enhance the achievements of education and health sector programmes. Improving the quality of services, increasing marginalized groups' access to services, prioritizing expenditure within sectors and achieving better governance merit special consideration.

***People living in rural and remote areas, the poor and women need to be targeted***

- Despite the improved coverage of education and health services in most countries, certain groups of the population have been left behind and opportunities remain unevenly distributed. Three main groups, people living in rural and remote areas, poor people and women, need to be targeted in order to achieve better results.

- More public resources should be devoted to rural and remote areas where they are most needed. Balanced development of rural areas will help to manage rural-to-urban migration. Within urban areas, slums and localities of poor people should be targeted for enhanced public funds for education and health.

- Education and health indicators based on national averages are not satisfactory in many countries. The situation of the poor is likely to be much worse in those countries, since the poor tend to have limited access to education and health services. This, in turn, keeps them poor so that the vicious cycle of poverty continues. Poor children should therefore be given scholarships, free textbooks and uniforms, and the access of the poor to public health facilities should be enhanced.

- Gender inequalities continue to be serious in many countries. Certain affirmative measures can help to enhance female access to education. There is a need to make parents, particularly in rural areas, aware of the importance of girls' education through publicity campaigns. Scholarship schemes, free textbooks and other supplies for girls can also attract them to schools. Enhancing the representation of women in management positions in the education and health sectors should help to take better account of the concerns and needs of women.

***Reprioritization of expenditure within the education and health sectors can improve achievements***

- Even with a fixed amount of resources, better outcomes could be achieved through reprioritizing expenditure within sectors according to need and importance. Developing countries need quality education at all levels, including tertiary education to grasp new technologies. ICT should be promoted in education at all levels. However, for countries with currently low enrolment ratios, the highest priority should be given to universal primary education, followed by improvements in secondary and higher education.
- Within the health sector, more emphasis is usually given to curative rather than preventive services. However, preventive measures for improving health, such as access to safe drinking water, adequate sanitation and mass vaccination against communicable diseases, are also very important and can reduce the need for curative services. Priority should be given to providing primary health care for all, particularly in rural and remote areas and for disadvantaged groups.
- In many countries, the education and health sectors are under enormous stress owing to population pressures. One of the most important health interventions is giving greater attention to reproductive health, not only to control the spread of sexually transmitted diseases such as HIV/AIDS but also to limit fertility through family planning, including access to contraception.

***Good governance to improve access and quality***

- By improving governance, resources can be saved and utilized to improve access to and the quality of education and health services. More effective implementation of checks and balances and greater decentralization in the provision of education and health services can help to check the wastage and leakage of resources.
- While better education and health outcomes contribute to economic growth, the causality also runs in the reverse direction. Financial resources for education and health can be made available more easily in a growing economy. Therefore, policies aimed at broad-based growth should be vigorously pursued.

## TRENDS IN PUBLIC EXPENDITURE ON EDUCATION AND HEALTH

The main source of comparable time-series data on public expenditure in countries of the region is IMF.[2] Generally, the reported data cover only central government expenditure on various components of social services, including education and health. Social services are also provided by state or provincial and local governments and, for some

[2] The data are reported in the *Government Finance Statistics Yearbook* of IMF.

countries, these lower-level governments have the major responsibility for providing such services. IMF also provides data on lower-level government expenditure on social services for some countries.[3] For other countries with no such reported data, the actual expenditure on social services will be understated. The public expenditure data reported in table III.1 are mainly from IMF, supplemented by national and other sources.

***Rising trend of public expenditure on social services***

Before examining public expenditure on education and health, a brief look at public expenditure on all social services combined may help to discern the evolution of government policy towards the social sector in different countries. Over the last two decades, there has been a generally rising trend in public expenditure on social services as a percentage of GDP, which increased in most developing countries of the region between 1980 and 2000 (table III.1). The share of social services in total public expenditure exhibits a similar trend. This suggests that social services have been gaining importance in public policy in developing countries. However, there are linkages between economic growth and public expenditure. A sudden drop in the economic growth of a country can adversely affect public expenditure on social services. For example, in the wake of the economic crisis of 1997, public expenditure on social services as a percentage of total government expenditure decreased in Indonesia and Thailand.[4] Rapidly growing public debt can also reduce the share of social services in total public expenditure.

***Data limitations make cross country comparisons difficult***

Because of data limitations, strict comparisons across countries may not be possible. However, there is no clear indication that countries with higher GDP per capita devote a larger share of their public expenditure budget to social services. For example, countries devoting more than 40 per cent of the public budget to social services in 2000 were a very diverse group, including Maldives, Mongolia and Samoa, as well as Malaysia, Singapore and Thailand.

## Public expenditure on education

***Share of education in the government budget increased in many countries***

Generally, the education sector claims the largest share of public expenditure devoted to social services in developing countries of the region. Out of 32 economies listed in table III.1, 15 devoted more than 15 per cent of total public expenditure to education in 2000. Kyrgyzstan, Malaysia, Papua New Guinea, the Republic of Korea, Samoa, Singapore and Thailand achieved the highest share of around 20 per cent. In terms

[3] The countries have been identified in tables III.1 and III.2.

[4] The countries most severely affected by the economic crisis were Indonesia, the Republic of Korea and Thailand. Time-series data from 1997 onwards on social services are available for Indonesia and Thailand only.

**Table III.1. Public expenditure on education, health and combined social services in selected economies of the ESCAP region in 1980 and 2000**

| | *Percentage of GDP* | | | | | | *Percentage of total public expenditure* | | | | | |
|---|---|---|---|---|---|---|---|---|---|---|---|---|
| | *Education* | | *Health* | | *Social services* | | *Education* | | *Health* | | *Social services* | |
| | *1980* | *2000* | *1980* | *2000* | *1980* | *2000* | *1980* | *2000* | *1980* | *2000* | *1980* | *2000* |
| **South and South-West Asia** | | | | | | | | | | | | |
| Bangladesh | 1.2 | .. | 0.6 | .. | 1.8 | .. | 11.5 | .. | 6.4 | .. | 18.2 | .. |
| Bhutan | .. | 5.2 | .. | 3.5 | .. | 10.3 | .. | 13.4 | .. | 9.2 | .. | 26.8 |
| India[a] | 2.9 | 3.1 | 0.9 | 1.3 | 5.6 | 6.3 | 11.6 | 11.2 | 3.5 | 4.8 | 22.0 | 22.4 |
| Iran (Islamic Republic of) | 8.2 | 4.1 | 2.4 | 1.4 | 14.4 | 11.1 | 21.3 | 18.6 | 6.4 | 6.5 | 37.5 | 50.4 |
| Maldives | 1.5 | 6.8 | 1.1 | 3.9 | 6.9 | 15.4 | 4.7 | 17.8 | 3.5 | 10.2 | 21.6 | 40.5 |
| Nepal | 1.4 | 2.5 | 0.6 | 0.9 | 2.3 | 4.7 | 9.9 | 15.3 | 3.9 | 5.7 | 16.1 | 29.5 |
| Pakistan[a] | 1.4 | 1.7 | 0.7 | 0.7 | 2.6 | 2.6 | 7.7 | 7.2 | 3.2 | 3.0 | 11.4 | 10.8 |
| Sri Lanka | 2.8 | 2.5 | 2.0 | 1.6 | 10.3 | 7.4 | 6.7 | 9.6 | 4.9 | 6.4 | 25.0 | 29.1 |
| Turkey | 3.1 | 3.8 | 0.8 | 1.3 | 5.2 | 9.3 | 14.2 | 9.6 | 3.6 | 3.4 | 24.0 | 23.6 |
| **South-East Asia** | | | | | | | | | | | | |
| Cambodia | .. | 1.5 | .. | 1.0 | .. | 2.8 | .. | 16.2 | .. | 10.7 | .. | 29.3 |
| Indonesia[a] | 2.9 | 1.3[b] | 0.7 | 0.5[b] | 4.5 | 6.2[b] | 11.0 | 6.4[b] | 2.6 | 2.3[b] | 16.8 | 30.7[b] |
| Malaysia[a] | 5.2 | 4.5[c] | 1.5 | 1.2[c] | 8.9 | 8.6[c] | 18.3 | 21.6[c] | 5.1 | 5.9[c] | 31.1 | 41.4[c] |
| Myanmar | 1.7 | 0.8[b] | 0.8 | 0.3[b] | 4.3 | 1.3[b] | 10.6 | 7.9[b] | 5.3 | 2.7[b] | 27.2 | 13.6[b] |
| Philippines | 1.7 | 3.7 | 0.6 | 0.4 | 3.3 | 5.2 | 13.0 | 18.6 | 4.5 | 2.3 | 24.9 | 26.2 |
| Singapore | 2.9 | 4.0 | 1.4 | 1.0 | 6.1 | 7.6 | 14.6 | 21.0 | 7.0 | 5.1 | 30.6 | 40.5 |
| Thailand[a] | 3.7 | 4.0[d] | 0.8 | 1.5[d] | 5.5 | 7.6[d] | 16.7 | 22.4[d] | 3.4 | 8.4[d] | 24.8 | 42.1[d] |
| Viet Nam | .. | 2.9 | .. | 0.8 | .. | 6.3 | .. | 13.9 | .. | 4.0 | .. | 30.4 |
| **East and North-East Asia** | | | | | | | | | | | | |
| China[a] | .. | 2.1[b] | .. | 0.7[b] | .. | 7.5[b] | .. | 8.6[b] | .. | 2.7[b] | .. | 30.1[b] |
| Hong Kong, China | 2.4 | 4.1 | 1.2 | 2.6 | 7.7 | 14.5 | 15.3 | 18.6 | 7.5 | 11.6 | 49.8 | 65.9 |
| Mongolia | .. | 2.7 | .. | 1.7 | .. | 13.0 | .. | 8.7 | .. | 5.5 | .. | 42.4 |
| Republic of Korea | 3.0 | 3.6[c] | .. | 2.1[c] | 4.6 | 6.1[c] | 17.1 | 20.5[c] | .. | 9.4[c] | 26.6 | 35.2[c] |
| **Pacific island economies** | | | | | | | | | | | | |
| Cook Islands | .. | 3.6 | .. | 2.9 | .. | 10.4 | .. | 10.5 | .. | 8.6 | .. | 30.4 |
| Fiji | 5.3 | 5.4[e] | 2.1 | 2.6[e] | 9.0 | 10.3[e] | 20.4 | 18.2[e] | 8.1 | 8.7[e] | 34.7 | 34.7[e] |
| Papua New Guinea | 5.2 | 6.2[b] | 2.7 | 1.9[b] | 9.6 | 9.7[b] | 16.5 | 22.1[b] | 8.6 | 6.9[b] | 30.2 | 34.6[b] |
| Samoa | 4.2 | 4.8 | 3.4 | 3.9 | 7.8 | 9.7 | 11.0 | 21.9 | 9.0 | 17.8 | 20.4 | 44.4 |
| Solomon Islands | 4.1 | .. | 3.2 | .. | 9.6 | .. | 13.5 | .. | 10.7 | .. | 31.7 | .. |

*(Continued on next page)*

**Table III.1** *(continued)*

| | *Percentage of GDP* | | | | | | *Percentage of total public expenditure* | | | | | |
|---|---|---|---|---|---|---|---|---|---|---|---|---|
| | *Education* | | *Health* | | *Social services* | | *Education* | | *Health* | | *Social services* | |
| | *1980* | *2000* | *1980* | *2000* | *1980* | *2000* | *1980* | *2000* | *1980* | *2000* | *1980* | *2000* |
| **North and Central Asia** | | | | | | | | | | | | |
| Azerbaijan[a] | .. | 4.5[b] | .. | 1.2[b] | .. | 14.3[b] | .. | 15.8[b] | .. | 4.0[b] | .. | 49.6[b] |
| Georgia[a] | .. | 1.4 | .. | 0.4 | .. | 5.6 | .. | 12.3 | .. | 3.6 | .. | 49.3 |
| Kazakhstan[a] | .. | 3.1 | .. | 2.0 | .. | 12.9 | .. | 12.6 | .. | 8.1 | .. | 51.9 |
| Kyrgyzstan | .. | 3.7 | .. | 2.1 | .. | 9.2 | .. | 19.5 | .. | 11.0 | .. | 48.5 |
| Russian Federation[a] | .. | 2.9 | .. | 2.0 | .. | 16.6 | .. | 8.0 | .. | 5.5 | .. | 45.4 |
| Tajikistan[a] | .. | 2.3 | .. | 0.9 | .. | 7.0 | .. | 14.2 | .. | 5.8 | .. | 43.1 |

*Sources:* IMF, *Government Finance Statistics Yearbook*, various issues and *International Financial Statistics Yearbook 2001;* ESCAP, *Statistical Yearbook for Asia and the Pacific*, various issues; Inter-State Statistical Committee of the Commonwealth of Independent States, *Statistical Abstract 1998* (Moscow, 1999); and national sources.

*Notes:* Social services include education, health, social security and welfare, housing and community amenities, recreation, culture and religious affairs.

Strict comparisons across countries may not be possible owing to possible differences in the classification of public expenditure.

[a] Including central, state or local government expenditure.
[b] 1999.
[c] 1997.
[d] Not including state or local level expenditure and thus not comparable with 1980 data.
[e] 1996.

of GDP, most of these economies were spending 4 per cent or more (mostly 4-5 per cent) on education. Other economies with public expenditure on education of over 4 per cent of GDP were Azerbaijan; Bhutan; Fiji; Hong Kong, China; the Islamic Republic of Iran; and Maldives. Most economies in the region were able to raise the share of public expenditure going to education between 1980 and 2000. Out of 18 developing economies (with data for both 1980 and 2000) in table III.1, 11 recorded an increase.

Some limited information is available on the distribution of public expenditure on various levels of education (table III.2). In more than half of the countries with data on all levels of education, primary education accounts for the highest share, followed by secondary and tertiary education. However, there are a good number of countries (mostly transitional economies) with higher expenditure on secondary than primary education. Between 1980 and 1996, the budget shares of secondary and tertiary education increased in several countries, reflecting demographic changes and a growing emphasis on education, including higher education, where unit costs are relatively high.

**Table III.2. Shares of primary, secondary and tertiary education in total public expenditure on education in selected countries of the ESCAP region, 1980 and 1996**

| | *Percentage distribution of current expenditure on education by level* | | | | | | | |
|---|---|---|---|---|---|---|---|---|
| | *1980* | | | | *1996* | | | |
| | *Primary* | *Secondary* | *Tertiary* | *Others* | *Primary* | *Secondary* | *Tertiary* | *Others* |
| Armenia | .. | .. | .. | .. | 15.8 | 63.0 | 13.2 | 8.0 |
| Azerbaijan | .. | .. | .. | .. | 14.6 | 63.9 | 7.5 | 13.9 |
| Bangladesh | 45.3 | 39.2 | 12.9 | 2.6 | 44.8 | 43.8 | 7.9 | 3.5 |
| Bhutan | .. | .. | .. | .. | 44.0[a] | 35.6[a] | 20.4[a] | 0.0 |
| China | 27.6 | 34.3 | 20.0 | 18.1 | 37.4 | 32.2 | 15.6 | 14.8 |
| India | 38.2 | 25.8 | 15.4 | 20.6 | 39.4 | 40.5 | 20.1 | 0.0 |
| Indonesia | .. | .. | .. | .. | .. | 73.5[b] | 24.4 | 2.1 |
| Iran (Islamic Republic of) | 43.7 | 38.1 | 7.1 | 11.2 | 36.5 | 46.5 | 2.1 | 14.9 |
| Kazakhstan | .. | .. | .. | .. | 10.4 | 61.1 | 13.4 | 15.1 |
| Kyrgyzstan | .. | .. | .. | .. | 6.6 | 68.0 | 14.1 | 11.2 |
| Lao People's Democratic Republic | .. | .. | .. | .. | 54.9 | 26.4 | 7.9 | 10.8 |
| Malaysia | 35.0 | 34.0 | 12.4 | 18.5 | 37.3 | 35.5 | 20.2 | 7.0 |
| Mongolia | 10.4 | 52.6 | 16.6 | 20.5 | 19.9 | 56.0 | 14.3 | 9.8 |
| Nepal | .. | 58.7[b] | 35.0 | 6.3 | 49.3 | 20.9 | 17.9 | 11.9 |
| Pakistan | 39.4 | 31.0 | 18.8 | 10.7 | 47.7 | 29.6 | 13.2 | 9.5 |
| Philippines | 61.4 | 15.7 | 22.1 | 0.8 | 54.7 | 23.5 | 17.8 | 3.9 |
| Republic of Korea | 49.9 | 33.2 | 8.7 | 8.2 | 45.3[c] | 36.6[c] | 8.0[c] | 10.0[c] |
| Russian Federation | .. | .. | .. | .. | 23.2[c] | 57.4[c] | 19.3[c] | 0.0 |
| Singapore | 35.8 | 41.1 | 17.1 | 6.1 | 25.7[c] | 34.6[c] | 34.8[c] | 4.9[c] |
| Sri Lanka | .. | 91.1[b] | 8.9 | .. | 0.0 | 74.8[b] | 9.3 | 16.0 |
| Tajikistan | 8.1 | 51.4 | 8.1 | 27.0 | 14.9 | 71.2 | 7.1 | 6.8 |
| Thailand | 58.5 | 16.7 | 19.3 | 5.5 | 50.4 | 20.0 | 16.4 | 13.3 |
| Turkey | 43.7 | 22.9 | 28.3 | 5.1 | 43.3[c] | 22.0[c] | 34.7[c] | 0.0 |
| Viet Nam | .. | .. | .. | .. | 43.0 | 26.0 | 22.0 | 9.0 |

*Source:* UNESCO, Institute for Statistics, <http://www.uis.unesco.org>, 30 October 2002.

*Note:* Expenditure on primary education includes pre-primary education.

[a] 1997.

[b] Including primary education.

[c] 1995.

***Public expenditure plays a major role in the provision of education***

Data on the mix between private and public expenditure on education are available only for a small number of countries (figure III.1). The share of private expenditure in total expenditure on education was 41 to 44 per cent in Kazakhstan, the Philippines, the Republic of Korea and Thailand. Malaysia had the lowest share, at 2 per cent, reflecting heavy investment by the public sector. In Cambodia and India, around 25 per cent of education expenditure came from private sources. On the basis of this limited empirical evidence, it can be concluded that the role of public expenditure in the provision of education is clearly dominant.

**Figure III.1. Share of private expenditure in total expenditure on education in selected countries, 1998**

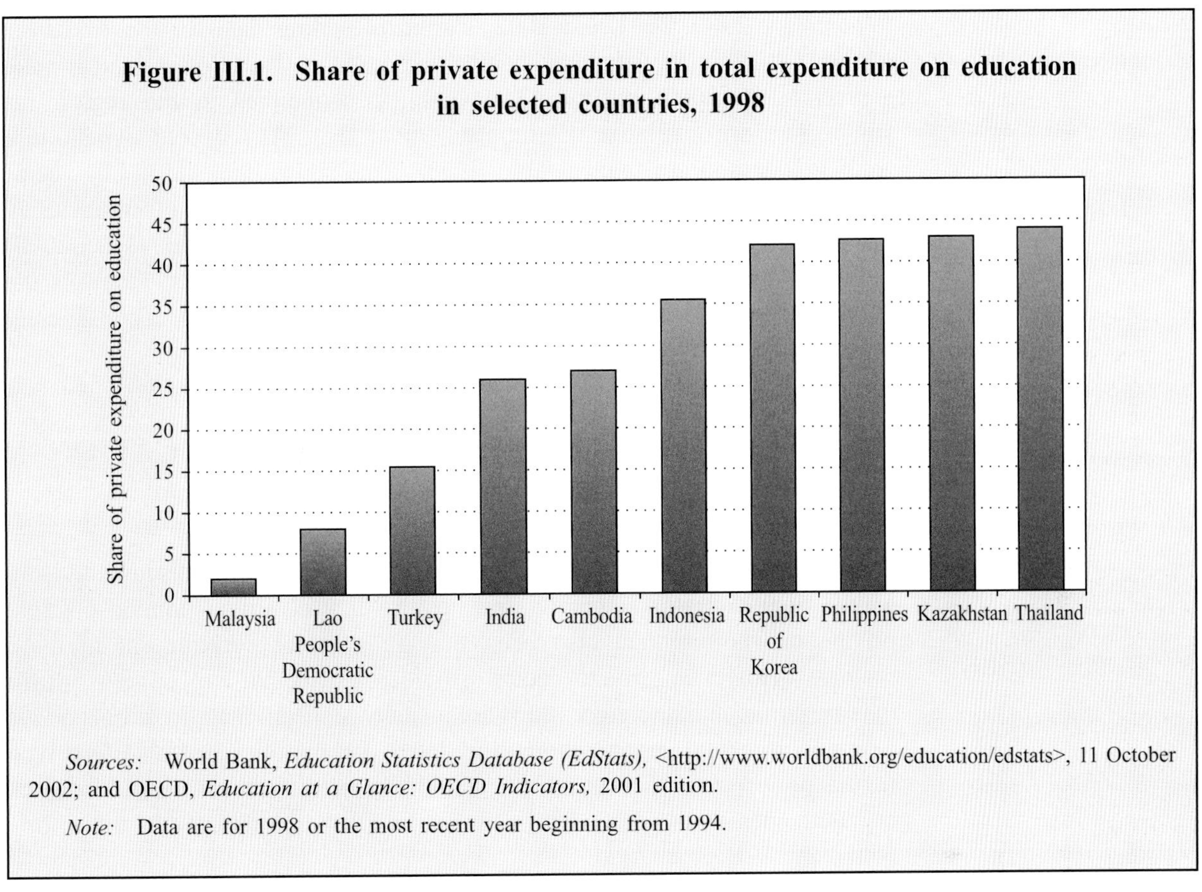


*Sources:* World Bank, *Education Statistics Database (EdStats),* <http://www.worldbank.org/education/edstats>, 11 October 2002; and OECD, *Education at a Glance: OECD Indicators,* 2001 edition.

*Note:* Data are for 1998 or the most recent year beginning from 1994.

## Public expenditure on health

***The share of health in total public expenditure increased in most countries***

As in the case of education, there is diversity in the levels and trends of public expenditure on health. Among developing economies, 5 spent more than 10 per cent of their total budget on health in 2000, 10 spent less than 5 per cent and the rest fell in between (table III.1). With respect to GDP, less than 2 per cent was being spent on health in 2000 in a large number of economies. Pacific island countries generally had a higher share, mainly funded through foreign assistance. Some countries with smaller populations, such as Bhutan, Cook Islands, Fiji, Maldives and Samoa, were spending more than 2 per cent of GDP on health. A comparison of shares of expenditure on health in total public expenditure between 1980 and 2000 presents mixed results. Out of 18 economies, 10 witnessed an increase and the remainder a decrease.

***The public sector is the major provider of health-care services***

Individuals and families spend a significant share of their income on health-care services, including traditional medicines. Therefore, in order to have a better picture of spending on health, it is important to know the amount of private expenditure on health. WHO, in its *World Health*

*Reports* for 2000, 2001 and 2002, started providing data for the first time on the distribution of total health expenditure by private and public sources.[5] In 2000, out of 43 developing economies in the region for which data are available, 19 reported more than 50 per cent expenditure from private sources (annex table III.1). This shows that the public sector is still the main provider of health services in the majority of countries in the region. Since the annual data available are for six years (1995-2000) only, not much can be said about emerging trends. However, China is the only country in which the share of private expenditure rose consistently over the five-year period.[6]

## OUTPUTS AND OUTCOMES OF THE EDUCATION AND HEALTH SECTORS

In the previous section, public expenditure was discussed as a source of finance for education and health. It was further pointed out that private expenditure had also been making a major contribution to these sectors. However, private sector providers' principal objective is profit maximization and therefore they are usually concentrated in urban areas. Non-governmental organizations and local communities are also involved in the provision of education and health services. Therefore, the outputs and outcomes of the two sectors cannot be attributed entirely to the efforts of the public sector alone.

***Not only supply but actual utilization of services is important***

Public expenditure mainly contributes to the supply side by making education and health facilities available. The actual utilization of these services by people can produce only positive results. It is possible that the services may remain underutilized even when they are free. For example, poor people may not be able to send their children to school because of the high opportunity cost involved, since children of the poor start working at a younger age and help their parents to earn a livelihood. Demand for education and health is also dependent on the overall development of a country.[7] For example, education and health facilities in rural areas can be utilized only if they are accessible by road and transport is available.

---

[5] *The World Health Report 2002: Reducing Risks, Promoting Healthy Life* contains data for 1995-2000.

[6] A recent study reveals that this trend began much earlier; the share of private expenditure in total health expenditure rose from 23 per cent in 1980 to more than 50 per cent in 1995. For further details, see Dezhi Yu, "Market-based reforms and changes in China's health care system", in Mwabu, Ugaz and White, eds., op. cit.

[7] ESCAP, *Survey 1996,* chapter V, "The role of public expenditure in the provision of social services".

***Achievements of the education and health sectors are linked to public expenditure***

It needs to be emphasized that the public sector still plays a major role in the provision of education and health services in most countries of the region. The achievements of the education and health sectors are also linked to the public expenditure devoted to them. A simple look at the cross-country data on public expenditure and achievement indicators suggests some intuitively appealing relationships (figure III.2). The relationships between public education expenditure as a percentage of GDP and the adult literacy rate as well as the youth literacy rate appear positive, that is, countries with higher public expenditure on education have achieved better outcomes. The relationship between

**Figure III.2. Relationship between public expenditure and achievement indicators of education and health of selected countries**

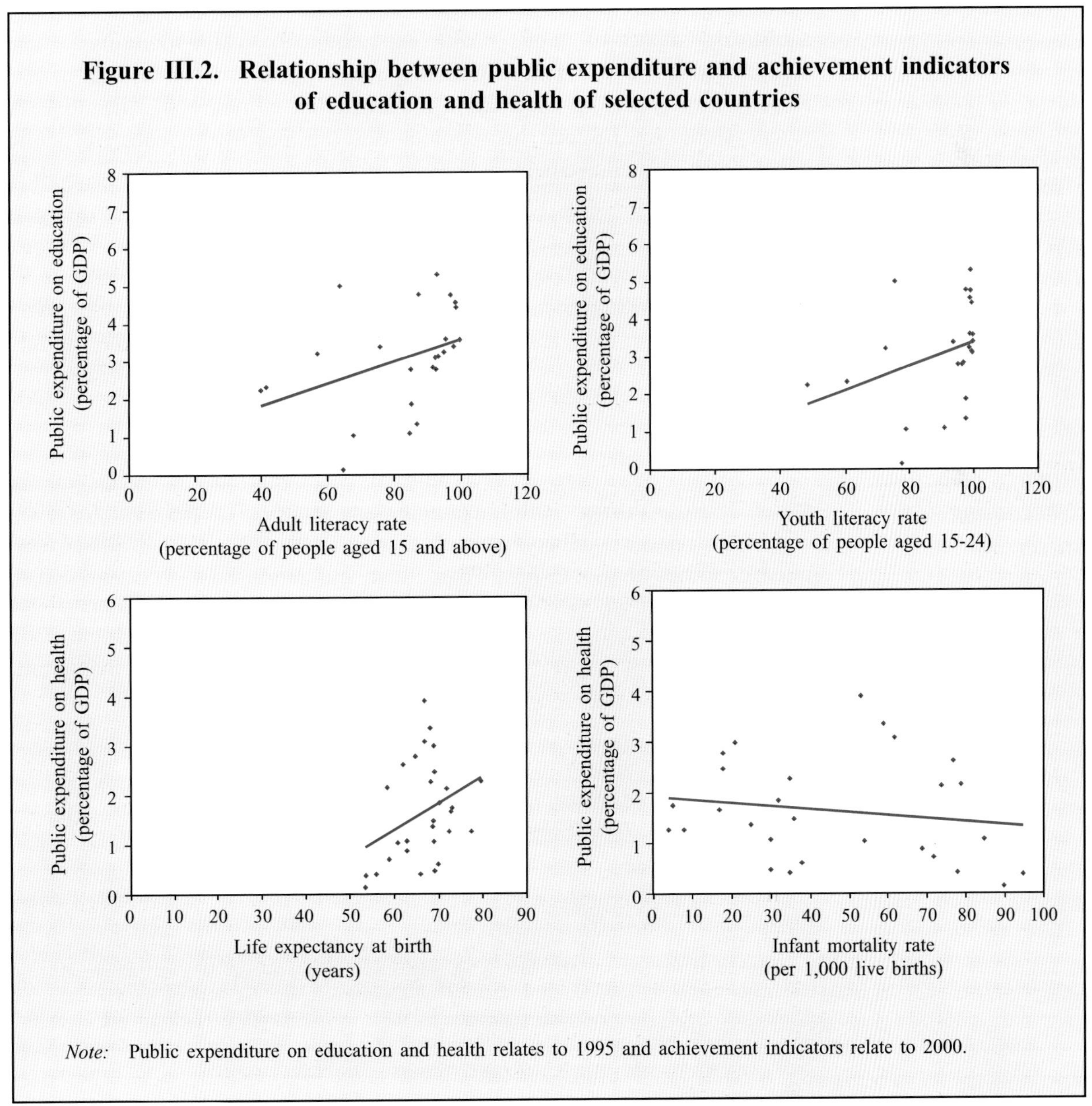


*Note:* Public expenditure on education and health relates to 1995 and achievement indicators relate to 2000.

public health expenditure and life expectancy also looks positive, whereas the relationship with the infant mortality rate appears negative, as can be expected. Since the impact of public expenditure on achievement indicators is likely to be felt with some time lag, the data on public expenditure in the figure are for 1995, as against achievement indicators for 2000. The pattern of results remains similar if public expenditure data for 1990 are tried instead of 1995. The results also do not change much even when both public expenditure and achievement indicators relate to 2000.[8]

A more rigorous study using multiple regression analysis and data from over 60 developing countries of the world brings out the statistically significant impact of public health expenditure on child mortality.[9] The study also shows that in addition to public expenditure on health, access to electricity and child vaccination reduces child mortality significantly. A recent study by ESCAP also points out the positive impact of public expenditure on achievement indicators of the education and health sectors as well as the economic growth of countries in the region.[10]

With these few observations, the outputs and outcomes of the education and health sectors are discussed in terms of various indicators.

## Education

***Primary education is becoming universal***

Primary education is becoming universal in most countries of the region. Gross primary enrolment rates are around 100 per cent (or even higher) in a large number of countries and areas (table III.3).[11] By 1980, most countries in South-East Asia, East and North-East Asia and North

---

[8] The results in all the experiments remain similar even when public expenditure on education/health as a percentage of total public expenditure rather than GDP is used.

[9] L. Wang, "Health outcomes in poor countries and policy options: empirical findings from demographic and health surveys", World Bank Working Paper 2831, April 2002.

[10] M. Aynul Hasan, "Role of human capital in economic development: some myths and realities", in ESCAP, *Development Planning in a Market Economy* (United Nations publication, Sales No. E.02.II.F.24).

[11] Gross enrolment ratio is defined as the number of students enrolled in a level of education, regardless of age, as a percentage of the population of official school age for that level. The gross enrolment rate can be more than 100, implying that there are substantial numbers of over-aged students and grade repeaters. By contrast, the net enrolment ratio represents the number of enrolled students of a particular age (as defined by the education system concerned) over the total population in the corresponding age bracket. Net enrolment ratio data are available only for a smaller number of countries, particularly at the secondary and higher education levels as well as for earlier years. Therefore, long-term analysis is carried out here with gross enrolment ratios.

**Table III.3. Gross enrolment ratios by education levels in selected economies of the ESCAP region, 1980 and 1998**

| | *Enrolment ratio (1980)* | | | *Enrolment ratio (1998)*[a] | | | *Combined primary, secondary and tertiary enrolment ratio (1999)* | |
|---|---|---|---|---|---|---|---|---|
| | *Primary* | *Secondary* | *Tertiary* | *Primary* | *Secondary* | *Tertiary* | *Male* | *Female* |
| **South and South-West Asia** | | | | | | | | |
| Bangladesh | 61 | 18 | 3 | 122 | 47 | 5 | 41 | 33 |
| Bhutan | 15 | .. | .. | 73 | .. | .. | .. | .. |
| India | 83 | 30 | 5 | 100 | 49 | 7 | 62 | 49 |
| Iran (Islamic Republic of) | 87 | 42 | .. | 98 | 77 | 18 | 76 | 69 |
| Maldives | 146 | 4 | .. | 128 | 69 | .. | 77 | 77 |
| Nepal | 86 | 22 | 3 | 114 | 48 | 5 | 67 | 52 |
| Pakistan | 40 | 14 | .. | 86 | 37 | 3 | 51 | 28 |
| Sri Lanka | 103 | 55 | 3 | 111 | 75 | 5 | 68 | 71 |
| Turkey | 96 | 35 | 5 | 107 | 70 | 21 | 68 | 55 |
| **South-East Asia** | | | | | | | | |
| Brunei Darussalam | 109 | 61 | 1 | 106 | 77 | 7 | 76 | 77 |
| Cambodia | 139 | .. | .. | 119 | 24 | 1 | 71 | 54 |
| Indonesia | 107 | 29 | 4 | 113 | 56 | 11 | 68 | 61 |
| Lao People's Democratic Republic | 114 | 21 | .. | 112 | 33 | 3 | 65 | 52 |
| Malaysia | 93 | 48 | 4 | 101 | 98 | 12 | 64 | 67 |
| Myanmar | 91 | 22 | 5 | 121 | 36 | 5 | 55 | 55 |
| Philippines | 112 | 64 | 24 | 117 | 78 | 29 | 80 | 84 |
| Singapore | 108 | 60 | 8 | 94 | 74 | 39 | 76 | 75 |
| Thailand | 99 | 29 | 15 | 94 | 88 | 30 | 60 | 61 |
| Viet Nam | 109 | 42 | 2 | 114 | 61 | 11 | 69 | 64 |
| **East and North-East Asia** | | | | | | | | |
| China | 113 | 46 | 2 | 123 | 70 | 6 | 73 | 73 |
| Hong Kong, China | 107 | 64 | 10 | 94 | 73 | 22 | 61 | 66 |
| Mongolia | 107 | 92 | 22 | 94 | 56 | 25 | 51 | 64 |
| Republic of Korea | 110 | 78 | 15 | 94 | 102 | 68 | 95 | 85 |
| **Pacific island economies** | | | | | | | | |
| Fiji | 119 | 55 | 3 | 128 | 64 | 12 | 84 | 83 |
| Papua New Guinea | 59 | 12 | 2 | 85 | 22 | 3 | 42 | 35 |
| Samoa | .. | .. | .. | 100 | 62 | 5 | 63 | 67 |
| Solomon Islands | 76 | 16 | .. | 97 | 17 | .. | .. | .. |
| **North and Central Asia** | | | | | | | | |
| Armenia | .. | .. | .. | 87 | 90 | 12 | 82 | 77 |
| Azerbaijan | 115 | 95 | 24 | 106 | 84 | 22 | 70 | 72 |
| Georgia | 93 | 109 | 30 | 95 | 79 | 42 | 69 | 71 |
| Kazakhstan | 85 | 93 | 34 | 98 | 87 | 33 | 73 | 81 |
| Kyrgyzstan | 116 | 110 | 16 | 104 | 86 | 30 | 65 | 70 |
| Russian Federation | 102 | 96 | 46 | 107 | 87 | 43 | 75 | 82 |
| Tajikistan | .. | .. | 24 | 95 | 78 | 20 | 72 | 63 |
| Turkmenistan | .. | .. | 23 | .. | .. | 22 | 81 | 81 |
| Uzbekistan | 81 | 106 | 29 | 78 | 94 | 32 | 79 | 74 |

*Sources:* UNESCO, Institute for Statistics web site <http://www.uis.unesco.org/en/stats/stats0.htm>, 19 July 2002; UNDP, *Human Development Report 2002* (New York, Oxford University Press, 2002); and World Bank, *World Development Indicators,* 2001 and 2002 (Washington, 2001 and 2002).

[a] 1998 or the most recent year for which data are available. In most cases data relate to 1998 or 1997.

and Central Asia had already achieved universal primary education. Countries in South Asia made considerable progress over the last two decades in raising primary enrolment rates. However, the enrolment ratios in Bhutan (73 per cent) and Pakistan (86 per cent) in 1998 require improvement. Similarly, Papua New Guinea (85 per cent), Armenia (87 per cent) and Uzbekistan (78 per cent) need to enhance their efforts. Since for most countries, overall gross primary enrolment ratios are around 100, male and female gaps in enrolment ratios cannot be pronounced. In fact, male-female gaps are only visible in some countries in South Asia and they are also closing over time.

***Diversity of success at the secondary level of education***

Success at the secondary level of education is more diversified (table III.3). In 1998, gross enrolment ratios were more than 75 per cent in all countries in North and Central Asia. Although the performance of these transitional economies is better than that of many other countries, some deterioration over time is visible as their enrolment ratios were even better prior to their transition. The performance of countries in South-East Asia and East and North-East Asia is also comparatively better. Malaysia (98 per cent), Thailand (88 per cent) and the Republic of Korea (102 per cent) showed the highest enrolment ratios. The ratios ranged from 70 to 78 per cent for Brunei Darussalam; China; Hong Kong, China; the Philippines; and Singapore, but were very low for Cambodia (24 per cent), the Lao People's Democratic Republic (33 per cent) and Myanmar (36 per cent), all of which happen to be least developed countries. Indonesia, Mongolia and Viet Nam had enrolment ratios ranging from 56 to 61 per cent. It is obvious that many countries in South-East Asia and East and North-East Asia have to accelerate their efforts to raise enrolment ratios to more satisfactory levels.

The enrolment ratios were generally low in South Asia, ranging from 37 per cent in Pakistan to 77 per cent in Sri Lanka. However, there has been a major improvement over the last two decades. For example, in the case of Pakistan, the enrolment ratio of only 14 per cent in 1980 rose to 37 per cent in 1998. Some Pacific island countries also need to intensify their efforts to improve their low enrolment ratios.

Male-female gaps in enrolment ratios at the secondary level are much more pronounced, particularly for most countries in South Asia plus other countries with lower enrolment ratios, with the exception of Mongolia, which had a higher ratio for females than for males.

***Low enrolment ratio at the tertiary level***

At the tertiary level, the enrolment ratios were generally low in 1998, ranging from 1 per cent (for Cambodia) to 68 per cent (for the Republic of Korea). Out of 33 countries given in the table for which data were available, only 17 had enrolment ratios 20 per cent or more. Male-female gaps existed here also but, interestingly, many countries reported higher enrolment ratios for females. Most of these are transitional economies of North and Central Asia.

***Dropouts and grade repetition are problems***

Enrolment ratios reveal neither the quality of education nor how many students actually completed their particular levels of education. Dropouts and grade repetitions are serious problems in many developing countries. Poor children are sometimes forced to withdraw from school to help their parents because of financial constraints. Additionally, a lack of facilities in schools and an uninteresting curriculum discourage students from continuing their education. Data on children starting primary school who eventually reach grade 5 are available for only a small number of countries. While in most countries the rate was over 90 per cent, countries in South Asia and least developed countries did not fare well in general.[12]

With the expansion of enrolments, one would expect greater pressure on school facilities and rising pupil-teacher ratios. However, those ratios at the primary and secondary levels fell between 1980 and 2000 in a large number of countries, as shown in annex table III.2, reflecting enhanced investment by countries to improve the quality of education. Some countries showed an upward trend in pupil-teacher ratios, particularly at the secondary level.

***Adult and youth literacy rates are linked to enrolment ratios at the primary level***

The previous discussion was in terms of output indicators. The outcome of the education sector is usually measured through literacy indicators. A person is considered literate who can with understanding both read and write a short, simple statement about everyday life. Adult literacy measures the percentage of literate people in the age group 15 and above. Adult literacy rates are generally high in those countries with high enrolment ratios at the primary level (table III.4). Some countries in South Asia, as well as Cambodia, the Lao People's Democratic Republic and Papua New Guinea had low literacy rates in 2000. Efforts by countries in the education sector during the last decade are better reflected in youth literacy rates (15-24 age group). Youth literacy was nearly universal in a large number of countries (table III.4). Countries with low rates need to intensify their efforts to raise enrolment ratios, particularly of females, in primary education and to ensure that students complete their primary education.

---

[12] For details, see *Survey 2002*, pp. 203-205.

**Table III.4. Adult and youth literacy rates in selected economies of the ESCAP region**

| | *Adult literacy (percentage of people aged 15 and above)* | | *Youth literacy (percentage of people aged 15-24)* | |
|---|---|---|---|---|
| | *1980* | *2000* | *1980* | *2000* |
| **South and South-West Asia** | | | | |
| Afghanistan | 18 | .. | 30 | .. |
| Bangladesh | 29 | 40 | 36 | 51 |
| India | 41 | 57 | 55 | 73 |
| Iran (Islamic Republic of) | 50 | 76 | 73 | 94 |
| Maldives | 92 | 97 | 97 | 99 |
| Nepal | 22 | 42 | 33 | 60 |
| Pakistan | 28 | 43 | 37 | 57 |
| Sri Lanka | 85 | 92 | 93 | 97 |
| Turkey | 68 | 85 | 88 | 97 |
| **South-East Asia** | | | | |
| Brunei Darussalam | 77 | 92 | 94 | 99 |
| Cambodia | 55 | 68 | 67 | 79 |
| Indonesia | 69 | 87 | 89 | 98 |
| Lao People's Democratic Republic | 48 | 65 | 63 | 71 |
| Malaysia | 71 | 87 | 90 | 98 |
| Myanmar | 76 | 85 | 85 | 91 |
| Philippines | 88 | 95 | 95 | 99 |
| Singapore | 83 | 92 | 97 | 100 |
| Thailand | 88 | 96 | 97 | 99 |
| Viet Nam | 87 | 93 | 95 | 97 |
| **East and North-East Asia** | | | | |
| China | 67 | 85 | 91 | 98 |
| Hong Kong, China | 85 | 93 | 96 | 99 |
| Mongolia | 97 | 98 | 99 | 99 |
| Republic of Korea | 93 | 98 | 100 | 100 |
| **Pacific island economies** | | | | |
| Fiji | 82 | 93 | 95 | 99 |
| Papua New Guinea | 48 | 64 | 61 | 76 |
| Samoa | 97 | 99 | 99 | 99 |
| **North and Central Asia** | | | | |
| Armenia | 96 | 98 | 99 | 100 |
| Kazakhstan | 98 | 99 | 100 | 100 |
| Russian Federation | 99 | 100 | 100 | 100 |
| Tajikistan | 96 | 99 | 100 | 100 |
| Uzbekistan | 98 | 99 | 100 | 100 |

*Sources:* World Bank, *World Development Indicators 2001* (CD-ROM); and UNESCO, Institute for Statistics, Estimates and projections, July 2002 assessment, <http://www.uis.unesco.org>, 17 September 2002.

## Health

Outputs of the health sector are discussed in terms of coverage of people by health services in various forms, including access to health services in general, the doctor-patient ratio, the number of births attended by skilled health personnel and the immunization of children against diphtheria, pertussis and tetanus (DPT).

***Access to health services does not mean their utilization***

Data on access to health services are available for a small group of countries (table III.5), and the latest data only cover the period 1990-1995. In many countries in the group, more than 80 per cent of the population had access to some health services. This access was universal in the Republic of Korea and Singapore. It is important to note that there is no one-to-one correspondence between access to health services and utilization of health services. Poor people usually do not have enough resources to pay for health services. At public hospitals where medical services are subsidized or free, there are discouraging factors such as long queues and poor quality.

***Doctor-patient ratios improved over time***

The doctor-patient ratio improved considerably in most countries between the 1980s and 1990s (table III.5). However, vast differences exist among countries. Despite improving doctor-patient ratios over time in most countries, rural and remote areas continue to face serious shortages of doctors and other trained medical staff. Doctors are reluctant to go to these areas owing to the poor living conditions there and the lack of proper facilities in the hospitals.

The coverage of health services is also measured by the proportion of births attended by skilled health personnel, such as physicians, nurses, midwives and primary health-care workers trained in midwifery skills. In some countries of the region, births attended by skilled health personnel were below 50 per cent in recent years (table III.5). The rates were particularly low in countries with high maternal mortality ratios, some of which are in South Asia.

***Huge success in immunization of children***

All countries achieved huge success in terms of immunization of children against DPT. This was the result of the national immunization campaigns launched in most countries. However, there are still many countries that need to improve the coverage further. Out of 35 countries in the table with data on the immunization of children against DPT, 13 had less than 80 per cent coverage. Interestingly, some countries have seen a deterioration in the coverage in 1999 compared with 1990. Therefore, sustained efforts are required to keep the immunization rates at high levels, particularly in those countries where child mortality rates are still high.

**Table III.5. Some health coverage indicators in selected economies of the ESCAP region**

| | Population with access to health services (percentage) | | Physicians (per 100,000 people) | | Births attended by skilled health staff (percentage of total) | | DPT3 immunization coverage (percentage) | |
|---|---|---|---|---|---|---|---|---|
| | 1985-1987 | 1990-1995 | 1984 | 1990-1999 | 1983-1988 | 1995-2000 | 1980 | 1999 |
| **South and South-West Asia** | | | | | | | | |
| Afghanistan | 29 | .. | .. | .. | 8 | .. | 4 | 35 |
| Bangladesh | 45 | 45 | 7 | 20 | 5 | 13 | 1[a] | 72 |
| Bhutan | 65 | .. | 2 | 16 | 7 | .. | 6 | 88 |
| India | .. | 85 | 18 | 48 | 33 | 42 | 6 | 55 |
| Iran (Islamic Republic of) | 78 | 88 | 17 | 85 | 82 | .. | .. | 99 |
| Maldives | .. | .. | .. | 40 | .. | .. | 4 | 92 |
| Nepal | .. | .. | 1 | 4 | 6 | 12 | 8 | 76 |
| Pakistan | 55 | 55 | 16 | 57 | 24 | 20 | 2 | 56 |
| Sri Lanka | 93 | 93 | 8 | 36 | 87 | .. | 46 | 99 |
| Turkey | .. | .. | 33 | 121 | 78 | 81 | 42 | 79 |
| **South-East Asia** | | | | | | | | |
| Brunei Darussalam | .. | .. | .. | 85 | .. | 99 | .. | 92 |
| Cambodia | 53 | 53 | .. | 30 | 47 | 34 | 17[b] | 49 |
| Indonesia | 80 | 93 | 5 | 16 | 31 | 56 | 1[a] | 72 |
| Lao People's Democratic Republic | 67 | 67 | 34 | 24 | .. | 21 | 7 | 56 |
| Malaysia | .. | .. | 24 | 66 | 82 | 96 | 67 | 93 |
| Myanmar | 33 | 60 | 12 | 30 | 57 | .. | 4 | 83 |
| Philippines | .. | 71 | 7 | 123 | 57 | 56 | 47 | 79 |
| Singapore | 100 | 100 | 35 | 163 | 100 | 100 | 85 | 94 |
| Thailand | 70 | 90 | 7 | 24 | 40 | 85 | 49 | 97 |
| Viet Nam | 80 | 90 | 46 | 48 | 99 | 70 | 4 | 93 |
| **East and North-East Asia** | | | | | | | | |
| China | .. | 88 | 46 | 162 | .. | 70 | 58[c] | 90 |
| Democratic People's Republic of Korea | .. | .. | .. | .. | 65 | .. | .. | 37 |
| Hong Kong, China | .. | .. | 43 | .. | 92 | 100 | .. | .. |
| Mongolia | .. | 95 | .. | 243 | 99 | 94 | 76 | 94 |
| Republic of Korea | 93 | 100 | 39 | 136 | 70 | 76 | 61[a] | 74 |
| **Pacific island economies** | | | | | | | | |
| Fiji | .. | .. | .. | 48 | .. | 100 | 68 | 86 |
| Papua New Guinea | .. | 96 | 7 | 7 | 34 | 53 | 32 | 56 |
| Samoa | .. | .. | .. | 34 | .. | 100 | .. | .. |
| Solomon Islands | .. | .. | .. | 14 | .. | 85 | .. | .. |
| Vanuatu | .. | .. | .. | 12 | .. | 89 | .. | .. |

*(Continued on next page)*

**Table III.5** *(continued)*

| | *Population with access to health services (percentage)* | | *Physicians (per 100,000 people)* | | *Births attended by skilled health staff (percentage of total)* | | *DPT3 immunization coverage (percentage)* | |
|---|---|---|---|---|---|---|---|---|
| | *1985-1987* | *1990-1995* | *1984* | *1990-1999* | *1983-1988* | *1995-2000* | *1980* | *1999* |
| **North and Central Asia** | | | | | | | | |
| Armenia | .. | .. | .. | 316 | .. | 97 | .. | 91 |
| Azerbaijan | .. | .. | .. | 360 | .. | 88 | .. | 99 |
| Georgia | .. | .. | .. | 436 | .. | 96 | .. | 90 |
| Kazakhstan | .. | .. | .. | 353 | .. | 99 | .. | 98 |
| Kyrgyzstan | .. | .. | .. | 301 | .. | 98 | .. | 98 |
| Russian Federation | .. | .. | .. | 421 | 98 | 99 | .. | 95 |
| Tajikistan | .. | .. | .. | 201 | .. | 71 | 82[d] | 82 |
| Turkmenistan | .. | .. | .. | 300 | .. | 97 | .. | 98 |
| Uzbekistan | .. | .. | .. | 309 | .. | 96 | 98[a] | 99 |

*Sources:* UNDP, *Human Development Report,* 1990, 1998 and 2002; and WHO/UNICEF, *Review of National Immunization Coverage,* various issues; and WHO/UNICEF database <http://www.childinfo.org/eddb/immuni/database.htm>.

[a] 1981.
[b] 1984.
[c] 1983.
[d] 1985.

***Life expectancy increased and infant mortality rates fell***

Outcomes of the health sector are discussed in terms of two selected indicators: life expectancy at birth and infant mortality rate. Most countries have shown a considerable achievement in raising life expectancy over the last two decades. In a number of countries, the increase in life expectancy was around 10 years. For example, a child born in Indonesia today can expect to live 66 years, 11 years longer than one born in 1980 (table III.6). Life expectancy at birth in India improved from 54 to 63 years over the period 1980-2000. The increase was more marked in the case of countries with initially low rates. Despite this closing gap, large differences among developing countries still exist. At present, life expectancy varies from 78 years in Singapore to 43 years in Afghanistan. The significant increase in life expectancy over time has been achieved particularly as a result of a sharp drop in infant mortality rates.[13] Bhutan's rate of 135 in 1980 was one of the highest; it came down to 77 in 2000. In Nepal it fell from 133 to 72 over the same period. Infant mortality virtually disappeared (the rate being 5 or less) in the Republic of Korea and Singapore.

[13] The infant mortality rate is the number of babies out of every 1,000 live births who die before their first birthday.

**Table III.6. Life expectancy and infant mortality rates in selected economies of the ESCAP region**

| | *Life expectancy at birth (years)* | | *Infant mortality rate (per 1,000 live births)* | |
|---|---|---|---|---|
| | *1980* | *2000* | *1980* | *2000* |
| **South and South-West Asia** | | | | |
| Afghanistan | 40 | 43 | 183 | 165 |
| Bangladesh | 49 | 61 | 129 | 54 |
| Bhutan | .. | 62 | 135 | 77 |
| India | 54 | 63 | 113 | 69 |
| Iran (Islamic Republic of) | 58 | 69 | 92 | 36 |
| Maldives | 56 | 68 | 115 | 59 |
| Nepal | 48 | 59 | 133 | 72 |
| Pakistan | 55 | 63 | 105 | 85 |
| Sri Lanka | 68 | 73 | 35 | 17 |
| Turkey | 61 | 70 | 103 | 38 |
| **South-East Asia** | | | | |
| Brunei Darussalam | 71 | 76 | 19 | 6 |
| Cambodia | 40 | 54 | 110 | 95 |
| Indonesia | 55 | 66 | 79 | 35 |
| Lao People's Democratic Republic | 45 | 54 | 135 | 90 |
| Malaysia | 67 | 73 | 31 | 8 |
| Myanmar | 51 | 56 | 94 | 78 |
| Philippines | 61 | 69 | 55 | 30 |
| Singapore | 71 | 78 | 11 | 4 |
| Thailand | 64 | 69 | 45 | 25 |
| Viet Nam | 60 | 69 | 50 | 30 |
| **East and North-East Asia** | | | | |
| China | 67 | 70 | 49 | 32 |
| Democratic People's Republic of Korea | 67 | 61 | 32 | 23 |
| Hong Kong, China | 74 | 80 | .. | .. |
| Mongolia | 58 | 67 | 97 | 62 |
| Republic of Korea | 67 | 73 | 16 | 5 |
| **Pacific island economies** | | | | |
| Fiji | 64 | 69 | 34 | 18 |
| Kiribati | .. | 62 | .. | 52 |
| New Caledonia | 67 | 73 | .. | .. |
| Papua New Guinea | 51 | 59 | 79 | 79 |
| Samoa | 63 | 69 | 70 | 21 |
| Solomon Islands | 60 | 69 | 43 | 21 |
| Vanuatu | .. | 68 | 77 | 35 |

*(Continued on next page)*

**Table III.6** *(continued)*

| | *Life expectancy at birth (years)* | | *Infant mortality rate (per 1,000 live births)* | |
|---|---|---|---|---|
| | *1980* | *2000* | *1980* | *2000* |
| **North and Central Asia** | | | | |
| Armenia | 73 | 74 | 22 | 25 |
| Azerbaijan | 69 | 72 | 76 | 74 |
| Georgia | 71 | 73 | 34 | 24 |
| Kazakhstan | 67 | 65 | 50 | 60 |
| Kyrgyzstan | 65 | 67 | 90 | 53 |
| Russian Federation | 67 | 65 | 28 | 18 |
| Tajikistan | 66 | 69 | 67 | 54 |
| Turkmenistan | 64 | 66 | 67 | 52 |
| Uzbekistan | 67 | 70 | 47 | 51 |

*Sources:* World Bank, *World Development Indicators 2002* (CD-ROM); and UNICEF Statistics web site <http://www.childinfo.org/cmr/revis/db1.htm>.

## ISSUES CONCERNING THE MOBILIZATION OF RESOURCES AND IMPROVING THEIR EFFECTIVENESS IN PROVIDING EDUCATION AND HEALTH

As discussed in the previous section, there appear to be strong linkages between resources devoted to education and health and the achievements of these sectors. Generally, countries with higher public expenditure show better outputs and outcomes. The results also depend on the effective and efficient utilization of resources. Therefore, the remaining part of this chapter addresses the following two questions:

1. How should additional resources for education and health be mobilized?
2. How can the effectiveness and efficiency of resources devoted to education and health be enhanced?

### Generating additional resources for education and health

Huge financial resources are needed for the expansion and upgrading of education and health services in most countries of the region. As discussed in the previous section, the sectoral allocation of public funds varies greatly across countries. In many countries, the education and health sectors have lower shares compared with other sectors, including defence and general administration. Shifting them from other sectors with low productivity would increase resources for education and health. Moreover, multiple channels of financing are required to raise sufficient resources. These include both the public and private sectors, communities and non-governmental organizations, donors and multilateral organizations. A brief discussion on each of these follows.

### Tax revenues

***Tax reforms to raise more revenue***

As discussed earlier, the public sector continues to play a major role in the provision of education and health in countries of the region. Education and health are in the nature of public goods and their economic and social benefits extend beyond the persons directly benefiting from them. The role of the public sector will remain important and therefore more public resources are needed to expand access to and improve the quality of education and health. The most obvious public source of finance is tax revenues, which are reliable and sustainable. Countries have been reforming their tax systems and many have introduced VAT. Tax revenues should be enhanced by expanding the tax base and improving tax administration.

### User charges

***Some user charges should be introduced to improve the quality of services***

Generally, the education and health services provided by the public sector are free of charge or are available at nominal charge. It is possible that people may be willing to pay some user charges for services of improved quality because the alternative to better-quality public services is the private sector with much higher fees and user charges. Owing to the lack of resources, public schools are starved of funds. They demand payments under different guises other than fees, and parents make these payments to save their children from punishment and humiliation.[14] Moreover, resource constraints lead to deterioration in the quality of education. Some parents shift their children to private schools, where the fees are much higher. Therefore, parents may be willing to pay some fees for better-quality education. A similar argument applies to the health sector. Equity considerations require that mechanisms be devised so that the poor are not barred from using these services because of lack of income.

***Primary education should be free***

One of the millennium development goals is universal primary education and this can be achieved only when children from all income groups, particularly the poor, have access to primary education. Unit costs at the primary level are low. A strong case can therefore be made for free primary education. Charging fees at the secondary and tertiary levels

---

[14] N.N. Nguyen, "Trends in the education sector from 1993-98", World Bank Policy Research Working Paper 2891, September 2002.

is generally recommended, especially for tertiary education. Students from rich families usually benefit more from tertiary education. On equity grounds, it makes no sense to subsidize the rich.[15] There is also scope for greater resort to user charges for hospital-based curative health. Resources generated through partial cost recovery can be used to provide social services to the poor in the form of scholarships, grants, loans for higher education and free/subsidized medical services.

Disease and illness can bring severe hardships even to those with good incomes. Private medical insurance is one way to spread the risk. Some subsidy element can be introduced by the Government for lower-income groups. However, the poor cannot join such a scheme because of their extremely low incomes. Therefore, public provision of health services is needed for the poor.

### *Involvement of the community and non-governmental organizations*

***Communities should be encouraged to contribute to the provision of education and health***

The active involvement of communities can augment resources for education and health. Communities can make contributions in kind and/or cash, including land and labour for building schools and hospitals. Communities can provide furniture, textbooks, equipment and teaching aids for schools. Community involvement has been utilized effectively in some countries to achieve the desired objectives in the education sector. For example, in Pakistan, where female literacy is low, some pilot projects were initiated targeting girls' enrolment in Balochistan, the largest province in terms of area but the most sparsely populated.[16] In one project in a rural area, the Government pays for locally recruited female teachers, training and supplies, while the village provides school premises and monitors teacher and student attendance. The establishment of such schools has helped to increase the enrolment of girls.

Local communities can be encouraged through incentive schemes in which each dollar that the community raises for social services would be augmented through co-financing by the national Government. The resources generated in this way, for example, can be used for the provision of health services.[17] This method offers a way of risk spreading especially for low-income groups, which can face financial catastrophe in

---

[15] ESCAP, *Human Resources Development in the Asian and Pacific Region: Health, Education and Employment Attainments* (United Nations publication, Sales No. E.01.II.F.35).

[16] J. Kim, H. Alderman and P.F. Orazem, "Evaluation of the Balochistan rural girls' fellowship program: will rural families pay to send girls to school?", World Bank Departmental Working Paper 22983 (Washington, 1999).

[17] For further details, see WHO, *Macroeconomics and Health: Investing in Health for Economic Development*, report of the Commission on Macroeconomics and Health (Geneva, December 2001).

case of illness. The only problem with this type of scheme is that rich communities are usually in a better position to raise funds and so benefit from co-financing. Poor communities can be left behind under such schemes. Therefore, it is important that national Governments make extra resources available for the general development of poor communities.

***Non-governmental organizations can mobilize resources and provide leadership for advocacy***

Non-governmental organizations have been active in the education and health sectors in most countries. They can mobilize resources from within and outside a country. They can provide leadership for advocacy and in mobilizing the public for good causes. They can come up with innovative schemes. An interesting example in this regard is that of a non-governmental organization providing health services in Bangladesh. Gonoshasthya Kendra, translated as the People's Health Centre, has been operating at Savar, Bangladesh, since 1972.[18] It provides health care with minimum expenditure. Common diseases are treated through the use of trained paramedics; young rural boys and girls, usually with secondary school education, sometimes less, are trained by qualified doctors to undertake the task of delivering health services to the doorsteps of the people. The recurring costs of the health services are recovered from the participants in the programme. Initially, a health insurance scheme was introduced which consisted of a small admission fee and a nominal monthly premium charge to be paid per family for the services received. The insurance scheme did not receive an enthusiastic response because residents were generally landless and extremely poor and it was revised as a result. Under the revised scheme, the residents in the project area are divided into three groups, namely, the poor, middle-income and rich. The rich and the middle-income classes are charged a renewable admission fee and a nominal charge per visit plus any treatment costs. The visit charge for those belonging to the middle-income group is lower than that for the rich. The poor do not have to pay any admission fee or treatment costs and only a token visit charge is levied on them. The involvement of such non-governmental organizations should be encouraged to enhance the provision of education and health services.

### *Private sector participation*

***Private sector participation raises the quality, efficiency and supply of services***

The rapid growth of the private sector in education and health reflects the growing demand for the services provided by the sector. Better quality and efficiency are the main reasons for the greater attraction of the private sector. Most Governments have encouraged private sector participation by loosening restrictions and allowing market forces to operate. In some countries, private-public partnerships are being promoted (see box III.1). The main motive of private sector providers is profit maximization and therefore their services are usually concentrated in urban

---

[18] ESCAP, *Regional Information Base on Poverty Issues: A Review of the Incidence of Poverty and Target Oriented Poverty Alleviation Programmes* (ST/ESCAP/1568).

## Box III.1. Public-private partnership in the education sector: afternoon school project in Pakistan

Recent education sector reforms in Pakistan aim to promote a public-private partnership to complement the existing national efforts to expand and improve educational facilities in the country. Under the planned public-private partnership, three key initiatives have been envisaged. The first covers a range of new incentives, such as free land, liberal loans and concessions on electricity tariffs, to encourage the private sector to operate educational institutions. The second is known as the Adopt a School Programme, under which non-governmental organizations and educated individuals can enter into an agreement with the public sector to improve existing schools and the quality of education. The third initiative is the Afternoon School System under the Community Participation Project, under which the Government allows interested organizations and persons to establish afternoon schools in existing government school buildings and facilities.

### *Salient features of an afternoon school*

An afternoon school, called a Community Model School, is an independent entity which can be initiated, planned and launched under the Community Participation Project by any organization or individual from the community. An organization or individual interested in running an afternoon school has to sign an agreement with the Government and is called the licensee.

Considering the needs of the community, the afternoon schools usually offer a higher level of education than can be obtained in the regular morning session. For example, a primary school in the morning becomes a secondary school in the afternoon. This upgrading of the standard helps to meet the community's need for a higher level of education.

The licensees of the afternoon school can avail themselves of the following on-campus facilities available at the regular morning school:

1. School building; classrooms and office furniture and fixtures; school library; school science laboratory, with access to the equipment and non-consumable items; and main hall.
2. Free affiliation with the boards of intermediate and secondary education; regular status of afternoon school students; funds for deserving students from provincial education foundations; and teacher training programmes for afternoon school teachers.
3. The education department will permit licensees to hire the services of employees of the morning school as and when required with mutual understanding and consent.

The licensee setting up the Community Model School will have the discretion to hire and fire teachers, negotiate and pay salaries and receive fees and funds (remaining within the upper limit as fixed by the Government). Problems and difficulties arising in the afternoon school will be handled through discussion with the headmaster/headmistress of the morning school. The licensee will pay 100 per cent of the electricity, gas and water bills for both the morning and afternoon schools; this will be considered a contribution by the community. In fact, an afternoon school is an improved form of private school with the cooperation of the Government. A separate name has been proposed for the afternoon school, namely, the Community Model Elementary/Secondary/Higher Secondary School, depending on its specific teaching level.

### *Assessment of the afternoon school system and future prospects*

The afternoon school system was started as a pilot project in part of the province of Punjab in February 2001. Following its success, the system was launched in the whole province in May 2001 and other provinces followed suit. By August 2002, about 7,000 schools had been upgraded and improved through afternoon shifts and Adopt a School Programmes in the country. In the beginning, there was great enthusiasm in the non-governmental organization sector for this scheme but subsequently the tempo slowed. Generally, the private sector is interested in afternoon schools for boys in urban areas and for girls to a limited extent in rural areas where there are no girls' schools. The scheme is a novel one but after an initial excellent spurt its pace subsequently slackened. It needs more vigorous publicity and the local community has to be motivated if the scheme is to realize its full potential.

areas. Private sector participation raises quality, efficiency and the supply of services, which allows the enhanced allocation of public resources in rural and remote areas as well as slums in urban areas, where they are most needed. Moreover, Governments should have proper regulatory regimes in place to maintain education and health service standards.

### *Foreign aid and debt relief*

***Governments of developing countries face severe resource constraints***

The lack of education and health services in developing countries is partly due to the low incomes of individuals and families. Governments want to provide such services to all but are unable to do so as there are limited funds available to meet so many competing demands. Many Governments have borrowed heavily in the past and a major part of their revenue is spent on debt-servicing, including foreign debt. Therefore, rich countries can assist poor countries in the provision of education and health services, which are in the nature of global public goods whose benefits extend beyond national boundaries. For example, lack of education and the wide spread of diseases breed instability in poor countries, which can rebound on rich countries as well. Communicable diseases in one country can spread rapidly across international boundaries. Therefore, it is in the interests of rich countries to help poor countries to improve access to education and health.

Huge amounts of financial resources are needed for education and health in developing countries. A recent study estimates minimum financing needs to be around $30 to $40 per person annually to cover essential medical interventions, including those needed to fight the AIDS pandemic.[19] However, actual health spending is considerably lower; the least developed countries average approximately $13 per person annually in total health expenditure, of which budgetary outlays are just $7, and the other low-income countries average approximately $24 per capita annually, of which budgetary outlays are $13. Therefore, the study recommends that developing countries enhance their efforts to mobilize domestic resources. In addition, the efficiency of domestic resource spending should be increased, including through better prioritization of health services and the encouragement of community-financing schemes to ensure improved risk pooling for poor households. The study proposes a financing strategy under which an increase in domestic budgetary resources for health of 1 per cent of GDP by 2007 and up to 2 per cent of GDP by 2015 is envisaged. For education, the initial target should be to raise public expenditure to 3 per cent of GDP, which has already been achieved by several countries in South-East Asia.[20] The advantages of education are so great that public expenditure should be raised gradually to 5 per cent of GDP.

---

[19] WHO, op. cit.

[20] ADB, *Education and National Development in Asia: Trends, Issues, Policies and Strategies,* Manila, 2001.

***More foreign aid and debt relief for the provision of education and health services are needed***

The health study referred to earlier notes that even with more efficient allocation and greater resource mobilization, the levels of funding necessary to cover essential health services are far beyond the financial means of many developing countries. Donor finance will be needed to close the financing gap. The study estimates that a worldwide scaling-up of health investments for low-income countries to provide the essential interventions of $30 to $40 per person will require approximately $27 billion a year in donor grants by 2007, compared with the amount of around $6 billion a year that is currently provided.

The Governments of many developing countries in the region have borrowed heavily in the past. Foreign debt-servicing is increasingly becoming a major expenditure item in the budgets of such countries. Therefore, debt relief for heavily indebted countries linked to increased spending of the resulting savings on social services can generate the needed resources. The World Bank's heavily indebted poor countries (HIPC) initiative aimed at reducing the debt-servicing of these countries should be expanded by increasing the number of countries and deepening the amount of debt reduction on offer. Moreover, this debt reduction strategy for the development of the social sector and poverty reduction should constitute only a small part of the needed increment in donor assistance.[21]

***Effective utilization of foreign aid is very important***

The effective utilization of aid in developing countries is very important since this will encourage people and their Governments in donor countries to be more supportive of increases in funding. For this, developing countries should set clear and quantifiable targets for coverage and outcomes in the education and health sectors. Moreover, the projects should be designed, implemented and evaluated in a transparent manner.

## Improving the effectiveness of resources

In addition to mobilizing more resources, the achievements of the education and health sectors can be enhanced through more effective and efficient use of resources. Improving the quality of services, enhancing access to the services by the targeted groups, prioritizing expenditure within sectors and ensuring good governance merit special consideration to achieve this objective.

### *Improving quality*

***Problem of poor quality is widespread***

While all developing countries agree on the need to improve the quality of education and health services, the real challenge is how to translate their resolve into viable policies. In addition, most Governments

[21] WHO, op. cit.

face resource shortages and there is a question of a trade-off between expanding access to, and the quality of, services. Usually expansion of access wins because it is more sellable politically.[22]

***More resources and their better management to improve quality are needed***

Quality is a broad concept since it can be viewed in terms of inputs, outputs and outcomes. The poor quality of education and health services is visible in poor physical facilities in general, poorly maintained buildings, lack of teaching materials in schools, poor teacher training, lack of motivated teachers, uninteresting curriculum, shortage of medicines in hospitals, lack of diagnostic equipment and shortages of trained medical personnel.[23] There is a need to improve the inputs going to the education and health sectors. Better management of resources and the use of more modern technologies can add to the quality of services.

It is not easy to ascertain changes in quality in terms of outputs and outcomes. One way in which poor quality in education can manifest itself is through high dropout and grade repetition rates. As discussed earlier, there has been a reduction in the number of dropouts in the last decade and as a result the number of students completing four years of primary education has increased. However, some countries, mostly in South Asia, are still facing serious problems. Dropout rates are influenced by factors internal and external to the education system.[24] External factors deal with general poverty and parents' perceptions of the role of schooling in improving the quality of life. Internal factors include inappropriate and irrelevant curricula, poorly trained teachers, lack of textbooks and other education materials, and poor physical facilities in schools. The greater involvement of parents and communities is needed to reduce dropout numbers and repetition rates. Reform in the curricula in a manner that relates to local needs, and flexible school hours, particularly in rural areas, which take into account family work schedules, can also be helpful.

***Falling population growth rates should help to improve the quality of services***

Demographic dynamics also play an important role in influencing the quality and quantity of schooling. Countries in which fertility rates have already slowed considerably will face less pressure on education systems as the demand for primary education will decrease and more resources can be devoted to improving the quality of education. Projections show that between 2000 and 2010 the share of the primary school-age population (6-11) in the total population will fall in most countries in the region.[25] In fact, the absolute numbers of this age group

---

22 ADB, op. cit.

23 ESCAP, *Public Expenditure in the Provision of Social Services in Bangladesh and Nepal* (ST/ESCAP/1607).

24 ESCAP, *Survey 1993*, p. 115.

25 Ibid., 2001.

will decline in 2010 as compared with 2000 in a large number of countries. In the following countries, the average annual rate of reduction will be over 1 per cent: Armenia, Azerbaijan, China, Georgia, Islamic Republic of Iran, Kazakhstan, Kyrgyzstan, Mongolia, Russian Federation, Singapore, Tajikistan, Uzbekistan and Viet Nam. Beyond 2010, it appears that the primary and secondary school-age population will become relatively more stable. Population growth rates have been coming down in all the countries and this will make it easier to provide better-quality education and health services.

***Poor quality can lead to the underutilization of services***

Poor quality can lead to the underutilization of services and wastage of resources.[26] This is true in the case of medical services in rural areas in many developing countries. Governments have set up primary health-care centres in rural areas. However, people in rural areas are reluctant to visit these centres even though their services are available free of charge because of a lack of medicines and medical staff. They prefer to go to cities to deal with health problems, putting more pressure on already overcrowded public hospitals. It is important to improve the quality of medical facilities in rural areas so as to increase their utilization and check the wastage of resources.

### *Equity in access*

The coverage of education and health services expanded in most countries of the region. However, certain groups of the population did not benefit enough and opportunities remained unevenly distributed. Three main groups, people living in rural and remote areas, poor people and women, have been identified for discussion.

### *Access by rural and remote areas*

***Rural and remote areas tend to lag behind***

Over the years, all the countries in the region have made progress in terms of economic and social development. However, significant disparities remain between rural and urban areas and among regions within countries.[27] The incidence of absolute poverty is much higher in rural than in urban areas in most countries. For example, in Bangladesh in 1996, only 14 per cent of the urban population was poor as against around 40 per cent of the rural population. In the Philippines in 2000, the corresponding figures were 24 and 54 per cent. The rate of reduction in urban poverty

[26] G. Mwabu, "User charges for health care: a review of the underlying theory and assumptions", in Mwabu, Ugaz and White, eds., op. cit.

[27] For details, see ESCAP, *Reducing Disparities: Balanced Development of Urban and Rural Areas and Regions within the Countries of Asia and the Pacific* (United Nations publication, Sales No. E.01.II.F.24).

**Table III.7. Child mortality rates in rural and urban areas in selected countries**

| | Year | Infant mortality rate | | Under-5 mortality rate | |
|---|---|---|---|---|---|
| | | Rural | Urban | Rural | Urban |
| Bangladesh | 1994 | 103 | 81 | 153 | 114 |
| | 1997 | 91 | 73 | 131 | 96 |
| Indonesia | 1991 | 81 | 57 | 117 | 84 |
| | 1997 | 58 | 36 | 79 | 48 |
| Philippines | 1993 | 44 | 32 | 73 | 53 |
| | 1998 | 40 | 31 | 63 | 46 |

*Source:* L. Wang, "Health outcomes in poor countries and policy options: empirical findings from demographic and health surveys", World Bank Working Paper 2831, April 2002.

has been relatively faster in a majority of countries. The performance of rural areas in terms of social indicators has also been worse than that in urban areas. The rural-urban breakdown of mortality rates for infants and children under five years of age for a few countries is given in table III.7. Not only are the rates higher in rural areas but they have also declined more slowly over time as compared with urban areas.

***Rapid rural-to-urban migration owing to lack of opportunities and social services in rural areas***

Partly because of better opportunities and social services in urban areas, people are migrating from rural to urban areas. This, coupled with the reclassification of some rural areas as urban areas over time, is adding to rapid urbanization in the region. In 1980, one in four people in the developing countries of the region lived in urban areas. The situation changed to one in three in 2000. By 2025, roughly half of the population will be living in urban areas. This will put more pressure on the social services in these areas; within big cities, the size and number of slums will increase in the absence of appropriate policies to absorb the growing influx of rural migrants.

In addition to rural-urban differences, remote areas and regions of particularly large countries tend to lag behind. In Thailand, there is a strong regional dimension to absolute poverty. Historically, the North-East has been the poorest region in the country, followed by the South, North and Central regions; Bangkok has the lowest incidence of poverty. Similarly, there are major differences in the development of various regions within China, India and Indonesia. Remote areas experience deficiencies in all forms of infrastructure, including transport links. Frequently, outmigration has resulted in a brain drain and left a population with depleted human capital. This has added to the urgent need for more public investment in human capital in remote areas.

***Enhanced public resources for rural and remote areas***

More public resources should be devoted to rural and remote areas where they are most needed. Balanced development of the rural areas will help to manage rural-to-urban migration. Within urban areas, the slums and localities of poor people should be targeted for enhanced public funds for education and health. If it is not possible to build schools and hospitals within slums, these should be built near them so that access by slum-dwellers is convenient. One serious problem in rural and remote areas is the shortage of qualified staff in schools and hospitals. Owing to the lack of facilities, teachers, and particularly doctors, do not want to go to these areas. Teachers and doctors from their own areas should be appointed and be given some added incentives to encourage them to stay. Moreover, local communities should be involved in order to improve the relevance of education and health services to local needs.

### *Access by the poor*

***Incidence of poverty is quite high in many countries***

Around two thirds of the world's poor live in Asia and the Pacific. Absolute poverty is a major problem faced by most developing countries in the region. In many countries, more than one third of the population lives on less than a dollar a day.[28] Education and health indicators, as discussed earlier, are not satisfactory in many countries. Those indicators are national averages; the situation of the poor is expected to be much worse in these countries. The poor tend to have much less access to education and health services, which in turn keeps them poor and the vicious cycle of poverty continues.

***School enrolment ratios demonstrate large gaps between the children of the rich and the poor***

There are often large gaps in the school enrolment of children of the rich and the poor within countries. In Bangladesh in 1996-1997, 67 per cent of poor 6-14-year-olds were in school, compared with 83 per cent of rich children of the same age group.[29] In Turkey, in 1998, the gap between rich and poor was also quite pronounced: 60 per cent enrolment for poor children as against 85 per cent for rich children. In Viet Nam, enrolment in primary education became more equitable in the 1990s.[30] However, gaps in enrolment in secondary and post-secondary education between the rich and the poor are still large. At the lower secondary level, for example, the net enrolment rate for the poorest quintile in 1998 was only about one third of that for the richest quintile. For higher education, the enrolment rates of the rich have risen much faster than those of the poor in recent years, adding to existing inequities.

---

[28] The poverty line is defined in terms of purchasing power parity. For details see, World Bank, *World Development Report 2000/2001: Attacking Poverty* (New York, Oxford University Press, 2000).

[29] World Bank, *Poverty Trends and Voices of the Poor,* fourth edition (Washington, May 2001).

[30] Nguyen, op. cit.

## Box III.2. Thailand's new universal coverage health-care scheme

Along with strong economic growth in Thailand, its heath services have expanded dramatically in coverage and quality over the last few decades. The Government provides health services to all its employees and those of State enterprises. Health insurance has become a standard job benefit offered by private companies to their employees. For poor and other disadvantaged groups, including disabled persons, the aged and Buddhist monks, a health welfare programme providing free health care was started in 1975.[a] These people were issued cards to enable them to benefit from medical facilities at government hospitals and health clinics. In 2000, the actual number of cardholders was approximately 20 million (33 per cent of the population); the annual budget for the programme had increased substantially from 300 million baht in 1979 to 8,833 million baht in 2000. While many poor people benefited from the programme, it suffered from a problem of appropriate targeting. Some studies found that while the low-income cards were overissued in many provinces, less than one fifth of the poor received the cards and only one third of the cardholders actually belonged to the low-income group.[b] One of the main reasons for having a universal health coverage programme is so that all citizens can enjoy quality health services at nominal cost and health-care expenditure is not a constraint on obtaining the health services.

In April 2001, the Government launched a new health-care scheme to cover every Thai citizen who was not currently under any other public insurance scheme. Under this priority programme of the current administration, the insured receives medical treatment from participating government and private hospitals for only 30 baht (approximately $0.75) a visit. The bulk of the cost of the service is covered by a central government subsidy. Under the system, health-care providers are compensated according to the number of registered patients they have. In addition to an annual allowance of 1,252 baht (approximately $30) per patient, resource-strapped hospitals can draw on a 3 billion baht contingency fund and claim fees for referral patients.

To participate in the scheme, the prospective beneficiaries must register with their local medical authority to obtain a universal health card or "gold card". This card must be shown together with the individual's national identification card when that person applies for health services through government or private sector health service providers registered under this scheme. There is a referral system for more complicated ailments, under which the primary health centre or local hospital can refer the patient to another hospital. The insured can access any government health services in case of emergency or accident. At present, the service package includes most health services except cosmetic care, obstetric delivery beyond two pregnancies, drug addiction treatment, organ transplants, infertility treatment and other high-cost interventions. However, with additional resources and the inclusion of more diseases, the coverage could expand over time.[c]

The new universal health scheme has resulted in an overhaul of the health-care system in Thailand, putting medical services within the reach of all citizens, rich and poor, young and old. For millions of rural poor people, the 30 baht health-care scheme is a blessing, ensuring their access to basic health services.

Providing universal health care requires a huge financial outlay. The fiscal budget allocation for this scheme for 2002 was 52 billion baht and in January 2003 the Government allocated an additional 5.7 billion baht to meet the expenses of the scheme.[d] The original budget estimate for full implementation of the project was much higher, at 90 billion baht.[e] Financing the programme will increase Thailand's total health expenditure dramatically in the coming years and could worsen the country's budget deficit. The Government has reassured the public that the bulk of the funds will come from budget reallocations, the reduction of administrative costs through the use of modern technology and the rationalization of the Government's current annual spending on health-care initiatives.

---

[a] Viroj NaRanong and Anchana NaRanong, *Social Protection in Health for the Poor in Thailand: From Welfare to Universal Coverage* (executive summary) (http://www.info.tdri.or.th/poverty/abstract/vn.htm, 20 December 2002).

[b] Ibid.

[c] Nutta Sreshthaputra and Kaemthong Indaratna, "The universal coverage policy of Thailand: an introduction", paper prepared for the Asia-Pacific Health Economics Network, 19 July 2001, (<http://www.unescap.org/aphen/thailand_universal_coverage.htm>, 30 December 2002).

[d] *Bangkok Post,* 14 January 2003.

[e] Government Public Relations Department of Thailand, "A new low-cost medical welfare scheme in Thailand" (<http://www.thaimain.org>, 3 March 2001).

The implementation of the 30 baht health-care scheme is facing difficult and challenging problems, especially among health service providers. The subsidy provided by the Government is insufficient to cover the cost of providing services under the scheme to patients, particularly those with serious health conditions. Some hospitals could face severe financial hardships and consequently some of them are reluctant to offer their services to beneficiaries of the scheme. There is also the problem of proper targeting of beneficiaries. Owing to loose registration procedures, many holders of other insurance schemes are also benefiting from the scheme.

The quality of health services in urban areas is relatively better than in rural areas. This can attract patients from rural areas and lead to the overcrowding of health facilities in urban areas. Therefore, it is important to maintain quality health services across the country. Moreover, without quality health services, people will be reluctant to use the services, which could result in the initiative becoming a low-quality health scheme for the poor. Adequate resources will be needed to maintain the quality of the health service and public resources could be shifted to this priority area. Since coverage under the scheme is universal, people from all income groups can benefit equally from the scheme. As people from higher income groups are able to afford higher charges for health services, the hospital charges could be raised above 30 baht per visit for such people. This would generate additional resources for the scheme. Progressive taxation could also be used to mobilize more public resources for this important initiative. The Government is aware of the problems and weaknesses of the scheme and is determined to address them.

Thailand's health experiment with universal health coverage could prove a model for other developing countries. Therefore, it is important for the scheme to succeed in providing sustained quality health care. Appropriate financing mechanisms will be the key to the sustainability of the scheme in the long run.

The poor are unable to send their children to school even when there are no fees. These children help their parents to earn a livelihood and the opportunity costs of sending children to school are high. Therefore, the children of the poor should be given scholarships as well as free textbooks and uniforms. Moreover, public resources should be spent more on basic education, where the children of the poor are well represented.[31]

***The poor suffer more from the burden of disease***

Poor people tend to suffer more from the burden of disease because they lack access to clean water and sanitation, safe housing and adequate nutrition. Furthermore, the poor are much less likely to seek medical care, even when it is urgently needed, because of their lack of the out-of-pocket resources needed to cover health outlays. Children born into poor families have a higher probability of dying at a young age than those born into better-off families. For example, the infant mortality rate for the poorest 20 per cent of children is twice as high as for the richest 20 per cent in Nepal and the Philippines. In Indonesia, a medically trained person attended only 21 per cent of births of the rural poor as against 78 per cent of the rural rich in 1997; the comparative figures for urban areas were 78 and 93 per cent. Therefore, the quality of public health facilities should be improved and the access of the poor to such facilities enhanced. Innovative approaches and increased allocation of resources are needed to reach the poor (see box III.2).

[31] A number of highly qualified individuals from developing countries migrate to developed countries. Public financing of tertiary education under these circumstances needs to be re-evaluated.

### *Access by females*

Today there is greater awareness of prevailing gender inequities. International and non-governmental organizations have played a major role in bringing this about. The growing realization by societies and Governments that economic and social development cannot be achieved without the active participation of women has also helped the cause of women.

***Gender disparities remain serious***

Despite these efforts, gender inequalities remain serious in many countries. Some of these inequalities were pointed out earlier in the chapter. In addition, adult literacy rates in 2000 were generally lower for females than for males in most countries. In some countries the differences were very pronounced. For example, in Nepal, the adult literacy rate for females was only 24 per cent as against 60 per cent for males (table III.8). The performance of some other South Asian countries

**Table III.8. Adult literacy and life expectancy by gender in selected countries of the ESCAP region, 2000**

| | *Adult literacy rate (percentage aged 15 and above) 2000* | | *Life expectancy at birth (years) 2000* | |
|---|---|---|---|---|
| | *Male* | *Female* | *Male* | *Female* |
| Bangladesh | 52 | 30 | 59 | 60 |
| Cambodia | 80 | 57 | 54 | 59 |
| China | 92 | 76 | 69 | 73 |
| Fiji | 95 | 91 | 67 | 71 |
| India | 68 | 45 | 63 | 64 |
| Indonesia | 92 | 82 | 64 | 68 |
| Lao People's Democratic Republic | 64 | 33 | 52 | 55 |
| Malaysia | 91 | 83 | 70 | 75 |
| Nepal | 60 | 24 | 59 | 58 |
| Pakistan | 58 | 28 | 60 | 60 |
| Papua New Guinea | 71 | 57 | 56 | 58 |
| Philippines | 96 | 95 | 67 | 71 |
| Republic of Korea | 99 | 96 | 71 | 79 |
| Russian Federation | 100 | 99 | 60 | 73 |
| Samoa | 81 | 79 | 66 | 73 |
| Singapore | 96 | 88 | 75 | 80 |
| Sri Lanka | 94 | 89 | 70 | 75 |
| Tajikistan | 100 | 99 | 65 | 71 |
| Thailand | 97 | 94 | 67 | 73 |
| Uzbekistan | 100 | 99 | 66 | 72 |
| Viet Nam | 96 | 91 | 66 | 71 |

*Source:* UNDP, *Human Development Report 2002* (New York, Oxford University Press, 2002).

was also dismal. Gender differences in adult literacy were quite visible in Cambodia, the Lao People's Democratic Republic and Papua New Guinea. In terms of life expectancy, females fared better than males in almost all countries. However, countries with relatively low female adult literacy rates tend to have comparable life expectancy of females and males.

***Affirmative measures are needed to close gender gaps***

Certain measures can help to enhance female access to education. Generally, girls from poor families and those living in rural areas tend to have lower enrolment ratios. There is a need to make parents aware of the importance of girls' education through publicity campaigns. Local communities and Governments, as well as non-governmental organizations, should be closely involved in this endeavour.

Scholarship schemes, free textbooks and other supplies for girls can also attract them to schools and encourage them to complete their education. In Bangladesh, a scholarship scheme for girls in secondary school was started in 1982, which helped to raise the enrolment ratio of girls in the project area. In the early 1990s, the scholarship scheme was extended to all rural areas in the country. This not only raised girls' enrolment ratios at the secondary level but also subsequently pushed up the number of girls entering intermediate colleges.

Schooling should respond to the cultural and practical concerns of girls. Schools in the neighbourhood with female teachers and appropriate sanitation facilities should encourage parents to send their daughters to school. In rural areas, girls usually help their parents with household chores. Therefore, flexibility in school hours can facilitate girls' attendance at the school. The close involvement of parents in setting school hours, particularly for girls, is important for enhancing school enrolment ratios.

***More women in management positions in the education and health sectors should help in responding to the needs of women***

Access to reproductive health services is very important for women. Such services are lacking in many countries. As discussed earlier, less than 50 per cent of births are attended by skilled health personnel in a number of countries in the region. Therefore, more resources should be devoted to the health-care needs of women. Enhancing the share of women in management positions in the education and health sectors should help to take better account of the concerns and needs of women.

### *Intrasectoral prioritization*

Even with a fixed amount of resources, better outcomes can be achieved through reprioritizing expenditure within sectors according to needs and importance. It is important to assess the existing needs of countries and how they are being met by existing education and health systems, as priorities can vary across countries and within countries over time.

***Need for reprioritization of the allocation of resources within the education sector***

For most countries, there is a need to have arrangements for education at all levels. "The emphasis on primary and secondary education should not lead to the neglect of tertiary education, as it was important that the economy of a country should be able to benefit from modern technology."[32] Moreover, different levels of education are interdependent. Higher-level quality education is needed to carry out teaching at lower levels. ICT should be promoted in education at all levels, as future jobs will increasingly require this knowledge.[33]

The allocation of resources for different levels of education can be prioritized. For countries with low enrolment ratios, the highest priority should be given to universal primary education, followed by improvements in secondary and higher education. Some countries already have free compulsory education at lower levels (see box III.3). The more developed countries in East Asia and South-East Asia have to focus on improving both the access to and the quality of higher or tertiary education, including placing more emphasis on grasping new technologies and scientific research.

***Technical and vocational education may help to deal with the problem of unemployment***

Many countries in the region are facing serious problems of unemployment and underemployment. Therefore, technical and vocational training at the upper secondary level can help. In the past, some countries achieved limited success; technical and vocational schools accounted for less than 10 per cent of all upper secondary enrolments in Bangladesh and Pakistan by around the mid-1990s. Economies showing a high proportion of technical and vocational enrolments were China (60 per cent), Hong Kong, China (58 per cent), Thailand (48 per cent), Republic of Korea (41 per cent) and Singapore (38 per cent).[34] Since the costs of technical and vocational education are usually higher than those of general education, it is important for the former to respond to the needs of the country. To this end, the private sector should be closely involved in designing technical and vocational education curricula.

***Preventive measures are equally important for improving health***

Within the health sector more emphasis is usually given to curative rather than preventive health services. However, preventive measures for health improvement, such as access to safe drinking water, adequate sanitation and mass vaccination against communicable diseases are also very important and can reduce the need for curative services. The priority for public health expenditure should be to provide primary health care to

---

[32] ESCAP, *Growth with Equity: Policy Lessons from the Experiences of Selected Asian Countries* (United Nations publication, Sales No. E.00.II.F.14), p. 6.

[33] This is also needed to contain the widening digital divide among and within countries.

[34] Keith M. Lewin, "Educational development in Asia: issues in planning, policy and finance", *Asian Development Review,* vol. 15, No. 2, 1997.

## Box III.3. Universal 11-year compulsory education in the Democratic People's Republic of Korea

The Democratic People's Republic of Korea is among the countries providing compulsory education for children. The universal compulsory primary education system in the country took effect from August 1956, with the ensuing disappearance of school fees in primary schools. From November 1958, the universal compulsory secondary education system was put into effect and the school fee system in secondary schools was abolished. Universal free education was introduced at all levels in April 1959. In April 1967, universal compulsory 9-year technical education was introduced and universal 11-year compulsory education was successfully enforced in September 1975, enabling the younger generation to have access to secondary education and learn the basics of modern science and technology.

Universal 11-year compulsory education, which is now in force in the country, consists of compulsory 1-year pre-school education and compulsory 10-year school education (4-year primary and 6-year senior middle school). The education system provides free pre-school, primary and secondary education to all children ranging from 5 to 16 years of age. Thus, not only is 100 per cent enrolment firmly secured for school-age children but usually there are no dropouts.

During those years the students theoretically acquire valuable scientific and technical knowledge, consolidate the knowledge acquired in the classroom and cultivate its application through observation and practical training such as experiments, practice, field trips and tours.

Whether they live in towns or in the countryside, and are male or female, all the students are given education without discrimination and use identical textbooks under the same free compulsory education system. Moreover, urban and rural students receive education in IT. Especially in urban schools, students learn how to drive a car and operate computers and machine tools, while in rural schools pupils learn how to drive a tractor and handle farm machines in keeping with rural conditions. Male students learn how to use machine tools, while female students learn sewing and cooking. After the years of compulsory education, students can go to various higher schools up to university level if they so wish.

While the national education goals and policies are in place (11-year compulsory schooling) and the commitment to "Education for All" is strong, their achievement has begun to suffer recently owing to financial constraints.

Economic difficulties since the early 1990s, resulting from the disintegration of the socialist market and a series of natural disasters, have gradually reduced the State's ability to provide quality basic education services for a large number of school-age children and the quality of education has been increasingly compromised. The curricula need to be updated. The lack of a budget for school maintenance has resulted in general deterioration of the education infrastructure.

Under these circumstances, the Government has given priority to the rehabilitation of educational facilities and has set as its general objective improving the quality of child care and 11-year compulsory and free education.

To this end, the Government has drawn up the following sustainable strategy for the development of basic education: to create better conditions for child care and education by increasing State investment and social support; to improve the content of education steadily in keeping with realistic requirements so that teachers can train children to develop with rich knowledge, sound morality and a strong physique; to improve the methods of education; and to improve the qualifications of teachers steadily by putting emphasis on the training of kindergarten and school teachers and in-service teacher training.

all, particularly to rural and remote areas and disadvantaged groups.[35] Public expenditure with a heavy bias towards high-tech curative services for the urban elite in big cities and not enough for essential interventions to control communicable diseases for the rural poor or to respond to the basic needs for the curative and maternal and child health services of the poor more generally, is misdirected.

*Planning for the medical needs of an ageing population*

The share of older persons in the general population is on the rise in many countries as a result of improvements in life expectancy. Therefore, countries have to take into account the medical needs of this group, which should be factored into the future planning for the sector. Usually, the health-care cost per person for older persons is much higher than that for younger ones.

Many countries are suffering from population pressures and their education and health sectors are under enormous stress. One of the most important health interventions is giving greater attention to reproductive health, not only to control the spread of sexually transmitted diseases such as HIV/AIDS but also to limit fertility through family planning, including access to contraception.

### Governance issues

*Good governance is the key to solving many problems*

Lack of good governance is as pervasive in the education and health sectors as in other public sectors in many developing countries. In fact, the poor quality of the services is partly due to leakages and mismanagement of resources. By improving governance, considerable resources can be saved and utilized for improving access to and the quality of services. One way to improve governance, which is already being increasingly accepted by developing countries, is the movement towards decentralization in the provision of education and health services. Decentralization not only relieves some of the burden on central bureaucracies but can increase the resource base through enhanced participation by the community and the private sector.[36] Moreover, allowing the direct involvement of community members will improve the relevance of education and health services to local needs. Along with decentralization, it is important that the capacity of institutions at the local level be strengthened so that they can fulfil their enhanced responsibilities more effectively.

---

[35] Most countries already have primary health-care centres to provide basic health services. The report of the Commission on Macroeconomics and Health by WHO (see note 11 above) calls these centres collectively the close-to-client system, which consists of relatively simple hospitals, where a great deal of work can be carried out by nurses and paramedical staff with varying degrees of training, including midwives. Patients with complicated diseases can be referred to medical doctors within the system.

[36] For a detailed discussion on relevant issues of decentralization, see C. Ugaz, "The role of the state in the provision of social services: decentralization and regulation", in Mwabu, Ugaz and White, eds., op. cit.

## Annex table III.1. Private expenditure on health as a percentage of total health expenditure in selected economies of the ESCAP region, 1995-2000

| | Private expenditure on health as percentage of total health expenditure | | | | | |
|---|---|---|---|---|---|---|
| | *1995* | *1996* | *1997* | *1998* | *1999* | *2000* |
| **South and South-West Asia** | | | | | | |
| Afghanistan | 50.0 | 50.0 | 47.4 | 42.3 | 43.1 | 36.5 |
| Bangladesh | 66.1 | 64.2 | 63.9 | 63.5 | 63.3 | 63.6 |
| Bhutan | 9.7 | 11.7 | 9.6 | 9.7 | 10.4 | 9.4 |
| India | 83.8 | 84.4 | 84.3 | 81.6 | 82.1 | 82.2 |
| Iran (Islamic Republic of) | 54.4 | 51.8 | 54.0 | 54.5 | 53.8 | 53.7 |
| Maldives | 16.2 | 15.5 | 18.1 | 18.2 | 17.5 | 16.6 |
| Nepal | 73.6 | 74.0 | 69.4 | 67.4 | 71.1 | 70.7 |
| Pakistan | 75.2 | 77.0 | 77.1 | 76.4 | 78.1 | 77.1 |
| Sri Lanka | 51.9 | 50.4 | 50.8 | 49.0 | 51.3 | 51.0 |
| Turkey | 29.7 | 30.8 | 28.4 | 28.1 | 28.9 | 28.9 |
| **South-East Asia** | | | | | | |
| Brunei Darussalam | 20.0 | 19.4 | 20.6 | 18.7 | 20.6 | 20.0 |
| Cambodia | 79.0 | 76.7 | 77.0 | 76.5 | 76.2 | 75.5 |
| Indonesia | 62.7 | 72.1 | 76.3 | 72.8 | 72.0 | 76.3 |
| Lao People's Democratic Republic | 52.9 | 58.0 | 61.5 | 64.0 | 63.0 | 62.0 |
| Malaysia | 43.9 | 41.7 | 42.4 | 42.3 | 40.2 | 41.2 |
| Myanmar | 81.0 | 82.7 | 85.7 | 89.4 | 88.3 | 82.9 |
| Philippines | 60.1 | 58.6 | 56.6 | 57.6 | 53.5 | 54.3 |
| Singapore | 58.2 | 59.8 | 60.5 | 58.0 | 61.2 | 64.3 |
| Thailand | 51.1 | 48.9 | 42.8 | 38.6 | 41.7 | 42.6 |
| Viet Nam | 59.6 | 65.2 | 68.8 | 70.9 | 75.6 | 74.2 |
| **East and North-East Asia** | | | | | | |
| China | 53.3 | 57.8 | 60.0 | 61.0 | 62.0 | 63.4 |
| Democratic People's Republic of Korea | 20.1 | 19.5 | 16.5 | 16.5 | 17.6 | 22.7 |
| Mongolia | 31.0 | 36.9 | 37.3 | 34.6 | 33.5 | 29.7 |
| Republic of Korea | 63.5 | 61.2 | 59.0 | 53.8 | 56.9 | 55.9 |
| **Pacific island economies** | | | | | | |
| Cook Islands | 21.1 | 33.3 | 32.9 | 31.7 | 36.6 | 37.2 |
| Fiji | 35.0 | 33.8 | 33.3 | 34.6 | 34.8 | 34.8 |
| Marshall Islands | 38.8 | 38.3 | 38.1 | 38.4 | 38.9 | 38.6 |
| Micronesia (Federated States of) | 42.9 | 44.0 | 43.3 | 44.7 | 45.4 | 46.3 |
| Nauru | 1.1 | 1.1 | 1.1 | 1.1 | 1.1 | 1.1 |
| Niue | 3.2 | 2.6 | 2.7 | 3.3 | 2.9 | 3.8 |
| Palau | 11.4 | 12.3 | 12.5 | 12.0 | 11.8 | 11.5 |
| Papua New Guinea | 8.4 | 10.1 | 10.6 | 9.1 | 10.1 | 11.4 |
| Samoa | 24.8 | 24.5 | 24.1 | 24.3 | 23.6 | 23.8 |
| Tonga | 56.7 | 56.7 | 53.2 | 53.9 | 54.1 | 53.2 |
| Tuvalu | 29.1 | 31.3 | 30.2 | 29.3 | 29.3 | 28.6 |
| Vanuatu | 33.9 | 42.4 | 35.8 | 34.6 | 39.7 | 39.1 |

*(Continued on next page)*

## Annex table III.1 *(continued)*

| | *Private expenditure on health as percentage of total health expenditure* | | | | | |
|---|---|---|---|---|---|---|
| | *1995* | *1996* | *1997* | *1998* | *1999* | *2000* |
| **North and Central Asia** | | | | | | |
| Armenia | 60.3 | 56.6 | 58.5 | 57.1 | 58.7 | 57.7 |
| Azerbaijan | 22.3 | 28.0 | 26.6 | 26.9 | 51.1 | 55.8 |
| Georgia | 87.1 | 86.1 | 85.3 | 86.7 | 89.8 | 89.5 |
| Kazakhstan | 18.2 | 23.7 | 23.6 | 29.4 | 29.1 | 26.8 |
| Russian Federation | 18.5 | 21.9 | 27.1 | 31.1 | 35.3 | 27.5 |
| Tajikistan | 39.5 | 36.9 | 34.0 | 35.0 | 15.4 | 19.2 |
| Uzbekistan | 22.7 | 17.5 | 17.9 | 15.3 | 21.2 | 22.5 |

*Source:* WHO, *World Health Report 2002* (Geneva, 2002).

**Annex table III.2. Pupil-teacher ratio at the primary and secondary levels of education in selected economies of the ESCAP region**

| | *Pupil-teacher ratio* | | | |
|---|---|---|---|---|
| | *Primary* | | *Secondary* | |
| | *1980* | *2000* | *1980* | *2000* |
| **South and South-West Asia** | | | | |
| Bangladesh | 54 | 59[a] | 24 | 22 |
| India | 45 | 43 | 22 | 32[b] |
| Nepal | 38 | 38 | 31 | 61[a] |
| Pakistan | 37 | 55 | 17 | 25 |
| Sri Lanka | 32[c] | 28[b] | .. | 22[b] |
| **South-East Asia** | | | | |
| Brunei Darussalam | 18 | 13 | 12 | 10[b] |
| Cambodia | 44 | 50 | 23[c] | 18 |
| Indonesia | 32 | 22 | 15 | 16 |
| Lao People's Democratic Republic | 30 | 30 | 19 | 21 |
| Malaysia | 27 | 20 | 23 | 19[a] |
| Myanmar | 52 | 33 | 34 | 30[a] |
| Philippines | 31 | 35[a] | 34 | 34[a] |
| Singapore | 31 | 25 | 19 | 22 |
| Thailand | 21[d] | 21 | 19 | 22 |
| Viet Nam | 39 | 30 | 25 | 28 |
| **East and North-East Asia** | | | | |
| China | 27 | 20 | 18 | 17 |
| Mongolia | 32 | 33 | 23 | 21 |
| Republic of Korea | 48 | 32 | 39 | 22 |
| **Pacific island economies** | | | | |
| Fiji | 28 | 23[a] | 19 | .. |
| Papua New Guinea | 31 | 36[a] | 21 | 22[a] |
| Samoa | 29 | 24 | 24 | 20 |
| Solomon Islands | 25 | 24[b] | 16 | .. |
| Tonga | 24 | 21 | 23[c] | 10[a] |
| Vanuatu | 24 | 24 | 13 | 26 |
| **North and Central Asia** | | | | |
| Georgia | 19 | 17 | 10 | 7 |
| Kyrgyzstan | 28 | 24 | 18 | 13[b] |
| Russian Federation | 28 | 19 | 16 | 12 |
| Uzbekistan | 24 | 21[b] | 15 | 9[b] |

*Sources:* UNESCO, Institute for Statistics database, <http://www.uis.unesco.org>, 11 October 2002 and *World Education Report 2000* (UNESCO Publishing, 2000).

[a] 1999.
[b] 1996.
[c] 1981.
[d] 1982.

# ENVIRONMENT-POVERTY NEXUS REVISITED: LINKAGES AND POLICY OPTIONS

## INTRODUCTION

*Rapid economic growth is a necessary condition for poverty eradication. However, fast economic growth is often accompanied by adverse environmental consequences*

The eradication of poverty is a major development challenge. Among the millennium development goals contained in the Millennium Declaration in General Assembly resolution 55/2 of 18 September 2002, adopted by 147 heads of State and Government and 189 Member States, the eradication of extreme poverty and hunger was underscored as the paramount goal.[1] Rapid economic growth is often seen as the key foundation for achieving poverty reduction. Recent findings by the World Bank provide additional evidence which strengthens this assertion.[2] While the linkage between economic growth and poverty reduction is generally obvious, the relationship between economic growth and improvement in the environment remains unclear.[3] In recent times, the fast economic growth in many countries, including developing countries of the Asian and Pacific region, where two thirds of the world's poor live, has often been accompanied by a range of adverse environmental impacts.[4] Apparently, there is a trade-off between

---

1 United Nations, "Road map towards the implementation of the United Nations Millennium Declaration", report of the Secretary-General (A/56/326), p. 56.

2 A World Bank study found that over the course of the 1990s, the 24 developing countries that increased their global trade and investment the most also increased income per person, much more than those that did not, by six percentage points more. In those countries, the number of people living on less than $1 per day dropped by 120 million between 1993 and 1998. See Colin Powell, "Only one Earth", *Bangkok Post,* 18 August 2002.

3 Environment relates to the biophysical environment which provides goods (natural resources) and ecosystem services used in producing agricultural, energy and other intermediate inputs, receives waste products from economic and human activities and provides recreation and beauty to mankind.

4 Asia's economic development over the past decades has come at a high environmental cost. See ADB, "New approach needed to halt Asia's rapid environmental decline", News Release No. 057/01, 18 June 2001 <http://www.adb.org/Documents/News/2001/nr2001057asp.>, 5 November 2002.

economic growth and environmental improvement; achieving both of these goals simultaneously may not be easy, especially in the early stage of development.[5]

***Developing countries have adopted policies and programmes to mitigate adverse environmental consequences, thereby strengthening the beneficial impact of economic growth on the poor, who are extremely vulnerable to environmental changes***

For many developing countries, the enhancement of economic growth is often the major macro-objective of economic development although the associated adverse environmental impacts are recognized. It is expected that sustainable poverty reduction will take place through a trickle-down of economic growth: the benefits of economic growth will percolate down to the poorer section of the population and increase their income. Under this premise, the tempo of economic growth is maintained as much as possible in order to maximize the pace of poverty reduction. In certain cases, policies and programmes are formulated to mitigate the adverse environmental impacts of economic growth and reverse environmental degradation. Against the background of possible positive linkages between the livelihood income and health of the poor and the environment, such action would lead to a reduction in poverty. In addition, there are certain poverty reduction policies which have a beneficial impact on the environment and certain environmental interventions targeted at the poor which enhance their livelihood income and health status. The aim of this chapter is to review and analyse the poverty-environment nexus against the background of the linkages between economic growth and the environment and the associated policies. An attempt is also made to identify modalities for strengthening the impact of the policies and to draw the attention of policy makers of the Asian and Pacific countries to the fact that environmental improvement strengthens the impact of economic growth on poverty reduction and that improving the environment is an important element of a pro-poor economic strategy.

This chapter has three specific objectives. First, an attempt will be made to identify, classify and analyse the major linkages between growth and the environment and between the environment and poverty (income and health of the poor). This will serve as a framework for understanding the objectives and impact of the relevant policies and programmes. Second,

---

[5] Deterioration of the environment could turn to improvement as economic development progresses and income increases up to a certain level. From a historical observation of trends in industrialized countries, this appears to be true; the achievement of both GDP growth and improvement in certain environmental indicators, such as air and water quality as well as a reduction in resource intensity, has been possible. It is seen that economic growth is gradually "de-coupled" with growth in energy demand. The above phenomenon might reflect progress towards less-polluting and more resource-efficient technologies as economies develop. It may also indicate a shift in industrial structure from resource-intensive industries to more knowledge-intensive industries as well as an increase in the relative importance of the service sector, which is less material resource-intensive compared with manufacturing sectors. Furthermore, industrialization and the rising incomes of these countries may be accompanied by increased awareness of and education on the benefits of improving local environmental quality, such as urban air quality.

policy options will be presented, elaborated and analysed, giving examples from Asian and Pacific countries. The conclusion will focus on suggestions for enhancing the effectiveness of policies and programmes in the context of achieving the millennium development goals following the Plan of Implementation of the World Summit on Sustainable Development.[6]

***Against the background of growth-environment and environment-poverty linkages, policy options for improving the environment and reducing poverty are analysed and conclusions on improving the effectiveness of policies presented***

Although absolute poverty in the Asian and Pacific region is predominantly a rural phenomenon, rapid urbanization and the expansion of urban-based economic activities have recently led to very substantial rural-urban migration. The migration process has, to some extent, helped to reduce population pressure on agricultural land and contributed to increasing agricultural productivity and reducing rural poverty. However, the migration has put pressure on housing and other services, leading to the development of slums, thus having an impact on the environment. The nature of poverty-environment interlinkages in urban areas is therefore somewhat different from that in a rural setting. The policies, especially those associated with the environment, also address different phenomena and issues. For example, vehicular pollution is an urban environmental problem while land degradation affects the lives of the rural poor. Rural-urban differences will be highlighted in appropriate places in this chapter and linkages and policies differentiated accordingly.

It is not possible to incorporate every aspect of the environment-poverty nexus in this limited review. For example, climate change is not dealt with, despite the realization that it has a major adverse impact on the poor, especially in the island developing countries. The review is selective and based on observations with regard to the broad priority issues and constraints faced by the member countries in formulating and implementing relevant policies for improving the environment, which contributes to the reduction of poverty.

## THE LINKAGES

### Economic growth-environment

There is little doubt that the fast economic growth in the region has contributed to the reduction of poverty in recent decades. Poverty in the region has declined dramatically since the 1970s, despite explosive population growth.[7] This fast growth, however, was achieved at the cost of environmental degradation, such as the depletion of natural resources,

---

6 *Report of the World Summit on Sustainable Development, Johannesburg, South Africa, 26 August-4 September 2002* (A/CONF.199/20), resolution 2, annex.

7 ADB, *Asian Environment Outlook 2001,* box 1-1 (<www.adb.org/documents/books/AEO/2001/aeo2001.pdf>, 14 January 2003).

***Increasing the production of agricultural and industrial goods, energy and services to cope with the increasing demand for human consumption has well-known detrimental impacts on the environment***

atmospheric pollution, the depletion of biodiversity, the drying-up of aquifers, the pollution of aquatic and marine ecosystems and the increasing production of wastes. The extent of the damage, however, varied from country to country and depended on a number of factors, including the state of economic development, industrial structure and technologies. Linkages between economic activities and the environment can be illustrated through the following observations:

- *Observation 1.* Most traditional economic activities comprise the transformation of resources into products and services useful to human beings. Thus, regardless of the income level or stage of development, practically any economic activity would alter the state of the environment in one way or another and has the potential to cause a number of negative impacts in the form of unsustainable depletion of resources and deterioration in the quality of resources and the environment. For example, agricultural activities for producing food and generating employment and income in rural areas are the major sources of methane flow to the atmosphere. Commercial energy is the most crucial input which enables economic activities to take place but is the major source of carbon dioxide emissions into the atmosphere and, together with manufacturing and other user sectors, contributes significantly to atmospheric and aquatic pollution.

- *Observation 2.* The environmental impacts of household consumption activities are no longer negligible. The use of resources such as freshwater and the production of wastes are examples of two such impacts. The consumption of various forms of energy, including the increasing use of fossil fuels by private vehicles, increases direct and indirect environmental stress through the burning of fuel.

- *Observation 3.* In the agricultural sector in the region, particularly in Asia, pressure to increase production and improve the yield to cope with the growing population has led to the intensive use of fertilizers, pesticides and water for irrigation. There is no doubt that this process has contributed to the substantial increase in agricultural production and associated beneficial effects, including the reduction of rural poverty. However, such resource-intensive agriculture has also posed various environmental problems which, in turn, have an adverse effect on agricultural productivity. For instance, the overexploitation of freshwater resources has in some cases resulted in the drying-up of spring-fed rivers; the intensive use of fertilizers and pesticides has contributed to water pollution; and the overuse of surface water for irrigation has resulted in aquifer depletion, land subsidence or sea-water/saline intrusion.

- *Observation 4.* In industry, the adverse environmental impacts of production activities are well known. For instance, the use of energy is essential for undertaking almost all industrial activities and operating transport infrastructure and services, but the production and use of a major part of the energy consumed in industry and transport have a detrimental environmental impact. However, the process of industrialization and economic development could entail improvement in resource efficiency and relative shifts into less resource-intensive industries, as well as the adoption of clean technologies and incremental improvements in the enforcement of environmental regulations, which have beneficial mitigating impacts. Nevertheless, rapid industrialization in the region, the resulting increase in energy production and consumption and the associated pollution have often outweighed such benefits.

## Environment-poverty

***The poor are disproportionately affected by environmental deterioration because of their locational disadvantages, higher dependence on environmental resources and insufficient assets for coping with environmental hazards***

Four observations highlight the strength and importance of the interlinkages between the environment and poverty:

- *Observation 1.* The poor live in places which are ecologically more vulnerable and are forced to earn their living from low-productivity natural resources.[8] The rural poor often live in low-lying, flood-prone areas, on steep mountain slopes or on dry land and possess low-productivity marginal land devoid of any irrigation facilities. The number of the rural poor in developing countries living on "marginal" land could be twice the number found on better-developed land.[9] The urban poor are found in the shanty towns of big cities, which are often built on flood-prone, low-lying areas or around city drains; many of the poor earn their livelihood from environmentally hazardous scavenging. Environmental deterioration in the form of land degradation, frequent flooding, increased pollution and other hazards reduces the income of both the rural and urban poor and worsens their health disproportionately by comparison with the rich.

---

[8] Fifty per cent of the poor in Asia are found in fragile ecosystems and mainly remote and ecologically vulnerable rural areas. See International Fund for Agricultural Development "Combating environmental degradation", (<http://www.ifad.org/events/past/hunger/envir.html>, 5 November 2002).

[9] Department for International Development, United Kingdom, European Commission, UNDP and World Bank, "Linking poverty reduction and environmental management, policy challenges and opportunities", January 2002, p. 5.

- *Observation 2.* It is commonly observed that poor households, especially in rural areas, derive their livelihood income from natural resources, for example, land resources for agriculture and water resources for fishing. It is also found that the poorer the household, the greater is the share of its income from environmental resources.[10] In addition to providing a livelihood, the environment plays a very significant part in influencing the health of the poor; while the incidence of disease in poor countries is about twice that of rich countries, the disease burden from environmental risks is 10 times greater in poor countries.[11] Environmental degradation has a disproportionate negative impact on both the livelihood and the health of the poor.

- *Observation 3.* It is apparent that the intensity of suffering of the poor from the adverse impacts of environmental shocks is much higher than that of the rich. However, because of the lack of proper assets, the poor are less capable of coping with those impacts. The vulnerability of the poor to environmental shocks is much higher than that of the rich in both rural and urban areas.

- *Observation 4.* Against the background of the observation that the poor, especially in rural areas, derive a large part of their livelihood income from environmental resources, especially land resources used for agriculture, some of the practices they follow can be damaging to the environment. Clearing forest areas to create land for agricultural use, including slash-and-burn practices, is an example showing that the poor are responsible for environmental degradation. Certain consumption practices of the poor, such as damaging the forest to acquire firewood to be used for cooking and heating could also be detrimental to the environment. The urban poor, most of whom live in shanty towns and ghettos, often create unhygienic sanitary conditions because of their lack of access to formal toilet facilities. However, there is overwhelming evidence[12] to show that the

---

[10] It may be worth mentioning that a similar situation exists even at the level of countries; the shares of GDP (and exports) originating from sectors whose production is directly connected with environmental resources in poor countries are higher than those in rich countries.

[11] "Linking poverty reduction ...", op. cit., pp. 5 and 8.

[12] As much as 70 per cent of the world's consumption of fossil fuels and 85 per cent of its chemical products are attributable to 25 per cent of the world's population who are not poor. The consumption pattern of forest products and many other commodities has the same direct inverse proportion to the size of the population of the top 20 per cent of the richest societies. See International Fund for Agricultural Development, op. cit.

impact of poverty on the environment is weak compared with the damage to livelihood and health which the poor suffer owing to environmental degradation not caused by them. Against this background, the impact of poverty on the environment will not be taken up explicitly in the present discussion and analysis.

It can be seen from the above arguments that the environment has strong linkages with the livelihood, health and vulnerability of the poor. These linkages need to be identified in some detail before options for appropriate policy interventions to benefit the poor can be studied.

"Environmental goods and services" which are crucial to all, particularly the poor, can be classified into three broad categories: natural resources, environmental conditions, including environmental stresses, and the ecosystem. The nature and extent of their linkages with poverty, encompassing the livelihood income and health of the poor, are somewhat different. These are discussed below.

### *Natural resources*

***Degradation of agricultural land, depletion of forests and fish stocks and the lack of access to safe drinking water have a major adverse impact on the income and health of the poor***

Natural environmental resources can be atmospheric, land-based or sea-based. Of these, the resources which have a major bearing on the poor's livelihood and health are the following:

- Land used for agricultural operations, including grazing land for animal husbandry, provides an important (often the only) source of rural livelihood. Land degradation, either natural or due to the overuse of chemical fertilizers, and the mechanization or depletion of groundwater, which increases soil salinity, could erode the most important modality of livelihood of the rural population, especially the rural poor, who do not possess the means to counter such adverse impacts.

- The widespread use of chemical fertilizer, pesticides and other chemicals for farming poses a formidable health hazard to the rural poor. Illiterate farm labourers who lack appropriate training in the use of poisonous chemicals are unable to read the instructions written on them and cannot afford protective devices can easily fall prey to a number of associated diseases.

- The poor, in both rural and urban areas, often do not have the luxury of access to safe drinking water. They have to rely on water sources which are frequently contaminated for various reasons. Water-related diseases such as diarrhoea and cholera kill a large number of people every year in the developing countries.[13] Any improvement in water quality is likely to yield rich dividends in terms of improving, the health standards and productivity of the poor.

- Fishing provides income and protein for the poor living near the sea, rivers, marshy lands and swamps. However, in many developing countries fishing sources are commercially over harvested in an unsustainable manner, which has a negative effect on the livelihood of the poor. Many commercial fishing ventures result in a number of adverse environmental impacts which could constitute health hazards for the poor who are associated with them. Coordinating policies and programmes at the regional and subregional levels aimed at the conservation and sustainable development of fisheries forms an important element of the Plan of Implementation of the World Summit on Sustainable Development, of which poverty reduction to achieve the relevant target is a major objective. Other areas highlighted in the Plan of Implementation that have implications for poverty are given in box IV.1.

- Forest products often provide livelihood income to the rural poor. Twigs and wood collected from forests provide a major part of the energy used by the poor for cooking and heating. Forests prevent soil erosion, flooding and mud slides in hilly areas during heavy rains. The unsustainable destruction of forests causes much misery to the poor, both directly and indirectly.

### *Environmental conditions*

***Deterioration of the environment in the form of increased indoor air pollution due to the use of biomass fuels and gradual as well as sudden atmospheric changes affect the income and health of the poor***

Worsening of the quality of atmospheric resources could be extremely harmful to the poorer sections of the population. There are two major environmental conditions which affect both the livelihood and health of the poor:

- Indoor air pollution due to the use of biomass fuels (e.g., wood, crop residue) for cooking and heating in poor households affects the health of a large number of people, causing various respiratory diseases. The incidence of this type of health hazard is higher in women and children as they face primary exposure. Nearly 2 million women and children die every year from indoor pollution.[14]

---

[13] A large number of people (2.1 million) die every year from diarrhoeal diseases (including cholera) associated with inadequate water supply, sanitation and hygiene. According to WHO, the majority are children in developing countries.

[14] "Linking poverty reduction ...", op. cit, p. 9.

## Box IV.1. Environment-poverty linkages and the Plan of Implementation of the World Summit on Sustainable Development

The Plan of Implementation of the World Summit on Sustainable Development specifies that the three components of sustainable development, economic development, social development and environmental protection, are interdependent and mutually reinforcing pillars. It also explicitly recognizes that poverty eradication and protecting and managing the natural resource base are overarching objectives of sustainable development. Against the background of the environment-poverty linkages discussed in this section and the large extent of the exposure of the poor to the degradation of environmental resources, which affects their livelihood income and health, the following areas and actions highlighted in the Plan of Implementation assume importance.

### *Water*

One of the major aims in this area is to launch a programme of action, with financial and technical assistance, to achieve the millennium development goal concerning safe drinking water, that is, to halve, by the year 2015, the proportion of people who are unable to reach or to afford safe drinking water.

Other action includes intensifying water pollution prevention to reduce health hazards and promoting ecosystems by introducing technologies for affordable sanitation and industrial and domestic waste-water treatment, by mitigating the effects of groundwater contamination and by establishing monitoring systems and effective legal frameworks at the national level. The need for prevention and protection measures to promote sustainable water use and to address water shortages is also emphasized.

### *Energy*

Governments, as well as relevant regional and international organizations and other relevant stakeholders, are required to implement, taking into account national and regional specificities and circumstances, the recommendations and conclusions of the Commission on Sustainable Development concerning energy for sustainable development adopted at its ninth session. These include integrating energy considerations, including energy efficiency, affordability and accessibility, into socio-economic programmes, especially into the policies of the major energy-consuming sectors, and into the planning, operation and maintenance of long-lived energy-consuming infrastructures, such as the public sector, transport, industry, agriculture, urban land use, tourism and construction. The development and dissemination of alternative energy technologies with the aim of giving a greater share of the energy mix to renewable energies, improving energy efficiency and placing greater reliance on advanced energy technologies, including cleaner fossil fuel technologies, were also recommended.

### *Health*

The objectives in this area include strengthening the capacity of health-care systems to deliver basic health services to all, in an efficient, accessible and affordable manner, aimed at preventing, controlling and treating diseases, and to reduce environmental health threats, in conformity with human rights and fundamental freedoms and consistent with national laws and cultural and religious values. Another objective is the implementation, within the agreed time frames, of all commitments made in the Declaration of Commitment on HIV/AIDS adopted by the General Assembly at its twenty-sixth special session, held in June 2001, emphasizing in particular the reduction by 2005 of HIV prevalence among young men and women aged 15 to 24 by 25 per cent in the most affected countries and by 25 per cent globally by 2010. Recognizing that many communicable diseases spread because of the existence of unhygienic and crowded living conditions, the Plan of Implementation aims at the achievement by 2020 of a significant improvement in the lives of at least 100 million slum dwellers, as proposed in the "Cities without Slums" initiative.

### *Agriculture*

Recognizing that sustainable agriculture and rural development are essential to poverty reduction, the implementation of an integrated approach to increase food production and enhance food security and food safety in an environmentally sustainable manner assumes importance. The Plan of Implementation emphasizes the need to achieve the Millennium Declaration target of halving by the year 2015 the proportion of the world's people who suffer from hunger. The relevant action includes the development and implementation of integrated land management and water-use plans based on the sustainable use of renewable resources and on integrated assessments of the socio-economic

*(Continued overleaf)*

*(Continued from preceding page)*

and environmental potentials. Strengthening the capacity of Governments, local authorities and communities to monitor and manage the quantity and quality of land and water resources and the adoption of policies and the implementation of laws that guarantee well-defined and enforceable land and water-use rights and promote legal security of tenure are important steps to be undertaken by Governments. Technical and financial assistance should be provided to developing countries as well as countries with economies in transition that are undertaking land tenure reform in order to enhance sustainable livelihoods.

***Biodiversity***

Biodiversity, which plays a critical role in overall sustainable development and poverty eradication, is currently being lost at an unprecedented rate owing to human activities. Several measures have been suggested to reverse this trend. These include the promotion of concrete international support and partnership for the conservation and sustainable use of biodiversity, including in ecosystems, at World Heritage sites and for the protection of endangered species, in particular through the appropriate channelling of financial resources and technology to developing countries and countries with economies in transition, and the provision of financial and technical support to developing countries, including capacity-building, in order to enhance indigenous and community-based biodiversity conservation efforts.

- As many of the poor live in ecologically vulnerable places (e.g., lowlands, mountain slopes, dry areas), atmospheric changes, both gradual (climate change) and sudden (disasters), can cause severe damage to the livelihood and health of the poor. Disasters, which include hurricanes, cyclones, floods and earthquakes, have been known to have a devastating impact on the poverty situation, giving rise a large number of "new poor" almost overnight. These concerns and the extent of such damage have been highlighted in a recent publication.[15]

## *Ecosystem*

Forests, grasslands and the coastal ecosystem, including coral reefs, provide a wide variety of services which contribute to the continuation of economic activities in both rural and urban areas. One important activity which exploits the existence of the natural ecosystem is ecotourism. Ecotourism is often labour-intensive and employs persons from the most vulnerable groups in rural areas, including those in remote and isolated areas and islands. Some examples of other ecosystem services include the provision of natural habitat for wild pollinators that are essential to food crops; watershed protection and the maintenance of hydrological regimes (recharging of water tables) by natural processes, including rainfall; and the natural breakdown of waste products and pollutants. It is apparent that the livelihood and health of a large number of the poor are intimately related to the activities facilitated by the ecosystem and its services, and any deterioration in their availability on quality could be detrimental to the reduction of poverty.

---

[15] M.H. Malik, "The new poor", ESCAP, *Bulletin on Asia-Pacific Perspectives 2001/02* (United Nations publication, Sales No. E.02.II.F.2), pp. 67-72.

Conservationists have shown concerns on this aspect. For example, it was indicated that the tourism development plan under the Government's economic stimulus scheme for the archipelago of Koh Chang in Thailand could threaten its rich biological diversity and genetic resources. Most of the projects under the tourism master plan are likely to cause damage to the island's ecosystem. A study has found that the island is home to 1,513 species, including ferns, mosses, algae, lichens, fungi, flowering plants and various insects. It is alleged that efforts to develop the area for tourism without addressing environmental concerns adequately, could destroy these rare species.

It has been found in another study that the construction of tourism facilities in Koh Chang would definitely drive away rare insects, particularly fireflies, which are a huge source of income for the local people.[16] Firefly watching is one of the island's most popular ecotourism activities. This perpetuates the dilemma of whether to develop a resort to generate income opportunities or to put greater emphasis on the protection of the natural ecology. Such trade-offs could occur in a range of other similar concerns.[17]

***While damage to the ecosystem owing to the promotion of growth-enhancing economic activities could take away the direct livelihood income of the poor, the trade-off between growth and environmental objectives often creates dilemmas***

## POLICY OPTIONS

Against the background of the linkages detailed in the previous section and the thrust of the chapter, environmental policies can be classified into two broad groups: those which aim at reducing the adverse environmental impacts of economic growth, leading to an improvement in the environment in general and a consequent beneficial impact on the poor, and those which are targeted specifically at the poor and have a positive impact on the environment. These are discussed below.

### Enhancing environment-friendly economic growth and development

At the United Nations Conference on Environment and Development, held at Rio de Janeiro in 1992, Governments committed themselves to adopting strategies for sustainable development (needs).[18] The challenge has been to achieve convergence between the growth and environment objectives of development through the integration of economic, social and environmental dimensions by the use of appropriate policies. These policies can be broadly classified as economic policies and institutional policies.

---

[16] Kultida Sanabuddhi, "Rush to boost tourism puts island in peril, say scientists", *Bangkok Post,* 28 November 2002.

[17] Raj Kumar, *The Forest Resources of Malaysia: Their Economics and Development* (Singapore, Oxford University Press, 1986), p. 79.

[18] Rio Declaration on Environment and Development (<http://www.unep.org/unep/rio.htm>, 9 November 2002).

### Economic policies

*National long-term planning mechanisms, strategic plans and sustainable development plans: the need for coordination*

Achieving economic, social and environmental objectives for a country requires coordination between many agents, namely, government, producers, consumers and domestic and foreign investors; policies, namely, sectoral, fiscal and monetary, and trade policies; and institutions, including regulatory agencies and the judiciary. There are various subdivisions within each group, for example, the Government consists of many ministries which deal with many areas, from finance to construction and the environment; and producers may be big corporate entities, SMEs or self-employed. It is only natural that there should be conflict between the objectives of so many entities. Bringing harmony into the functioning of these groups to enhance a country's welfare (of which poverty reduction and improving the environment are major components) calls for the recognition and identification of various trade-offs and the realignment of individual goals and policy instruments under a "win-lose as little as possible" framework.

National planning mechanisms which constitute the articulation of such a framework spell out the objectives, concerns, goals, policy options and strategies of various agents, groups and organizations. Whereas elaborate plans for socio-economic development have a long history, those which deal explicitly with environmental concerns and sustainable development issues are relatively recent and came into being to a considerable extent after the adoption of Agenda 21 at the Rio Conference.

***Sustainable development plans aim to minimize the adverse environmental impacts of economic growth through the promotion of conservation measures, the reduction of pollution and the use of clean production technologies***

A number of countries have formulated elaborate sustainable development plans. For example, in 1995, the Republic of Korea prepared Green Vision 21, which integrated long-term environmental policies with development needs. Under this broad vision, the relevant ministries, especially the Ministry of Environment, the Ministry of Commerce, Industry and Energy and the Ministry of Construction and Transportation, developed their own annual plans and strategies for action. Viet Nam's Environmental Vision 2020, National Strategy for Environmental Protection, 2001-2010 and National Environmental Action Plan, 2001-2005 address long- medium- and short-term issues of environment and economic growth. Official environment protection visions, integrating economic development and the environment, exist in at least 37 countries of the Asian and Pacific region.[19] Some examples of these are China's

[19] ESCAP and ADB, *State of the Environment in Asia and the Pacific 2000* (ST/ESCAP/2087).

Agenda 21, Vision 2020 (Malaysia), the Singapore Green Plan, 2012 National Conservation Strategies (India), the National Policy on the Environment (Uzbekistan), the National Strategy for Ecologically Sustainable Development (Australia) and the National Environment and Development Strategies, 1993 (Samoa). As examples, the major features of three selected sustainable development plans, the Singapore Green Plan, Australia's National Strategy for Ecologically Sustainable Development and China's Agenda 21, are given in table IV.1. The objectives of the plans are to ensure that economic growth and development take place with minimum damage to the environment. They emphasize the conservation of natural resources and the reduction of environmental pollution. The adoption of clean technologies has often been explicitly considered as a major modality for balancing growth and environment objectives. Strategies for achieving these objectives include raising environmental awareness and education and promotion of the 3P (people, public sector and private sector) partnership. Implementation methods incorporate a broad range of initiatives from the inclusion of environmental issues in school curricula to the formulation of legislation and laws to induce environmental protection. Financial resources for implementing environmental plans come primarily from Governments, and are augmented by bilateral and multilateral donors.

### *Sectoral policies*

***Sectoral policies and plans, including those which help to counter deforestation and river pollution, benefit the poor directly and help to fulfil national obligations under global conventions***

Visions and strategies of sustainable development must be supported by sectoral action plans that fulfil national obligations under global environmental conventions such as the need to contain greenhouse gas emissions, the conservation of biodiversity and the phasing-out of ozone-depleting substances, while ensuring adequate growth of the sector.

Sectoral plans and policies have also been developed to address concerns about agricultural land and water. Against the background of the importance of these sectors in the environment-rural poverty linkage, the associated policies require special mention. For example, forest land is often used to augment agricultural land and trees are cut indiscriminately to satisfy the growing demand for wood. In order to counter deforestation, which has a negative impact on the livelihood and vulnerability of the poor, especially in rural areas, a shift towards plantation forestry is a policy option which can be pursued. This type of shift will relieve the pressure on national forests and at the same time enable the development of reliable sources of industrial raw material and contribute to strengthening the income-earning potential of the persons associated with this sector.

**Table IV.1. Selected sustainable development plans**

| | *Objectives* | *Strategies* | *Implementation* | *Resource requirements* |
|---|---|---|---|---|
| Singapore Green Plan 2012 | • Aiming for an environmentally conscious nation, through promoting resource conservation and clean technology to protect both the local and global environments<br>• Aiming at strengthening environmental consciousness to promote personal responsibility for and civic commitment to the environment | • Key modalities for achieving the objectives include promoting waste management, conserving nature, ensuring clean air, increasing water supply, improving public health, forging and strengthening strategic partnerships with the private sector, enhancing international collaboration and encouraging, through incentives, the innovation of clean technology for environmental sustainability | • Government level:<br>- Strengthening the message of environmental sustainability among communities (employers, employees, civic groups, labour unions, educators and the media), through training in environmental skills and management, providing incentives and fostering greater collaboration among the communities<br>- Implementing nationwide initiatives such as public transport using compressed natural gas<br>- Including environmental issues in the school curricula to increase awareness<br>- Formulating and enforcing legislative measures to encourage environmental sustainability<br>- Complying with international agreements on the matter<br>• Partnerships:<br>- Between government agencies, non-governmental organizations, educational institutions, private and international organizations<br>- Close partnership among the 3Ps (people, public sector and private sector) to create environmental awareness and responsibility | • Government funding for public utilities development and training |
| National Strategy for Ecologically Sustainable Development (Australia) | • Enhancing individual and community well-being and welfare by following a path of economic development that safeguards the | • Ensuring that decision-making processes integrate both long- and short-term economic, environmental, social and equity considerations<br>• Incorporating the global dimensions of the | • Government level:<br>- Development of detailed environmental policies to be adopted at all levels of government<br>- National-level strategies on forests, waste management, biodiversity | • State and local government resources |

(Continued on next page)

**Table IV.1** *(continued)*

| | *Objectives* | *Strategies* | *Implementation* | *Resource requirements* |
|---|---|---|---|---|
| | welfare of future generations<br>• Providing for equity within and between generations<br>• Protecting biological diversity and maintaining essential ecological processes and life-support systems | environmental impacts of actions and policies in national policy formulation<br>• Developing a strong, growing and diversified economy which can enhance the capacity of environmental protection<br>• Maintaining international competitiveness in an environmentally sound manner | and rangeland management<br>- Legislation and government programmes stress environment and sustainable development objectives and principles, such as waste minimization and cleaner production<br>- Land-use and transport planning and natural resource management to be entrusted to State and local-level authorities<br>- Adopting cost-effective and flexible policy instruments, including valuation, pricing and incentive mechanisms<br>• Decisions and actions should provide for community involvement | |
| China's Agenda 21 | • Rapid economic growth and gradual improvements in the quality of development through relying on scientific and technological advances and improvements in the quality of labour<br>• Promoting the overall development and progress of society and establishing the social basis for sustainable development<br>• Controlling environmental pollution, improving the | • Focusing on economic development and the deepening of reforms and openness<br>• Strengthening the foundation for building capacity for sustainable development by:<br>- Establishing a policy framework for developing social and economic norms for sustainable development<br>- Developing planning, statistics and information support systems for social and economic development<br>- Improving education and raising awareness of sustainable development issues throughout the country<br>• Gradually popularizing sustainable agricultural | • Government level:<br>- Environmental protection has been included in annual and medium-term plans for national economic and social development, such as the five-year plans<br>- The Government has formulated and implemented a series of laws and policies concerning environmental protection<br>- Support from ministries, departments and local governments<br>- Bilateral and multilateral cooperation with countries and regions through consultation and dialogue, transfer of environmentally sound technologies and environmental protection agreements | • China's own resources to cover roughly 60 per cent of total funding while the remaining 40 per cent is to be covered from international funding; foreign Governments and international organizations have shown willingness to support this Agenda and its associated priority programmes |

*(Continued on next page)*

**Table IV.1** *(continued)*

| | *Objectives* | *Strategies* | *Implementation* | *Resource requirements* |
|---|---|---|---|---|
| | environment and protecting the resource base for sustainable development | techniques, while giving consideration to local situations<br>• Vigorously promoting cleaner production technologies, working hard to minimize the production of wastes, encouraging recycling, resource and energy saving and increasing efficiency of production<br>• Arranging for the development and popularization of important environmental pollution control techniques and equipment through technological skills training, establishing demonstration projects, raising fees for the discharge of pollutants and providing incentives such as preferential taxes for socially beneficial undertakings to control environmental pollution<br>• Emphasizing protection of water resources and treatment of waste water by preventing the spread of desertification and developing water-saving technologies that produce little or no waste<br>• Emphasizing protection and rational utilization of natural resources to protect species and improve environmental quality by disseminating scientific findings on environmental problems to raise awareness and promoting the production of "green products" and the use of renewable resources<br>• Working hard to improve land productivity and reduce the impact of natural disasters | - Establishment of a comprehensive natural resources and environment monitoring and management system | |

Several countries of the region are pursuing the development of plantation forests and simultaneously withdrawing national forests from the production of wood, which is used as industrial raw material. For example, China has one of the most extensive plantation forestry programmes in the region. It is planned to plant some 26 million hectares of forest in the Yangtze and Yellow river basins by 2030. In India, farmers in three states established a total of 26,000 ha of poplar plantations in 1990 which are now used to provide raw material for industries such as match boxes and plywood.

There have been changes in the policies and strategies for protecting and improving the quality of available freshwater resources. Instead of expanding the supply of freshwater, emphasis has been put on demand management and water-use efficiency, conservation and protection. An integrated approach to water resources management in line with Agenda 21 has been accepted as an effective policy option.

Multisectoral and multidisciplinary approaches are needed to rehabilitate degraded water quality and ensure the provision of a safe drinking water supply. In many countries of the region, this need has been translated into action plans for cleaning up rivers, canals, lakes and other water bodies: the Murray Darling Basin Agreement (Australia), the pollution control plans for three rivers (China), the Ganga Action Plan (India) and the Love Our Rivers Campaign (Malaysia) are some examples. The reduction of pollution loads through proper waste-water treatment, reuse and recycling of domestic sewage and industrial waste water, the introduction of appropriate low-waste technologies and strict control on industrial and municipal effluents are essential elements of these action plans.

### *Instruments for implementing policies: command and control and market-based instruments*

Command and control-based mechanisms utilize the power of the State in forcing the agents, that is, producers and consumers, to adhere to environmental standards. For example, the management of forest resources in many countries uses a system of awarding licences for logging with the threat of cancellation as a penalty mechanism. In another sector, fishing, in which many of the poor earn their livelihood, a quota system is applied to keep the catch within sustainable limits. A number of countries have used command and control mechanisms to regulate effluents, emissions and disposable wastes.

***Command and control measures utilize the power of the State in forcing consumers and producers to adhere to environmental norms and good practices***

Command and control measures have often focused on particular sectors which are of primary importance to the poor. For example, Indonesia's PROKASIH Programme, started in 1989, aimed at ensuring that industries install waste-water treatment systems. Initially, attention was focused on the worst industrial pollution occurring near 24 highly polluted rivers with the goal of reducing their pollution load by 50 per cent.[20] The objective was subsequently expanded; more rivers were brought within the purview of the control measures and the pollution standards were also increased. Command and control measures have also been applied to control air pollution. For example, a unique Vehicle Quota System to control the number of vehicles is in operation in Singapore, thereby reducing traffic congestion and emissions from fossil fuel. Under this system the number of new vehicles allowed for registration is predetermined annually. The quota for new vehicles takes into account the prevailing traffic conditions and the number of vehicles taken off the road permanently, while the supply-demand condition of the market determines the price of new vehicles.[21]

***Market-based fiscal incentive-disincentive systems influence the behaviour of producers and consumers by providing them with a choice as to the extent and nature of responses for reducing environmental damage, and are easy to administer***

The requirement for the success of the command and control system is the ability to use the power of the State to identify violations by continuous policing and then to enforce the associated penalties. These actions require substantial financial and human resources and a well-functioning judicial system. In most countries, resources are scarce and the judicial system is slow in handling non-criminal cases. A market-based fiscal incentive, a disincentive system which seeks to influence the behaviour of producers and consumers by enabling them to choose the most appropriate measures based on their own assessed cost and benefit, is considered a viable and often preferable alternative to the direct command and control system and is implemented in various countries of the region. In contrast to command and control measures, these are self-regulatory in nature and require less policing and fewer court actions. As these instruments are often administered at the local level, like other fiscal instruments, they result in increased revenue/savings for local governments and municipalities. Some of the popular market-based instruments are user charges, an increase/decrease in targeted subsidies and a deposit refund system. These are described in table IV.2 below.

---

[20] ESCAP and ADB, op. cit., p. 265.

[21] D. Goh, "Certificates of entitlement" (<http://www.geocities.com/MotorCity/Pit/8858/singapore/taxes.htm>, 9 November 2002).

**Table IV.2. Market-based instruments for environmental management[a]**

| *Instrument* | *Modus operandi* | *Examples* |
|---|---|---|
| Environmental tax | Charged to polluters as the cost of neutralizing pollution and environmental damage | Industries in Singapore are allowed to discharge effluent (containing biodegradable pollutants) directly in public sewage on payment of a tariff which allows the recovery of the additional cost of sewage treatment. In the Philippines, the polluters are required to pay a fee for every unit of pollution they discharge. The emission tax structure consists of 4,500 pesos/ton of particulate matter emitted in excess of the allowance limit and 14,200 pesos/ton of sulphur dioxide emitted for manufacturing industries. Taxes for power-generating plants are 1,750.86 pesos/ton of particulate matter and 40,725 pesos/ton of sulphur dioxide emitted. The nominal rates are adjusted periodically for inflation to maintain the deterrent impact in "real terms" |
| User charges | Charges are levied on the use of public good and natural resources for reducing environmental damage | Road pricing is practised in Singapore to reduce air pollution and congestion; peak hour road use in the city centre is taxed. To implement the road tax system efficiently, an electronic road pricing arrangement has been introduced; the system is designed to automate the pay-when-you-use principle. Charges are levied on a per-pass basis and vary according to the time and congestion levels. Indonesia plans to charge ecotourists for the use (enjoyment) of protected areas for the sustainable management of ecosystems |
| Increase/decrease in targeted subsidies | Eco-friendly actions are encouraged by providing subsidies/tax exemptions and these are reduced to curb environmentally damaging activities | Examples of incentives include a preferential low-interest loan for desertification control (China); incentives for wood substitution and subsidies to encourage the use of fuel-saving devices and alternative sources of energy supply, such as biogas and solar energy (India). Examples of disincentives include reduction of the domestic subsidy on coal from 61 per cent in 1984 to 11 per cent in the late 1990s to deter its use (China) |
| Deposit (fee) refund system | Used to encourage recycling activities; a deposit on the product is levied initially to be refunded to the consumer on the return of the recyclable waste | Examples include a deposit refund system for beer bottle recycling in Japan. The beer makers levy a fee on the beer bottles and containers, which is ultimately passed on to the consumer. A refund is provided when the bottles and containers are brought back for recycling. A similar system is used for soft drink bottles in India |

[a] ESCAP and ADB, *State of the Environment in Asia and the Pacific 2000* (ST/ESCAP/2087), p. 269.

### *Institutional policies and institutions*

***The existence of functioning institutions and the horizontal and vertical linkages between them are crucial for formulating and implementing effective environmental plans and policies***

Policies and programmes, whether economic, social or environmental, cannot be implemented effectively without the support of an interconnected network of institutions at different levels national, subnational and local. In addition to the apex institutions for example, parliament and the judiciary, institutions include administrative bodies, such as ministries, departments, councils and committees, which, in general, deal with policies and programmes belonging to specific areas. Institutional policies refer to the legal, normative and regulatory framework which enables the policies to generate the intended impact. For example, the environment ministry, the institution which is primarily responsible for implementing environmental policies, cannot carry out pollution control programmes (either through command and control or by using a market mechanism) without clearly defined pollution norms and legal penalties for not adhering to the norms.

Agenda 21 emphasizes the important role of institutions and institutional policies in underscoring the critical importance of reshaping the decision-making process in order to integrate environmental and

**Diagram**

**Institutional coordination for integrating development and the environment**

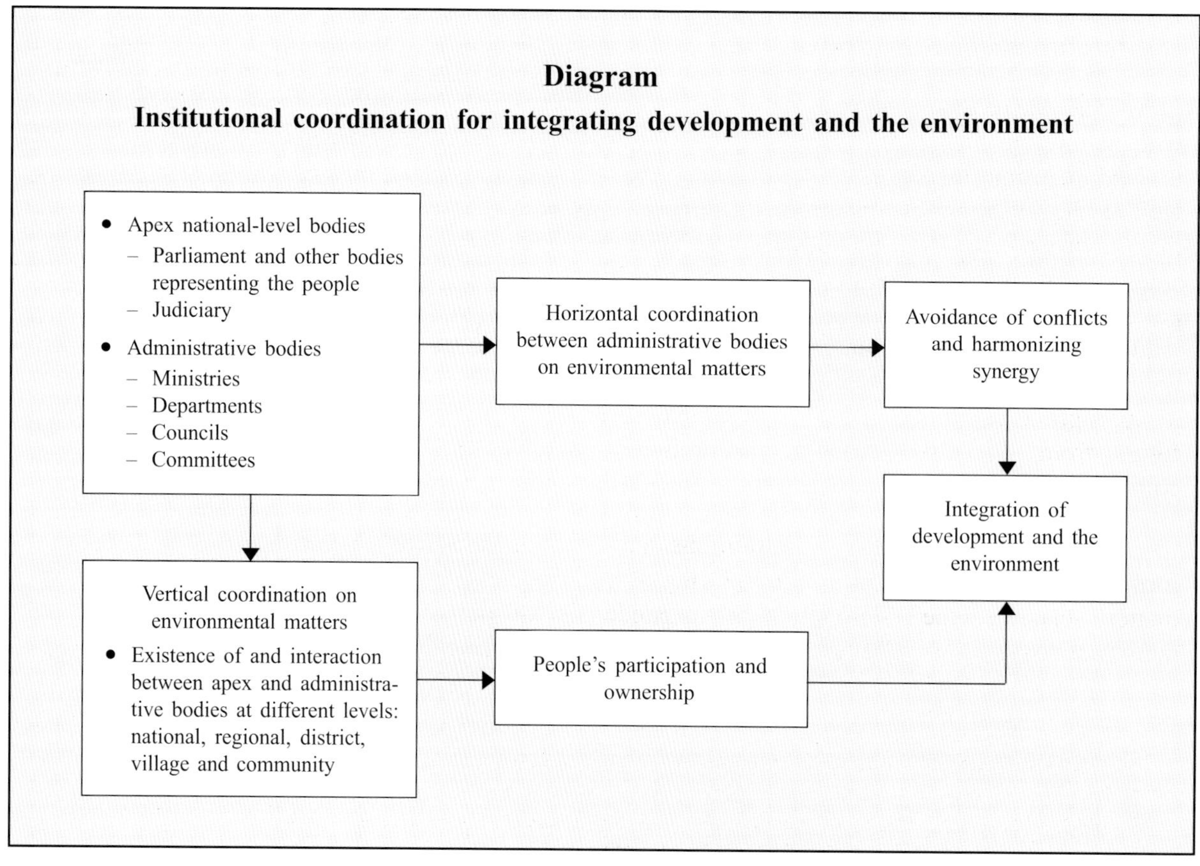

developmental concerns into decision-making.[22] To achieve this aim, the institutions and policies (which have a bearing on the environment) of various sectors/areas need to be well coordinated not only horizontally but also vertically. Horizontal coordination between institutions will avoid conflict and exploit complimentarities, thus enhancing the impact of policies. Vertical coordination requires the existence of institutions at different levels from the national to the community level, and interaction between them. It ensures people's participation and ownership, without which all policies, especially environmental policies, will not be effective (see diagram).

Although there is room for improvement in the coordination mechanisms, the modalities for horizontal coordination on environmental matters already exist in many Asian and Pacific countries. For example, in Tonga, the Development Coordination Committee is the paramount economic planning and coordinating body.[23] Its standing members are the Deputy Prime Minister and senior representatives of selected ministries. In Fiji, the National Planning Office is required to have discussions with all ministries during the preparation of policy. If policies have economic or financial implications, the Economic Strategy Committee, chaired by the Prime Minister and comprising such ministers as the Minister of Finance, reviews the policies. In Malaysia, the National Planning Council is the highest planning body in the country and is in charge of the coordination and implementation of development programmes.

The success of vertical coordination between institutions dealing with environmental matters depends on the emphasis given to decentralized decision-making and the creation of decentalized institutions as well as the linkages between them. Effective vertical coordination ensures that environmental issues and concerns at the local level, especially in small towns and rural areas, are given due consideration in designing policies and programmes. The involvement of local institutions in formulating and implementing policies is essential as they are directly in touch with problems in their areas of operation and may have useful insights as to appropriate solutions. Local institutional structures can comprise many forms, from municipal councils or commissions in urban areas to village councils in rural areas.

The role of subnational institutions and local governments in the formulation, implementation and monitoring of policies and programmes on matters related to the environment has expanded in the post-Rio era. In many countries, provincial-level environmental agencies have been set up

---

22 Sections 1 and 2 of Agenda 21 (<http://www.un.org/esa/sustdev/agenda21text.htm>, 9 November 2002).

23 ESCAP, *Integrating Environmental Considerations into Economic Policy Making: Institutional Issues,* Development Papers, No. 21 (ST/ESCAP/1990).

***Decentralization of institutions to the provincial and local levels is an important precondition for the success of environmental plans and policies***

and local governments have been given the responsibility for formulating and implementing local environmental protection plans (local Agenda 21). For example, in Japan, local authorities are involved in the implementation of environmental laws, regulations and guidelines and the measurement and control of pollution. Out of a total of 248 local governments in the Republic of Korea, 159 are formulating local environmental plans. Provinces, autonomous regions and municipalities in China have also formulated their own local Agenda 21 plans regarding management of the environment. Similar efforts have been made in many other countries, including Indonesia, Malaysia, the Philippines, Thailand and Viet Nam.[24]

The local municipal governments are in principle closest to urban environmental problems, such as air and water pollution and the lack of industrial waste disposal facilities. They are capable of participating effectively in the administration of control measures. In China, there are municipal environmental protection commissions consisting of local leaders, other commissions and bureaucrats. These commissions are responsible for implementing policies and coordinating activities at the local level; these, in turn, are assisted by the environmental protection departments of municipal governments. In Fiji, the Suva City Council is the largest local government entity and deals with environmental issues; in terms of implementation, it relies on different departments to carry out its plans. The Health Services Department in Fiji plays an important role as it is in charge of garbage collection, waste disposal and drainage control. The problem of squatters, with its serious environmental implications, is also addressed by the Health Services Department.

Village councils and committees are common in the rural areas. They can play a significant role in monitoring rural environmental problems, such as soil degradation, deforestation and depletion of fish stocks.

In Samoa, the traditional Polynesian decision-making system is reflected in the structure of most political and social organizations. Village councils decide on all matters pertaining to the village and its land and sea resources. One of the important features of this decision-making system is the emphasis placed on consensus. People avoid conflict by consensus agreement among peers. Meetings involve as many stakeholders as possible. In the villages, the village council discusses all matters concerning village life, especially when there are conflicts over resource use.

In Nepal, there are various district and village development committees. As a result of the decentralization policy, these committees are empowered to undertake village and district development activities. These activities have had a tremendous positive impact with regard to new road construction, irrigation, drinking water, forest management, etc.

---

[24] ESCAP and ADB, op. cit., pp. 260 and 261.

For instance, areas of degraded and semi-degraded forest land are allocated to these local bodies for management, controlled exploitation and reforestation. This has improved the quality of land and prevented the massive destruction of forests. The Annapurna Conservation Area Project in Nepal is an illustration of the successful decentralization of planning and decision-making.[25]

Although there have been several attempts to enhance the importance of local institutions, their role has been mostly confined to participating in environment-related activities in some specific sectors. There are very few mechanisms enabling local institutions to participate and provide inputs, directly or indirectly (through regional institutions), into the formulation of overall development policies and to voice their concerns on environmental matters. In order to overcome the limitations mentioned earlier, the creation of an apex local (urban or rural) council with representation from various local government departments would be beneficial and it could present local views in a regional council. In this way, local issues and concerns, including those related to the environment, would be directly presented at the regional level and indirectly in national policy-making bodies (through the regional entity).

Legislation, laws, rules and guidelines (norm-setting) aimed at improving the environment and conserving natural resources fall under the general rubric of institutional policies. A very good description of the subject can be found in an ESCAP publication[26] and is not reported here.

## Policies directed at the reduction of poverty as well as improvement of the environment

A large number of policies and programmes are available which address both poverty reduction and environmental improvement. These can be classified into two broad groups: the first group refers to those policies that strengthen the asset base of the poor and also help to protect the environment and the second includes those related to the improvement of governance, especially in the management and monitoring of the environment, and strengthening the coping mechanisms of the poor.

In the first group, major policies include ensuring the property rights of the poor, supporting rural community-based projects, especially social forestry, and giving the poor access to environmentally clean technologies.

---

25 ESCAP Virtual Conference, "The Annapurna Conservation Project (ACAP)" (<http://www.unescap.org/drpad/vc/conference/ex_np_125_acp. htm>, 11 November 2002).

26 ESCAP and ADB, op. cit., chap. 11.

### Property rights of the poor

***Conferring property rights on the poor could increase their income as well as provide the motivation for resource conservation***

The property rights to resources, that is, land, water and trees, play an important role in the environment-poverty linkage, especially in the rural areas. As the rural poor often rely on customary and informal arrangements, they are deprived of formal private property rights and, at times, exploited. Uncertain ownership conditions have a negative impact on agricultural productivity by inhibiting investment and reducing incentives for resource conservation. The situation can be reversed by ensuring property rights through policy interventions. For example, the formal issuance of legal titles in Thailand in 1984 was beneficial for agricultural productivity and thus provided the necessary incentive and financial resources for investing in soil and water conservation. A large number (15.5 million) of land titles were distributed to 2.2 million households, of which 35 per cent were below the poverty line. A study has shown that this action has resulted in an 8-27 per cent increase in agricultural output.[27] In India, tenancy reforms, the enactment of land ceiling legislation and the distribution of surplus (over ceiling) land to the poor was very successful in the State of West Bengal. The tenancy reform programme which began in the late 1960s through Operation Barga, a movement to register sharecroppers and provide them with tenurial security through legal enactment and social mobilization, was very beneficial to the landless poor. A large number of sharecroppers (1.5 million) were formally provided with security of tenure.[28] Of these, 38 per cent belonged to the downtrodden class ("dalits" and "scheduled castes", who are the poorest of the poor).

Although, by and large, providing ownership of land to the poor should enhance their income-earning capabilities and their interest in resource conservation, Governments have to make sure that the land does not end up with rich persons or speculators, which would defeat the objective of this policy.[29]

### Social forestry

***Social forestry is a very effective modality for poverty eradication and improvement of the environment***

Social forestry is the sustainable management of trees and forests by farmers, landowners, industries or community-based organizations in order to provide forest products and services to meet local needs. It is distinguished from commercial forestry by the extent of stakeholders' involvement, their decision-making powers and the benefits that accrue to them. The principal stakeholders in social forestry are the people who live in the local communities located close to the forest. Such communities often

---

27 "Linking poverty reduction ...", op. cit., p. 20.

28 Venkatesh Athreya, "A creditable record", *Frontline,* vol. 19, Issue 04 (<http://www.flonnet.com/fl1904/19040810.htm>, 2 August 2002).

29 "PM's title deeds proposal panned", *Bangkok Post,* 3 December 2002.

encompass a large number of poor people who cannot afford to live in better places. Fundamental to social forestry is the employment of these people to manage the trees so as to improve their economic and social condition.

Social forestry includes a wide range of activities, such as tree-planting, agroforestry, management of natural forests, watershed management and the collection of non-wood forest products. At times, social forestry touches upon other sectors, such as the energy sector, when families plant and harvest fuelwood for domestic cooking and heating, or the agricultural sector, when farmers use trees to enrich soil, produce fodder to feed livestock and plant windbreaks to protect crops. The importance of the sustainable development of forestry has been highlighted in the Plan of Implementation of the World Summit on Sustainable Development (see box IV.1).

A large number of countries in the Asian and Pacific region have adopted social forestry as an important modality for improving the environment and providing a livelihood income to the rural poor (see box IV.2.).

## Box IV.2. Social forestry in a Chinese village[a]

Nongla village of China, located in a bare limestone area, had been traditionally underdeveloped. Harsh living conditions and the shortage of water have hindered economic growth and perpetuated poverty. As a result of the efforts of villagers in afforestation over the past 10 years, about 72 per cent of village-owned land has now been planted with Chinese medicinal herbs and fruit trees. As a consequence, the land under forest cover in and around the village reached 90 per cent and villagers' per capita annual cash income rose to 3,180 yuan ($383) in 2001, a big increase from 100 yuan ($12) 20 years ago.

Before social forestry was introduced, the villagers thought that their land could only be used to plant corn, the growth of which was frequently damaged by flooding. With the help of extension services provided by township, country and autonomous regional level governments, the villagers have acquired the skill to grow medicinal plants.

The village is an example of success in both poverty reduction and sustainable development through the sensible development of local resources as well as protection of the environment.

---

[a] Paper prepared by Wang Tong, Senior Research Fellow, State Council Economic Restructuring Office, Beijing (unpublished).

In recognition of its great benefits, the Government of Indonesia has given social forestry considerable importance in its official five-year development plans and has actively supported projects in this area.[30] The Kaltim social forestry project in Indonesia aims at generating local capacity in social forestry through professional development research,

---

30 Forestry Profiles, Indonesia: Kaltim Social Forestry Project (<http://www.rcfa-cfan.org/english/profile.14.html>, 3 November 2002).

curriculum development and training-extension activities. Greater capacity in social forestry facilitates greater community participation in the management of East Kalimantan's forests. The project has the following major objectives:

- Protecting and managing the environment by limiting resource degradation and expanding the environmental benefits of trees through the introduction of agroforestry systems to enhance farm and pasture productivity, protecting of household and community food and fuelwood supplies, conserving natural forests, expanding the area of protected areas under joint community-Government management and using trees in the conservation of soil and water resources
- Supporting private sector development by increasing the sustainable output of economic products from tree and forest resources, expanding the development of forest industries on an appropriate scale to expand cash incomes on a locally sustainable basis, creating professional opportunities for local social forestry and natural resource management and expanding the knowledge base regarding sustainable economic uses for natural forest products in the tropics
- Developing sustainable infrastructure services by initiating self-sustaining education programmes in social forestry at the community, technical and professional levels by increasing the capacity of the educational infrastructure in the following areas: practical soil conservation; forest management; family fuelwood supply and use; agricultural and pastoral fire management; watershed management; extension and communication skills in participatory needs assessment; planning, monitoring and evaluation; resource monitoring; integrated resource management and protection; and soil and water conservation

In India, 16 social forestry projects, under which 2.6 million ha have been brought under forest cover, were completed from 1979 to 1999. Currently there are 18 ongoing projects aiming to cover 2.6 million ha for tree planting of land.[31]

### *Access of the poor to environmentally clean technologies*

One of the areas in which simple technology could bring immediate benefit to the poor as well as to the environment is an improvement in cooking stove technology to reduce air pollution and associated acute

---

[31] National Forestry Action Programme India, "Completed projects" (<http://envfor.delhi.nic.in/nfap/complete-project.html>, 13 November 2002).

respiratory infections. It has been pointed out that such diseases are largely responsible for the dismal health standards of the poor. In the Asian and Pacific region, India has long been engaged in designing, producing and marketing improved cooking stoves in rural areas. Its experience has shown that the task of improving the health of the poor by introducing redesigned cooking stoves should focus not only on the engineering side of the technology but also on the social, cultural and financial aspects.

***The provision of environmentally clean technologies to the poor can go a long way towards improving their health***

The objectives of improving cooking stoves have been to conserve and optimize the use of fuelwood, especially in the rural and semi-urban areas, help to alleviate deforestation, reduce the drudgery associated with cooking, especially for women, and the health hazards caused by smoke and heat exposure in the kitchen and bring about improvements in household sanitation and general living conditions.

A multimodal and multi-agency approach was adopted to popularize the use of the stove. State government agencies, autonomous bodies and voluntary organizations have taken part in the process. A pool of self-employed workers was created and given the responsibility for installation and maintenance. The Government's strategy also placed emphasis on providing the poor with subsidies for purchasing improved stoves based on geographical and indicator targeting, the introduction of incentive schemes for field-level functionaries and wider publicity through radio, television and other local media.

Two major policies which have a direct bearing on environmental resources are the implementation of anti-corruption measures and the incorporation of elements of the environment-poverty nexus in environmental monitoring systems. Last, but not least, plans, programmes and policies to minimize the adverse impacts of natural disasters are expected to go a long way in benefiting the poor. These are discussed below.

### *Implementing anti-corruption measures*

Corruption is directly related to the unsustainable management of natural resources, especially forestry resources. According to *State of the Forest: Indonesia* released early in 2002, corruption and lawlessness had been fuelling illegal logging in Indonesia, resulting in a doubling of the countries' deforestation rates in the late 1990s.[32] The report concluded that such massive deforestation was the result of a corrupt political and

***Anti-corruption measures and disaster management plans and policies have a strong beneficial impact on the poor***

[32] World Resources Institute, "Corruption, lawlessness fuel epidemic of illegal logging in Indonesia" (<http://www.wri.org/press/indoforest.html>, 8 August 2002).

economic system that regarded natural resources as a source of private revenue. Echoing similar concern, a recent report by FAO identified corruption and illegal forest practices as the biggest threat to successful forest management.[33]

Corrupt practices can be reduced by providing quality information on the state of natural resources, effective publicity concerning corruption practices and anti-corruption laws, the agencies responsible and the penalties applied and by ensuring that violators are punished. With regard to the forestry sector, strict law enforcement, including deterrent punishment in tandem with a programme to address corruption within the enforcement agencies, is essential and urgently needed if corruption in this sector is to be controlled.

### *Disaster management plans and policies*

The poor are disproportionately vulnerable to environmental shocks in the form of natural disasters. Natural calamities such as cyclones, typhoons, flood and mud slides occur fairly regularly and affect many countries. The Asian and Pacific region has been one of the worst hit in terms of natural disasters, accounting for 50 per cent of the world's major emergencies. During the rainy season of 2002, more than 20 countries in the region suffered serious flooding, resulting in the deaths of 2,300 people and forcing 16 million people from their homes.[34] In Thailand alone, floods affected 7 million hectares of farmland and 80,000 people needed treatment for water-borne, flood-related diseases. While not all natural disasters can be predicted or prevented, policies and programmes can be formulated and implemented to mitigate the loss of life and property of the affected people and avoid destitution. A plan of action for disaster management can be formulated and periodically updated. In India, the elements of such a plan are forecasting and operating warning systems; maintaining uninterrupted communication between potential disaster-prone communities/areas and the Government; giving wide publicity to warnings of impending calamities and disaster preparedness and relief measures through all channels of communications (including television, radio and the press); arranging for transport, with particular reference to evacuation and the movement of essential commodities; making essential goods and services available at reasonable prices (or for free) in disaster-struck

---

[33] "Corruption threatens forests: FAO", *Dawn,* 4 October 2001 <http://www.dawn.com/2001/10/04/int13.htm>, 3 November 2002).

[34] "Effective disaster management needed in Asia and Pacific", Press release No. G/35/2002 (United Nations Information Service, Bangkok).

## Box IV.3. Disaster relief plan of Thailand[a]

Nationwide, 1,408 villages in 34 provinces have been identified as being at high risk for floods and mud slides. Local authorities in these areas have been instructed to be on high alert since the rainy season began. While the Interior Ministry focused on disaster relief, other agencies, including the Forestry Department, were busy restoring areas at risk with a view to reducing their vulnerability to disasters.

Flood-related disasters have been brought under the National Civil Disaster Relief Committee. Information centres, early warning systems and disaster relief drills have been introduced in high-risk areas. The 24-hour alert system is operated from the Interior Ministry's information centre. With help from the Meteorological Department, the Ministry monitors weather conditions.

Evacuation procedures are also part of the plan. Drills have been held in 14 of 16 target provinces. Local authorities have been told to exercise precautions. Safe places have been identified at each spot in the event of an emergency. About one billion baht was set aside for the evacuation process.

---

[a] *Bangkok Post*, 12 August 2002.

areas; and ensuring the availability of medicines.[35] In Thailand, the disaster relief plan has recently been overhauled to increase its effectiveness (see box IV.3).

### *Strengthening environment-poverty monitoring*

There are substantial lacunae in the availability of data that capture environment-poverty interlinkages. In many cases, environmental data focus on environmental changes without measuring their impact on the poor, and poverty data do not capture environmental concerns. This situation can be remedied by devising appropriate environment-poverty indicators. Indicators such as deaths from acute respiratory infection by income class could quantify the state of environmental health. Similarly, the extent of dependency indicated by the proportion of income generated by using primarily natural resources can be an indicator of poverty; a reduction in the extent of dependency can indicate a possible reduction in poverty. Substantial research has already been done to identify effective environment-poverty indicators.[36] However, efforts to collect country-level data on these indicators are not really adequate. Institutional mechanisms are also needed through which the information on these indicators could be analysed and used for designing policies to improve the environment and reduce poverty.

---

[35] National Disaster Management, Ministry of Home Affairs, Government of India, "Contingency action plan" (<http://www.ndmindia.nic.in/manageplan/intro.html>, 9 August 2002).

[36] "Linking poverty reduction ...", op. cit., p. 17.

## CONCLUSION

***The relatively intangible nature of environmental costs, negative externalities associated with such costs as well as the existence of free-rider problems are reasons for market failure***

The aim of this chapter has been modest. An attempt has been made to review the interlinkages between the environment and poverty and selected policies and programmes which can minimize the adverse environmental impacts of economic growth. Against the background of the positive linkage between improvement in the environment and the reduction of poverty it can be argued that policies and programmes for improving the environment could form an important element of a pro-poor economic strategy to strengthen the impact of economic growth on poverty reduction. It is also found that certain policies (such as providing resource rights to the poor) centred directly on the poor people can improve the environment, and environmental interventions such as the prevention of land degradation and controlling indoor smoke pollution from cooking can improve the income and health of the poor.

Despite the existence and application of a large number of policies and programmes, the track record for improving the state of the environment in the Asian and Pacific region does not denote the success of such instruments.[37] The limited success of environmental policies is due to the economic aspects of the environment, which make the associated policies difficult to implement.

Conceptually, there are three aspects associated with the environment which have an impact on the extent of environmental degradation, especially that created by human activities, and on the effectiveness of the policies for reversing such damage.

First, a significant part of the environmental costs of human activities is intangible and thus difficult to quantify in monetary terms. Environmental impacts often occur over the long term, even beyond the generation of those responsible. Thus people (polluters) do not fully realize the costs (environmental degradation) of their actions. Second, the environment has negative externalities, that is, the social costs of environmental degradation are always much higher than the private costs. It is difficult to design deterrent policies and instruments which reflect the true social costs. Third, the environment is a typical public good. It is non-rival in type: the quantity available for other people does not fall when someone consumes it. It is also non-excludable; it is prohibitively costly to provide a "good environment" only to those who pay for it and prevent or exclude others from obtaining it. This is responsible for the "free-rider phenomenon" in the area of the environment: other agents are allowed to benefit, at no cost, from the effort of one agent to improve the environment. Under these circumstances, it is very difficult to provide a "good environment" through the market, where private motives are the major driving force.

---

[37] ESCAP and ADB, op. cit.

***Securing stakeholders' ownership through vigorous awareness-building campaigns, decentralizing responsibilities for designing and implementing environmental policies and programmes, ensuring coordination between agents, policy makers and institutions and the maintenance of good governance are expected to improve the effectiveness of environmental policies***

The Government's role in designing and ensuring the success of policies and programmes for improving the environment cannot be exaggerated. In this regard, on the basis of the issues discussed in the previous paragraphs, certain broad observations can be made on the modalities for improving the effectiveness of environmental policies and programmes.

First, the role of awareness-building of various agents, that is, consumers, producers, government bureaucrats and politicians, concerning different aspects of the environment is essential in securing stakeholder ownership in designing and implementing environmental policies. The use of all available media and means of communication, such as newspapers, television and the Internet, to focus group discussions/seminars for disseminating information on the various social costs of environmental degradation and the benefits achievable from improvement, is highly recommended.

Second, the decentralization of the responsibilities for designing and implementing environmental programmes and policies is required for success. In formulating policies and programmes concerning the environment, the local-level state of the environment within a national environmental plan should be considered. The national plan is required to mainstream environmental issues and concerns, many of which have long-term implications, in the national development strategy, which often incorporates specific targets for economic growth.

Third, the crucial importance of coordination needs to be highlighted in both the design and implementation of environmental policies. Environmental issues are cross-cutting and involve a large number of sectors and a variety of agents, sometimes with conflicting interests. Broad consensus-building through proper coordination is required to ensure the equal commitment of various stakeholder groups to environmental causes.

Fourth, maintaining good governance in executing policies and programmes in the area of the environment is of prime importance. Policies need to be designed in a participatory and transparent manner. Keeping in mind the public-good nature of environment, including natural resources and the high negative externalities (the social cost being much higher than the private cost) associated with environmental degradation, environmental policies require a corruption-free administration in order to ensure their success.

Improvement of the environment is beneficial to everybody, to those currently living and those who are yet to be born. However, compared with the rich, the poor are more exposed to various types of environmental damage and thus stand to gain more from the improvement of the environment, which makes the associated policies truly pro-poor. Designing and implementing environmental policies are complex tasks; the multiplicity of agents with conflicting interests and the high negative externalities make the tasks these more difficult. The commitment of national Governments in this difficult area is of crucial importance. With respect to the Asian and Pacific countries, there is need for a periodic review of the environment policies and programmes and environmental situation of various countries, along with the strategies to reduce poverty. Through this exercise, Governments will be able to take stock of the situation and, if needed, readjust their priorities so as to achieve real sustainable development and poverty reduction.

Since the 1957 issue, the *Economic and Social Survey of Asia and the Pacific* has, in addition to a review of the current situation of the region, contained a study or studies of some major aspect or problem of the economies of the Asian and Pacific region, as specified below:

1957: Postwar problems of economic development
1958: Review of postwar industrialization
1959: Foreign trade of ECAFE primary exporting countries
1960: Public finance in the postwar period
1961: Economic growth of ECAFE countries
1962: Asia's trade with western Europe
1963: Imports substitution and export diversification
1964: Economic development and the role of the agricultural sector
1965: Economic development and human resources
1966: Aspects of the finance of development
1967: Policies and planning for export
1968: Economic problems of export-dependent countries. Implications of economic controls and liberalization
1969: Strategies for agricultural development. Intraregional trade as a growth strategy
1970: The role of foreign private investment in economic development and cooperation in the ECAFE region. Problems and prospects of the ECAFE region in the Second Development Decade
1971: Economic growth and social justice. Economic growth and employment. Economic growth and income distribution
1972: First biennial review of social and economic developments in ECAFE developing countries during the Second United Nations Development Decade
1973: Education and employment
1974: Mid-term review and appraisal of the International Development Strategy for the Second United Nations Development Decade in the ESCAP region, 1974
1975: Rural development, the small farmer and institutional reform
1976: Biennial review and appraisal of the International Development Strategy at the regional level for the Second United Nations Development Decade in the ESCAP region, 1976
1977: The international economic crises and developing Asia and the Pacific
1978: Biennial review and appraisal at the regional level of the International Development Strategy for the Second United Nations Development Decade
1979: Regional development strategy for the 1980s
1980: Short-term economic policy aspects of the energy situation in the ESCAP region
1981: Recent economic developments in major subregions of the ESCAP region
1982: Fiscal policy for development in the ESCAP region
1983: Implementing the International Development Strategy: major issues facing the developing ESCAP region
1984: Financing development
1985: Trade, trade policies and development
1986: Human resources development in Asia and the Pacific: problems, policies and perspectives
1987: International trade in primary commodities
1988: Recent economic and social developments
1989: Patterns of economic growth and structural transformation in the least developed and Pacific island countries of the ESCAP region: implications for development policy and planning for the 1990s
1990: Infrastructure development in the developing ESCAP region: needs, issues and policy options
1991: Challenges of macroeconomic management in the developing ESCAP region
1992: Expansion of investment and intraregional trade as a vehicle for enhancing regional economic cooperation and development in Asia and the Pacific
1993: Fiscal reform. Economic transformation and social development. Population dynamics: implications for development
1995: Reform and liberalization of the financial sector. Social security
1996: Enhancing the role of the private sector in development. The role of public expenditure in the provision of social services
1997: External financial and investment flows. Transport and communications
1998: Managing the external sector. Growth and equity
1999: Social impact of the economic crisis. Information technology, globalization, economic security and development
2000: Social security and safety nets. Economic and financial monitoring and surveillance
2001: Socio-economic implications of demographic dynamics. Financing for development
2002: The feasibility of achieving the millennium development goals in Asia and the Pacific. Regional development cooperation in Asia and the Pacific

This publication may be obtained from bookstores and distributors throughout the world. Please consult your bookstore or write to any of the following:


Sales Section
Room DC2-0853
United Nations Secretariat
New York, NY 10017
USA

Tel: (212) 963-8302
Fax: (212) 963-4116
E-mail: publications@un.org

Sales Section
United Nations Office at Geneva
Palais des Nations
CH-1211 Geneva 10
Switzerland

Tel: (41) (22) 917-1234
Fax: (41) (22) 917-0123
E-mail: unpubli@unog.ch

Chief
Conference Management Unit
Conference Services Section
Administrative Services Division
Economic and Social Commission for
Asia and the Pacific (ESCAP)
United Nations Building
Rajadamnern Avenue
Bangkok 10200, Thailand

Tel: (662) 288-1234
Fax: (662) 288-1000
E-mail: likitnukul.unescap@un.org


For further information on publications in this series, please address your enquiries to:


Chief
Poverty and Development Division
Economic and Social Commission for
Asia and the Pacific (ESCAP)
Rajadamnern Avenue
Bangkok 10200, Thailand

Tel: (662) 288-1610
Fax: (662) 288-1000, 288-3007
Cable: ESCAP BANGKOK

# READERSHIP SURVEY

The Poverty and Development Division of ESCAP is undertaking an evaluation of this publication, ***Economic and Social Survey of Asia and the Pacific 2003,*** with a view to making future issues more useful for our readers. We would appreciate it if you could complete this questionnaire and return it, at your earliest convenience, to:

Chief
Poverty and Development Division
ESCAP, United Nations Building
Rajadamnern Avenue
Bangkok 10200, THAILAND

## QUESTIONNAIRE

| | *Excellent* | *Very good* | *Average* | *Poor* |
|---|---|---|---|---|
| **1. Please indicate your assessment of the *quality* of the publication on:** | | | | |
| • Presentation/format | 4 | 3 | 2 | 1 |
| • Readability | 4 | 3 | 2 | 1 |
| • Timeliness of information | 4 | 3 | 2 | 1 |
| • Coverage of subject matter | 4 | 3 | 2 | 1 |
| • Analytical rigour | 4 | 3 | 2 | 1 |
| • Overall quality | 4 | 3 | 2 | 1 |
| **2. How *useful* is the publication for your work?** | | | | |
| • Provision of information | 4 | 3 | 2 | 1 |
| • Clarification of issues | 4 | 3 | 2 | 1 |
| • Its findings | 4 | 3 | 2 | 1 |
| • Policy suggestions | 4 | 3 | 2 | 1 |
| • Overall usefulness | 4 | 3 | 2 | 1 |

**3. Please give examples of how this publication has contributed to your work:**

.............................................................................................................................................

.............................................................................................................................................

.............................................................................................................................................

.............................................................................................................................................

**4. Suggestions for improving the publication:**

.................................................................................................................................................

.................................................................................................................................................

.................................................................................................................................................

.................................................................................................................................................

**5. Your background information, please:**

Name: .........................................................................................................................................

Title/position: ............................................................................................................................

Institution: .................................................................................................................................

Office address: ..........................................................................................................................

.................................................................................................................................................

**Please use additional sheets of paper, if required, to answer the questions.**
**Thank you for your kind cooperation in completing this questionnaire.**